THE MODERN PREACHER AND THE ANCIENT TEXT

Interpreting and Preaching Biblical Literature

by

SIDNEY GREIDANUS

WILLIAM B. EERDMANS PUBLISHING COMPANY
GRAND RAPIDS, MICHIGAN

INTER-VARSITY PRESS
LEICESTER

Copyright © 1988 by Sidney Greidanus

First published 1988 by Wm. B. Eerdmans Publishing Co.
255 Jefferson Ave. S.E., Grand Rapids, Mich. 49503

First British edition published 1988
through special arrangement with Eerdmans
by Inter-Varsity Press,
38 De Montfort Street,
Leicester, England LE1 7GP

Library of Congress Cataloging-in-Publication Data

Greidanus, Sidney, 1935-
    The modern preacher and the ancient text: interpreting and
preaching biblical literature / by Sidney Greidanus.
        p.   cm.
    Bibliography: p. 342
    Includes indexes.
    ISBN 0-8028-0360-1
    1. Bible—Homiletical use. 2. Preaching. I. Title.
BS534.5.G74   1988
251—dc19   88-24046
                                                   CIP

Eerdmans ISBN 0-8028-0360-1
IVP ISBN 0 85111 573 X

CONTENTS

FOREWORD

One of the needs of busy pastors and aspiring preachers is to have access to the fruit of biblical scholarship which is frequently hidden in scholarly journals and distant libraries. A felt need at many seminaries is a tool to bridge the gap between the department of biblical studies and that of homiletics. This book seeks to fill both of these needs. It brings together the results of recent biblical scholarship as they pertain to preaching, and it links the disciplines of biblical hermeneutics and homiletics.

In fusing hermeneutics and homiletics, I am building on my doctoral dissertation of 1970, *Sola Scriptura: Problems and Principles in Preaching Historical Texts.* In the present volume cross-fertilization takes place not only between hermeneutics and homiletics but also between historical and literary studies. For biblical studies has recently entered into a new world: it has undergone a paradigm shift from historical to literary studies so that scholarly interest today is focused not so much on history as on *genres* of biblical literature—with a concomitant shift in homiletics to *forms* of sermons. These paradigm shifts open up exciting new possibilities for preaching but also some precarious hazards. In this book I wish to alert preachers to the possibilities as well as the hazards.

One of the risks in writing on this subject is that, because of the knowledge explosion, one spreads oneself too thin. This study deals with issues in history, hermeneutics, homiletics, Hebrew narrative, prophecy, the Gospels and Epistles—each of them specialties in their own right. What encouraged me to carry out this broad inquiry is that preachers cannot be experts in all of these areas and yet they need to be knowledgeable about them in order to preach responsibly. I was also motivated by the fact that I presently teach courses in many of the above-named fields so that my research could enrich my teaching and my teaching benefit my writing. In addition, experts in history, literature, systematic theology, Old Testament, New Testament, and homiletics—as well as some pastors and church members—were willing to read all or parts of this study and to serve me with advice.

I have generally followed *The Chicago Manual of Style* (1982). The references in the notes usually contain only enough information to find the item in the Bibliography. For items not selected for the Bibliography, complete information is provided in the note itself. The notes also contain standard abbreviations for various periodicals. The complete title of the periodical may be found in the list of Abbreviations.

The Scripture Index lists only the biblical texts that are discussed, used as examples, or quoted, and not other references. The detailed Subject Index can be used not only for finding the places where a particular topic is discussed but also for reading up on a specific topic, for example, chiasm, as this is discussed in various chapters and illustrated in the chapters on Hebrew narrative, prophecy, Gospels, and Epistles.

In *The Modern Preacher and the Ancient Text* I seek to set forth a responsible, contemporary method of biblical interpretation and preaching. I have developed this method with the help of and in conversation with biblical scholars of various convictions and faith commitments. Although I cannot agree with them all, I have learned from all. In the notes and Bibliography I have acknowledged my indebtedness; here I simply wish to express my sincere thanks to these scholars for sharing their insights, their convictions, and the results of their research. May this study serve to raise awareness of the homiletical significance of contemporary biblical scholarship, and may this awareness, in turn, lead to better biblical preaching, to the upbuilding of the church, and to the glory of God.

Edmonton, Canada   SIDNEY GREIDANUS

ACKNOWLEDGMENTS

Since many people were involved in one way or another in the production of this book, I would like to express publicly my deep appreciation for their work. I cannot mention all by name but must make a few exceptions.

Most of the research for this project took place during a sabbatical in 1985-86. Dr. Anthony Thiselton provided splendid advice for making the most of our five-month stay in England. My research got off to a fine start in the excellent research library of Tyndale House, Cambridge. I thank its staff as well as the staff of the University of Cambridge. Next my family and I became part of the community of St. John's College, Nottingham. We express our sincere gratitude to all of you for your warm hospitality. I thank especially the library staffs at St. John's College, the University of Nottingham, and the University of Sheffield. I also appreciated being part of the doctoral seminars organized by the Biblical Studies Department of the University of Sheffield.

In Edmonton, Canada, I made good use of The King's College library and those of the University of Alberta, North American Baptist Divinity School, St. Stephen's Theological College, St. Joseph's College, Concordia College, and Newman Theological College. While in Grand Rapids, Michigan, I was served well by the excellent library of Calvin College and Theological Seminary. I thank the staff of all these institutions for their work on my behalf, and especially the staff at The King's College and its librarian, Simona Maaskant, for tracking down and loaning books and articles from as far away as Singapore and South Africa.

Many relatives, friends, and colleagues were willing to proofread all or parts of this book; in fact, I was pleasantly surprised that not one person turned me down. For their thoroughgoing criticisms and helpful suggestions, I am especially indebted to Prof. John Stek of the Old Testament Department at Calvin Theological Seminary in Grand Rapids and to Dr. George Vandervelde, Senior Member in Systematic Theology at the Institute for Christian Studies in Toronto. For reading the entire manuscript and commenting in various places, I am also extremely grateful to Dr. David Holwerda, Professor of New Testament, and Dr. Carl Kromminga, Professor of Homiletics, both at Calvin Theological Seminary; Rev. Morris Greidanus, pastor, Grand Rapids; Rev. Gorden Pols, pastor, Edmonton; Roy Berkenbosch, seminary student and youth pastor, Edmonton; and Vern Gleddie, rancher, Edmonton. Two of my colleagues at The King's College read chapters touching their fields, Dr. Harry Groenewold, history, and Dr. Keith Ward, English. Harold Jansen, my student assistant in the summer of 1987, not only provided valuable service in proofreading but commendably performed numerous other functions in helping me prepare this book and its indexes for publication. I should also like to mention the fine work of the William B. Eerdmans Publishing Company and especially that of editor Gary Lee. To all these people I express my heartfelt gratitude for their time, efforts, and comments.

My wife Marie has been involved from the beginning in countless aspects of this project. I thank her for her encouragement, her dedication to the project, and her cheerful performance of innumerable tasks. Our son Nathan also deserves a word of thanks for his cooperation and for his willingness to leave friends behind in order to be with us in England.

I am thankful to the Lord for surrounding me with relatives and friends, for providing health, strength, and opportunities to complete this project, and for granting wisdom and insight especially when I became bogged down in complicated foundational issues.

The writing of this book was greatly facilitated by the sabbatical policy of The King's College—a young, Christian liberal arts college in Edmonton, Canada. I thank the Senate and Board of the College for granting me a year's sabbatical, and my colleagues for taking up the slack while I was gone. Since this book is one of the firstfruits of the College's sabbatical policy, it is only fitting that it be dedicated to The King's College community.

To The King's College, Edmonton,
Its Staff, Students, and Supporters

ABBREVIATIONS

AB	Anchor Bible
ATR	*Anglican Theological Review*
BETS	*Bulletin of the Evangelical Theological Society*
Bib	*Biblica*
BSac	*Bibliotheca Sacra*
BTB	*Biblical Theology Bulletin*
CBQ	*Catholic Biblical Quarterly*
CTJ	*Calvin Theological Journal*
CTM	*Concordia Theological Monthly*
EvQ	*Evangelical Quarterly*
ExpTim	*Expository Times*
FOTL	Forms of the Old Testament Literature
GTJ	*Grace Theological Journal*
HorBT	*Horizons of Biblical Theology*
IB	*Interpreter's Bible*
IDB	*Interpreter's Dictionary of the Bible*
IDBSup	*Interpreter's Dictionary of the Bible—Supplementary Volume*
Int	*Interpretation*
JAAR	*Journal of the American Academy of Religion*
JBL	*Journal of Biblical Literature*
JETS	*Journal of the Evangelical Theological Society*
JR	*Journal of Religion*
JSNT	*Journal for the Study of the New Testament*
JSOT	*Journal for the Study of the Old Testament*
JSOTSup	Journal for the Study of the Old Testament—Supplement Series
KD	*Kerygma und Dogma*
MT	Masoretic (Hebrew) Text
NCBC	New Century Bible Commentary
NICOT	New International Commentary on the Old Testament
NovT	*Novum Testamentum*
NTS	*New Testament Studies*
OTL	Old Testament Library
RevExp	*Review and Expositor*

SBT	Studies in Biblical Theology
SEAJT	*South East Asia Journal of Theology*
Sem	*Semitics*
SJT	*Scottish Journal of Theology*
SR	*Studies in Religion*
SWJT	*Southwestern Journal of Theology*
TDNT	*Theological Dictionary of the New Testament*
TDOT	*Theological Dictionary of the Old Testament*
TynBul	*Tyndale Bulletin*
VT	*Vetus Testamentum*
VTSup	Vetus Testamentum, Supplements
WTJ	*Westminster Theological Journal*
ZTK	*Zeitschrift für Theologie und Kirche*

CHAPTER 1

Biblical Preaching

PAUL charges Timothy: "Preach the word, be urgent in season and out of season, convince, rebuke, and exhort, be unfailing in patience and in teaching" (2 Tim 4:2). This charge to preach the word follows immediately upon the classic passage on the inspiration of Scripture in 3:16: "All scripture is inspired by God and profitable for teaching, for reproof, for correction, and for training in righteousness." Evidently, the charge to preach the word is closely connected to the fact that all Scripture is inspired by God. In this first chapter we shall explore the connection between the Bible and contemporary preaching.

PREACHING THEN AND NOW

Old Testament Prophets

IN Old Testament times, the prophets in particular proclaimed the word of God. Gerhard von Rad reminds us that "for the prophets the word of God is a distinct reality that encounters them almost as something material. They therefore see the relationship of this word to history as also something almost material, in any case as an indescribably effective power."[1] For example, Isaiah shows the effective power of God's word when he compares it with the rain that waters the earth, "making it bring forth and sprout, giving seed to the sower and bread to the eater, so shall my word be that goes forth from my mouth; it shall not return to me empty, but it shall accomplish that which I purpose, and prosper in the thing for which I sent it" (55:10-11).

---

1. Von Rad, *God at Work in Israel*, 149. Cf. Schmidt, *TDOT*, III, 120-25.

God's Word

The prophets were keenly aware of the fact that the word was God's word, not theirs. God communicated his word to them; he put his words in their mouth (Jer 1:9); he gave "their spirits access to his Word";[2] he inspired them. The New Testament confirms this view when it declares that "no prophecy ever came by the impulse of man, but men moved by the Holy Spirit spoke from God" (2 Pet 1:21). Because God gave them his word, the prophets were able to proclaim: "Thus says the Lord," and "Hear the word of the Lord!"[3]

Since the prophets proclaimed *God's* word, their preaching was authoritative. This relationship suggests that the authority of the prophets did not reside, ultimately, in their person, their calling, or their office; rather, their authority was founded in the word of God they proclaimed.[4] The Lord said to Jeremiah (15:19), "If you utter what is precious, and not what is worthless, you shall be as my mouth." But he also said: "Do not listen to the words of the prophets who prophesy to you, filling you with vain hopes; they speak visions of their own minds, not from the mouth of the Lord. . . . Let him who has my word speak my word faithfully" (Jer 23:16, 28; cf. 27:14, 16).

God's Deed

For us today, words are often cheap. We think of words merely as something which is said. "Action speaks louder than words," we say, and thus we tend to separate words and action and ascribe greater value to action than to words. Although we would hesitate to call God's words "cheap," we often cheapen God's words by separating them from his deeds and thinking about his words merely as words *about* his deeds. The Bible, however, does not separate God's words from his deeds. God's words are his deeds in the sense that they accomplish his purposes. "By the word of the Lord the heavens were made, and all their host by the breath of his mouth. . . . For he spoke, and it came to be; he commanded, and it stood forth" (Ps 33:6, 9; cf. 107:20; 147:18). Similarly, God's word proclaimed by the prophets is not merely information about God's deeds but is itself a deed which accomplishes God's purposes.[5] For example, the Lord told

---

2. Von Rad, *God at Work*, 153. Cf. Schmidt, *TDOT*, III, 100.

3. Victor Furnish observes that "these announcements punctuate every paragraph of the prophetic preaching. The prophets are not thereby trying to . . . dignify their own status as 'inspired men.' Rather, they are trying to underscore the urgency and importance of their message by showing that it is not really 'their' message' at all, but God's" (*Int* 17/1 [1963] 49).

4. Cf. Furnish: "The authority of the prophetic preaching did not reside in the *speaker*, but in the words of which he was the spokesman" (ibid., 50).

5. Furnish argues cogently that "the prophet's word did not just discuss an event; it *was* an event. The word uttered is a deed done. . . . It was a word in which Yahweh

Jeremiah: "Behold, I have put my words in your mouth. See, I have set you this day over nations and over kingdoms, to pluck up and to break down, to destroy and to overthrow, to build and to plant" (Jer 1:9-10; cf. 5:14).

Whenever the prophets faithfully proclaimed the word of God, therefore, that word was not merely something "which was said," information about God's will for the present or his plan for the future, but that word was a deed of God, setting in motion the content of the message. The Hebrew mind understood this relation more readily than we do, for the word *dabar* could mean "word" or "deed" or both. In any event, the preaching of the prophets must be understood in a deeper sense than is conveyed in the English notion of *word*. That deeper sense is not that the word had magical power (see Chapter 10 below) but, as Abraham Heschel puts it, that "divine power bursts in the words."[6]

In fact, the preaching of the prophets was part and parcel of God's redemptive activity on earth. Donald Miller articulates this idea dramatically: "When . . . the prophets announced the word of God to men, they were not merely making speeches or just trading with ideas about God. Their word was rather . . . an embodiment of the agony of redemption, initiated at the Exodus but straining to be brought to fulfillment in a yet greater deliverance."[7]

New Testament Apostles

"IN many and various ways God spoke of old to our fathers by the prophets; but in these last days he has spoken to us by a Son" (Heb 1:1-2). The astounding new element of New Testament revelation is that God sent his own Son into the world: "the Word became flesh!" "No one has ever seen God," writes John; "the only Son, who is in the bosom of the Father, he has made him known" (1:14, 18). In the life, death, and resurrection of Jesus Christ, God laid the foundation for the redemption of all people, but this redemptive event had to be proclaimed in order to become effective. Paul in particular underscores the indispensability of preaching. After quoting the Old Testament promise that "every one who calls upon the name of the Lord will be saved," he asks in Rom 10:14-15: "But how are men to call upon him in whom they have not believed? And how are they to believe in him of whom they have never heard? And how are they to hear without a preacher? And how can men preach unless they are sent?"

---

himself was actively present and decisively accomplishing his purposes" (ibid., 51; cf. Schmidt, *TDOT*, III, 115-18).

6. Heschel, *Prophets*, I, 22.

7. Miller, *Fire in Thy Mouth*, 22.

God's Representatives

God sent apostles to proclaim his word. "An apostle is 'one who is sent' as the fully certified representative of another."[8] The apostles represented God himself as they proclaimed his word. During his ministry, Jesus had sent out his disciples, charging them, "Go . . . to the lost sheep of the house of Israel. And preach as you go, saying, 'The kingdom of heaven is at hand.'" In this commissioning, Jesus made unmistakably clear that the disciples in their preaching represented him and, ultimately, the Father: "He who receives you receives me, and he who receives me receives him who sent me" (Matt 10:5-7, 40). After his resurrection Jesus broadened the mandate: "Go therefore and make disciples of all nations." But here, too, there was no question as to whom the disciples represented in their mission in the world: "Lo, I am with you always, to the close of the age" (Matt 28:19-20).

That the apostles in their preaching represented God is clearly demonstrated by several words the New Testament uses for preachers and preaching. The first word is *keryx* (herald) and its derivatives. In New Testament times heralds proclaimed publicly the message that was given to them by their master. It is important to note that the message did not originate with the heralds but with their master. In delivering their master's message, therefore, heralds represented their master.[9] The same idea comes to expression in the word "ambassador." In 2 Cor 5:20 Paul writes of himself and his fellow preachers: "So we are ambassadors for Christ, God making his appeal through us. We beseech you on behalf of Christ, be reconciled to God." Ambassadors, of course, do not speak for themselves nor act on their own behalf but speak and act on behalf of their sender. So, says Paul, God himself is "making his appeal through us" because we, as preachers, are sent by God and represent God; we plead with you on behalf of Christ because "we are ambassadors for Christ."

God's Word

Accordingly, the apostles recognize that they speak on behalf of God and, in fact, proclaim the very word of God. Just like the Old Testament prophets, Paul frequently calls his messages "the word of God" or "the word of the Lord."[10] Perhaps the clearest passage in this respect is Paul's statement

8. Furnish, *Int* 17/1 (1963) 55. See Ridderbos, *Paul*, 448-50.

9. See G. Friedrich, *TDNT*, III, 687-88. Cf. Furnish, *Int* 17/1 (1963) 55. Stott elucidates six biblical metaphors of the preacher and concludes: "What is immediately notable about these six pictures is their emphasis on the 'givenness' of the message. Preachers are not to invent it; it has been entrusted to them" (*Between Two Worlds*, 135-37).

10. K. Runia notes that Paul uses these phrases not only for "the written Word of the Old Testament" but also for the word preached in New Testament times. "Here we meet with the real secret of all apostolic preaching: it is God's own Word. He Himself

to the Thessalonians: "And we also thank God constantly for this, that when you received the word of God which you heard from us, you accepted it not as the word of men but as what it really is, the word of God, which is at work in you believers" (1 Thess 2:13).

God's Deed

Paul's conviction that the preached word of God "is at work in you believers" is similar to the view of the Old Testament prophets that God's word is God's deed: God's word goes out into the world as a powerful force that accomplishes his purposes. Peter also echoes this belief when he reminds his readers: "You have been born anew . . . through the living and abiding word of God." If anyone should wonder what that word of God is precisely, Peter explains: "That word is the good news which was preached to you" (1 Pet 1:23, 25). Like the prophets and Paul, Peter is convinced of the power of the preached word. That power is not some magical force in the words themselves but is the power of God whose word it is, for the gospel "is the power of God for salvation to every one who has faith" (Rom 1:16). The New Testament, therefore, views preaching as "God in action."[11] Preaching is not merely a word *about* God and his redemptive acts but a word *of* God and as such is itself a redemptive event.

Exposition of Scripture

Thus far we have noted some striking similarities between the preaching of the prophets and that of the apostles: both represented God, both spoke his word, both understood God's word to be God's deed. One difference between the preaching of the prophets and that of the apostles, aside from the contents, lies in the sources used for their preaching. Whereas the prophets usually received the word of the Lord via vision, dream, or audition, the apostles usually based their preaching on what they had "seen and heard" (1 John 1:3), the Word made flesh in fulfillment of the Scriptures. As such, their preaching moved toward exposition of the Scriptures.[12] From the letters of Paul it is apparent that his preaching was not only exposition of the Old Testament Scriptures but also transmission of

---

is speaking. This is also the meaning of the genitive in terms such as 'the Word *of God*' and 'the Word *of the Lord*.' This genitive does not primarily indicate the person about whom the Word speaks, but the person whose Word it is" (*TynBul* 29 [1978] 23, 25).

11. Haddon Robinson, *BSac* 131 (1974) 56.

12. Judging by the sermonic material in the first half of Acts, Gustaf Wingren concludes that "the original *kerygma* . . . is clearly and obviously exposition of Scripture. Central to what is proclaimed is an event, the death and resurrection of Christ, and the message has its full meaning as a message only because of the fact that these events are set forth as the 'fulfillment of the Scriptures' (Acts 2.17, 25; 3.18, 24; 10.43 and many others)" (*Living Word*, 17).

New Testament traditions. "Now I would remind you, brethren, in what terms I preached to you the gospel. . . . For I delivered to you as of first importance *what I also received*, that Christ died for our sins in accordance with the scriptures, that he was buried, that he was raised on the third day in accordance with the scriptures, and that he appeared to Cephas, then to the twelve" (1 Cor 15:1-5, my emphasis). But whether the apostles proclaimed the fulfillment of the Old Testament Scriptures or delivered eyewitness accounts or New Testament traditions, their preaching was inspired by the same Spirit who had earlier inspired the Old Testament prophets (see 1 Cor 2:13; cf. Rom 15:19).

Preaching and Teaching

The New Testament uses as many as thirty-three different verbs to describe what we usually cover with the single word *preaching*. The most significant of these verbs are *keryssein* (to proclaim as a herald), *euangelizesthai* (to announce good news), *martyrein* (to testify, witness), *didaskein* (to teach), *propheteuein* (to prophesy), and *parakalein* (to exhort).[13] These words and others show the rich variety of preaching in the early church.

C. H. Dodd promoted the theory that the early church distinguished sharply between proclamation in a missionary setting and teaching in an established church: "The New Testament writers draw a clear distinction between preaching and teaching. . . . Teaching *(didaskein)* is in a large majority of cases ethical instruction. . . . Preaching, on the other hand, is public proclamation of Christianity to the non-Christian world."[14] This distinction, which appears so simple, has led to "considerable confusion" in homiletical writings.[15] Moreover, it has led to "tragic" results in the pulpit, for Dodd's distinction between proclamation and teaching, between *kerygma* and *didache*, drove some preachers into opposing camps: supporters of dialectical theology opting for the kerygmatic principle and supporters of progressive religious education opting for the opposite pole of "personal, moral, and psychological development of Christian individuals."[16]

The New Testament, however, does not separate preaching and teach-

---

13. See Friedrich, *TDNT*, III, 703. For a description of the meaning of these six verbs, see Runia, *TynBul* 29 (1978) 7-20.

14. Dodd, *Apostolic Preaching and Its Developments*, 7; cf. p. 8: "For the early Church, then, to preach the Gospel was by no means the same thing as to deliver moral instruction or exhortation."

15. Davis, *Design for Preaching*, 106.

16. T. Hall, *Future Shape of Preaching*, 106. See further pp. 106-7: "The end result was tragic: inside the Christian community, the function of the preacher was reduced to an exercise in Christian moralism—often torn loose from any detectable grounding in the Christian gospel itself; and beyond the fellowship of believers, the presentation of the gospel to the world . . . took the form of a paradoxical, dialectic-kerygmatic cry in the night."

ing into such rigid, ironclad categories. Matthew relates that Jesus was "teaching [didaskon] in their synagogues and preaching [kerysson] the gospel of the kingdom" (4:23; cf. 9:35; 11:1). Luke similarly reports that Jesus "taught [edidasken] in their synagogues" and a little later that Jesus "was preaching [kerysson] in the synagogues" (4:15, 44). In Rome Paul was engaged in "preaching [kerysson] the kingdom of God and teaching [didaskon] about the Lord Jesus Christ" (Acts 28:31). Thus, in one and the same place, both kinds of activity went on: teaching and proclaiming. Although preaching in a mission situation must have had a different emphasis than preaching in an established church, there appears to be a developing consensus today that "preaching and teaching were never sharply separated by the first Christians and should not be separated by us today."[17] The church needs to hear the kerygma as well as the teaching, and unbelievers need to receive teaching as well as the kerygma. Consequently, preaching can be seen as an activity with many facets—facets which are highlighted by such New Testament words as *proclaiming, announcing good news, witnessing, teaching, prophesying,* and *exhorting.* Although one facet or another may certainly be accentuated to match the text and the contemporary audience, preaching cannot be reduced to only one of its many facets.

Preachers Today

PREACHERS today are neither Old Testament prophets nor New Testament apostles. Unless one would be guilty of both presumption and anachronism, one must constantly keep in mind the great difference between preachers then and preachers now. Preachers today do not receive their messages directly from God the way the prophets did. Nor can preachers today claim with the apostles that they were "eyewitnesses" (2 Pet 1:16; cf. Luke 1:2). And yet, provided their sermons are biblical, preachers today may also claim to bring the word of God.

God's Word
As we noticed in the partial shift from the direct revelation of vision or

17. Ibid., 105, referring to R. C. Worley's *Preaching and Teaching in the Earliest Church* (Philadelphia: Westminster, 1967). See also Wingren, *Living Word,* 18-19. Cf. Runia, *TynBul* 29 (1978) 14: "Apparently, the two activities are inseparable, and the various passages clearly show that teaching was not restricted to believers but was aimed at any one who listened in the various places where teaching took place"; and p. 23: "There is no indication in Paul's letters that he makes a fundamental difference between two kinds of preaching, the one *extra muros* and the other *intra muros.*" Runia states that "'teaching' and 'preaching' belong together," and that "'teaching' is the necessary consequence and follow-up of 'preaching'" (p. 15). Cf. Davis, *Design for Preaching,* 123-25.

audition received by the prophets to the exposition of Scripture by the apostles, one does not necessarily need direct revelation in order to speak God's word—God can speak his word mediately, by means of the exposition of prior revelation. One need not even be an eyewitness of Jesus' life, death, and resurrection in order to speak God's word—Paul can instruct young Timothy to "preach the word" (2 Tim 4:2; cf. 1 Cor 16:10). In order to demonstrate that preachers other than apostles can bring God's own word, Klaas Runia appeals particularly to 2 Cor 5:18-20, where Paul writes that "God gave *us* the ministry of reconciliation." Along with many commentators, Runia suggests that with the word *us* Paul means himself and "'his assistants' or 'other preachers of the Gospel.'" If this identification of "us" is correct, argues Runia, "it also means that the following words apply to *all* preachers of the Gospel: 'We are ambassadors for Christ, God making his appeal through us.' If today's preacher brings the same message of reconciliation as Paul and the other apostles, God also speaks through him. Then his word too is not just a human word, but the Word of God himself."[18]

Even more than the apostles, of course, today's preachers are dependent on the Scriptures as their source of revelation. The sermon as an exposition of the Scriptures can trace its roots from the Old Testament priesthood (Deut 31:9-13; Neh 8:1-8) to the synagogue (see Luke 4:16-27; Acts 13:14-41; 17:1-3) to the New Testament church. Some have sought to articulate the difference between the biblical preachers and their contemporary counterparts as follows: "The Old Testament and the New Testament organs of revelation came forward, saying: 'Thus says the Lord.' . . . But the New Testament preacher must say, if he would speak strictly: 'Thus has the Lord written.'"[19] Technically, in terms of the source of revelation, this formulation is correct, but materially, in terms of the reality of God's word, contemporary preachers should also be able to say: "Thus says the Lord." For the Spirit who spoke through the prophets is still speaking today through preaching which passes on the messages of God's prophets and apostles. Although the Spirit's speaking is by no means limited to preachers (think of parents, teachers, friends, and neighbors through whom the Spirit speaks today), contemporary preachers have a special responsibility to proclaim the word of the Lord. No less than their biblical counterparts, contemporary preachers are called to be channels of the word of God. The metaphors of herald and ambassador apply as much to them as they did to the apostles.[20] This high view of preaching

18. Runia, *TynBul* 29 (1978) 32.
19. Samuel Volbeda, *Pastoral Genius of Preaching*, 24.
20. "A herald never comes with his own authority or with his own message. He is backed by a higher power; he is the mouthpiece of his lord. In like manner Christ stands behind the preachers of his Word with his authority. . . . God speaks through

came to clear expression in the Reformed *Second Helvetic Confession* of 1566: *Praedicatio verbi Dei est verbum Dei* (the preaching of the word of God is the word of God).

God's Deed

But if God speaks through contemporary preachers, then this word of God is also God's deed today, a redemptive event.[21] This view reflects Paul's amazing statement that the gospel is "the power of God for salvation to every one who has faith" (Rom 1:16; cf. 1 Cor 1:18). Contemporary preaching of the gospel, therefore, is an indispensable link in the chain of God's redemptive activity which runs from Old Testament times to the last day (Matt 24:14). God uses contemporary preaching to bring his salvation to people today, to build his church, to bring in his kingdom. In short, contemporary biblical preaching is nothing less than a redemptive event.

This high view of preaching can never be the boast of preachers, of course; it can only underscore their responsibility. For with the prophets we noticed that their authority did not reside, ultimately, in their calling or office but in the words they spoke, whether they were from the Lord. So it is with preachers today: they have a word from the Lord, but only if they speak the *Lord's* word. The only norm we have today for judging whether preachers speak the word of the Lord is the Bible.[22]

Since the Bible is the normative source of revelation for contemporary preachers, they must bind themselves to the Scriptures if they would preach the word of God. In other words, they must preach biblically.

---

them. They have an official task; they are ambassadors of Christ. It seems as if *they* speak, but in reality *God* speaks" (R. Schippers, *Van den Dienst des Woords* [Goes: Oosterbaan & Le Cointre, 1944], 17, 19, translated and quoted in my *Sola Scriptura*, 160). Cf. Daane, *Preaching with Confidence*, 8-16.

21. Friedrich states: "The word proclaimed is a divine Word, and as such it is an effective force which creates what it proclaims. Hence preaching is no mere impartation of facts. It is event" (*TDNT*, III, 711; cf. p. 710). Miller makes the same point by describing the sermon as "an act wherein the crucified, risen Lord personally confronts men either to save or to judge them. . . . In a real sermon . . . Christ is the Preacher. The Preacher speaks through the preacher." "True preaching . . . is not achieved until the words of the preacher become the Deed of God" (*Fire in Thy Mouth*, 17, 24). See also my *Sola Scriptura*, 154-57. Similar thoughts about preaching are expressed today in Roman Catholic circles. Writes J. Kahmann, "As a message of salvation . . . the preaching is in fact a coming of God into this world. It is not merely a presentation of salvation, an announcement of God's plan with the requirements to be met by mankind, but it is an act of salvation by God" (*The Bible on the Preaching of the Word*, 109).

22. Haddon Robinson remarks that "the man in the pulpit faces the pressing temptation to deliver some message other than that of the Scriptures—a political system (either right-wing or left-wing), a theory of economics, a new religious philosophy, old religious slogans, a trend in psychology. . . . Yet when a preacher fails to preach the Scriptures, he abandons his authority. He confronts his hearers no longer with a word from God but only with another word from men" (*Biblical Preaching*, 18).

What this means concretely is the concern of all the following chapters. At this stage, however, we need to examine the foundations of these chapters with a general discussion of the meaning of "binding oneself to the Scriptures." The question is, What is involved in preaching biblically? Leander Keck suggests that at least two elements must be given their due: "Preaching is truly biblical when (a) the Bible governs the content of the sermon and when (b) the function of the sermon is analogous to that of the text. In other words, preaching is biblical when it imparts a Bible-shaped word in a Bible-like way."[23] Under the heading of "Expository Preaching" we shall discuss the "Bible-shaped word," and under the heading of "The Form of Biblical Preaching" the "Bible-like way."

EXPOSITORY PREACHING

WHEN Paul charged young Timothy to "preach the word," he intended not simply that Timothy mount a pulpit and speak but that he base his spoken word on the written (and heard) word (see 1 Tim 4:13; 2 Tim 2:2, 15). If the Scriptures were a prerequisite for Timothy's preaching, they are so even more for contemporary preachers, for the latter have no other source of revelation. If contemporary preachers wish to preach the word, they will need to proclaim relevantly the word that was long ago inscribed in Scripture. To preach the word today means, therefore, to pass on to the church here and now the message of the Bible. The call to preach the word is a call to preach biblically.

The Category of Expository Preaching

Confusing Categories

Biblical preaching has often been identified with expository preaching, especially in contrast to topical preaching. Unfortunately, some homileticians brought confusion into the terminology when they contrasted the category of "expository preaching" not only with the category of "topical preaching" but also with that of "textual preaching." With that complication, the term *expository preaching* took on so many misleading connotations as to make it practically useless. For example, in contrast to textual preaching, it has been claimed that expository preaching "grows out of a Bible passage longer than two or three verses," that "both the main points *and the subpoints* of the sermon are derived from the text"; that it is "verse-by-verse explanation of a chosen passage," or "consecutive interpretation and practical enforcement of a book in the sacred canon."[24]

---

23. Keck, *Bible in the Pulpit*, 106.
24. For the first view, see Blackwood, *Preparation of Sermons*, 69; cf. idem, *Preach-*

Small wonder that the distinction between expository preaching and textual preaching has been called "an act not of discrimination but of confusion," for with all these additional connotations, the term *expository preaching* has lost its original, plain meaning—"to exposit the Word of God."[25] The way out of the confusion is to disregard all the barnacle-like connotations that have encrusted the term "expository preaching" and concentrate on the original meaning of the term.

The Heart of Expository Preaching

Expository preaching is "Bible-centered preaching." That is, it is handling the text "in such a way that its real and essential meaning as it existed in the mind of the particular Biblical writer and as it exists in the light of the over-all context of Scripture is made plain and applied to the present-day needs of the hearers."[26] Thus one might say that expository preaching is preaching biblically. But "expository preaching" is more than a mere synonym for biblical preaching; it describes what is involved in biblical preaching, namely, the exposition of a biblical passage (or passages). John Stott elucidates this point as follows: "Whether it [the text] is long or short, our responsibility as expositors is to open it up in such a way that it speaks its message clearly, plainly, accurately, relevantly, without addition, subtraction or falsification. In expository preaching the biblical text is neither a conventional introduction to a sermon on a largely different theme, nor a convenient peg on which to hang a ragbag of miscellaneous thoughts, but a master which dictates and controls what is said."[27]

A Classification of Sermon Types

In order to keep our terminology straight and not compare apples with oranges, it may be helpful to introduce a classification scheme for differ-

---

ing from the Bible, 38-39. For the second, see Mickelsen, *Interpreting the Bible*, 365 (my emphasis). For the last, see Blackwood, *Preaching from the Bible*, 39; and Miller, *Way to Biblical Preaching*, 17-36.

25. See Daane, *Preaching with Confidence*, 52. William Thompson remarks that "the terms expository preaching and textual preaching are at least worthless—perhaps dangerous, if they keep us from understanding what *biblical* preaching is" (*Preaching Biblically*, 10). Dwight Stevenson suggests that the "traditional distinction between textual and expository preaching is superficial and . . . ought to be discarded" (*In the Biblical Preacher's Workshop*, 61).

26. Merrill Unger, *Principles of Expository Preaching*, 33. Cf. Robinson, *Biblical Preaching*, 20; and Liefeld, *NT Exposition*, 6-7. Miller claims that "all true preaching is expository preaching, and that preaching which is not expository is not preaching" (*Way to Biblical Preaching*, 22). Cf. Daane, *Preaching with Confidence*, 55-56: "If expository preaching means 'setting forth' biblical truth (and it literally does), then all preaching should be expository. . . . All authentic preaching is exposition of Scripture." Cf. Stott, *Between Two Worlds*, 125.

27. Stott, *Between Two Worlds*, 126. See also Barth, *Preaching of the Gospel*, 15, 43-49.

ent types of sermons. I suggest that sermons be classified, in descending order, by the following criteria: biblical content, use of text, and length of text. The classification, then, shows contrastable sermon types along the horizontal lines.

CATEGORIES	TYPES OF SERMONS			
Biblical content	Biblical Sermon			Nonbiblical Sermon
Use of text	Textual or Expository Sermon		Topical-Biblical Sermon	Topical Sermon
Length of text	Textual Unit	Verse or clause	Nontextual	Nontextual

We shall have occasion later to refer again to this diagram. For now the points to be noted are that expository preaching may indeed be contrasted with topical-biblical and topical-nonbiblical preaching, but questions concerning the length of a text are of a different order.

The Necessity of Expository Preaching

The Question of Authority

The necessity of expository preaching shows itself most clearly when the question of authority is raised. By whose authority do preachers preach? Whose word do they bring? If preachers preach their own word, the congregation may listen politely but has every right to disregard the sermon as just another person's opinion. If contemporary preachers preach with authority, however, the congregation can no longer dismiss their sermons as merely personal opinions but must respond to them as authoritative messages. The only proper authority for preaching is divine authority—the authority of God's heralds, his ambassadors, his agents. Heralds and ambassadors, we have seen, do not speak their own word but that of their sender. Contemporary preachers, similarly, if they wish to speak with divine authority, must speak not their own word but that of their Sender.[28]

Accordingly, if preachers wish to preach with divine authority, they must proclaim the message of the inspired Scriptures, for the Scriptures alone are the word of God written; the Scriptures alone have divine authority. If preachers wish to preach with divine authority, they must submit themselves, their thoughts and opinions, to the Scriptures and echo

---

28. "To be the agent of God's authority is to bear witness to what God has done for men in Christ, as this is recorded in the Bible" (Miller, *Fire in Thy Mouth*, 109). Or, more succinctly, every sermon should be "a manifestation of the Incarnate Word from the Written Word by the spoken word" (B. L. Manning as quoted by Taylor, "Shaping Sermons," 142).

the word of God. Preachers are literally to be *ministers* of the word. Thus preaching with authority is synonymous with true expository preaching. "Preaching which severs itself . . . from the Bible can have little or no valid authority over men's minds or hearts," asserts Miller, "for it is an irreverent assumption of authority which no living man may rightly claim. . . . The only right we have to preach is to preach Christ as he makes himself known through the Scriptures of the Old and New Testament."[29]

The Bible as the Source for Preaching

Not only does the Bible provide divine authority for preaching, it is also the *only* normative source for contemporary preaching. Donald Miller asks, "Why . . . does the Bible remain unique and authoritative for preaching? Why is the canon closed and a clear line of demarcation drawn between the history of redemption in the Bible and church history? The answer to this is to be seen in the light of the fact that revelation lies primarily in the unfolding drama of redemptive history, rather than in a set of religious ideas. Since the Bible is the record of the redemptive history, it remains permanently normative."[30] This answer is valid as far as it goes, but there is more to the uniqueness of the Bible than simply being "the record of the redemptive history." The Bible is unique and indispensable for preaching because it provides the definitive *interpretation* of God's acts in history; the Bible is the source for contemporary preaching because it alone provides the normative *proclamation* of God's acts of redemption and the response he requires. The Bible itself, therefore, can be seen as preaching: authoritative proclamation for future generations of God's good news of salvation. As such the Bible is the only normative source for contemporary preaching.

From the beginning the church recognized the Bible as the source for preaching (see, e.g., Luke 4:16-27; the sermonic material in Acts; 1 Tim 4:13). At certain points in history (A.D. 367, 393, 397), however, the church *officially* acknowledged the biblical books as canonical, as the *standard* for faith and practice. In the Belgic Confession of 1561 we hear the following profession of the church: "We receive all these books, and these only, as holy and canonical, for the regulation, foundation, and confirmation of our faith" (art. 5). In line with that faith commitment, contemporary preachers are to use "all these books, and these only" as the source for their preaching. This is not an impossible task since, as we have seen, the

---

29. Miller, *Fire in Thy Mouth,* 112. Cf. Smith, *Interpreting the Gospels for Preaching,* 54. According to John Bright, "There can . . . be no substitute for biblical preaching. Biblical preaching is the only kind that carries with it authority. . . . Since the recognized authority is for us the Bible, it is biblical preaching or no preaching with authority" (*Authority of the OT,* 166).

30. Miller, *Fire in Thy Mouth,* 55.

Bible is essentially God's proclamation to future generations. As proclamation, the Bible is the ideal source for further preaching; as canon, it is the only normative source.

Using the Bible as the source for preaching undoubtedly places a heavy responsibility on preachers, for they must seek to do justice to the Scriptures as well as to the contemporary situation in which the word must be spoken. Paul reminded Timothy of this responsibility in a word that is equally applicable to contemporary preachers: "Do your best to present yourself to God as one approved, a workman who has no need to be ashamed, rightly handling the word of truth" (2 Tim 2:15).

The Bible as the Criterion of Preaching

The affirmation that the Bible serves as source for preaching and lends authority to preaching does not entail that the congregation must blindly accept whatever is said, for the other side of the coin is that the Bible also functions as the criterion of preaching. Paul reminds the Corinthians that even the word of New Testament prophets is not simply to be accepted but should first be *weighed* (1 Cor 14:29). In 1 Thess 5:20-21 he encourages the congregation, "Do not despise prophesying, but *test* everything." And in Gal 1:8 he goes so far as to say, "Even if we, or an angel from heaven, should preach to you a gospel contrary to that which we preached to you, let him be accursed." Someone may claim to speak the word of God, but that claim does not necessarily make it so. Someone may have been called and ordained to the office of preacher, but that office does not automatically transform the preacher's words into the word of God. The sermon is the word of God "only in so far as the ambassador does not deviate from his Sender; the sermon requires unconditional submission only in so far as it correctly interprets the normative, infallible Word of God."[31] Hence the hearers will have to test the word that is spoken to see if it is indeed worthy of acceptance as the word of God.

Testing, of course, must be done with a certain standard, a criterion. But what standard shall we use for testing sermons? The standard surely cannot be personal likes or dislikes. The only standard we have today is the canon, the Bible. Sermons, therefore, must be tested against the Scriptures. Although we shall explore later what this means in detail, it may be helpful at this point to call to mind a few key testing criteria provided by the Bible.[32] The first and foundational criterion is that sermons must be

---

31. H. J. Spier, "De Woorddienst," *Cursus* I (1943), lesson vi.11, as translated in my *Sola Scriptura*, 160. See also Runia, *TynBul* 29 (1978) 43-46. Cf. Daane, *Preaching with Confidence*, 49: "If what the minister proclaims are human insights, however perceptive—mere human words even though they are pearls of wisdom—what is happening is not what the Bible regards as preaching."

32. See my article "On Criticizing Sermons," *The Banner* 119 (Aug 13, 1984) 8-9.

biblical, that is, they must pass on the meaning and intent of Scripture. A second criterion, implied in the first, is that sermons must be God-centered (or Christ-centered) rather than human-centered. If the Bible can indeed be characterized as God's *self*-revelation, then any biblical sermon will have to manifest that same quality by being *God*-centered and not human-centered (see further Chapter 5 below). A third criterion is that sermons must be good news. If one of the main New Testament words for preaching is "to announce good news" (*euangelizomai*), and if one may characterize as "good news" not only the Gospels but the entire Bible, then our sermons ought also to measure up to this standard so that they are indeed *good* news.

Expository Preaching and the Bible

The outstanding characteristic of expository preaching is that it uses the Bible as the source for its preaching; it seeks to give an exposition of a biblical passage. By contrast, nonbiblical topical preaching presents neither text nor exposition. Although it is possible to preach topical sermons that are biblical, in actual practice they often turn out to be flights of fancy which have little or nothing to do with biblical thought.[33] Moreover, it is extremely difficult for the congregation to test topical preaching by the criterion of the Bible. But an expository sermon purposely seeks to set forth a biblical message on the basis of a biblical text; "The expositor is only to provide mouth and lips for the passage itself so that the Word may advance."[34]

At heart, expository preaching is not just a method but a commitment, a view of the essence of preaching, a homiletical approach to preach the Scriptures.[35] This underlying commitment, in turn, is bound to reveal itself in a method in which preachers tie themselves to the Scriptures and, as heralds of Christ, seek to proclaim only that which the Scriptures proclaim.

Advantages of Expository Preaching

EXPOSITORY preaching has many advantages over topical preaching.

33. James Smart observes that "the topical form of sermon, which seems to have the widest appeal today, . . . usually permits the Biblical text to be touched only lightly. There is not room in it for any very careful exposition. . . . It inhibits the function of the sermon as a channel between the Scriptures and the church of today" (*Strange Silence of the Bible in the Church*, 22).

34. G. Wingren, *Living Word*, 201.

35. Cf. H. Robinson: "Expository preaching at its core is more a philosophy than a method. Whether or not a man can be called an expositor starts with his purpose and with his honest answer to the question: 'Do you, as a preacher, endeavor to bend your thought to the Scriptures, or do you use the Scriptures to support your thought?'" (*Biblical Preaching*, 20).

John Stott lists four major benefits: (1) It sets limits, that is, "it restricts us to the scriptural text" and does not allow us to invent our own message. (2) It demands integrity, that is, it confronts the preacher with the question, "What did the original author intend his words to mean?" (3) It identifies the pitfalls to be avoided. Stott mentions two main pitfalls: forgetfulness and disloyalty. "The forgetful expositor loses sight of his text by going off at a tangent and following his own fancy. The disloyal expositor appears to remain with his text, but strains and stretches it into something quite different from its original and natural meaning." (4) It gives us confidence to preach, for we are not expounding our own fallible views but the word of God.[36] All of these benefits are advantages for the preacher.

In the light of our discussion, we can also enumerate specific benefits of expository preaching for the church. First, expository preaching causes the *Scriptures* to be heard in church, thus enabling the members to gain an understanding of the Scriptures. Second, more so than topical preaching, expository preaching gives the hearers a measure of assurance that they are hearing the word of God. Finally, expository preaching aids the critical functioning of the church since it provides the hearers with textual limits for testing the spoken word against the written word; thus the hearers can decide more responsibly whether a message deserves acceptance.

THE FORM OF BIBLICAL PREACHING

THUS far we have looked at expository preaching mainly in terms of biblical content. A related aspect that is gaining increasing recognition today is the question of form. It has been suggested that "the distinguishing mark [of expository preaching] is that it is biblical both in form and in content."[37] In line with this suggestion, Richard Jensen surmises that "our style of exegesis for preaching may have to undergo some radical shifts. Exegesis has been directed primarily at the question of content. A holistic exegesis must be directed at both form and content. It is not enough to get the meaning out of the text and into the sermon. We must pay attention to the total configuration of textual form/content."[38]

Biblical Forms and Hermeneutics

THE recognition of different forms ("forms" used here in a general, nontechnical sense) of biblical literature is important for hermeneutics be-

---

36. Stott, *Between Two Worlds*, 126-33. Cf. Liefeld, *NT Exposition*, 10-13.
37. Bryant Kirkland, *Pulpit Digest* 45 (1965) 11.
38. Jensen, *Telling the Story*, 129.

cause it provides the initial clue to the meaning of a passage. Grant Osborne states that "genre plays a positive role as a hermeneutical device for determining the *sensus literalis* or intended meaning of the text. Genre is more than a means of classifying literary types; it is an epistemological tool for unlocking meaning in individual texts."[39]

The Interpreter's Expectations

Basically, our perception of the literary form of a text functions like a presupposition that influences and screens the meaning we perceive. The reason for this subtle influence of form is that our perception of a form sets our expectations and guides the questions we ask.[40] In fact, the mistaken interpretation resulting from understanding a particular form as if it were a different form has been called a "genre mistake."[41] A genre mistake takes place, for example, when the genre of prophecy or apocalypse is understood as historical narrative, or when a parable is understood as historical narrative, or when descriptive statement is understood as prescriptive. A genre mistake leads to faulty interpretation because the interpreter will ask the wrong questions. In a negative way, then, genre mistake alerts us to the fact that one's perception of the literary form of the text determines the questions one asks.

Asking the Right Questions

Of course, interpreters understand texts only by asking questions and receiving answers. Asking the right questions is of crucial importance, for asking the wrong questions will undoubtedly result in receiving wrong answers. One of the weighty issues in hermeneutics is, therefore, how to ask the right questions. The literary critic Leland Ryken emphasizes continually that the interpreter must ask questions of the text "that are appropriate to its literary form." "Any piece of writing must be read in terms of what it is. . . . When we fail to ask literary questions we go astray, interpreting figurative expressions as if they were intended literally, looking for theological propositions in a lyric poem that contains mainly an outpouring of human emotion . . . , allegorizing the Song of Solomon."[42]

---

39. Osborne, *Trinity Journal* 4/2 (1983) 24. J. Barton even claims: "It is not too much to say that it is impossible to understand any text without at least an implicit recognition of the genre to which it belongs" (*Reading the OT*, 16).

40. See E. D. Hirsch, *Validity in Interpretation*, 74: "An interpreter's preliminary generic conception of a text is constitutive of everything that he subsequently understands, and that this remains the case unless and until that generic conception is altered." Cf. p. 76: "All understanding of verbal meanings is necessarily genre-bound. . . . The genre-bound character of understanding is, of course, a version of the hermeneutic circle." Cf. Gunn, *Story of King David*, 19.

41. Patrick, "Political Exegesis," 143.

42. Ryken, *Christian Imagination*, 175, 179-80.

Hence the hermeneutical significance of recognizing biblical literary forms is that such discernment guides the interpreter in asking the right questions—questions that are appropriate to the form of the text.

Biblical Forms and Homiletics

BECAUSE of the monotonous similarity of all sermon forms, the sermon has sometimes disparagingly been defined as "three points and a poem." Today some preachers are moving away from monotony of form by taking their cue from the richness of biblical forms. Fred Craddock would have the preacher ask himself "why the Gospel should always be impaled upon the frame of Aristotelian logic, when his muscles twitch and his nerves tingle to mount the pulpit not with three points but with the Gospel as narrative or parable or poem or myth or song."[43] Don Wardlaw similarly decries the "assumption that preaching as such seems to mean finding sensible, orderly things to say *about* scriptural texts, rather than letting those texts say things their own way." Wardlaw continues: "When preachers feel they have not preached a passage of Scripture unless they have dissected and rearranged that Word into a lawyer's brief, they in reality make the Word of God subservient to one particular, technical kind of reason."[44]

Biblical Forms and Sermon Forms

In looking for forms of preaching that do justice to the biblical text, it is quite appropriate to look to the textual forms since most of them reflect the original preaching underlying the Bible. The form that occurs most frequently in the Bible is narrative. Richard Jensen contends, "If the text 'makes its point' in story form then we ought to seriously consider constructing a sermon that is faithful to the content and the form of the biblical text. . . . Why should we de-story these stories in our sermons and simply pass on the point of the story to our listeners?"[45]

Many sermons in the past tended to be strictly didactic, feeding the

---

43. Craddock, *As One Without Authority*, 45. Cf. pp. 143-44: "Why should the multitude of forms and moods within biblical literature . . . be brought together in one unvarying mold, and that copied from Greek rhetoricians of centuries ago? An unnecessary monotony results, but more profoundly, there is an inner conflict between the content of the sermon and its form. . . . The content calls for singing but the form is quite prosaic; the message has wings but the structure is quite pedestrian."

44. Wardlaw, "Need for New Shapes," 13, 16.

45. Jensen, *Telling the Story*, 128. See also Elizabeth Achtemeier: "Because the story of God's salvation of humankind is presented to us through the heart-stirring genres of the Bible, it therefore follows that if we are to proclaim that story, we should do so in words and forms that will produce the same telling effects. Why turn God's love into a proposition . . . ?" (*Creative Preaching*, 46).

congregation a diet of propositional truths.[46] Wardlaw points out that whereas form and content were "classically treated as separate, ultimate categories," in our contemporary society they are viewed as "a dynamic fusion in which meaningful form of any kind participates in the content it embodies. For the preacher, this means that a sermon's form should necessarily work in union with its substance. . . . The more integral a sermon's form is to its content, the Word in Scripture, the better chance that Word in Scripture has to be heard and felt by today's congregations."[47] Although not everyone agrees that the form of the text should be carried through in the sermon,[48] the attempt to do so opens up some exciting possibilities, provided preachers are sensitive to the canonical context of these forms.

Copying Biblical Forms?

The goal of shaping the sermon according to the form of the text obviously cannot be to copy slavishly the biblical form—that endeavor would falter immediately in cases where the text is a psalm or an epistle. Rather, the goal is to study carefully the form of the text and how it, in its literary context, plays its part in carrying the message to its intended effect with the hearers. David Buttrick uses the example of miracle stories, which "were designed to evoke a 'wow!' from listeners. The wise preacher will guess that a turgid apologetic for miracles or, worse, any rational explanation of miracles may scuttle the sense of 'wow' and, therefore, be homiletically inappropriate. If a passage wants to provoke amazement, it would seem homiletically respectful to aim at the effect."[49]

Although the "wow!" may not hold for all miracle stories—and here the canonical context is certainly decisive—whenever a text seeks to evoke amazement, the sermon should seek the same effect and not undercut it with its very form. Or, to take another example, suppose one's text is a hymn of praise. The text says "Praise God!" and wants people who hear it to praise God. But "if the sermon is the result of boiling down this poetic text to some abstract idea, the sermon is not really preaching the text."[50] The point is that the form of a sermon can undercut the message

---

46. It must also be said, however, that homileticians in the past were not blind to the fact that people can be fed and influenced in ways other than purely intellectual— witness the division of preaching texts into didactic (teaching), protreptic (exhorting), and empoetic (affecting) texts; see Hoekstra, *Gereformeerde Homiletiek*, 321-52.

47. Wardlaw, "Shaping Sermons by Context," 60. Ronald Allen suggests similarly that following the textual form in preaching is "to communicate the text in the fullness of both its cognitive (discursive, rational) and intuitive (tacit, feeling) dimensions of meaning" ("Shaping Sermons by Language," 30).

48. For example, Adams, *Preaching with Purpose*, 57.

49. Buttrick, *Int* 35/1 (1981) 51.

50. Willimon, *Preaching*, 68-69.

of a text and thus distort it. Conversely, the form of a sermon, if appropriate, can help the message get across as originally intended.

Again, the goal of shaping the sermon according to the form of the text cannot be slavish imitation. One might speak instead of *respect* for the text. What this means concretely will differ from sermon to sermon and from text to text. For example, a sermon on a narrative text can follow the plot of the narrative, while a sermon on a poetic text can follow the movement of its images.[51] Thus the form of the text provides clues for shaping the sermon so that it will do justice to the original formed content as it affected the original hearers.

Classification of Biblical Forms

WE shall conclude this introductory chapter with a brief discussion of the classification of biblical forms. The classification of various forms is complex because biblical literature comes in many different forms at many different levels—all overlapping and interspersed. Moreover, the word *form* is ambiguous, since it can indicate forms of literature at all levels but also, as a technical term introduced by form criticism, preliterary or literary units at the most elementary level. For the sake of clarity, we shall distinguish the forms of biblical literature at three levels: the level of the Bible as a whole, the level of major literary types or "genres," and the level of smaller literary units or "forms."

The Kerygmatic Form of the Bible

We have already noted that the form of the Bible as a whole is proclamation, preaching. As such, biblical literature reveals both its origin, which was mainly preaching, and its goal, which is preaching. One way to become aware of the significance of the kerygmatic form of the Bible is to contrast this form with other possible forms: the Bible was not written in the form of a theological tome or of a scientific treatise; the Bible was not written in the form of a handbook of world history or of a newspaper report; the Bible comes in the form of proclamation, that is, direct address, personal appeal. It is with this biblical, kerygmatic form in mind that many are calling for a change in contemporary forms of preaching.[52] At this level the call for a biblical form of preaching is usually a justified call

---

51. See Ronand Allen, "Shaping Sermons by Language," 35-36.

52. Thorwald Lorenzen argues that "the responsible sermon must in its form correspond to the subject which it tries to communicate. If God as the 'Coming One' wants to come in the preaching event and modify the existence of the hearer, then one cannot underhandedly change the preaching situation into a theology lecture or a history class" (*SJT* 33 [1980] 467).

for a form of preaching that is not scientific, theoretical, objective, or abstract but one that is proclamation, relevant address, personal appeal.

Genres and Forms

At the level of major literary types we find various genres of literature in the Bible but little agreement among biblical scholars regarding their number and classification. For example, David Clines suggests that "story and poem" are the major literary types of the Old Testament: "Overarching the multiplicity of literary forms *(Gattungen)* discovered within Old Testament literature are these two catch-all forms of story and poem."[53] Walter Kaiser argues for "five basic literary forms used by the Biblical writers. . . . (1) prose, (2) poetry, (3) narrative, (4) wisdom, and (5) apocalyptic."[54] Dealing with both Old and New Testament genres, Gordon Fee and Douglas Stuart divide the biblical literature over ten chapters: Epistles, Old Testament narratives, Acts, Gospels, Parables, Law(s), Prophets, Psalms, Wisdom, and Revelation.[55]

Aside from disagreement about the number and identity of major literary types, discussions on literary forms are often confusing because the smaller "forms" of literature are not clearly distinguished from the larger "genres." A "literary genre" has been defined as "a group of written texts marked by distinctive recurring characteristics which constitute a recognizable and coherent type of writing."[56] This definition, as well as others, can apply to major literary genres as well as to smaller literary forms. Matters are further complicated by the mixture of genres so that, for example, prophecy is found in the genre of narrative and narrative in the genre of prophecy.[57]

We need not become unduly involved in a classification system of literary types, but as already intimated, it is helpful to draw a clear distinction between major literary types or "genres" and subtypes or "forms" that make up a major type. J. Arthur Baird offers such a distinction: "The concept of 'form' has been applied since Gunkel to the small individual

53. Clines, *Int* 34/2 (1980) 117-18.

54. Kaiser, *Toward an Exegetical Theology,* 91. Note that Kaiser (pp. 91-92) sees historical narrative as "a type of prose writing" but lists it separately because of "special problems."

55. Fee and Stuart, *How to Read the Bible.*

56. Collins, *Semeia* 14 (1979) 1. Cf. Barton, *Reading the OT,* 16: "By 'genre' is meant any recognizable and distinguishable type of writing or speech . . . which operates within certain conventions that are in principle . . . stateable."

57. Cf. Osborne, *Trinity Journal* 4/2 (1983) 6, 9. Buss speaks of "a multidimensional array of overlapping forms" ("Understanding Communication," 11). On the "fluid concept of genre" see Longman, *Literary Approaches,* 78-80. Thompson observes aptly that "it is easy in dealing with genre to become involved in the debate over how many ways you can slice the Scriptures" (*Preaching Biblically,* 62).

units representing the materials out of which the literary work is composed. . . . Form . . . is a category for analyzing relatively small, individual units of literary material." But genre "is a category for classifying literary works as a whole. As such it is a collective category that requires many individual units often . . . of different types, which taken together constitute the characteristic features of the Genre."[58] This basic distinction will be beneficial for understanding the organization of the following chapters. All the same, we ought not to become rigid about a certain classification system: the distinction between genre and form is not always clear, and the various genres, far from being airtight compartments, often overlap with one another and, of course, may contain similar "forms." In spite of this fluidity, a fruitful distinction between certain genres can be made for the sake of focusing hermeneutical and homiletical questions upon texts of a similar type.

Biblical Genres

Distinguishing between only two types of literature, prose and poetry (or "story and poetry") is too general to be particularly helpful. Prose and poetry, in fact, are found in all the major biblical genres and thus, though contributing to their makeup, are distinctive of neither.

Most biblical scholars seem to agree that Hebrew narrative, prophecy, wisdom, gospels, and epistles are major biblical genres. There is disagreement, however, about law, parables, psalms, apocalyptic literature, and the book of Acts. Although both law and parables satisfy the definition of "a group of written texts marked by distinctive recurring characteristics," it is also clear that both function as subtypes of broader biblical genres: law especially in Hebrew narrative,[59] in gospels, and in epistles, and parables especially in the gospels but also in Hebrew narrative and in prophecy. However, psalms are not only "a group of written texts marked by distinctive recurring characteristics," but are also found in their own unique collection in the book of Psalms. The same is true for apocalyptic literature, which, while found in various genres such as prophecy and gospels, has found a home in its own unique book, Revelation. I would therefore be inclined to include psalms and apocalyptic literature among the major biblical genres, while I would subsume law and parables as "forms" contained in various genres.

The last borderline case is the book of Acts, which some classify

---

58. Baird, *SBL Proceedings*, 1972, II, 386-88. Cf. William Doty, *Contemporary NT Interpretation*, 167; and Stuart, *OT Exegesis*, 107.

59. Even in the book of Leviticus, "all the laws are set within a narrative framework," according to G. J. Wenham, *The Book of Leviticus*, NICOT (Grand Rapids: Eerdmans, 1979), 5. Cf. David Damrosch, "Leviticus," in *The Literary Guide to the Bible*, ed. Robert Alter and Frank Kermode (Cambridge: Harvard University, 1987), 66-77.

alongside gospel, epistle, and apocalypse as a separate genre and others ignore altogether. Acts cannot, of course, be classified as a subtype of other New Testament genres. The alternative, however, of making Acts a separate genre is not very satisfactory either since Acts is a continuation of the Gospel of Luke. Another possibility is to cover both Acts and Luke, as well as the other Gospels, under the genre of New Testament narrative. Although this alternative would solve the problem and at the same time nicely parallel Old Testament narrative, the disadvantage is that gospel is a well-established genre. For our purposes, the most satisfactory solution seems to be not to classify Acts as a separate genre but to treat it in connection with our discussion on the genre of gospel (New Testament narrative) as a unique continuation of the Gospel of Luke.

With these borderline cases more or less settled, we can diagram these genres and their relationship to "forms" as follows:

CATEGORIES	FORMS OF BIBLICAL LITERATURE					
The Bible as a Whole	Proclamation					
"Genres"	Narrative Wisdom Gospel Apocalypse Prophecy Psalm Epistle					
"Forms"	Law	Dream	Lament	Parable	Miracle	Exhortation
	Autobiography	Funeral dirge		Lawsuit		Pronouncement
	Report	Royal accession		Passion	Etc.	
	Subforms					

Note that "forms" such as law, parable, and miracle are now parts of the canonical "genres"; although they may be treated separately because of their distinctive form, in the final analysis they can be validly understood only in the context of their biblical genre.

The next chapters deal with hermeneutical and homiletical issues relevant to all biblical genres, while the final chapters focus this general discussion on specific genres of biblical literature. For these final chapters I have selected for special consideration the four major genres of biblical literature: Hebrew narrative, prophecy, gospel, and epistle. These four genres not only cover most of the biblical books but also allow for some discussion of prose and poetry. Before examining the hermeneutical and homiletical issues, however, we will discuss in Chapter 2 an even more fundamental subject, the historical foundations of biblical preaching.

CHAPTER 2

Historical Foundations

THE message of all biblical genres of literature is in one way or another dependent on the reality of specific historical events proclaimed in the Bible. It is not accidental that by far the largest genre of biblical literature is that of historical narrative (found in most of Hebrew narrative, the Gospels, Acts, and to some extent in the Prophets, Psalms, and Epistles). The faith of Israel and the faith of historical Christianity is founded not in lofty ideas or ideals but in God's acts in human history.

Unfortunately, the historicity of the events proclaimed in Scripture is under a cloud of suspicion today, and as long as that suspicion (or skepticism) remains, these narratives and other genres cannot be preached with the same point and conviction as they were by their biblical authors. In his day, Paul already had to confront people who, because of their dualistic worldview, doubted Jesus' bodily resurrection. Paul clearly perceived the implications of this skepticism for his preaching: "If Christ has not been raised, then our preaching is in vain and your faith is in vain." More than that, Paul asserts, "We are even found to be misrepresenting God, because we testified of God that he raised Christ, whom he did not raise if it is true that the dead are not raised" (1 Cor 15:14-15).

Before all else, therefore, it is necessary for preachers to be clear on the historical foundations of their message. The issue is, Is the Bible historically reliable or is it not? Do we approach the Bible with skepticism or with confidence? Since "the historical accuracy of what purports to be historical narrative" is usually ascertained by historical criticism,[1] we need to examine the procedures and presuppositions of the historical-critical method.

---

1. Marshall, "Historical Criticism," 126.

THE HISTORICAL-CRITICAL METHOD

ANALYZING the historical-critical method is complicated by the fact that different biblical scholars used the method with different sets of presuppositions, thus obtaining different results.[2] Consequently, it may be more appropriate to speak of "historical-critical methods" (plural) rather than of "the historical-critical method" (singular). Nevertheless, when one speaks of the historical-critical method today, one can with some justification speak of a specific historical-critical method which is informed and guided by a specific set of shared presuppositions. Although these presuppositions are seldom acknowledged, in 1898 Ernst Troeltsch forthrightly brought some of them out into the open.[3] In fact, without calling attention to it, Troeltsch actually laid bare two layers of presuppositions, the bottom layer supporting the upper layer. The upper layer he called "principles," of which there are three: criticism, analogy, and correlation. Troeltsch acknowledged that these principles were founded on two underlying assumptions: the "fundamental similarity" of all historical texts, and the "fundamental similarity of all historical events."[4] Accordingly, the in-depth picture of the historical-critical method may be sketched as follows:

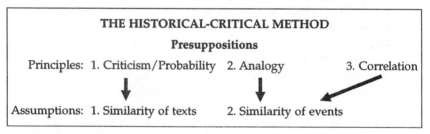

THE HISTORICAL-CRITICAL METHOD

Presuppositions

Principles: 1. Criticism/Probability   2. Analogy   3. Correlation

Assumptions: 1. Similarity of texts   2. Similarity of events

We shall first examine each principle and its underlying assumption, then appraise these presuppositions critically, and finally offer an alternative.

Analysis

The Principle of Criticism/Probability
The first principle Troeltsch lists is the principle of criticism, which he explains as follows: "In the field of history one can give only probability judgments . . . of a greater or lesser degree, and therefore every tradition must first be given its appropriate degree of probability." Troeltsch insists that this principle be applied impartially to all historical traditions, in-

2. Rogerson, *OT Criticism*, 82-83; see also p. 140: "Their starting points varied considerably and fundamentally affected how criticism was employed." On pre-understanding and its role, see Ferguson, *Biblical Hermeneutics*, 6-22.

3. Troeltsch, *Gesammelte Schriften*, II, 729-53. I am responsible for the translation of the following quotations from German into English.

4. Ibid., 732.

cluding biblical traditions. In other words, the Bible is to be treated like any other document. Troeltsch admits that this principle of criticism applied equally to all documents rests on a prior assumption, namely, that of the fundamental similarity or homogeneity *(die prinzipielle Gleichartigkeit)* of all ways of passing on traditions *(Überlieferungsweisen)*.[5]

This first principle, it should be noted, is two-pronged. It states not only that all historical documents must receive the same critical treatment but also that questions of historicity can receive only probability judgments. Since Troeltsch linked this principle of criticism with "probability" and spoke of "the implied uncertainty of its results,"[6] some have described this principle as "methodological doubt," and others as "systematic skepticism."[7] Although Troeltsch himself did not make this explicit, it is fair to say that one of the underlying assumptions of the historical-critical method as generally practiced is that all historical documents must be approached with an attitude of doubt. Consequently, the two-pronged principle of criticism/probability turns out to be supported by an underlying assumption which is also two-pronged: similarity of texts and an approach marked by doubt.

The Principle of Analogy

The second presupposition, linked to the first, is the principle of analogy. According to Troeltsch: "The means by which criticism becomes possible is the employment of analogy. The analogy of what takes place before our eyes . . . is the key to criticism. . . . Correspondence with normal, customary, or at least repeatedly attested ways of occurrence . . . , as we know them, is the mark of probability for occurrences which criticism can acknowledge as really having happened." In other words, correspondence with occurrences as we know them in the present is the standard for judging the reality of events in the past. At this point, too, Troeltsch is aware of an underlying ontological assumption, namely, that of "the fundamental similarity *[die prinzipielle Gleichartigkeit]* of all historical events."[8]

The Principle of Correlation .

From this "fundamental similarity of all historical events" follows, for Troeltsch, the third principle, which he calls the principle of correlation. "If the leveling significance of the analogy is possible only on the basis of the coherence and similarity of humanity and its historical activities, then with it the third historical presupposition is also given, namely, the interaction

---

5. Ibid., 731 and 732.
6. Ibid., 740.
7. For the former, see Krentz, *Historical-Critical Method,* 55. For the latter, see Stuhlmacher, *Historical Criticism,* 45.
8. Troeltsch, *Gesammelte Schriften,* II, 732.

of all human phenomena in such a way that no change can take place at any point without a change in the preceding and the following; all events exist in a firm correlative coherence and must necessarily develop into a movement in which each and every event coheres and every progression is related to others."[9] The principle of correlation, in short, holds that an event must be understood in the context of the whole of history, in terms of its causes and its effects, its antecedents and its consequences.

Although Troeltsch linked the principle of correlation specifically to the assumption of the similarity of all events, his writings reveal that he grounded this principle of correlation in a more direct, ontological assumption, namely, that history is a coherent, unified web of immanent causes and effects.[10] In other words, in studying history one eliminates a priori the possibility of a transcendent cause. This assumption about history is held not only by Troeltsch but also today by adherents of naturalism, positivism, and other "isms" who view history as a closed continuum of a series of causes and effects.

It appears, then, that each of the "principles" of the historical-critical method rests on a prior assumption. Instead of the earlier sketch, therefore, a more accurate, in-depth picture of the historical-critical method would look as follows:

THE HISTORICAL-CRITICAL METHOD

Presuppositions:

Principles:	1. Criticism/Probability	2. Analogy	3. Correlation
	↑↓ ↑↓	↑↓	↑↓
Assumptions:	1. Similarity/Doubt of texts	2. Similarity of events	3. Closed universe

---

Results of the Historical-Critical Method

The above three principles together with their underlying assumptions are still used by many contemporary biblical scholars as they employ the historical-critical method. Although this method has booked many gains, the overall results in biblical studies have been the separation of the biblical narrative from its underlying history and such extreme skepticism with respect to the historicity of biblical events that some biblical scholars have fled from history into the safety of a nonhistorical or suprahistorical realm. For example, having surrendered nearly all historicity of the New Testament to the historical-critical method, Rudolf Bultmann "retreated with his

9. Ibid., 733.
10. See, e.g., ibid., 732 and 737; also idem, *ZTK* 8 (1898) 5.

revelation into the area of existential meaning in the historicity (*Geschicht-lichkeit*) of the individual."[11] His pupils Willi Marxen and Hans Conzelmann, also skeptical about the historicity of the Gospels, opt for the theological meanings they discover with their redaction criticism. Similarly, Norman Perrin uses redaction criticism to pit theology against history, as if there were an antithesis between the two.[12] It could be argued that the recent paradigm shift from historical criticism to literary criticism is partly the result of the uncertainty brought on by the historical-critical method—although other motives may share responsibility for this shift.[13]

In any event, in Old Testament as well as New Testament studies the historical-critical method has left us with a problem of major proportions: two widely divergent pictures of biblical history. In New Testament studies we are confronted with the well-known discrepancy between the "historical Jesus," that is, Jesus as reconstructed by the historical-critical method, and the "kerygmatic Christ," that is, Jesus as presented in the Gospels. Similarly, in Old Testament studies we are left with two pictures of Israel. Gerhard von Rad speaks for many when he says:

> These two pictures of Israel's history lie before us—that of modern critical scholarship and that which the faith of Israel constructed—and for the present, we must reconcile ourselves to both of them. . . . The one is rational and "objective"; that is, with the aid of historical method and *presupposing the similarity of all historical occurrence*, it constructs a critical picture of the history as it really was in Israel. . . .
>
> The other activity is confessional and personally involved in the events to the point of fervour. . . . Historical investigation searches for a critically assured minimum—the kerygmatic picture tends towards a theological maximum. The fact that these two views of Israel's history are so divergent is one of the most serious burdens imposed today upon biblical scholarship.[14]

It is clear that the historical-critical method by its very principles and assumptions has driven biblical interpreters into a corner. Instead of trying to escape from that corner by way of a nonhistorical *Geschichte* or by way of the aesthetic structure of the *story*, however, a sounder route to follow is to question the principles and assumptions of the historical-critical method that gave rise to the problem in the first place. It speaks well for von Rad that he experiences the discrepancy between the two pictures as a serious burden. What is surprising is that he does not question the validity of the historical-critical method and its presuppositions. Can it be

11. Braaten, *History and Hermeneutics*, 21. Cf. Ferguson, *Biblical Hermeneutics*, 41-64.
12. For example, Perrin, *Resurrection*, 81. See Hooker, "In His Own Image," 36-38.
13. Hasel, *JSOT* 31 (1985) 34-37.
14. Von Rad, *OT Theology*, I, 107-8 (my emphasis). Cf. Eichrodt's evaluation of von Rad's method in *Theology of the OT*, I, 512-16.

that the historical-critical method is an improper tool to recover the real
history of Israel and the real historical Jesus? John Bright, for one, sees the
problem in the field of method:

> Where the earliest history of Israel is concerned, one may find head-on
> clashes of opinion at almost every point, together with totally divergent re-
> constructions of the whole. . . .
>
> Now it must be stressed that this confusion reflects an unsolved prob-
> lem of method. All these reconstructions, diverse as they are, are made on
> the basis of the same traditions and . . . the same external evidence. The
> question is not, therefore, primarily one of the field of evidence, but of the
> evaluation of that evidence. . . . It is without doubt the most pressing prob-
> lem confronting the historiography of Israel that the question of method as
> it applies to this problem be given an answer.[15]

It is necessary, therefore, to evaluate critically the historical-critical
method and its commonly held presuppositions.

Appraisal

Criticism and the Bible

We saw that the first principle, criticism, is two-pronged. The first prong,
that the Scriptures should receive the same critical treatment as other historical documents, rests on the assumption of the fundamental similarity
of all historical documents. Although this assumption does not do justice
to the Bible, which as the word of God is quite different from other documents, our acceptance of the Bible as the word of God cannot remove it
from historical criticism. Since the word of God comes to us in human
form, the Bible can indeed be subjected to the same historical-critical
method that is applied to other historical documents. It should be noted,
however, that the Bible is subject to the same critical inquiry as other
documents not only because of its similarity to other documents but in
spite of its dissimilarity. In any event, the Bible demands no special treatment; nor, of course, should it be subjected, as happens, to harsher criteria
than are applied to other ancient documents. The critical question here is,
What *kind* of historical-critical method is applied to the Bible?

Probability and Doubt

The second prong of the principle of criticism is that a historian can give
only probability judgments concerning the historical reliability of documents. Since documents can range from spurious to accurate, the above
statement rings true. Moreover, in view of the extreme complexity of history (see Chapter 4 below), no historical document can ever fully record

15. Bright, *Early Israel in Recent History Writing*, 15.

the intricacies of historical events. Hence the principle of probability judgments appears to be valid.

The assumption behind this notion of probability, the assumption of methodological doubt, is, however, more open to criticism. Since a historian should not be gullible, a measure of doubt is obviously quite in order when first approaching a historical document. But the question is, How radical should that doubt be? And how long should it persist? Some have argued that the roots of the historical-critical method can be traced back to Descartes, whose radical doubt in philosophy was transferred into the field of history.[16] It certainly appears that this kind of radical doubt motivates some biblical critics who approach the Bible with the assumption that there is little or no "hard" history in the Bible.[17] Because of the historical-critical method's approach of doubt, the burden of proof has shifted so that now the biblical reports are required to *prove* their historicity.[18]

But what evidence will satisfy biblical critics that a narrative is historically reliable? Some have stated that one should accept nothing in the Old Testament as historical fact "until it can be demonstrated as such by extrabiblical evidence." But this criterion is obviously unreasonable, for "many of the scriptural records have to do with people and situations that were of no interest whatever to non-Hebrews who might otherwise have provided confirmatory source material."[19] Moreover, many other reasons could be given for the silence of extrabiblical sources on biblical history: it might, indeed, be "no interest," or "no occasion," or "no knowledge," or "no time or writing materials," or "the evidence perished or is still to be found." In any case, by itself an argument from silence can neither prove nor disprove biblical historicity.[20]

Analogy and the Similarity of All Events

The second principle, that of analogy, is indeed an important principle for advancing knowledge: we learn by comparing the unknown with the already known. As a principle for the historical-critical method, however,

---

16. See Lyon, "Evangelicals and Critical Historical Method," 138-39.

17. See Anthony Hanson on the unexamined assumption "that virtually no trustworthy historical information can have survived the period of oral transmission" ("Quandary of Historical Scepticism," 75).

18. See, e.g., Norman Perrin, *Rediscovering*, 39: "The nature of the synoptic tradition is such that the burden of proof will be upon the claim to authenticity." Cf. George Ramsey, *Quest for the Historical Israel*, 101: "When the principal features and developments in a story can be attributed to literary devices and motives, the burden of proof should be placed upon the person who maintains that the story contains historical reminiscences."

19. See Harrison, *Biblical Criticism*, 5-6. For references see Merrill, *BSac* 140 (1983) 305.

20. Cf. Kitchen, *TynBul* 17 (1966) 67.

analogy has two drawbacks. The first drawback is that this principle is extremely *subjectivistic* and hence becomes an arbitrary criterion in determining what is historical and what is not. For the principle of analogy posits that the probability of the historicity of reported events is to be judged by the critic's experience. The narrower one's experience, therefore, the more one will have to dismiss as unhistorical; and the broader one's experience, the less one will have to dismiss as unhistorical.

I suspect, however, that most critics would understand analogy in a broader sense than analogy with one's personal experience. But even a broader criterion such as analogy with the experience of contemporary humanity, if applied rigorously, would screen out all *unique* events. Thus the second drawback comes into view: this principle is *reductionistic*. Analogy by itself, even when broadly conceived, cannot confirm the historicity of Luther nailing "his ninety-five theses to the door of the Castle Church in Wittenberg in 1517"; it cannot confirm the historicity of "the first human landing on the moon," nor any other first, because there is no analogy.[21] Since analogy, strictly speaking, cannot confirm the historicity of unique events, this principle will tend to declare as unhistorical what we know as a matter of fact to be historical. Happily, contemporary unique events are not completely at the mercy of analogy; by way of contemporary eyewitnesses, they assert their historicity in spite of the lack of analogy. Unique events of the past do not have such living corroborators, however, and hence tend to be summarily declared "nonhistorical."

One class of unique biblical events that are commonly dismissed with the principle of analogy are the miracles—often summarily labeled as fiction or myth. I may protest, of course, that I have experienced miracles in the present and that therefore, by way of analogy, I need not disallow miracles from having taken place in the past. But Troeltsch closes the door to that use of analogy by coupling analogy with the underlying assumption of "the fundamental similarity of all historical events"—events understood as "natural" events. In fact, he writes, "this omnipotence of analogy includes the fundamental similarity of all historical events."[22] This combination of analogy and the similarity of all events effectively blocks out all unique events such as miracles, and in that sense the historical-critical method is bound to be reductionistic.

Sometimes the principle of analogy is presented under the innocent term of "commonsense judgments."[23] Naturally people cannot cross a sea on foot; naturally blind men do not receive sight; naturally people do not rise from the dead. But why are these things naturally so? It appears that

21. Abraham, *Divine Revelation*, 103.
22. Troeltsch, *Gesammelte Schriften*, II, 732.
23. Ramsey, *Quest for the Historical Israel*, 15-16.

behind these "commonsense judgments" lies the principle of analogy, and behind the principle of analogy lies the assumption of the similarity of all events, and behind the assumption of the similarity of all events lies the nineteenth-century philosophy of Positivism. The so-called commonsense judgment turns out to be rather more than common sense; in fact, it is a judgment which is "anti-historical in the sense that it involves measuring the past by the standards of the present."[24] Further, this judgment is made on the basis of a rather restricted view of reality—"a narrow concept of reality according to which 'dead men do not rise.'"[25] This reduced view of reality functions as the standard by which the probability of past events are judged. Small wonder that reported miracles are blocked out and labeled nonhistorical. That conclusion is not the result of careful, critical work but is already given in the premises.

Several biblical scholars have warned against absolutizing the principle of analogy. Edgar Krentz asserts: "That a reported event bursts analogies with otherwise real events is still no reason to dispute its factualism. Thus the resurrection cannot be rejected through the use of analogical reasoning."[26] And John Goldingay observes aptly: "If it is unscientific to be gullible about what purports to be miracle, it is also unscientific arbitrarily to rule out the possibility that an event may be unique, miraculous. Historical sources must be treated on their merits as sources, rather than prejudged by means of presuppositions."[27]

Correlation in a Closed Universe

The third principle, correlation, confirms that the historical-critical method as commonly used is reductionistic. Not only is the method unable to handle unique events, but correlation shows that it cannot take into account *all* factors operating in history. The principle of correlation starts out well enough with the requirement that each event be understood in terms of its causes and effects as part of the whole web of history. But it becomes problematic when it is fused with the assumption that historical events can be explained exhaustively in terms of intraworldly causality. Troeltsch asserts pointedly that the totality of history "knows no point outside this mutual influence and interlacing."[28] Elsewhere, in discussing supernaturalism, he insists that the historical-critical method,

24. See Richardson, *History Sacred and Profane,* 110; also Lonergan, *Method in Theology,* 225-26.

25. Pannenberg, *Jesus—God and Man,* 109.

26. Krentz, *Historical-Critical Method,* 82. Cf. Nations, *SJT* 36/1 (1983) 62: "The criteria by which historical method functions (e.g. the principle of analogy) are inadequate in dealing with historical novelty."

27. Goldingay, *TynBul* 23 (1972) 89.

28. Troeltsch, *Gesammelte Schriften,* II, 732; cf. 737.

once accepted, knows no boundaries but can be applied to the supernatural as well; however, "having been formed according to natural events, when the method is applied to the supernatural, it necessarily dissolves the latter into natural categories."[29]

As formulated by Troeltsch, therefore, the principle of correlation is unable to acknowledge a transcendent God's acts in history; it has a built-in blind spot for divine causation in history. On this account, too, it must declare all reported miracles nonhistorical. Bultmann underscores this point as follows: "The historical method includes the presupposition that history is a unity in the sense of a closed continuum of effects in which individual events are connected by the succession of cause and effect. . . . This closedness means that the continuum of historical happenings cannot be rent by the interference of supernatural, transcendent powers and that therefore there is no 'miracle' in this sense of the word."[30] In other words, the assumption that we live in a closed universe decides in advance that miracles are impossible.

The question may now be raised whether immanentism, positivism, naturalism, or some other "ism" that assumes a closed universe is able to account adequately for all events taking place in human history. Or, to put the question differently, Can a method that excludes from the outset any particular solution claim to be scientific? Robert Lyon contends that such a method is provincial rather than scientific. "This is not to argue that any and all supernatural claims be accepted; rather it is to say that a truly scientific method will not and cannot limit automatically the boundaries of explanation."[31]

Those who do automatically limit the boundaries of explanation by subscribing to the accepted historical-critical method are methodologically committed to some form of immanentism or naturalism. Walter Wink labels this "a secularist perspective" and "functional, methodological atheism."[32] Troeltsch did indeed refer to his method as a "secular, historical method,"[33] and it is clear that atheists would feel quite at home with his method and its presuppositions. It must be recognized, however, that deists (in the technical sense) can find themselves equally well in this method. But biblical theists, if they are consistent, will have to demur because this historical-critical method cuts the heart out of the biblical message. For theists there is no conceivable reason why historical events need to be understood exclusively in terms of immanent causality. On the contrary, the heart of the biblical message is that God acts in human history; in fact, as Jer 9:24 puts

29. Troeltsch, ZTK 8 (1898) 5.
30. Bultmann, Existence and Faith, 291-92.
31. Lyon, "Evangelicals and Critical Historical Method," 145-46.
32. Wink, Bible in Human Transformation, 38.
33. Troeltsch, Gesammelte Schriften, II, 740; cf. p. 745.

it: "Let him who glories glory in this, that he understands and knows me, that I am the Lord who practice steadfast love, justice, and righteousness in the earth; for in these things I delight, says the Lord."

Some theologians argue, however, that a Christian may personally believe in God, but as a scientific historian one must leave God out of account. For example, James Barr asserts: "We do not apply the term 'history' to a form of investigation which resorts to divine agency as a mode of explanation."[34] Although it must be admitted that acknowledging divine causality introduces a complicating dimension into the method, can one, to avoid this complexity, simply exclude God from the discipline of history by definition? Can one simply pronounce that the historian as historian cannot take God into account? Surprisingly, even Lyon argues in a similar vein. He writes that acts of God such as Jesus' virgin birth and resurrection, "even though they may have happened and may truly be part of history, . . . will never achieve the status of historical facts because they are not subject to either verification or refutation." A historian qua historian cannot take God's acts into account because "they can be neither substantiated nor disproved." According to Lyon, "A historical fact is a historian's fact."[35]

But the question may be raised, Does not this line of argumentation put the cart before the horse? Should not a historical method suit reality rather than reality be reduced to suit an immanentistic or naturalistic method?[36] Although Lyon may remember that his definition of "historical facts" covers only a part of reality and not all actual events, others identify "historical facts" with all actual events and use his definition to deny a priori the historicity of the acts of God proclaimed in the Bible. Moreover, the historical-critical method seeks to discern whether recorded events indeed took place in the past—at least, it seeks to determine the probability of recorded events having taken place. The method cannot, in the nature of the case, decide whether *God* led Israel out of Egypt, but it ought to be able to determine the probability of the Exodus having taken place. It cannot decide whether *God* raised Jesus from the dead, but it ought to be able to determine the probability of Jesus' resurrection. The biblical proclamation that *God* works his redemption through certain events is indeed beyond the reach of a historical-critical method; this mes-

34. Barr, *JR* 56 (1976) 8.

35. Lyon, "Evangelicals and Critical Historical Method," 150. Cf. Smart, *Strange Silence*, 108-16.

36. See Marshall, *Luke*, 28-32; idem, *I Believe*, 243-46; Voskuil, *Pro Rege* 16/3 (1988) 2-12. Contemporary attempts to remove God from the discipline of history may well be motivated by the concern to make history into a hard science like the natural sciences (see Richardson, *History Sacred and Profane*, 109-10), but even natural sciences should attempt to explain all factors in their field and not arbitrarily cut out complicating factors.

sage can be accepted only by faith. But the question of the probability of these events having *taken place* is a historical question that ought not to be dismissed a priori by immanentistic presuppositions.

The accepted historical-critical method shows its bias when it first eliminates God as a factor in history and then declares certain reported events unhistorical because they speak of God's acts in history. Aside from pointing out the obvious circularity in this argument, I would make the following observations: If a historical-critical method, by definition or otherwise, cannot acknowledge all factors in history, it loses the right to make subsequent judgments concerning the historicity of reported events. Now the historical-critical method, as a matter of fact, has been making probability judgments regarding the historicity of reported events. That being the case, the method—if it is to be credible—must of necessity take into account all possible factors that may be operative in history.

The Failure of the Historical-Critical Method

All biblical scholars will agree, I think, that the Bible testifies to God acting in history. Disagreement takes place with respect to acknowledging the truth of that claim: Did God really act in history or was this testimony only what Israel or the early church believed? But if all agree that the Bible testifies that God acts in history, then all should also agree that the naturalistic historical-critical method is out of tune with the Bible and does not seek to understand the Bible on its own terms. The naturalistic historical-critical method seeks to assess the Bible from a standpoint, a worldview, grounded outside the Bible—a post-Enlightenment worldview rather than the biblical worldview. In other words, the Bible is pressed into a foreign mold and the resultant strain leads to all kinds of aberrations: historical narrative in the Bible is summarily labeled fiction or legend or myth, and interpretation, ironically, turns into unabashed allegorical interpretation, as, for example, when Jesus' resurrection is interpreted as "Jesus being risen into the kerygma of the church."[37]

Both Old Testament and New Testament scholars have pointed out the failure of the historical-critical method to do justice to the essence of the biblical message. Claus Westermann remarks: "The nineteenth century [notion] of history alone cannot be the standard for an Old Testament theology because it *a priori* excludes an act of God as an integral part of history."[38] George Ladd asserts similarly that "the historical-critical method is not an adequate method to interpret the theology of the New Testament because its presuppositions limit its findings to the exclusion of the central biblical message."[39]

37. Perrin, *Introduction*, 242, in agreement with Bultmann.
38. Westermann, *Elements of OT Theology*, 12.
39. Ladd, *Int* 25/1 (1971) 51-52.

Given its presuppositions, one is not surprised that the historical-critical method constructed pictures of Israel and of Jesus quite different from those in the Bible. The problem, however, appears to be not so much with the biblical pictures as with the method that, because of its presuppositions, is unable to focus properly on the pictures. Gerhard Hasel has summarized the issue well:

> We are, therefore, led to conclude that the crisis respecting history in Biblical theology is not so much a result of the scientific study of the evidences, but stems from the historical-critical method's inadequacy to deal with the role of transcendence in history due to its philosophical presuppositions about the nature of history. If the reality of the Biblical text testifies to a supra-historical dimension which transcends the self-imposed limitations of the historical-critical method, then one must employ a method that can account for this dimension and can probe into all the layers of depth of historical experience and deal adequately and properly with the Scripture's claim to truth.[40]

In the following section we shall seek to discern the foundations of such a method.

A HOLISTIC HISTORICAL-CRITICAL METHOD

A historical-critical method that would do justice to the Scriptures must make a radical break with the assumptions held by Troeltsch. Peter Stuhlmacher's proposal to add to the principles of analogy and correlation the principle of "hearing" (Vernehmen)[41] is a halfway measure that cannot succeed because it builds the contradiction between "naturalism" and "supernaturalism" right into the method. Moreover, the problem is not with the principles of probability, analogy, and correlation as such; the problem lies rather at the deeper level of the assumptions that support and shape these principles. Carl Braaten underscores aptly "the need for a new concept of history which is freed from a mechanistic and positivistic definition of the nature of history."[42] And Wolfhart Pannenberg claims rightly that "the principles of historical research do not have to be essentially and unavoidably imprisoned within an anthropocentric world view."[43]

In setting forth the contours of a more holistic historical-critical method, shaped by the biblical worldview, we are aided by the analysis of Troeltsch, for he correctly pinpointed three crucial areas where any

---

40. Hasel, *OT Theology*, 174. Cf. Krentz, *Historical-Critical Method*, 68-69.
41. Stuhlmacher, *Historical Criticism*, 85. See also the critique of Childs, *NT as Canon*, 46.
42. Braaten, *History and Hermeneutics*, 100.
43. Pannenberg, *Basic Questions*, I, 40.

method is guided by prior assumptions. These areas concern, first, one's attitude toward the text: Should one approach a document with doubt or with confidence in its reliability? Second, one's view of historical events: In applying analogy, as we invariably do, should one assume that all events are similar or must one leave room for the unique? Third, one's view of history: In applying correlation, as we must, do we reckon only with immanent or so-called natural causes, or can a transcendent God be acknowledged as Lord of history? Since this last assumption is the most basic and comprehensive because it expresses one's worldview, we shall start with this third assumption and work through the presuppositions in reverse order.

Correlation in an Open Universe

AN obvious but important observation is that the principle of correlation is a valid principle only as long as it is open to all possible causes in history. Now the Scriptures clearly proclaim that God, though transcendent, works in history. We can liken God's work in history to his work in creation: as God is Lord of creation, so he is Lord of its history; and as God transcends creation and yet works in it, so also God transcends world history and yet works in it. Further, the biblical testimony is clear that God acts not only in the history of Israel but also in the history of other nations (e.g., Amos 1–2; 9:7; Rom 1–2). In fact, the prophets proclaim that God uses and directs pagan nations such as Assyria and Babylon to punish his people Israel (e.g., Isa 10; Habakkuk). Yahweh, then, is seen as "the supreme and undisputed controller of history"—all history.[44]

God's Rule and Human Initiative
The fact that God governs history does not rule out, however, human freedom, initiative, and responsibility. Here we face the old paradox of divine sovereignty and human responsibility—a paradox in which neither pole may be emphasized to the exclusion of the other but both must be held together. Stressing only divine sovereignty eliminates human causality in history and leads to determinism. Stressing only human responsibility leads, as we have seen, to various forms of naturalism. The Bible chooses neither the one nor the other but presents both together. What this means for our view of history is suggestively portrayed by J. Langmead Casserley:

> The doctrine of providence asserts the notion of an ultimate and absolute power which is at the same time magnificently, infinitely tolerant. According to this doctrine, God creates freedom and yet dares to preordain the

44. Rowley, Re-Discovery of the OT, 72.

consummation. . . . This doctrine implies that history will always have direction, point, and shape, because God has preordained the consummation, and yet, on the other hand, that it must inevitably appear haphazard and sporadic, a thing of jerks, fits, and starts, filled with recurrent episodes of tragedy and failure, because the creation of genuine freedom is essential to the attainment of the divine purpose.[45]

God's Mediate and Immediate Acts

The Bible shows that God works in history in two ways. Usually God works in unobtrusive, natural ways—ways so natural, in fact, that an unbeliever can easily deny God's activity since the natural causation is so obvious. But in and through these so-called natural causes, the eye of faith discerns God at work: the eye of faith sees snow and ice, rain and wind, not so much as results of "natural laws" but as the creation's response to the word of God (Ps 147:15-18); faith sees God's hand in the conception and birth of a baby (e.g., Gen 4:1; 21:1); faith sees God at work even in Pharaoh's refusal to let the people go (Exod 4:21) and in the Babylonian armies marching against Jerusalem (Hab 1:5-6). God, we could say, is *the* all-pervading cause in the natural order of things, both in creation and in human history. But God himself transcends that order and is not bound always to act according to the order we usually perceive. God can indeed act in extra-ordinary ways. As Casserley puts it: "In the Bible we are sometimes confronted with events in which the Lord God, as the Bible says, 'lays bare his holy arm' and acts, so to speak, nakedly and unmistakably. Here we encounter testimonies to events of a supernatural or miraculous kind, which, if we grant that they have occurred at all, cannot possibly bear any other explanation."[46]

In comparing these two types of God's activity, Casserley makes the point that "the most important ground of the assertion that God is the 'living God who acts' is to be found not in his veiled activity but in his naked activity. . . . For the biblical mind the living God is, above all, revealed in the naked acts."[47] This observation goes far toward explaining the atheistic results of a naturalistic historical-critical method, for once one allows such a method to dismiss God's "naked acts" as unhistorical, the critic has effectively removed God from history since God's "veiled acts" will not resist a totally naturalistic explanation. It would be well, therefore, to delve further into the issue of God's immediate acts.

Miracles

Miracles are often dismissed because they have been defined as "viola-

J. V. Langmes l

45. Casserley, *Toward a Theology of History*, 92-93.   London : Mowbray 1965,
46. Ibid., 123.
47. Ibid., 123-24.

tions of natural law" and even as "'unlawful' occurrences."[48] But these definitions and caricatures are far removed from biblical thinking because they define miracles in terms of a seventeenth-century notion of natural law (Hume).[49] Even today, such definitions often proceed from an atheistic or deistic assumption that nature is autonomous, a law unto itself. From this assumption atheists will conclude that miracles are naturally impossible, while some theists argue that God is able to break natural law, the supernatural overcoming the natural.

The Bible, however, does not set God and nature over against each other as two autonomous entities. On the contrary, nature is God's handiwork which responds obediently to his bidding: "He sends forth his command to the earth; his word runs swiftly," and God's creation responds with snow, ice, or rain—whatever God's word calls for (Ps 147:15-18; cf. 148:8). Hence the regular patterns we observe in creation are not immutable laws of autonomous nature but rather creation's regular responses to the constancy of God's words or laws (see Gen 8:22).[50] The sovereign God is not locked into these regular patterns, however; he is free, naturally, to vary his word, and then creation responds in unique ways.

It must also be recognized that according to the Bible God performs many of his miracles by "natural" means. For example, the miraculous conception of Samuel to the barren Hannah came about by quite natural means: "Elkanah knew Hannah his wife, and the Lord remembered her" (1 Sam 1:19). Similarly, the miracle of Israel crossing the Sea of Reeds on dry ground was accomplished by natural means: "The Lord drove the sea back by a strong east wind all night, and made the sea dry land" (Exod 14:21). Later, the crossing of the Jordan may well have been made possible by a landslide at Adam blocking the water of the Jordan, thus drying up the riverbed opposite Jericho (Josh 3:16). Should we deny that these were miracles because the Bible points to so-called natural causes? But then we may overlook that God works in regular, natural ways as well as unique ways, mediately as well as immediately. It is clear, moreover, that Israel celebrated these events as miracles not because they "violated natural law" but because they were unexpected and therefore surprising; the timing of these events clearly revealed God at work. Hence these miracles were perceived as fulfillment of God's prior promises or his answer to

48. Ramsey, *Quest for the Historical Israel*, 108.

49. Note Hume's definition of a miracle: "A miracle may be accurately defined [as] a transgression of a law of nature by a particular volition of the Deity, or by the interposition of some invisible agent." And again: "A miracle is a violation of the laws of nature." David Hume, *Enquiries Concerning Human Understanding and Concerning the Principles of Morals*, 3rd. ed., ed. L. A. Selby-Bigge (Oxford: Clarendon, 1975), 115 n. 1 and 114. For a discussion on Bultmann's views, see Thiselton, *Two Horizons*, 260-61.

50. See further my "The Universal Dimension of Law in the Hebrew Scriptures," *SR* 14/1 (1985) 39-51, and the references there.

prayer. As Goldingay notes with respect to the Exodus, "The marvel was not essentially something quite inexplicable, but something quite unexpected. It intervened to break the bounds of what could have been envisaged in the situation, and Israel responded with wonder."[51]

Another problem with defining miracles as "violations of natural law" is that this definition overlooks the fact that we now live in a fallen creation where, for example, enslavement, sickness, and death appear to be natural. Is it indeed the case that liberation, healing, and resurrection from the dead are contrary to the "laws of nature"? They may be contrary to what we have come to expect in this world, but from the perspective of God's good creation and his coming kingdom, enslavement, sickness, and death are unnatural, and liberation, healing, and eternal life are natural (Gen 2–3; Rev 21:4). From that perspective, then, miracles are not to be seen as "unnatural" but as signs of God's kingdom breaking into our fallen world, provisional indications of the restoration of God's creation to its original goodness.[52]

Accordingly, miracles should be thought of not as "violations of natural law" but as outstanding, exceptional acts of God, signs which point to God's power and faithfulness (cf. Ps 107:20), events which create a sense of wonder. In agreement with biblical teaching, miracles have been defined as occasional evidences of direct divine power in actions striking and unusual, yet by their "beneficence pointing to the goodness of God."[53] Miracles, in short, are signs of God's kingdom.

We should also note, contrary to much scholarly opinion, that substantiating the *historicity* of miraculous events is not beyond the reach of historians; just like other events, their probability can be proved or disproved by the usual historian's tools: eyewitness accounts and other sources. The historian Paul Merkley asserts that historians base their conclusions regarding historicity on the credibility of the witnesses. "The question is this: on what basis do we generally believe what a historical testimony tells us? The answer is: we believe when and insofar as we have confidence in the author of the testimony. . . . His credentials as a witness come down to these two: (a). was he there? and (b). would he lie to us (or

51. Goldingay, *Approaches to OT Interpretation*, 80-81.
52. See Diemer, *Nature and Miracle,* especially p. 25: "Through the signs and wonders the disintegrating power of sin is broken and its results overcome. What occurs is not a supernatural interference in the positive consequences of a natural process, but a fully natural interference in the negative consequence of a sinful process." Cf. Bright, *Kingdom of God*, 218: Jesus' "miracles are 'mighty works' ('powers,' *dunameis*) of the Kingdom of God, which in them advertises its presence. . . . In them the grip of the Adversary—who has enthralled men in bonds of disease, madness, death, and sin—begins to be loosened."
53. An unknown author quoted by Rhodes, *Mighty Acts of God*, 303. See further pp. 301-7.

could he have been deceived?)."[54] These types of questions can be put to witnesses of all kinds of events, including those of miracles. In fact, this is precisely the historical evidence marshalled by Luke and Paul for the resurrection of Christ (see Luke 1:1-4 and 1 Cor 15:3-8). Historians, then, ought to be able to reach some conclusions regarding the probability of a miracle having taken place. What is beyond the historian's ability, of course, is to verify that it was *God* who caused the miracle; the fact that *God* worked the miracle was and remains a matter of acceptance by faith.

The Biblical Worldview

The biblical worldview, then, holds that God acts in history, both mediately and immediately. God acts in history, but not to the exclusion of human freedom and initiative. Consequently, in contrast to the naturalistic worldview with its closed continuum, the biblical worldview is open to the activity of God. As A. Berkeley Mickelsen puts it, "The world is a controlled continuum, and it is God who exercises the control."[55] This biblical worldview is the proper foundation for the principle of correlation.[56]

Allowing the principle of correlation to be shaped by the biblical worldview does not mean that one has stopped being scientific or critical; on the contrary, this worldview enables one to be open to all factors of history. As William Abraham correctly points out, it does not at all follow "that one can only be critical if one is committed to a *material* conception of correlation. Failure to see this stems principally from a failure to see that to accept direct divine action is to widen rather than abandon the principle of correlation."[57]

Analogy and Unique Events

IN deciding for the biblical worldview, the case for the principle of analogy has also been decided. Analogy is still a valuable tool, but it operates in a very different context from that of the naturalistic model which assumed the similarity of all events. The biblical worldview holds that all events are not similar, for God need not always speak the same word.

54. Merkley, *EvQ* 58 (1986) 332. See also Anderson, *Understanding the OT*, 23: "It is in the concrete affairs and relationships of people that God makes himself known. No external historical study can demonstrate that the Exodus was an act of God; but to Israel this 'political' event was the medium through which God's presence and purpose were disclosed. . . . Thus Israel's sacred history does not belong to a completely different sphere from that with which the historian can deal."

55. Mickelsen, *Interpreting the Bible*, 60.

56. On contextual hermeneutics and the hermeneutical circle at the level of the interpreter's and the Bible's worldview, see Padilla, "Interpreted Word," 297-308.

57. Abraham, *Divine Revelation*, 111.

Two Kinds of Events

Basically the biblical worldview leads one to recognize that events can be of two kinds: in most events God works unobtrusively through "natural" causation; but some events are surprising, unique, "naked" acts of God, miracles. The recognition of these two kinds of events does not derail the principle of analogy, for God continues to work in history today the same way he did in the past: mediately and immediately. Thus, operating in the context of the biblical worldview, the principle of analogy can accept that unique events took place in the past because they also take place in the present. God answers prayer today: he protects us, heals us, saves us— both mediately and immediately. Given this present experience of God's acts, one cannot use the principle of analogy to declare unhistorical God's reported acts in the past.

Unique Events

Wolfhart Pannenberg shifts the focus of analogy from the discovery of similarity to the search for the unique and distinctive in historical events. "It is characteristic of the activity of the transcendent God . . . that it constantly gives rise to something new in reality, something never before present. For this reason, theology is interested primarily in the individual, particular, and contingent. In the revelatory history, the stress falls not least upon the new, upon that which is peculiar to the particular event." By this route Pannenberg denies the principle of analogy the right to judge the historicity of reported events: "If analogies . . . are used . . . in awareness of the limit of their validity, they hardly can serve in Troeltsch's way as the criterion for the reality of an event. . . . The fact that a reported event breaks the analogy of what is otherwise . . . frequently attested is not in itself sufficient grounds to contest its factuality."[58]

Since neither correlation nor analogy can contest a reported event's factuality, the weight for determining historicity shifts away from prior assumptions to the place where the issue should have been decided in the first place, the documents themselves. This shift brings us back to the principle of criticism.

The Principle of Criticism

WE have noted how radical criticism turned the principle of criticism into methodological doubt about the historical reliability of the Scriptures; the burden of proof was shifted from the detractors of Scripture's historical reliability to the Scriptures themselves; and not only were the biblical

---

58. Respectively, Pannenberg, *Basic Questions*, I, 48; idem, *KD* 5 (1959) 266, as quoted in James Robinson, "Revelation as Word and as History," 31.

narratives required to prove their historicity, the proof demanded was often quite unreasonable, such as extrabiblical evidence. Although no historical critic should be gullible, unreasonable criteria and continued doubt in the face of reliable witnesses are also less than scientific.

Criteria for Historicity

It may be helpful to recall that Troeltsch, with the first prong of the principle of criticism, assumed the "fundamental similarity of all traditions," so that all traditions can be subjected to the same criticism. The intent, obviously, was to view the Bible on a par with all other traditions so that it could not be exempted from historical criticism. Since the Bible comes to us in human form, we can agree that, though God's word, it can be subjected to criticism. But then the same kind of criticism should be applied to the Bible that is applied to other documents—not more demanding—and the same kind of criteria should be used—not more stringent or unrealistic ones.

A few New Testament scholars have developed a number of criteria for assessing the authenticity of Jesus' words and deeds. Although there is no agreement on their number or their definitions, it is worthwhile to take note of the major criteria. The first and most controversial is the criterion of *dissimilarity*. Perrin calls this "the fundamental criterion" and explains it as follows: "Sayings and parables may be accepted as authentic if they can be shown to be dissimilar to characteristic emphases of both Judaism and early Christianity." Perrin acknowledges the obvious flaw of this criterion, that "it misses material in which Jesus is at one with his Jewish heritage and the later church at one with him, and that by concentrating on what is different it may present a distorted picture of the message of Jesus." But, he says, "it is only a starting point; its use must always be supplemented by the use of other criteria."[59] In a thorough critique, however, Morna Hooker asserts not only that this criterion leads to "serious distortion" but that "the method dictates its own conclusions" and that "the application of the method is bound to be subjective."[60] The

---

59. Perrin, *Introduction*, 281-82. Note that this is more flexible than his earlier statement in *Rediscovering*, 39: "If we are to ascribe a saying to Jesus . . . , we must be able to show that the saying comes neither from the Church nor from ancient Judaism. This seems to many to be too much to ask, but nothing less will do justice to the challenge of the burden of proof. There is no other way to reasonable certainty that we have reached the historical Jesus."

60. Hooker, *NTS* 17 (1970-71) 481-82. Ladd, calls this criterion "highly arbitrary" (*NT and Criticism*, 163). Goetz and Blomberg comment that it "makes Jesus a man without parallel in history since he neither depends on his predecessors nor influences his followers at any point" (*JSNT* 11 [1981] 43). For a detailed critique of this criterion, see Hooker, *NTS* 17 (1970-71) 480-86; idem, *Theology* 75 (1972) 574-81; Osborne, *JETS* 21/2 (1978) 117-30.

charge of subjective application is borne out by the fact that Perrin uses this criterion mainly in a negative way, while Morna Hooker, I. Howard Marshall, René Latourelle, and others use it in a positive way to increase "confidence about a saying."[61]

A second criterion is that of *multiple attestation*. Latourelle employs a broader definition of this criterion than does Perrin. Latourelle states that multiple attestation accepts as "authentic an evangelical datum solidly attested to in all the sources (or most of them) of the Gospels . . . and in other writings of the New Testament." This criterion applies particularly to "establishing the essential characteristics of . . . the preaching and the activity of Jesus."[62]

A third criterion is that of *coherence:* "A saying or act of Jesus may be considered as authentic when it is in strict conformity not only with the epoch and environment of Jesus (the linguistic, geographic, social, political, religious environment), but also and above all closely coherent with the essential teaching, the heart of the message of Jesus, that is, the arrival and the instauration of the messianic Kingdom."[63]

For Latourelle the most important criterion is his fourth, the criterion of *necessary explanation*. He describes it as follows: "If, before a considerable collection of facts or of data, which require a coherent and sufficient explanation, there is offered an explanation which clarifies and brings together in harmony all these elements (which, otherwise, would remain enigmas), we may conclude that we are in the presence of an authentic datum (fact, deed, attitude, word of Jesus)."[64] An example may clarify what Latourelle has in mind:

> In the case of miracles, we find ourselves before a dozen important facts, which the most severe criticism cannot challenge, and which require adequate explanation: the popular enthusiasm on the appearance of Jesus, the apostles' belief He is the Messiah, the place of miracles in the synoptic and Johannine tradition, the hatred of the high priests and of the Pharisees due to the prodigies worked by Jesus, the constant link between the miracles and the message of Jesus about the decisive coming of the Kingdom, the place of miracles in the early kerygma, the close relationship between the

---

61. Hooker, *NTS* 17 (1970-71) 486. Cf. Marshall's critique and use of this criterion in *I Believe*, 201-3; and Latourelle, *Finding Jesus*, 223-26.

62. Latourelle, *Finding Jesus*, 221 and 223. Cf. Perrin's different definition: "Themes or concerns may be accepted as authentic if they occur in different literary forms within the tradition" (*Introduction*, 221).

63. Latourelle, *Finding Jesus*, 228.

64. Ibid., 229. The intent of this criterion appears to be close to Marshall's proposal of "the criterion of traditional continuity": "The question the historian must ask at this point is: what historical cause must be postulated in order to explain the origin of this tradition?" (*I Believe*, 207).

claims of Jesus that He is the Son of the Father and the miracles as signs of His might. All these facts demand an explanation, a sufficient reason.[65]

The result of applying these criteria to the Gospels is that the burden of proof for authenticity seems to be shifting again. Whereas Perrin had stated unequivocally that "the nature of the synoptic tradition is such that the burden of proof will be upon the claim to authenticity," Latourelle and others consider that "the burden of proof is not on those who acknowledge Jesus as the source of the words and actions preserved in the Gospels but on those who consider them as interpolations or as inventions of the early Church. . . . This change of attitude is attributable largely to recent researches on the criteria of authenticity."[66] For his part Marshall concludes, "Over against the scepticism of radical scholars we have been able to show that the tradition can be viewed in a positive way, and that there is good reason to regard it as reliable unless the contrary can be clearly shown."[67]

Biblical scholars can also learn from the criteria for historicity which historians apply to nonbiblical documents. K. A. Kitchen describes four basic principles that scholars use in ancient Near Eastern studies: (1) the primary importance of facts, (2) a positive attitude to source material, (3) the inconclusive nature of negative evidence, and (4) a proper approach to apparent discrepancies. At this juncture we are interested primarily in the second item, the attitude with which scholars approach their ancient Near Eastern documents. Kitchen writes: "It is normal practice to assume the general reliability of statements in our sources, unless there is good, explicit evidence to the contrary. Unreliability, secondary origins, dishonesty of a writer, or tendentious traits—all these must be clearly proved by adduction of tangible evidence, and not merely inferred to support a theory."[68]

Confidence in Reliability

It appears, then, that many scholars approach general historical documents not with radical doubt but with a "positive attitude" so that the burden of proof for denial of historicity rests on the critic and not on the

---

65. Latourelle, *Finding Jesus,* 229-31.

66. See Perrin, *Rediscovering,* 39; Latourelle, *Finding Jesus,* 239.

67. Marshall, *I Believe,* 211. Cf. p. 200: "A tradition which purports to be recording what Jesus said must be reckoned to be doing precisely this unless there are clear signs to the contrary; in general these signs are lacking." See also the quotation of Jeremias (*NT Theology,* I, 37): "We are justified in drawing up the following principle of method: In the synoptic tradition it is the inauthenticity, and not the authenticity, of the sayings of Jesus that must be demonstrated."

68. Kitchen, *Ancient Orient,* 29; the four basic principles are given on pp. 28-33.

ancient document. Accordingly, one would expect the same approach to the Bible: a positive attitude, or what we might call confidence in the Bible's reliability, with the burden of proof for denying the historicity of any particular narrative on the critic.[69]

Archeological studies confirm that confidence in the historical reliability of Scripture is not misplaced. With respect to the Old Testament, R. K. Harrison, among others, asserts that "comparative historiographic studies have shown that, along with the Hittites, the ancient Hebrews were the most accurate, objective, and responsible recorders of Near Eastern history. . . . As a result, it is possible to view with a new degree of confidence and respect those early traditions of the Hebrews that purport to be historiographic in nature."[70] As far as the New Testament is concerned, Robert Stein reviews six arguments "frequently raised in support of the substantive accuracy of the gospel accounts"—arguments such as the existence of eyewitnesses who could have pointed out errors when the tradition was fixed, the existence of a responsible center of leadership in Jerusalem, the high regard in which New Testament authors held the traditions, the faithfulness of the church in transmitting difficult sayings of Jesus (e.g., Mark 10:18; 13:32), the ability to remember traditions in an oral society, and so on. Stein concludes that these arguments are "sufficient to establish that the burden of proof ought to be with those scholars who deny the historicity of the gospel materials."[71]

There are good reasons, therefore, to approach the biblical text not with doubt but with confidence in its historical reliability. This confidence does not mean, of course, that one stops one's critical investigation at that point; nor does it mean that one should expect to find historical reporting that conforms to modern Western standards of so-called objectivity and accuracy. Only a study of the text itself will show how the authors wrote history, to what standards they conformed, what artistic freedom they had, and whether they intended to write history (see Chapter 4 below). But before one gets into such detailed study of the text, one's attitude toward the text ought to be brought out into the open since this attitude

---

69. Cf. Goetz and Blomberg, *JSNT* 11 (1981) 40-42; Marshall, "Historical Criticism," 134; and H. Berkhof, *Christian Faith*, 270-71.

70. Harrison, *Biblical Criticism*, 5; cf. p. 9: "The current flow of archaeological discoveries tends to confirm, rather than repudiate, the claim of the Old Testament to historicity." Cf. W. F. Albright, *Archaeology and the Religion of Israel*, 5th ed. (New York: Doubleday, 1969), 169: "There can be no doubt that archaeology has confirmed the substantial historicity of Old Testament tradition." See further Bright, *Early Israel*, 88, 125; de Vaux, *Bible and the Ancient Near East*, 60, 114-19; Hasel, *JSOT* 31 (1985) 34; Herion, *JSOT* 21 (1981) 37-40; Kitchen, *Bible in Its World*, 73; Merrill, *BSac* 140 (1983) 306.

71. Stein, *Gospel Perspectives*, 226-27. See further Latourelle, *Finding Jesus*, 239; Mosley, *NTS* 12 (1965) 10-26; and on the resurrection of Jesus, see Richardson, *History Sacred and Profane*, 197-212.

will influence the results of further analysis. Should the biblical text be approached with an attitude of doubt as if it were a spurious document or with confidence in its reliability? It appears that there are sufficient reasons for approaching the biblical text with confidence. Obviously, this confidence is all the more sure for the person who accepts the Bible as God's word, for if the inspiration of the Bible (2 Tim 3:16; 2 Pet 1:21) means anything, it is that the Bible is trustworthy in what it intends to teach.[72]

In contrast to the picture of the naturalistic historical-critical method, we may therefore sketch the in-depth picture of a holistic historical-critical method somewhat as follows:

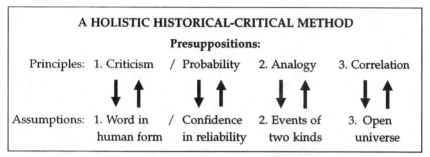

A HOLISTIC HISTORICAL-CRITICAL METHOD
Presuppositions:

Principles: 1. Criticism   / Probability   2. Analogy   3. Correlation

Assumptions: 1. Word in   / Confidence   2. Events of   3. Open
              human form   in reliability   two kinds   universe

This kind of holistic historical-critical method will be able to assess the historicity of biblical narrative without the subjectivism and reductionism inherent in the naturalistic historical-critical method. In other words, it will be able to render a more valid assessment of biblical historicity than does the "accepted" method. Moreover, it allows subsequently for a more valid interpretation of biblical narrative, for it permits one to recognize historical narrative in the Scriptures for what it is and to interpret it as historical narrative and not just as myth, legend, parable, or mere story.

Chapter 4 will deal more specifically with biblical history writing, but first we shall turn to issues in holistic literary interpretation.

72. See Armerding, *OT and Criticism*, 46.

CHAPTER 3

Literary Interpretation

IN both Old Testament and New Testament interpretation, critical methodologies have forced biblical scholars into such a high degree of specialization that a perspective of the whole was (and often still is) nonexistent. Interpreters have tended to focus on details of the text or its prehistory rather than on the text in its biblical context. This atomistic approach has led to a crisis in homiletics: biblical texts are perceived not only to be distant and objective but also irrelevant for contemporary congregations. The homiletician Dwight Stevenson tried to overcome fragmentation by advocating sermons on whole Bible books. This kind of sermon may "provide one way . . . for a return from the fragmented world of textual preaching to the wholeness of the biblical view upon life and destiny."[1] But to overcome the perceived irrelevance of biblical texts requires not simply new homiletical techniques but a holistic hermeneutical approach.

HOLISTIC INTERPRETATION

Contemporary Atomistic Approaches

"MANY will agree," writes Brevard Childs, "that we have entered into a period in which the analytical concerns of biblical exegesis have largely replaced the older and broader synthetic interests within both the disciplines of Old and New Testaments."[2] David Clines underscores this observation by calling attention to atomistic approaches in hermeneutics today: "The tendency toward atomism is amply revealed by the contents pages of our learned journals." He suggests that "the atomism of contem-

---

1. Stevenson, *Preaching on the Books of the OT*, ix.
2. Childs, *HorBT* 4/1 (1982) 1.

porary Biblical scholarship is founded ultimately on a scientific model of knowledge. This may be called the pyramid view of the accumulation of knowledge. Each worker is content to have made his little contribution . . . which with any luck will form part of a vast structure." Clines goes on to argue, however, that even if this pyramid model fits "normal" science, which is arguable, it certainly does not fit biblical studies. Although "Old Testament study in some of its aspects (e.g., philology, archaeology) bears a certain resemblance to natural science, the model still gravely distorts the reality of our discipline. . . . It is a mistake to believe that we can ever manage in Biblical studies without both holistic and atomistic work."[3]

Increasingly, biblical scholars are realizing that an atomistic approach by itself cannot possibly do justice to the biblical text. In the 1950s form criticism, which had been studying small, independent units, was augmented or, for some, replaced by redaction criticism, which sought to understand whole books in terms of the "theology" of the author or redactor. In 1968 James Muilenburg declared his dissatisfaction with mere form criticism and launched an era of rhetorical criticism. In the 1970s Brevard Childs embarked upon a different type of holistic approach which he called the canonical approach. In 1981 Walter Kaiser promoted a "syntactical-theological method" which included the formulation of biblical principles for today.[4] All in all, there appears to be a growing awareness among contemporary biblical interpreters that, by themselves, some critical methodologies hinder the biblical texts from speaking relevantly and that only a more holistic approach will do justice to the Scriptures.

Dimensions of a Holistic Alternative

A holistic hermeneutical method seeks to take into account *all* aspects that contribute to the meaning of biblical texts and attempts to understand these aspects in the light of the whole—and vice versa. Clines asserts that "the holistic, total view, while always open to revision in the light of the merest detail, must have the last word in interpretation. In the quest for meaning, the essence, message, function, purpose . . . of the work as a whole is our ultimate ambition."[5]

Traditional exegesis viewed biblical interpretation as consisting of two major dimensions: the grammatical and the historical. While before the rise of Enlightenment higher criticism biblical texts were studied primarily for their theology (doctrine), afterward they were studied primarily for their historical data. Recently another shift has taken place—a shift from the historical to the literary dimension of biblical texts. David

3. Clines, *Theme of the Pentateuch*, 7-9.
4. Kaiser, *Toward an Exegetical Theology*.
5. Clines, *Beginning OT Study*, 35.

Robertson, among others, describes this change in emphasis from history to literature as a paradigm shift: "One can say, then, that the *paradigm* which has governed practically all modern research on the Bible is history. Scholars operating under this paradigm have either remarked on the literary quality of a text as an aside or have engaged in literary tasks for the purpose of answering historical questions (e.g., the attempt to establish the authentic sayings of Jesus by form criticism)." Today, by contrast, "the paradigm, or controlling idea, guiding the research of literary critics is . . . literature. Consideration of the Bible as literature is itself the beginning and end of scholarly endeavor. The Bible is taken first and finally as a literary object."[6] This paradigm shift to the literary dimension, like the earlier exclusive emphasis on the historical dimension, is itself indicative, of course, of an atomistic approach insofar as not all aspects are taken into account. For example, many new literary critics, especially structuralists, contend that it is irrelevant whether a text describes historical events or, for that matter, whether a text is sacred.[7] Others reject this one-sidedness, however, and claim that "diachronic and synchronic study of the Bible, historical critical and literary structural approaches, possess a complementary relationship to each other."[8]

Besides these historical and literary dimensions, a third area of interest, the "theological," was revived in this century. For example, James Smart remarks that "the Scriptures are a theological as well as a historical entity and they demand for their scientific investigation a methodology that is as responsible theologically as it is historically." Smart cautions that one should not view these two elements as existing "in separate compartments, the theological being an additional compartment added on to an untheological historical one. The theological and the historical content of Scripture are not two separate realities but are one reality with two aspects, each inseparable from the other and interfused with it."[9] Although I believe that all aspects of a holistic approach can be covered adequately with the literary and historical dimensions—the goal of both being the "theological" message—a separate discussion on theological interpretation can highlight certain aspects that are easily overlooked today.

The following three chapters will therefore be used to discuss sepa-

6. Robertson, *IDBSup*, 547-48. Cf. Macky, "The Coming Revolution: The New Literary Approach to NT Interpretation," in *Guide to Contemporary Hermeneutics*, 263-79.

7. Robertson, *IDBSup*, 548.

8. Polzin, *Moses and the Deuteronomist*, 2. Sternberg argues for the unity of "ideology, historiography and aesthetics": "Where does aesthetics end and ideology begin? How does one differentiate either from history? The finished narrative is all of these and none: it constitutes a whole greater than the sum not only of its parts but also of their regulating forces" (*Poetics*, 48).

9. Smart, *Strange Silence*, 78.

rately the literary, historical, and theological dimensions of holistic interpretation. It will be clear that this division of interpretation into different dimensions is made to facilitate analysis and not to set forth a particular order, for the actual process of interpretation is an integrated, unified whole.

METHODS OF LITERARY INTERPRETATION

IN literary interpretation (broadly conceived as inclusive of grammatical concerns) one commonly raises questions concerning the text's genre of literature, rhetorical devices, figures of speech, grammar, syntax, etc., in order to determine the meaning of the words in their immediate context and, ultimately, in the context of the whole document and of the entire Bible. Contemporary interpreters are confronted by so many different methods in biblical interpretation that the methods and their ambiguous terminological distinctions threaten to get in the way of interpretation.[10] In what follows I shall highlight only those methods which, in my opinion, contribute to an understanding of the text for purposes of preaching. One may also note that although I have grouped these methods together under literary interpretation, some can equally be classified under historical or theological interpretation. For example, methods such as source criticism and form criticism also have a bearing on historical matters, "to reconstruct the events of the past,"[11] and redaction criticism and biblical theology focus on theological aspects, the "theology" of an author/redactor or the "theological" themes of a book. This overlap only underscores the point made earlier that literary, historical, and theological questions are so intertwined that these three dimensions should not be thought of as rigid, disconnected categories.

Source Criticism

SOURCE criticism was originally called "literary criticism,"[12] but, as the name "source criticism" denotes more specifically, its concern is not with every literary aspect but mainly with the written sources underlying the biblical text. Source criticism came to classic expression in the work of Julius Wellhausen at the end of the nineteenth century. When source criticism can lay bare the documents an author had at his disposal, it provides

10. Knierim's irritation is understandable: "The situation is a nuisance, and students as well as experts could spend their hours on more important things than on the analysis of the same words for different things or on different words for the same things in the various methodological and exegetical publications" ("Criticism of Literary Features," 147).

11. J. Maxwell Miller, *OT and the Historian*, 14.

12. Knierim, "Criticism of Literary Features," 130-31.

an important service for determining the message the author (redactor) sought to bring, for it enables us to observe the deliberate changes made in the original documents.

Hypotheses

Unfortunately, the work of source criticism is often hypothetical, especially with respect to the sources of the Pentateuch. For, whereas New Testament source critics are at least able to exhibit a copy of Mark (which in its first edition as *Ur-Markus* was presumably a source for Matthew and Luke), Old Testament source critics have been unable to present any comparable evidence that their widely acclaimed sources such as J and E ever did exist as separate, written sources. Wellhausen's documentary hypothesis, for all its later modifications, has remained just that—a hypothesis. Consequently, there is little agreement among biblical scholars regarding underlying sources.[13] Moreover, other hypotheses might account for the textual givens equally well or better.[14] In any event, "much of the old source criticism and of the hypotheses it produced remains conjectural and problematic."[15]

Source Criticism and Preaching

The fatal flaw of source criticism for preaching is that it is largely speculation, for one can hardly preach the sure word of God on the basis of speculation. This is not to deny that biblical authors frequently used sources but to warn against basing sermons on hypothetical constructs.[16] Although source criticism may be beneficial at times for discovering the specific meaning of a passage, its speculative character calls for extreme caution. Moreover, it must be remembered that the preacher's task is not to preach the sources of the biblical text but the biblical text itself (see Chapter 1 above).

Form Criticism

IN comparing source criticism with form criticism, Gene Tucker calls attention to the fact that the primary concern of source (or literary) criticism is the literary stage of the material, whereas the task of form criticism is to identify the literary forms of the material, their structures, intentions, and

13. Even "among those who assume the existence of Pentateuchal sources, the opinions conflict sharply" (ibid., 132).

14. See, e.g., Armerding, *OT and Criticism*, 21-42; Kitchen, *Ancient Orient and OT*, 112-35.

15. LaSor, Hubbard, and Bush, *OT Survey*, 65.

16. "That there are sources is hard to doubt; that they can be extirpated so certainly from the closely-knit corpus that finally emerged is another matter" (ibid.).

settings, in order to understand the oral or preliterary stage of their development.[17]

Forms

In 1906 Hermann Gunkel became the first to apply form criticism to the Old Testament, classifying prose narrative into such forms as myth, folktale, saga, romance (novelette), legend, and historical narrative.[18] Between 1919 and 1921, K. L. Schmidt, Martin Dibelius, and Rudolf Bultmann each published a book applying form criticism to the New Testament. Dibelius, for example, listed five categories of Gospel pericopes apart from the passion narrative: paradigm (pronouncement-story), tales (miracle-stories), legends, myths, and exhortations.[19] In the light of the presuppositions of the historical-critical method (see Chapter 2 above), one may well wonder the extent to which these categories and their labels give expression to a naturalistic worldview that prejudges the historicity of the events described in forms like "legend" and "myth." Certainly, a warning is in order against limiting form-critical work "by naturalistic presuppositions."[20] But form criticism faces other objections as well.

Atomism

Form critics have been accused of an atomistic approach that neglects the larger context: "The form critics have tended to lose sight of the forest by concentrating on the individual trees: by dealing exhaustively with individual pericopes . . . and, in general, small blocks of material, they have sometimes neglected to regard biblical books as individual entities."[21] It has also been pointed out that a familiar form can be used in a different setting than expected, thus altering the meaning of that form. For example, Isaiah (14:4-21) uses the form of a funeral dirge not for a funeral but as a parody to prophesy the imminent death of the king of Babylon, while Amos (5:1-2) uses the funeral dirge to prophesy the fall of the nation of Israel.[22] Moreover, as Carl Armerding observes, "form-critical research can never replace the grammatical, historical, theological study of the text. Whether a particular form is used consciously or unconsciously, it is merely the vehicle for that which the inspired writer wishes to con-

17. Tucker, *Form Criticism of the OT*, 1, 18.
18. Gunkel quoted by Tucker, ibid., 24.
19. Explained by Travis, "Form Criticism," 155-57.
20. See, e.g., Armerding, *OT and Criticism*, 63-64. Cf. Caird's criticism of Bultmann's use of "emotive names (Legend and Myth), which inevitably implied a negative judgment of historicity," and a "bland dogmatism" that "the early church had no interest in the historical Jesus" (*ExpTim* 87 [1976] 139-41).
21. Greenwood, *JBL* 89 (1970) 418. For a rejection of the charge, see Tucker, *Form Criticism of the OT*, 12-13.
22. See, e.g., von Rad, *OT Theology*, II, 38.

vey. The medium is certainly important, but the medium is not the entire message."[23]

Conjecture

Questions are also being raised about form criticism researching the *pre-history* of the text. Especially with respect to positing the *Sitz im Leben*, the communal life-setting, of different forms, form criticism is open to the same charge as was source criticism, the charge of speculation. D. A. Carson contends that "radical form criticism assumes we have a much greater knowledge of the life-settings of the church than we do. All we think we know of such settings is derived from speculation based on form-critical theories and fertile imaginations."[24] The same can be said about life-settings in ancient Israel.

Aside from the hypothetical nature of researching a text's prehistory, other questions concern the value of this study: "The question that many are raising these days . . . is: What is the *relative* value of going behind the final text into previous levels of tradition. . . ? How much light does the prehistory of the text throw upon the final text—the one that has functioned in Judaism and Christianity and the one that we read today?"[25] Clines decries the "obsession" with "the study of the origins and development of the extant Biblical text"—what he calls "geneticism." In Old Testament studies, "the sources and pre-history of our present texts are for the most part entirely hypothetical, and . . . in any case, a work of art, such as a good deal of Old Testament literature undoubtedly is, yields its significance to the observer as a whole and through the articulation of its parts in its present form."[26] With some modifications, the same might be said for New Testament studies.

Form Criticism and Preaching

The value of form criticism for preaching lies particularly in its emphasis on acknowledging that different forms of literature make their point in different ways—both in the past and for the present. For example, Old Testament laws are to be understood and applied differently than historical narratives, and both of these differently than parables. Traditional exegesis, of course, was not unaware of different forms, but form criticism

23. Armerding, *OT and Criticism*, 63.
24. Carson, "Redaction Criticism," 124-25.
25. Anderson, "New Frontier of Rhetorical Criticism," xvii. Cf. Frye, "Literary Perspective," 212: "In much that is written about the Gospels, more attention is devoted to the hypothesized stages of formation than to the actual literature as we have it—more attention to how the Gospels may have been developed and composed than to what they actually say."
26. Clines, *Theme of the Pentateuch*, 9.

attempts to delineate the forms more precisely. Not all proposed forms are valid categories, however; nor are all proposed forms homiletically significant. For example, Gunkel's distinctions among myth, folktale, and legend are of questionable hermeneutical and homiletical value.[27] Moreover, the speculation of form criticism regarding life-settings of various forms makes a poor basis for preaching the sure word of God. Although awareness of specific forms can help a preacher in discovering the point of certain texts, a preacher's task is not to preach prebiblical forms as they functioned in their original context but to preach textual units in their biblical and historical contexts (see Chapter 1 above).

In the light of the criticism leveled at source criticism, form criticism, and other methods studying the *pre*history of biblical texts (e.g., tradition criticism),[28] it is not surprising to observe a shift in biblical studies. Biblical scholars are increasingly gravitating to studying the texts in their present literary form. Rudolf Smend remarks that "the final written form of the material . . . is not only a neglected and hence fertile field, but also a more certain one, since the finalised texts are not imaginary entities. Here we are less under the influence of speculations, but can make observations on material that clearly lies before us, and are often also in a position to prove and disprove."[29]

Redaction Criticism

IN the 1950s, Bultmann's pupils, Bornkamm, Conzelmann, and Marxsen, developed a method for investigating the Gospels that has become known as redaction criticism. Marxsen introduced the term *Redaktionsgeschichte* to indicate the change from form criticism; his concern was not with the "oral smaller units" but with "the larger written wholes," while at the same time he gave more credit to the evangelists as "authors" than form critics had done.[30] In contrast to source criticism and form criticism, which "tended to fragment and atomize the gospels," redaction criticism "arose as a more holistic approach dedicated to viewing the gospels as they

---

27. For example, in *Value of the Historical-Critical Method upon Preaching the OT*, Scroggs fails, by and large, in his stated objective of positing different homiletical guidelines for preaching saga, historical narrative, and short stories.

28. For OT tradition criticism and related methods, see, e.g., Knierim, "Criticism of Literary Features," 146-50; for its NT counterpart, see Doty, *Contemporary NT Interpretation*, 75-78.

29. Smend, *JSOT* 16 (1980) 45.

30. See James Robinson, "On the *Gattung* of Mark and John," 100. For the individual contributions made by Bornkamm, Conzelmann, and Marxsen, see Smalley, "Redaction Criticism," 183-84.

stand as individual entities."[31] Although the method started with the Gospels, it was soon applied to Old Testament books as well. The Old Testament scholar Rolf Rendtorff observes that "it is evident that the form-critical approach is not enough to explain the origin of the books of the Old Testament. The traditional material was collected by writers, worked over again, and interpreted theologically. These writers were not bound to fixed, pre-existing forms of expression, but made use of their own, further, theological conceptions."[32]

Aim and Method

Norman Perrin describes the aim of redaction criticism as "studying the theological motivation of an author as this is revealed in the collection, arrangement, editing, and modification of traditional material, and in the composition of new material or the creation of new forms within the traditions of early Christianity."[33] By means of redaction criticism the interpreter tries to discover the specific intention and contribution of a biblical author/redactor. The methodology is to study the composition of the book as a whole (hence the name "composition criticism" has been proposed), the vocabulary and comments of the author especially in his introduction, conclusion, the "seams," editorial links, and summaries, and particularly the author's use of sources as he inserts or omits words or phrases, highlights certain aspects, and rearranges the order.[34] It is well to underscore that redaction criticism views the author's "editing" not in terms of literary style but of theological intentionality. "The editors or authors of the larger works have a clearly recognizable theological purpose. They set their work in a particular theological perspective."[35]

Theology and History

Unfortunately, redaction criticism is not as holistic as it may first appear. In concentrating on the "theology" of individual authors or redactors, interpreters tend to overlook the significance of the incorporation of the author's work in the one Bible. Moreover, redaction criticism can be used just as atomistically as Bultmann's form criticism when the historical dimension is crassly disregarded. Redaction critics such as Marxsen and Perrin play theology off against history; the motto seems to be: if the author had theological interests, he becomes historically questionable. Morna Hooker suggests that "redaction critics, too, may fairly be said to

---

31. Turner, GTJ 4/2 (1983) 264.
32. Rendtorff, Introduction, 127.
33. Perrin, What Is Redaction Criticism? 1.
34. See Smalley, "Redaction Criticism," 182-84; and Stein, JBL 88 (1969) 53.
35. Rendtorff, Introduction, 126. Cf. Stein, JBL 88 (1969) 46, 53-54.

have recreated the evangelists in their own image. For many of them, it is axiomatic that the evangelists had no interest in history, but were creative theologians." Hooker advises that "the twentieth-century critic must not build the first-century evangelist in his own image, and assume that because he himself has despaired of discovering certainty regarding the historicity of his material, and has come to terms with this by placing more and more emphasis on its theological meaning, the evangelists did the same."[36] It should be noted, however, that the antithesis between history and theology, the dualism between fact and value, is not inherent in the redaction-critical method as such but is located in the presuppositions of certain scholars who use that method. "There is no necessary reason why *Redaktionsgeschichte* should lead to the de-historicizing of the New Testament Gospel."[37]

Redaction Criticism and Preaching

Because redaction criticism is more holistic than source and form criticism, it is not surprising that this method has been described as "the most fruitful of all the disciplines of Synoptic study for the preacher."[38] This may be overstating the case somewhat, but it is certainly true that redaction criticism, with its emphasis on the composition of the whole book and its concern for the "theological" intention of the author, better enables the preacher to discern the specific message of the preaching text. Moreover, as Hooker points out, redaction criticism makes preachers aware of the fact that the evangelists themselves were preachers: "Even in the writing down of the material, the evangelists were attempting to do what Christian preachers have been trying to do ever since—to point to the significance of Jesus Christ for those who hear the gospel. The preacher's work is half done for him by the evangelists themselves."[39]

36. Hooker, "In His Own Image?" 30, 37-38. Cf. Caird, *ExpTim* 87 (1976) 171: "The real failings of the [redaction critical] school lie not in its aims or in its methods, but in its unexamined presuppositions. Most of its members are pupils of Bultmann, from whom they have inherited the curious notion that history is the antithesis both of preaching and of eschatology."

37. Lane, *BETS* 11 (1968) 32. See Kantzer, *Christianity Today* 29/15 (Oct 18, 1985) 66 (insert, p. 12): "Evangelicals . . . ought not to reject redaction criticism out of hand, because we would thereby lose a tool that can help us understand the Word of God better. . . . Rather, we ought to use redaction criticism cautiously, recognizing the dangers from its misuse, and avoiding the false presuppositions of those who employ it to lead away from the truth." Cf. Osborne, *JETS* 22/4 (1979) 305-22; 27/1 (1984) 27-30; 28/4 (1985) 399-410; Carson, "Redaction Criticism," *Scripture and Truth*, 119-42.

38. Hull, "Preaching on the Synoptic Gospels," 175.

39. Hooker, *Epworth Review* 3/1 (1976) 52.

Rhetorical Criticism

ANOTHER attempt at a more holistic interpretation is rhetorical criticism. James Muilenburg has been credited with launching rhetorical criticism in his presidential address to the Society of Biblical Literature in 1968. Muilenburg faulted form criticism for its exclusive attention to forms and neglecting biblical content. He stated frankly that form criticism "does not focus sufficient attention upon what is unique and unrepeatable, upon the particularity of the formulation. Moreover, form and content are inextricably related. They form an integral whole. The two are one."[40] In order to get beyond form criticism to a more holistic method of interpretation, Muilenburg proposed "rhetorical criticism." "What I am interested in, above all, is understanding the nature of Hebrew literary composition, exhibiting the structural patterns that are employed for the fashioning of a literary unit, whether in poetry or in prose, and discerning the many and various devices by which the predications are formulated and ordered into a unified whole. Such an enterprise I should describe as rhetoric and the methodology as rhetorical criticism."[41] Accordingly, rhetorical criticism began by focusing attention particularly on two areas: the relation of form and content and the structural patterns of the received text.

Form and Content

Rhetorical criticism looks on the biblical text as a work of art and therefore emphasizes the unity of form and content. Thus the interpreter cannot lay hold of the specific content of a text without paying close attention to the form into which the artist-author (redactor) has cast his message in that particular instance. Clines remarks that rhetorical criticism "is not a mechanical matter of identifying stylistic devices, but, on the premise of the unity of form and content of a work of art, moves towards the work's meaning and quiddity from the standpoint of form rather than of content, of the 'how said' rather than the 'what said.'"[42]

Notwithstanding the wave of enthusiasm for rhetorical criticism, it must also be recognized that "in the pursuit of this new venture . . . there

---

40. Muilenburg, *JBL* 88 (1969) 5. He continues: "Exclusive attention to the *Gattung* [form] may actually obscure the thought and intention of the writer or speaker. The passage must be read and heard precisely as it is spoken. It is the creative synthesis of the particular formation of the pericope with the content that makes it the distinctive composition that it is."

41. Ibid., 8.

42. Clines, *JSOTSup* 1 (1976) 37. Cf. Isaac Kikawada, *Sem* 5 (1977) 67: "In rhetorical criticism the Hebrew Bible is studied from a synchronistic perspective, in an effort to appreciate the received text and to describe not only what the text says but also how it conveys the message."

has been little unanimity except with regard to its general aim: the study of biblical literature as an art-form."[43] The lack of unanimity should not, however, cause us to overlook the important contribution that the perception of the unity of form and content makes to biblical interpretation. This holistic perspective points up that inquiring about form is already to inquire about meaning—and vice versa. In literary studies, "form is intrinsically related to content. . . . Ultimately form has to have content; it has to *contain* something. And conversely content has to take some shape; it has to *conform* to some recognizable or intelligible pattern. Therefore, to deal with one to the exclusion of the other is to surrender a significant part of the whole. Or, stating the process positively, in those instances when we press to discern the fullness of meaning, to deal with the one aspect is to invoke the other."[44]

Structural Patterns

In addition to a holistic perspective of form-content, rhetorical criticism is known for its interest in ancient composition techniques which biblical authors used in "prose" as well as "poetry."[45] In focusing on *how* the text conveys its message, rhetorical criticism has brought to light various structural patterns and literary devices that mark a literary unit and its structure. Muilenburg asserts that "the first concern of the rhetorical critic . . . is to define the limits or scope of the literary unit, to recognize precisely where and how it begins and where and how it ends." Defining the limits of the literary unit is important because each literary unit has a theme, and knowing where the unit ends enables us "to learn how its major motif, usually stated at the beginning, is resolved." The complicating factor that there may be "several points of climax" within a single literary unit is all the more reason to discern the whole unit and not "to resolve it into fragments."[46] But how does one go about discovering the limits of a literary unit? Muilenburg claims that "there are many marks of composition which indicate where the finale has been reached," and he lists two of these: "climactic or ballast lines, which may indeed appear at several junctures within a pericope, but at the close have an emphasis which bears the burden of the entire unit," and ring composition or *inclusio*, that is, "where the opening words are repeated or paraphrased at the close."[47]

---

43. Whybray, *JSOT* 27 (1983) 76.
44. R. L. Hicks, "Form and Content," 307.
45. Biblical "prose" and "poetry" cannot be distinguished as easily as has often been suggested. See Kugel, *Idea of Biblical Poetry*, 76-95, 302, and especially p. 85: "The distinction between 'poetry' and 'prose' is . . . not native to the texts."
46. Muilenburg, *JBL* 88 (1969) 8.
47. Ibid., 9.

"The second major concern of the rhetorical critic," according to Muilenburg, "is to recognize the structure of a composition and to discern the configuration of its component parts . . . , and to note the various rhetorical devices that are employed for marking, on the one hand, the sequence and movement of the pericope, and on the other, the shifts or breaks in the development of the writer's thought."[48] Among several rhetorical devices, Muilenburg highlights particularly parallel structures and repetition of key words or phrases: "Repetition serves many and diverse functions in the literary compositions of ancient Israel. . . . It served as an effective mnemonic device. It is the key word which may often guide us in our isolation of a literary unit, which gives to it its unity and focus, which helps us to articulate the structure of the composition and to discern the pattern or texture into which the words are woven."[49]

One of the clearest expositions of ancient structural patterns is offered by H. Van Dyke Parunak. He reminds us that biblical literature, in contrast to modern literature, is "essentially aural," that is, "it was intended to be understood with the ear, and not with the eye."[50] That fact presented the biblical authors with the limitation (from our perspective) of having to communicate in one dimension rather than two. Whereas modern authors can signal literary units with chapter headings, section titles, and paragraph indentations, ancient authors did not have that graphic dimension at their disposal. Whereas modern authors can give clues to their intended meaning by emphasizing words and phrases with italics or bold print and deemphasizing items with parentheses or with placement in footnotes or appendices, ancient authors did not have that graphic dimension at their disposal.[51] Hence both with respect to indicating the limits of a literary unit as well as giving clues to its intended meaning, ancient authors were dependent on other than modern, graphic techniques. Since their techniques had to be perceived aurally, they consisted primarily of structural patterns that could be sensed by ears attuned to those patterns. One such device, still used by preachers today in their aural proclamation, is repetition.

Repetition is apparently the basic building block of most ancient structural patterns. Simple repetition of words, phrases, and clauses is, of course, frequently found in biblical literature. As a literary device known as "the keyword technique," repetition of words or phrases is a device

---

48. Ibid., 9-10.

49. Ibid., 16. Cf. already in 1953 Muilenburg's "Hebrew Rhetoric: Repetition and Style," *VTSup* 1 (1953) 97-111.

50. Parunak, *Sem* 8 (1982) 2. Even today, communication for the ear requires different techniques than communication for the eye. See Davis, *Design for Preaching*, 164-71, 265-94, especially 288 about parallel construction and repeated constructions.

51. Parunak, *Bib* 62/2 (1981) 153.

that can mark literary units: "As long as a keyword persists, we know that we are still in the same literary unit. When one keyword disappears or another one appears, we recognize a structural division."[52]

From that simple scheme of repetition of a word or phrase, more complex schemes can be developed. Parunak elaborates as follows: "For simplicity let us assume that our text has only two kinds of units at one level, A and B. Let us form the simplest possible pattern from these units, the pair AB. If we repeat this unit by sliding . . . it along the one dimensional axis of speech, we produce ABAB. . . . Our other option in duplicating the basic unit is to reflect the unit on itself, producing either ABA or ABBA. . . . Mathematically, these are the only ways to duplicate a pattern in one dimension." Parunak recognizes, of course, that "more complex arrangements may be imagined," but his point is that all arrangements "can be reduced to repeated combinations" of the above two forms, the ABAB parallelism or alternation and the ABBA inverted parallelism or chiasm.[53]

Basically, therefore, the structural patterns at the disposal of ancient authors were fairly simple. And yet, as is evident from the literature, biblical authors were able to weave these simple components into extremely complex structures. Parunak tries to account for this complexity by noting that "more than one pattern may be active in a passage at a time," either by one pattern being embedded in another or running concurrent with another. "Once we recognize how patterns can combine dynamically through embedding and concurrence, we can tailor the pattern to fit the data, rather than the other way around."[54]

It may clarify matters to offer a brief explanation of each of the structural patterns which were depicted above in their relation to each other. *Repetition* is present "when the same sonal quantity, word, phrase, clause or even a literary type keeps on being repeated—$A \ldots A^1 \ldots A^2 \ldots A^3 \ldots$—throughout a literary composition and thereby draws attention to itself."[55] The purpose of repetition can vary: it can serve to express urgency, or "to center the thought," then again "to give continuity to the writer's thought"; sometimes it "indicates the structure of the poem, pointing to the separate divisions; at other times it may guide us in determining the extent of the literary unit."[56] (For an example, see the analysis of Gen 1 below.)

---

52. Parunak, *Sem* 8 (1982) 6.
53. Ibid., 8.
54. Ibid., 10, 12.
55. Edward Newing, *SEAJT* 22/2 (1981) 7.
56. Muilenburg, *VTSup* 1 (1953) 99; cf. p. 102 on repetition "to express urgency."

Parallelism, if synonymous, is a form of repetition: *AB AB.* For example, Isa 1:2a:

| Hear, | O heavens, | A B |
| and give ear, | O earth | A' B' |

Muilenburg correctly points out, however, that "parallelism is in reality very seldom precisely synonymous. The parallel line does not simply repeat what has been said, but enriches it, deepens it, transforms it by adding fresh nuances and bringing in new elements, renders it more concrete and vivid and telling."[57]

Chiasm is a form of inverted parallelism: *AB BA.* It consists of "a two-part structure or system in which the second half is a mirror image of the first, i.e. where the first term recurs last, and the last first."[58] Inverted parallelism is shown, for example, in Jer 30:17a:

| For I will restore | health to you, | A B |
| and your wounds | I will heal | B' A' |

A chiasm consisting of three or more elements in each panel, such as *ABCDEDCBA,* (sometimes called "introversion" or "concentric structure"), still displays the basic chiastic structure around a "central key pivot point which we call 'X.'"[59] Like repetition, chiasm can also serve various purposes. Chiasm can mark off a textual unit, for "it signals its own conclusion. If a reader has already encountered the sequence 'A B C,' the occurrence of 'C B A' will indicate the completion of a unit."[60] A second purpose of chiasm is to indicate where the emphasis falls, namely on the central element. In a sequence such as *ABCDCBA,* the emphasis would naturally fall on the central element *D*—naturally, for "the abrupt repetition by which the last elements of the first half of

57. Ibid., 98. For other forms of parallelism, see Chapter 10 below. See also Kugel, *Idea of Biblical Poetry;* Berlin, *Dynamics of Biblical Parallelism.*

58. John Welch, "Introduction," 10. Man, *BSac* 141 (1984) 154-55, notes that "the word 'chiasm' derives from the Greek verb *chiazoo,* meaning 'to mark with two lines crossing like a X (Chi).' . . . If the two mirrored halves of a simple chiastic structure . . . are placed one under the other and the lines are drawn connecting the corresponding elements, the lines form a shape resembling the capital Greek letter X (Chi):

59. Newing, *SEAJT* 22/2 (1981) 5; cf. the diagrams on pp. 8 and 9 on the "introverted structure of the Hexateuch." Breck insists rightly that chiasm should be distinguished from mere inverted parallelism: "The uniqueness of the chiastic structure lies in its focus on a *pivotal theme,* about which the other propositions of the literary unit are developed" (*BTB* 17 [1987] 71).

60. Parunak, *Bib* 62/2 (1981) 156.

the system become the first elements of the second half draws attention to the central terms."[61]

Inclusio or "envelope figure" or "ring composition" can be seen as a simple chiasm, namely, "a three-membered (A B A) chiasm whose outer members are short, compared with the center member."[62] A more detailed definition describes *inclusio* as "the use of assonance of consonants and/or syllables, words and their pairs, phrases, clauses, sentences and/or motifs, either singly or more often in multiples to bracket a sentence, set, paragraph, episode or pericope, narrative section or cycle, block of laws, book, national epic, or even the whole Hebrew and Christian Bibles, in order to define its limits."[63] The purposes for which *inclusio* are used can also vary. As can be seen, for example, in Psalms 8 and 103, *inclusio* can mark the limits of the literary unit or highlight the motif or both.

Rhetorical Criticism and Preaching

Although these structural patterns are all too often "passed off in the scholarly literature as mere literary niceties, a structural tour de force which serves only aesthetic ends,"[64] their value for biblical interpretation and preaching should be quite apparent. For if the biblical authors—in the New Testament as well as in the Old Testament and in "prose" as well as in "poetry"—did indeed use these structural patterns to mark their text in order to signal how they wished their work to be heard by their audience, contemporary expository preachers can also take advantage of these ancient markings. Let us look at several homiletical areas where these textual markings may be relevant.

The first area is that of text selection. As we shall see in Chapter 6 below, a preaching text must not be a fragment of a text but a literary unit. Since, as we have seen, the biblical authors used literary devices such as repetition (the keyword technique), chiasm, and *inclusio* to mark units and subunits in their work, the biblical authors themselves often provide the clues as to what would make for a proper preaching text. A related consideration for text selection is that "an inclusio, especially an external inclusio, is often used . . . to set off material that is peripheral to the course of the argument"—see, for example, 2 Chr 2:2-18; 6:12-13; Eph 3:1-14.[65] In defining the limits of a preaching text or reading selection, one may wish to concentrate on the main argument and consider skipping over a pas-

61. Stock, *BTB* 14/1 (1984) 23.
62. Parunak, *Bib* 62/2 (1981) 158.
63. Newing, *SEAJT* 22/2 (1981) 2; cf. p. 5.
64. Man, *BSac* 141 (1984) 147.
65. Parunak, *Bib* 62/2 (1981) 160-62. See further Chapter 9 below.

sage which the biblical author, had he lived today, might have placed in parentheses or a footnote. As the example of Eph 3:1-14 shows, however, sometimes these asides themselves make for good, unified preaching texts.

Another homiletical area where the structural patterns are relevant is that of theme formulation. As we shall see in Chapter 6, every sermon ought to have a theme. With their structural patterns, biblical authors provide contemporary preachers with clues to the theme or motif of the selected preaching text. *Inclusio* or repetition of a word, phrase, or clause may provide such a clue. For example, an investigation of Gen 1 reveals the following significant repetitions: 32 times "God," 8 times "God said," 7 times "God saw that it was good," and 6 times "there was evening . . . and morning." By way of the repetitions, the theocentric theme comes through loudly and clearly: the sovereign God created all things and he created them good. Moreover, by matching the repetitions with each other an intricate parallel structure is revealed:

	6 days	8 creative acts	7 times good
A	Day 1:	Light	good
B	Day 2:	Firmament	
C	Day 3:	Land	good
		Vegetation	good
A'	Day 4:	Sun, moon, stars	good
B'	Day 5:	Fish, birds	good
C'	Day 6	Animals	good
		Human beings	very good

The parallel structure accounts for the frequently observed discrepancy between the creation of light (Day 1) and that of the lightbearers (Day 4). It also allows for the polemical thrust against the worship of the Sun and Moon (pagan gods) by placing the creation of these "lights" between that of vegetation and fish. It further highlights progression from Day 1 to 3 and from Day 4 to 6. Did the author purposely skip the declaration that the creation of the firmament was "good" so that the climax "and behold, it was very good" might resound on the seventh (perfect) time? Whatever the case, the repetition and parallelism focuses attention on the theme that God sovereignly ordered his creation into a structured cosmos and that it was very good.

A chiastic structure is also able to reveal the theme of a passage because it focuses on the pivotal thought around which the passage turns.[66]

---

66. "Because of this central focus, genuine chiasmus is able to set in relief the central idea or theme the writer tries to express" (Breck, *BTB* 17 [1987] 71).

For example, in Gen 2:4b–3:24 we find the following structure:[67]

A		Narrative:	God, man	(2:4b-17)
			From *adamah* (ground) to garden	
	B	Narrative:	God, man, woman, animals	(2:18-25)
			Relationships among creatures	
			God's goodness in making a partner for man	
		C	Dialogue:	Serpent, woman	(3:1-5)
				Eating from the tree	
				Three statements	
			D	Narrative:	Woman, man	(3:6-8)
					They eat from the tree	
					The Fall: Rebellion in God's kingdom	
		C′	Dialogue:	God, man, woman	(3:9-13)
				Eating from the tree	
				Three questions and answers	
	B′	Monologue:	God, man, woman, serpent	(3:14-19)
			Relationships among the creatures	
			God's judgment and grace	
A′		Narrative:	God, man	(3:20-24)
			From garden to *adamah* (ground)	

Clearly the author's intention is to show us what happened to God's *good* creation. The pivotal point is D, human rebellion in God's kingdom; the "image of God" (1:27) wanted to be "like God" (3:5) and ended up hiding "from the presence of the Lord God" (3:8). Thus the focus and theme of a passage may be revealed by its structure, whether that be repetition, inclusion, parallelism, or chiasm.

The theme of a passage may also be pinpointed by another ancient method of emphasizing material—"the broken structure." Parunak points out that "a deviation from a regular structural pattern (whether alternating or chiastic) can give emphasis. In this case, the emphasized item is highlighted precisely because it does not fit into the expected symmetrical scheme."[68]

A third and related area where the structural patterns are relevant is that of understanding the text both in its parts and in its larger context. As far as understanding the parts of a text is concerned, parallel lines tend to elucidate each other. Parallel lines, of course, are found not only in obvious parallel structures but also in chiastic structures since they are forms of inverted parallelism. For example, the meaning of "desire" in Gen 3:16b, "your desire shall be for your husband," has always been

---

67. Adapted from Radday, "Chiasmus in Hebrew Biblical Narrative," 98-99. See also Jerome T. Walsh, "Genesis 2:4b–3:24: A Synchronic Approach," *JBL* 96/2 (1977) 161-77.

68. Parunak, *Bib* 62/2 (1981) 165.

rather vague. Does it indeed mean, as many commentators suggest, that a wife will have *sexual* desire for her husband in spite of his domination? Recently it has been observed that the "chiastic parallelism" of this verse indicates that the wife's desire is a desire to *rule* her husband.

| Your | desire shall be for | your husband, |
| and he | shall rule over | you. |

This interpretation is substantiated by the identical parallelism in Gen 4:7b where "sexual desire" is obviously impossible. God says to Cain:

| Its [sin's] | desire is for | you, |
| but you | must master | it.[69] |

As far as understanding a text in its larger context is concerned, being able to place a text in an overall chiastic structure of a section or book provides an important clue to the meaning of that particular text. "Where chiasmus is present, it has been found to hold a key to the perception of the central message of the book in question. This offers significant clues for understanding the unity of the writing, . . . and the meaningful relationships existing between seemingly repetitious sections in the book."[70]

Having set forth some of the benefits of rhetorical criticism for preaching, we should also note some of the possible pitfalls. Charles Conroy observes that "the search for chiasmus and other forms of structural geometry appears at times to exert a fatal fascination on students of biblical texts." As an antidote, he suggests that one first carry out "a detailed analysis of each pericope and of the intrinsic narrative dynamism of the story as a whole . . . [and] then erect such structural edifices as the text actually permits."[71] Although this reaction to some excesses is understandable, I do not believe that modern interpreters ought to leave for last what ancient hearers heard first, or at least were listening for. Surely, the structural patterns inserted by the author can form a valid guideline for discovering the meaning of a passage. Nevertheless, a note of caution is in order to be wary of discovering patterns where none was intended, and to be wary of imposing known structures on the text. Martin Kessler appropriately reminds us that "the ancient Hebrew writers used literary conventions creatively; though they seem always to have been aware of them, they felt quite free to modify, to transform, or even to turn them up-

---

69. See Bruce Waltke, "The Relationship of the Sexes in the Bible," *Crux* 19/3 (Sept 1983) 16, with credit to Susan Foh (*Women and the Word of God* [Grand Rapids: Baker, 1981], 67-69) for pointing out the parallel between Gen 3:16 and 4:7b. Cf. Foh's earlier article, "What Is the Woman's Desire?" *WTJ* 37 (1974) 376-83.

70. Welch, "Chiasmus in the NT," 248.

71. Conroy, *Absalom Absalom*, 145. Cf. Lundbom, *Jeremiah*, 19: "We must do more than be descriptive, which has been the tendency from Lowth on. Analysis of balancing patterns could go on *ad infinitum* without our knowing anything of their rhetorical value."

side down. The biblical student must therefore allow the literature to speak for itself; each literary piece must be permitted to set forth its own characteristic features."[72]

A second note of caution concerns the tendency of rhetorical criticism to concentrate on and isolate a subsidiary unit such as a narrative from its larger contexts. This temptation to isolate a unit may, ironically, reduce rhetorical criticism to but another form of atomism. Richard Lischer comments: "By isolating stories from their contexts in canon, theology, church, and history, the aesthetic approach does more than ignore the historical dimension in interpretation; it atomizes the community's experience of the gospel—of which texts are organic parts." As a result of isolating a narrative or a parable, the point and relevance which the text has as part of the canon is lost. Lischer asks, "When a New Testament parable is presented in isolation from the mission of Jesus and the church, what residual experience remains available to the congregation? What story lifted from its background still *works* on any but the moralistic or universalising levels?"[73] This point is well taken and is a pertinent reminder that rhetorical criticism, for all its helpful insights, is not the whole of biblical interpretation.

Biblical Theology

BIBLICAL theology is here used in the sense of the specific theological discipline which seeks to uncover "the theology which the Bible itself contains."[74] Of the several methods of interpretation being discussed in this chapter, biblical theology is the oldest, going back more than 200 years. The Biblical Theology Movement was influential particularly in the 1940s and 1950s when it formed a wholesome alternative to critical scholarship which had lost itself "in the minutiae of literary, philological, and historical problems. As a result the Bible had been hopelessly fragmented and the essential unity of the gospel was distorted and forgotten."[75] In contrast to these atomistic approaches, biblical theology offered a holistic perspective.

Although biblical theology has lost much of its popularity today, reports of its death are exaggerated.[76] In *Biblical Theology in Crisis* (1970), Brevard Childs focused attention on the problems of biblical theology but

72. Kessler, *Sem* 6 (1978) 45.
73. Lischer, *Int* 38 (1984) 27.
74. Hasel, *OT Theology*, 16. For a survey of the history of biblical theology, see ibid., 16-34.
75. Childs, *Biblical Theology in Crisis*, 15.
76. Barton, *Reading the OT*, 211: "The Biblical Theology movement . . . is dead and unlikely to revive." According to Childs, the demise of the Biblical Theology Movement may be dated to 1963 (*Biblical Theology in Crisis*, 85).

also advocated establishing "the discipline on a solid foundation while resisting the challenge of those denying the right of constructive theology to relate Bible and theology."[77] Later, in a journal called, significantly, *Horizons in Biblical Theology*, Childs wrote that "there remains a large and continuing expression of support for the need of some form of biblical theology."[78] For his part, Gerhard Hasel has documented the continuing popularity of Old Testament theology.[79] In evangelical circles biblical theology certainly retains much of its attraction.

The reason for looking at biblical theology in this chapter is that it brought out some important aspects of literary interpretation which are lacking in the more contemporary methods. We shall focus on three of these: its holistic approach, the longitudinal themes, and the idea of progressive revelation.

A Holistic Approach

The holistic approach of biblical theology is so all-encompassing that this method of interpretation could be discussed under all three dimensions of biblical interpretation: historical, theological, and literary. For, despite disagreements, the practitioners of biblical theology agreed at least on these points: that God reveals himself in history, that the biblical text is ultimately "theological" in nature, and that the Bible is a literary unity.[80] Unfortunately, the historical and literary dimensions were not always clearly distinguished; in some circles the text was often used merely as a window for viewing past historical events, with the result that the literary dimension never came clearly into focus.[81]

The holistic approach of biblical theology is also apparent in the various descriptions of the method. Geerhardus Vos defined biblical theology as "that branch of Exegetical Theology which deals with the process

77. Childs, *Biblical Theology in Crisis*, 93. Cf. p. 95: "The real question is not whether to do Biblical Theology or not, but rather what kind of Biblical Theology does one have!"

78. Childs, *HorBT* 4/1 (1982) 1.

79. In the first edition of *OT Theology* (1972), Hasel could still write: "The 'golden age' of OT theology began in the 1930s and continues to the present" (p. 32), and in the preface to the 1982 revised edition he observes: "A flood of studies on OT theology continues to pour forth with a steady pace since the appearance of this volume in 1972" (p. 7). Cf. Hasel, *HorBT* 4/1 (1982) 80: "We believe that the time for creative and critical reflection is here and that there is a distinct future for Biblical theology."

80. See Childs, *Biblical Theology in Crisis*, 32-44. Cf. Gamble, *Int* 7 (1953) 471-76.

81. See, e.g., my analysis of the redemptive-historical movement in Holland in the 1930s and 1940s—a movement which tended simply to identify historical texts and historical facts; *Sola Scriptura*, especially pp. 191-212. On the other hand, Gamble, *Int* 7 (1953) 471, claims that for biblical theologians "the message was expressed through literary forms, therefore literary principles were invariably at work. The biblical theologian recognizes that historical and literary study are absolute prerequisites to his work of theological interpretation."

of the self-revelation of God deposited in the Bible."[82] In this definition, one can sense the concern for the theological ("the self-revelation of God") and the historical ("process") dimensions. Gerhard Hasel places more weight on the literary dimension: "A Biblical theology has the task of providing summary interpretations of the final form of the individual Biblical documents or groups of writings and of presenting the longitudinal themes, motifs, and concepts that emerge from the Biblical materials."[83] Whatever the emphasis, we can learn from the holistic approach of biblical theology that a holistic literary method by itself is not sufficient for biblical interpretation but that it needs to be complemented by methods that do justice to the historical and theological dimensions of biblical literature.

Longitudinal Themes

In the literary dimension, biblical theology's holistic approach is demonstrated particularly by its concern for longitudinal themes that span not only individual books (the concern of redaction and rhetorical criticism) but several books and even both Testaments. In this search for themes, a perennial question has been, Is there in the Bible one, all-inclusive, overarching theme? In 1933 Walther Eichrodt breathed new life into biblical theology with his proposal that there is indeed such an all-encompassing biblical theme: the theme of covenant.[84] Unfortunately, the covenant theme, though central and spanning both Old Testament and New Testament, cannot naturally encompass all biblical themes, and it was not long till Eichrodt was accused of "artificially forcing" the biblical material into his scheme.[85] Other proposals for an all-encompassing theme followed: "the holiness of God," "God as the Lord," "the rulership of God," "the kingdom of God," "the promise of God," "the experience of God," "Israel's election as the people of God," "communion," "the name of God,"

---

82. Vos, *Biblical Theology*, 13. Cf. the descriptions of Floyd Filson: "Biblical theology is essentially an interpreted account of the biblical history, seen as the advancing work of God Himself" (quoted by Gamble, *Int* 7 [1953] 466), and Edmund Clowney: "Biblical theology as a distinct and fruitful study must take seriously both historical progression and theological unity in the Bible" (*Preaching and Biblical Theology*, 17).

83. Hasel, *HorBT* 4/1 (1982) 77. Cf. Hasel, *OT Theology*, 93.

84. "Eichrodt's theology was epoch-making because he broke decisively with the pattern of exposition current at the time, which sought structural unity from the categories of systematic theology. In its place Eichrodt displayed a cross-section of the OT defined by a category native to the OT witness" (Coats, "Theology of the Hebrew Bible," 244). Gamble, *Int* 7 (1953) 470, credits Eichrodt, along with C. H. Dodd, for "the revival of biblical theology."

85. For example, Gamble, *Int* 7 (1953) 470: "Undoubtedly Eichrodt holds too rigidly to the pattern he has adopted and at times artificially forces his material into an outline."

"the presence of God."[86] After recounting most of these proposals, Hasel concludes: "It is highly significant that virtually all of these suggestions have as their common denominator an aspect of God and/or his activity for the world or man. This inadvertently points to the fact that the OT is in its essence *theo*centric just as the NT is *christo*centric. In short, God is the dynamic, unifying center of the OT."[87]

With respect to the longitudinal themes, Hasel contends that they can be brought out best without the framework of a more specific overarching theme: "It is evident that even the most carefully worked out single center or formula will prove itself finally as one-sided, inadequate, and insufficient, if not outrightly erroneous, and therefore will lead to misconceptions." Consequently, he proposes that "an OT theology which recognizes God as the dynamic, unifying center provides the possibility to describe the rich and variegated theologies and to present the various longitudinal themes, motifs, and ideas."[88] On the one hand, Hasel and others voice a legitimate concern when they warn that a more specific theme would impose a straightjacket on the variety of themes in the Bible and might end up distorting them. On the other hand, lining up biblical theological themes side by side, as if they were all of the same rank, does not do justice to the biblical material either, for such an approach lacks the depth which the Bible itself provides. For example, the theme of the coming of the kingdom of God naturally encompasses the theme of the covenant, for covenant is a form of kingdom administration. And the theme of covenant, in turn, naturally encompasses the theme of law, for God's laws are covenant stipulations. My point is that for the sake of doing justice to the biblical material, the interpreter must try to visualize and classify the complex relationships and interrelationships among themes—constantly guarding, of course, against imposing a foreign system on the biblical material.

In any event, the discussion of a possible overarching theme has brought to light many genuine longitudinal themes which span individual books and Testaments: the rulership of God, the kingdom of God (realm), election (grace), the covenant, the promise of God, the presence of God, etc. Since, as is commonly acknowledged, every part must be interpreted in the light of the whole, every text must also be interpreted in the light of the larger biblical themes of which it forms a part.

Progressive Revelation
The idea of longitudinal themes is linked to the notion of progressive rev-

---

86. See Hasel, *OT Theology*, 119-43. On the "presence of God" theme, see Coats, "Theology of the Hebrew Bible," 245.

87. Hasel, *OT Theology*, 139-40.

88. Ibid., 134, 142.

elation, for the themes are not static entities but develop, change, and grow in the course of history. The idea of progressive revelation, in turn, is woven in with the conviction that revelation takes place in history and through history. The latter conviction "has come under increasing attack" of late, but Werner Lemke rightly argues that the concept of revelation through history "will always be of fundamental significance to those who choose to believe in the biblical God. For in contrast to other major religious traditions, at the center of which stands a philosophical metaphysics, a system of ethics, or a written code of conduct, the biblical tradition, whether in its Jewish or Christian manifestations, is first and foremost a story about God who acts on behalf of and through human beings in the context of specific and concrete historical events."[89]

Edmund Clowney explains the concept of progressive revelation as follows: "The Bible records revelation given in the course of history. This revelation . . . was given progressively, for the process of revelation accompanies the process of redemption. Since redemption does not proceed uniformly but in epochs determined by God's acts, so revelation has an epochal structure, manifested and marked in the canonical Scriptures."[90]

We can leave further discussion of progressive revelation for Chapter 5. The point here is simply that also in literary interpretation one must be aware of the progression taking place within the unity of Scripture; in other words, one must be aware of the fact that Scripture does not, in any one place, present static, full-grown concepts but the growing, changing ideas that are part and parcel of the forward movement of progressive revelation.

As far as literary interpretation is concerned, the idea of progressive revelation has implications in two directions. On the one hand, an interpreter must be careful not to read more into a text than is actually there at that particular stage of redemptive history. "It is a mark of *eis*egesis, not *ex*egesis, to borrow freight that appears chronologically later in the text and to transport it back and unload it on an earlier passage simply because both or all the passages involved share the same canon."[91] On the other hand, an interpreter, and certainly a preacher, cannot be satisfied with a descriptive analysis of the meaning of a text in its own particular historical context; one cannot present as gospel truth a message at a certain stage of its development but must follow it through the whole of the Bible, from seed to plant to flower. This deeper, fuller level of meaning has been called the *sensus plenior* (the fuller sense). Raymond Brown offers the following definition: "The *sensus plenior* is that additional, deeper meaning, intended by God but not clearly intended by the human author,

---

89. Lemke, *Int* 36 (1982) 46.
90. Clowney, *Preaching and Biblical Theology*, 15.
91. Kaiser, *Toward an Exegetical Theology*, 82.

which is seen to exist in the words of a Biblical text (or group of texts, or even a whole book) when they are studied in the light of further revelation." Here again interpretation is open to the abuse of subjective opinions being imposed on the text. Brown seeks to curb this abuse with two criteria: "The fuller sense must be a development of what is literally said in the passage," and "God must have willed that the fuller sense be contained in the literal sense."[92] William LaSor writes similarly that the quest for the fuller meaning "must always begin with the literal meaning of the text. *Sensus plenior* is not a substitute for a grammatico-historical exegesis, but a development from such exegesis. It is not a reading into the text of theological doctrines and dogmas; rather it is a reading out of the text the fullness of meaning required by God's complete revelation."[93]

Biblical Theology and Preaching

Clowney claims that "in all the wealth of fresh approaches to preaching there is none which has the significance or usefulness of that development in biblical studies which is generally called biblical theology."[94] Certainly biblical theology contains many fruitful insights for preaching. More than any of the other methods of interpretation, biblical theology underscores the importance of holistic interpretation, especially with respect to the historical and theological dimensions. Biblical theology may also be credited with a theocentric approach which at its best undercuts an anthropocentric, moralistic reading and preaching of the Bible.[95] Biblical theology further emphasizes the unity of the Bible and uncovers the connecting themes between the Old Testament and the New Testament, thus guiding the preacher from the Old Testament to the New Testament, and setting the direction for the word that should go out to the congregation today. Biblical theology also "exhibits the organic growth of the truths of Special Revelation. By doing this it enables one properly to distribute the emphasis among the several aspects of teaching and preaching. A leaf is not of the same importance as a twig, nor a twig as a branch, nor a branch as the trunk of the tree."[96] Finally, biblical theology makes the preacher aware of the fact that the Bible is not an assortment of similar parts (verses) which, like pizza, can be dished out at random; rather, each text must be understood in its own historical context and in the light of God's progressive revelation before it can be proclaimed as God's authoritative word for contemporary congregations.

---

92. Raymond Brown, "The 'Sensus Plenior' of Sacred Scripture," S.T.D. dissertation (Baltimore: St. Mary's University), 92, 145-46; see also LaSor, "Sensus Plenior," 275.

93. LaSor, *TynBul* 29 (1978) 59. On *sensus plenior* see further Chapter 5 below.

94. Clowney, *Preaching and Biblical Theology*, 10.

95. See my *Sola Scriptura*, especially pp. 65-86 and 140-52.

96. Vos, *Biblical Theology*, 26.

The Canonical Approach

ANOTHER form of holistic literary interpretation is the canonical approach. In the past most evangelical interpreters adhered implicitly to the canonical approach, but today this approach has been developed explicitly by Brevard Childs. This approach is sometimes called or confused with "canonical criticism," but Childs is "not happy with this term because it implies that the concern with canon is viewed as another historical-critical technique which can take its place alongside of source criticism, form criticism, rhetorical criticism and the like. I do not envision the approach to canon in this light. Rather, the issue at stake in canon turns on establishing a stance from which the Bible is to be read as Sacred Scripture."[97] "This is my concern," he writes elsewhere, "How does one read the Bible from within, read it as the Scripture of the church?"[98]

In direct contrast, therefore, to the standpoint of liberal critical scholars, Childs wishes to interpret the Scriptures from "within." "The critic presumes to stand above the text, outside the circle of tradition, and from this detached vantage point adjudicate the truth and error of the . . . Testament's time-conditionality. In contrast, the canonical interpreter stands within the received tradition, and, fully conscious of his own time-conditionality as well as that of the scriptures, strives critically to discern from its kerygmatic witness a way to God which overcomes the historical mooring of both text and reader."[99]

The canonical approach might best be described as a new biblical theology. In the chapter headings to *Biblical Theology in Crisis,* Childs already points out "The Need for a New Biblical Theology," and proposes "The Shape of a New Biblical Theology." Having indicated the "great confusion" in the Biblical Theology Movement with respect to the context for doing biblical theology, Childs announces his proposal for a new biblical theology as follows: "As a fresh alternative, we would like to defend the thesis that the canon of the Christian church is the most appropriate context from which to do Biblical Theology."[100]

---

97. Childs, *Int* 32 (1978) 54. The term "canonical criticism" is associated with J. A. Sanders; see Spina, "Canonical Criticism: Childs Versus Sanders," in *Interpreting God's Word Today,* 165-94.

98. Childs, *CTM* 43 (1972) 711.

99. Childs, *NT as Canon,* 51-52.

100. Childs, *Biblical Theology in Crisis,* 99. Childs argues that "one of the persistently weak points of the Biblical Theology Movement [the nonevangelical wing] was its failure to take the Biblical text seriously in its canonical form." Because of this hermeneutical uncertainty, he claims, the movement was "vulnerable to every shifting wind that blew, from Cullmann's 'salvation-history' to Bultmann's 'self-understanding' to Ebeling-Fuchs's 'linguisticality of being'" (p. 102). On Childs as promoter of a "new Biblical theology" see also Hasel, *OT Theology,* 87. Hasel, and most conservative theologians, would agree that biblical theology "is best conceived as an enterprise that is

In the writings of Childs, one can detect at least three reasons for selecting the canon as context for biblical interpretation: the canon is normative, it is the final literary form, and it is a channel for contemporary relevance. We shall take a closer look at each topic in turn.

The Canon as Norm

A major reason for selecting the canon, rather than history or earlier literary formations, as context is that only the canon is normative. "To do Biblical Theology within the context of the canon involves acknowledgment of the *normative* quality of the Biblical tradition. The Scriptures of the church provide the authoritative and definitive word that continues to shape and enliven the church."[101]

In selecting the canon as *the* context for biblical interpretation, Childs charts a different course from the diachronic approach of tradition criticism practiced by von Rad and others.[102] "The canonical form marks not only the place from which exegesis begins, but also it marks the place at which it ends. The text's pre-history and post-history are both subordinated to the form deemed canonical. The goal of the enterprise is to illuminate the writings which have been and continue to be received as authoritative by the community of faith."[103]

Childs acknowledges that canonical study shares a common interest with "several of the newer literary critical methods in its concern to do justice to the integrity of the text itself apart from diachronistic reconstruction." At the same time he insists that the canonical approach differs from and goes beyond literary approaches such as rhetorical criticism "by interpreting the biblical text in relation to a community of faith and practice for whom it served a particular theological role as possessing divine authority. . . . The canonical approach is concerned to understand the nature of the theological shape of the text rather than to recover an original literary or aesthetic unity."[104]

---

oriented by the canonical form of Scripture," *JSOT* 31 (1985) 44; at the same time, Hasel is also critical of aspects of Childs's methodology; see *OT Theology*, 91-92.

101. Childs, *Biblical Theology in Crisis*, 100. For argumentation that "the level of final composition . . . provides the clearest norm both for exegesis and for faith," see Dunn, "Levels of Canonical Authority," *HorBT* 4/1 (1982) 37-51.

102. See Hasel, *JSOT* 31 (1985) 40-41; see also the mediating position of Rendtorff, *Introduction*, 130-31.

103. Childs, *NT as Canon*, 48.

104. Childs, *Introduction*, 74. Cf. idem, *Exodus*, xiv: "From a literary point of view there is a great need to understand the present composition as a piece of literature with its own integrity. The concentration of critical scholars on form-critical and source analysis has tended to fragment the text and leave the reader with only bits and pieces. But an even more important reason for interpreting the final text is a theological one. It is the final text, the composite narrative, in its present shape which the church . . . accepted as canonical and thus the vehicle of revelation and instruction."

The Canon as the Final Form

Another reason for selecting the canon as context is that the canon is the final form of the biblical literature and as such "it alone bears witness to the full history of revelation." Childs acknowledges that "earlier stages in the development of the biblical tradition were often regarded as canonical prior to the establishment of the final form." But he argues that in spite of that earlier acceptance, the final form of the canon still exercised a critical function over the earlier stages: "A critical judgment is exercised in the way in which the earlier stages are handled. At times the material is passed on, complete with all of its original historical particularity. At other times the canonical process selects, rearranges, or expands the received traditions. The purpose of insisting on the authority of the final form is to preserve the canon's role of providing this critical norm."[105]

The selection of the final form as the context for biblical interpretation has direct hermeneutical implications. In response to reviewers of his *Introduction to the Old Testament as Scripture*, Childs reiterates: "The crucial point to make is that regardless of the exact nature of a text's prehistory, a new dynamic was unleashed for its interpretation when it was collected with other material and assigned a religious role as sacred scripture."[106] The hermeneutical implications of this position show up clearly when Childs contrasts the final canonical form with other forms that have been used as context. "To work with the final form is to resist any method which seeks critically to shift the canonical ordering. Such an exegetical move occurs when an overarching category such as *Heilsgeschichte* subordinates the unique canonical profile, or when an historical or rhetorical reconstruction attempts to refocus the picture according to its own standards of historical accuracy or literary aesthetics."[107]

The Canon as Channel

A third reason for selecting the canon as context is that the canon functions as a channel directing the message to the present. "The Scriptures of the church are not archives of the past but a channel of life for the continuing church, through which God instructs and admonishes his people. Implied in the use of the canon as a context for interpreting Scripture is a rejection of the method that would imprison the Bible within a context of the historical past. Rather, the appeal to the canon understands Scripture as a vehicle of a divine reality, which indeed encountered an ancient

105. Childs, *Int* 32 (1978) 47-48; cf. idem, *Introduction*, 75-76.
106. Childs, *JSOT* 16 (1980) 54.
107. Childs, *Int* 32 (1978) 48. Cf. idem, *CTM* 43 (1972) 721: "The present shape of the Pentateuch is a profoundly theological witness which is lost if its shape is destroyed in order to reconstruct a so-called objective, historical sequence."

people in the historical past, but which continues to confront the church through the pages of Scripture."[108]

Here again we notice how Childs contrasts his approach with other contemporary approaches. His view of many modern commentaries is that "there is little which quickens the mind, and nothing which touches the heart."[109] He blames the historical-critical method for this "utter sterility." The problem, he believes, lies in the slighting of the canon as context. "The usual critical method of biblical exegesis is, first, to seek to restore an original historical setting by stripping away those very elements which constitute the canonical shape. Little wonder that once the biblical text has been securely anchored in the historical past by 'decanonizing' it, the interpreter has difficulty applying it to the modern religious context."[110] For the canon was formed with the stated intent of passing on the authoritative tradition. Although "the motivations behind the canonical process were diverse and seldom discussed in the biblical text itself . . . , the one concern which is expressly mentioned is that a tradition from the past be transmitted in such a way that its authoritative claims be laid upon all successive generations of Israel. Such expressions of intent are found in the promulgation of the law (Deut. 31.9ff.), in the fixing of rituals (Ex. 12.14), and in the provisions for transmitting the sacred story (Ex. 12.26ff.)."[111]

It is the canon, therefore, that projects the biblical material in a relevant way. "Scripture became the vehicle by which the original historical events were faithfully remembered, but also theologically interpreted to function as revelation for the generations yet unborn. The decisive hermeneutical role of canon was to guide the church in moving from the past to the present."[112]

The Canonical Approach and Preaching

The relevance of the canonical approach for preaching will be evident. We shall highlight just a few points. First, the canonical approach is as holistic as were other forms of biblical theology, but it is more specific in taking the canon as its context. Selecting the canon as context does, of course, tend to shift the emphasis from the historical to the literary and theological dimensions, but it also makes the method less speculative since we have the canon, but not the history, directly before us.

108. Childs, *Biblical Theology in Crisis*, 99-100.
109. Childs, *CTM* 43 (1972) 710.
110. Childs, *Introduction*, 79. Cf. idem, *Int* 32 (1978) 49.
111. Childs, *Introduction*, 78.
112. Childs, *CTM* 43 (1972) 721. Cf. idem, *Int* 32 (1978) 47: "In sum, prophetic oracles which were directed to one generation were fashioned into Sacred Scripture by a canonical process to be used by another generation." Cf. idem, *NT as Canon*, 51.

Second, from the recognition of the canon's unique authority, it follows that preachers who desire to proclaim the authoritative word of God will have to base their messages on canonical texts understood in the context of the canon. In other words, the sole authority of the canon underscores the homiletical necessity of selecting preaching texts from the canon and interpreting these texts in the light of the canon. This procedure will also give preachers and congregations the assurance that the sermons are not the preacher's own eloquent ideas nor hypothetical scholarly reconstructions but the authoritative word of God (see Chapter 1 above).

Third, the canonical approach views the text not as an objective thing out there that must be *made* relevant but as part of the canon which is inherently relevant, for this channel was formed for the specific purpose of proclaiming God's good news to future generations. Childs claims with much justification: "Many of the modern problems of building hermeneutical bridges from the text to the sermon or from the past to the present arise from first treating the Bible as ancient graffiti and still expecting it to produce great spiritual truths."[113] These problems of irrelevance are largely the result of a faulty starting point. For "biblical texts are made relevant to today's community of faith and to the world . . . by faithfully hearing the intent of the literature which has already been shaped to confront its hearers with the divine imperative. Canon serves as a guarantee that the biblical material has not been collected for antiquarian reasons, but as an eternal Word of God laying claim on each new generation."[114]

HOLISTIC LITERARY INTERPRETATION

THIS completes the review of some of the more important methods of literary interpretation and their contributions for preaching. Structuralism has been omitted because, as an ideology, it is out of tune with Scripture,[115] while, as a method of analyzing surface structures, its concerns are largely covered by rhetorical criticism and the new literary criticism. We

---

113. Childs, *Biblical Theology in Crisis*, 146.

114. Childs, *Int* 32 (1978) 54. For Childs's perception of the contrast between his approach and redaction criticism, see idem, *Introduction*, 300-301, 383.

115. See, e.g., Hultgren, *Dialog* 21/2 (1982) 90: "Its lack of concern for, and even rejection in principle of the significance of historical context, cannot be accepted in a theological tradition and outlook which claims that God speaks his Word in particular situations." See also V. S. Poythress, "Philosophical Roots of Phenomenological and Structuralist Literary Criticism," *WTJ* 41/1 (1978) 165; idem, "Structuralism and Biblical Studies," *JETS* 21/3 (1978) 221; A. C. Thiselton, "Structuralism and Biblical Studies: Method or Ideology," *ExpTim* 89 (1978) 329-35; T. Longman, *Literary Approaches to Biblical Interpretation*, 27-37.

shall meet the new literary or narrative criticism, which analyzes biblical narratives as stories, in the chapters on Hebrew narratives and Gospels. All of the reviewed methods make valid contributions to biblical interpretation and preaching as they study pretextual sources, forms, authorial intention, textual structural patterns, biblical themes, and the normative context of the canon. Although some of the discussed methods are sometimes presented as the one and only method of interpretation, it has become apparent that each method highlights one or more aspects of biblical interpretation but none covers the whole of it.

Interrelationship of Literary Methods

BY adapting a sketch of the literary critic Abrams, John Barton offers an instructive diagram of the "interrelationship of critical methods." The diagram consists of four points, each of which can be the primary focus of a particular method. The four points are: (1) historical events or theological ideas; (2) author(s) or community; (3) the text; and (4) the reader.[116] According to Barton, "pre-critical study of the Bible assumes that the biblical record corresponds *directly* to external reality, whereas for the critical scholar it corresponds with reality only at second-hand (at best), *via* a primary correspondence with the intentions of some writer or writers."[117] Thus he suggests that with the rise of critical studies a shift took place from (1) historical events or theological ideas to (2) the author. This shift shows up in the focus of source criticism, form criticism, and redaction criticism, which Barton places all in the same family (2) because "the central concern is to find the meaning of a biblical text by locating its *author*." The next major shift in focus is the concentration on the text itself (3). Here Barton locates Childs,[118] canon criticism, and early structuralism, and we may add literary or narrative criticism. The final shift, to the reader (4), occurs in post-structuralism with its interest "in the relation between text and reader"—a shift which, according to Barton, has not arrived in biblical criticism as yet, though "'reader-response' criticism may well be heralding this arrival."[119]

Adapting Barton's data, we can locate the various methods of interpretation in the following diagram.

---

116. Barton, *Reading the OT*, 200-201. I have changed the numbers to coincide roughly with the historical order in which each topic became the center of attention.

117. Barton, *JSOT* 29 (1984) 24.

118. Note that Childs objects, and rightly so, to describing "a canonical approach simply as a form of structuralism" (*OT Theology*, 6).

119. Barton, *Reading the OT*, 201-3; idem, *JSOT* 29 (1984) 30. Longman places in this final category "ideological readers" such as "liberation theologians and feminist scholars" (*Literary Approaches*, 39).

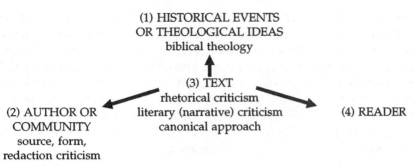

(1) HISTORICAL EVENTS
OR THEOLOGICAL IDEAS
biblical theology

(3) TEXT
rhetorical criticism
(2) AUTHOR OR   literary (narrative) criticism   (4) READER
COMMUNITY   canonical approach
source, form,
redaction criticism

Although the diagram is a very blunt instrument and measures along only one axis, it is helpful in showing the primary focus of each method of interpretation and the paradigm shifts that have taken place from biblical theology (1) to source, tradition, form, and redaction criticism (2), to rhetorical criticism and the canonical approach (3). Even more important, for our purposes, is the fact that the diagram portrays graphically that these methods concentrate on a specific area; they approach the text from their own particular standpoint and question it from their own particular perspective. Consequently, each of these literary methods, by itself, tends to be atomistic in not taking into account all aspects and dimensions of interpretation.[120] By contrast, holistic interpretation will need to take into account all these literary aspects as well as historical and theological dimensions.

Ahistorical Tendencies

THE diagram above also reveals a double shift away from historical studies: first from the historical events (1) to the historical sources and forms underlying the text (2), then from these historical sources, etc., to the text itself (3). It is no secret that these paradigm shifts from historical studies to literary studies have resulted in ahistorical tendencies in biblical studies. In some methods, such as rhetorical criticism, the historical background and historical referent (the events) are not necessarily denied, but in the interest of the "aesthetic dimension" historical and theological questions are often "bracketed out."[121] Other methods, such as structuralism and the new literary criticism, "may be described as inherently ahistorical."[122] These ahistorical tendencies in contemporary literary interpretation are forms of reductionism, for they rather arbitrarily eliminate a major facet of the interpretation process. Holistic interpretation requires that justice be done also to the historical and theological dimensions. In the next chapter we shall explore the historical dimension.

120. Tremper Longman states that each theory "leads to a new imbalance" (*JETS* 28/4 [1985] 388).
121. See Hultgren, *Dialog* 21/2 (1982) 88.
122. Robertson, *IDBSup*, 548.

CHAPTER 4

Historical Interpretation

HISTORICAL interpretation acknowledges that the text is a historical document and should be understood historically, that is, in terms of its own time, place, and culture. In historical interpretation one tries to answer the questions: Who wrote this text? to whom? when? where? and why? These questions focus on the identity of the author, the original audience, the approximate period of writing, the social and geographical setting (the provenance), and the purpose of writing. In short, historical interpretation involves "careful historical investigation of the biblical writings in order to set them squarely in the cultural, religious, political and literary environment of their own times,"[1] and to understand their message in that original context.

THE NEED FOR HISTORICAL INTERPRETATION

SINCE the need for historical interpretation is being challenged today both from the left (New Literary Criticism and Structuralism) and from the right (forms of Fundamentalism), it is appropriate first to review some of the reasons for historical interpretation.

Better Understanding

HISTORICAL interpretation is necessary, first of all, because all biblical texts are historical documents. Accordingly, to understand them, they must be heard today as they were heard in their original historical setting. As Perry Yoder puts it, "The words of Scripture came to their audience addressed to their situation. By uncovering that specific historical situa-

1. Stanton, *Ex Auditu* 1 (1985) 64.

tion, we can begin to catch a glimpse of why the words were written. This . . . allows us to see the reason or rationale behind what is written."[2] In other words, historical interpretation will help in determining the intention, the purpose, of a passage.

Since historical interpretation seeks to understand the words according to their original intent and meaning, it promotes authentic listening. One tries to place oneself among the original hearers and hear the message as they did. Placing oneself back in that distant and foreign culture leads to better understanding, for it enables one to comprehend the text in terms of its native culture, geography, and the like. For example, historical understanding will hear the words, "life for life, eye for eye, tooth for tooth" (Exod 21:23-24), not as a sanction, let alone a demand, for vengeance but as a critique of taking a life for a tooth.[3] In the New Testament, similarly, historical understanding will hear Paul's words that "the women should keep silence in the churches" (1 Cor 14:34) not as an absolute prohibition against women speaking (which would contradict 1 Cor 11:5) but as a prohibition against wives disturbing the service by questioning their husbands seated in the front section of the church.[4]

Leander Keck elucidates well the importance of historical interpretation for preaching: "To preach biblically is to take full account of the concrete issues to which the text is addressed in the first place; it is to reckon with the fact that what the biblical writers found necessary to say was determined not by truth in general but by needs in particular. The situation of the community, as perceived by the writer, set the agenda . . . ; the text is a selected and focused truth in the form of a literary response."[5]

Objective Point of Control

A further reason for historical interpretation is that it alone is able to provide an objective point of control for confirming the meaning of a particular passage. Gordon Fee and Douglas Stuart assert: "The only proper control for hermeneutics is to be found in the original intent of the biblical text. . . . In contrast to . . . [pure] subjectivity, we insist that the original meaning of the text—as much as it is in our power to discern it—is the objective point of control."[6] If one bypasses historical interpretation, one

2. Yoder, From Word to Life, 20.

3. See, e.g., Stendahl, Meanings, 6-7.

4. See, e.g., Donald Guthrie, in Eerdmans Handbook to the Bible, ed. David Alexander and Pat Alexander, rev. ed. (Grand Rapids: Eerdmans, 1983), 594.

5. Keck, Bible in the Pulpit, 115.

6. Fee and Stuart, How to Read the Bible, 26. Cf. Yoder, From Word to Life, 37: "If the church is to hear the voice of Scripture in what is said, rather than its own voice, it must seek the original historical meaning of the words."

loses not only the historical dimension of the text but also control of its intended meaning.

Historical interpretation not only offers an objective point of control against subjective and arbitrary interpretations but also functions positively to keep the interpreter on track with respect to the specific point of the text. Krister Stendahl suggests two advantages of historical interpretation: "Its first advantage is that it guards against apologetic softenings and harmonizations, against conscious and unconscious modernizations in the interest of making the Bible more acceptable and conterminous with religious and ethical sentiments and concerns of the contemporary reader." A second advantage, he suggests, is "its fostering great respect for the diversity within the Scriptures."[7] Matthew does not bring exactly the same message as Luke does—and historical interpretation helps one discern the difference.

Historical interpretation in the sense of understanding a document in its original historical-cultural context applies to all genres of biblical literature, narrative as well as prophecy, gospel as well as epistle. In what follows, however, we shall focus particularly on the most common of all biblical genres, historical narrative, for *holistic* historical interpretation also needs to consider the historical referent (the events referred to) of passages purporting to be historical. To bracket out their historical referent, as proposed by some of the recent literary methods, is obviously reductionistic. But to read historical narrative as if it were just plain history does not do justice to its literary dimension. Consequently, we need to explore some of the complexities of biblical history writing.

BIBLICAL HISTORY WRITING

As any dictionary will show, the term *history* has various meanings. The major distinction to observe is that the term "may refer either to past events in general, or to a reconstruction of these events, usually in roughly chronological order."[8] For the sake of clarity, we shall use the term *history* only for the past events themselves, and the term *history writing* for the writing or "reconstruction of these events."[9] Before examining

7. Stendahl, *Meanings*, 2.

8. Miller, *OT and the Historian*, 11. See Lemke, *Int* 36 (1982) 38: "History . . . has been variously understood as a sequence of human events of the past, as that which is factual in contrast to that which is mythical or legendary, as an existential moment for decision, or as future possibility."

9. Van Seters's definition of history writing as "national" history writing appears to be arbitrarily narrow and exclusive; see *In Search of History*, 1-6. Better is Bernard Anderson's definition: "An event is a meaningful happening in the life of a people. And history is the narration of these experienced events—events so memorable that

biblical history writing, we need first to take a brief look at the complexity of history itself.

Historical Events

HISTORICAL events can be defined simply as that which happened in the past, but given scholarly disagreement about historical events, that definition is deceptively simple. In order to appreciate their complexity, we shall note five characteristics of historical events: they are past, unverifiable, multidimensional, ambiguous, and inherently meaningful.

Past

Although historical events carry their significance far beyond their own time, the events as such no longer exist in the present: they are *past*. Moreover, historical events are *einmalig*, that is, unique in the sense that they will never be repeated in exactly the same way. Since historical events are *past* as well as *einmalig*, the events themselves are out of our reach. The only things we can reach are the sources that inform us about the events. As Alan Richardson puts it: "Doubtless in the sense of 'what happened' the facts are indeed immutable, but in this sense they are just what the historian can never directly know. It is not the reality which the historian takes apart, but only 'sources.'"[10] In our interpretation of the Bible, too, it is well to remember that we are a large step removed from the facts themselves; we know the facts only through the sources.

Unverifiable

The obvious truth that historical events are past has a frequently forgotten implication: events can seldom be verified. James Jennings elucidates that, even with eyewitnesses, "events are often unverifiable, especially in regard to detail." He instructively uses the example of the Warren Commission, which tried to reconstruct the facts of President Kennedy's assassination. "Despite the presence of television crews, movie cameras, hundreds of still cameras, thousands of eyewitnesses, and patient analysis, it could still not be proven whether the alleged assassin was the assassin, or whether he acted alone or had accomplices." This contemporary attempt to reconstruct the facts enables Jennings to draw several important observations about interpreting historical writings in general: "First, the

---

they are preserved in the oral memory and eventually written down in records" (*Understanding the OT*, 22).

10. Richardson, *History Sacred and Profane*, 191. Cf. p. 210: "The historian cannot observe events in history: he can only infer them. . . . 'Facts' must always remain inferences from evidence, and the historian's judgments of evidence, critically displayed before him, remain judgments."

event itself is out of reach. It can never be reconstructed in its entirety. Second, evidence is crucial, but is always and necessarily limited. Absence of evidence does not disprove the event. Third, it should be obvious that decisive weight must be given to what is probable, since absolute proof is frequently impossible."[11]

Multidimensional

To add to the complexity of understanding history, historical events are multidimensional, that is, they carry meanings at many different levels. The philosopher Herman Dooyeweerd has demonstrated that each event (and each thing) contains at least fifteen levels or sides of meaning, ranging from the basic arithmetic modality to the complex modality of faith.[12] For our purposes it is sufficient to note that each event has many sides of meaning and that, therefore, each event can be interpreted from many different sides, say, the economic side, the social side, the political side, or the side of faith. For example, David's capture of Jerusalem is meaningful economically in view of the cost involved in taking the city and the resultant gain, socially in view of subduing the Jebusites, politically in view of unifying the nation of Israel with a new capital, ethically in view of the way the war was conducted, cultically in providing a central place for the worship of Yahweh, and much more. A historian could legitimately set forth these and many more interpretations of one and the same event.

To get some idea of the complexity of history and history writing, one might think of a single historical event as a many-sided molecule; history, then, can be likened to an ocean of billions of many-sided molecules, all connected with each other in an infinite variety of ways. In view of this complexity, it is evident that no one can write a complete history; no one can duplicate the past in all its intricate detail and interconnections. In writing history, therefore, historians cannot help but be selective—selective not only in choosing which events they will write about but also which *side* of the events they will write about. For example, a historian may choose to write a political history, or a social history, or a history of art. This choice "will not only influence the limits of his study; it will necessarily bring certain facts into prominence or allow others to recede into the background. Different aspects of the same fact will acquire a special significance according to the context in which it is placed."[13]

---

11. Jennings, "Interpreting the Historical Books," 43.
12. See Dooyeweerd, *Roots of Western Culture* (Toronto: Wedge, 1979), especially pp. 40-47; idem, *In the Twilight of Western Thought* (Nutley, NJ: Craig, 1975), especially pp. 7-11. For a more comprehensive treatment of the modal scale, see idem, *A New Critique of Theoretical Thought* (Philadelphia: Presbyterian and Reformed, 1955), II, 3-426. A popular introduction to Dooyeweerd's thought is given in L. Kalsbeek, *Contours of a Christian Philosophy* (Toronto: Wedge, 1975).
13. Turner, *Historicity and the Gospels*, 17.

This multidimensional character of historical events must be kept in mind when interpreting Scripture; one cannot legitimately expect a complete history writing in any sense of the term. Perhaps John had this in mind when he concluded his Gospel with the words: "There are also many other things which Jesus did; were every one of them to be written, I suppose that the world itself could not contain the books that would be written" (21:25). A complete history writing is an impossibility. Consequently, a crucial question for biblical interpretation is, Which events did the author select and which side of these events did he wish to highlight?

Ambiguous

Historical events are not only past, unverifiable, and multidimensional, they are also ambiguous, that is, they are open to various interpretations. Take, for example, the fact that Cyrus II overthrew the Babylonian empire around 539 B.C. Cyrus himself "assigns the credit to Marduk, god of Babylon, who was desirous of punishing his own people," while Isa 45:1-6 credits Yahweh, the God of Israel.[14] Or take the New Testament fact of the empty tomb: at the time one person interpreted that fact as the removal of Jesus' body, while another interpreted it as Jesus' resurrection (John 20:2, 8). The fact of the empty tomb could bear both, and more, interpretations, "but the angel's announcement provided the definitive explanation of the empty tomb: 'He is not here; for he has risen.'"[15] As Bertil Albrektson writes concerning the Old Testament: the events as such "are ambiguous. Something must be given in addition to the events: the *word* of revelation." And again: "The bare facts of history are usually capable of several different interpretations, and the inner meaning of the events, Yhwh's purpose behind the occurrences, is not clear unless it is disclosed in words which Yhwh speaks to his chosen messengers."[16]

Inherently Meaningful

Lest the above point be misunderstood in the sense of a separation between fact and meaning, we need to add that historical events are inherently meaningful. In contrast to Positivism, which searches for the "bare facts" and thus attempts to separate fact and meaning,[17] we need to emphasize, as is increasingly acknowledged today, that there are no meaningless facts. René Latourelle aptly observes: "At the end of exploration, the historian finds himself ever in the face of events and of a meaning.

---

14. Ramsey, *Quest for the Historical Israel*, 118.
15. Harris, *Easter in Durham*, 16.
16. Albrektson, *History and the Gods*, 118, 119.
17. See Pannenberg, "Revelation of God," 126-31; Klooster, *CTJ* 11/1 (1976) 28-32; Latourelle, *Finding Jesus*, 114-23.

Never does he reach 'meaningless' events."[18] Some facts, naturally, are more significant than others; but all facts—whether it be the birth of a baby or the capture of a city—all facts are inherently meaningful. For a Christian whose presupposition is that we live in a world created and governed by an all-wise God, all historical events are bound to be meaningful. Meaning, therefore, is not something the history writer (Bible writer) adds to so-called bare facts like icing on a cake; on the contrary, meaning is drawn by the biblical author from the events themselves.

The Bible presents many interpretations of historical events; it even presents different interpretations of one and the same event in, say, the Synoptic Gospels. Although these interpretations may come many years after the events, they draw out of the events what was present in their initial happening. In other words, biblical interpretations of historical events can be seen as revelation of meanings already present, but perhaps not perceived, when the events occurred. Klaas Runia summarizes the relevance of this point:

> Contrary to modern theology, scripture itself everywhere presupposes that we have to do with an interpretation of an actual history of salvation. We do not meet with . . . bare facts, but always with *interpreted* facts. The interpretation belongs to the fact, just as much as the fact is the presupposition of the interpretation. . . . The fact itself becomes transparent as to its actual meaning (i.e., as to its revelatory and saving dimension) only in the interpretation. Likewise, the interpretation is a message of revelation and salvation only when it interprets a real fact. In other words, fact and interpretation together are *die Sache*.[19]

History Writing

WITH these five characteristics of history in mind, we can now address the issue of history writing, particularly as this pertains to the interpretation of historical narrative in the Bible.

Interpretations of Events

Our definitions of history and history writing above make clear that the Bible contains not history but history writing. This is but another way of stating the obvious but frequently overlooked fact that the Bible confronts us not directly with history but with *literature* about history. In other words, what we find in the Bible are not the events themselves but partic-

18. Latourelle, *Finding Jesus*, 123.
19. Runia, *CTJ* 19/2 (1984) 149. Cf. p. 150: "When, for instance, in the gospels and the epistles the apostles interpret Jesus Christ, both as to his person and as to his work, they do not put their own subjective interpretation upon his person and work, but derive it from his person and work."

ular interpretations of certain events. Like all history writers, the biblical authors had to select carefully which remembered or recorded events they would write about and which aspect of these events they would highlight (see, e.g., Luke 1:3). Although the events themselves were rich in meaning, they could be understood in different ways and did not always disclose their deepest meaning. Consider the Exodus event: even though the miracles revealed that God was leading his people out of slavery, the event as such did not answer the question, Why? "Was it because of the faithfulness of the Hebrews, their piety and righteousness," or was it because of God's love "for an insignificant and unworthy nation?"[20] In Deut 7:6-8 the biblical author clearly shows that the motivation of the Exodus was God's love. Or, to take an example from the New Testament, Jesus' crucifixion, as a historical event, can be understood in various ways, but only the biblical author gives the further understanding, which was not plain from the event as such, that God through Christ was "making peace by the blood of his cross" (Col 1:20). Although, as we saw earlier, one must guard against separating fact and meaning, one can say that the biblical authors reveal a deeper dimension of the meaning of certain events than was obvious from the events themselves.

Prophetic Interpretations

The disclosure of this deeper dimension of meaning has often been called prophetic interpretation. For instance, Marten Woudstra writes: "Ordinary historiography may highlight natural causes and enlarge upon subjective motives. Not so with biblical historiography. It is essentially prophetic in character. It views events not from a purely human standpoint but from that of God himself."[21] With respect to the New Testament, this special way of writing history has often been called "kerygmatic" history writing. Both the words *prophetic* and *kerygmatic* underscore the special nature of biblical history writing.

This special character of biblical history writing should guide interpreters in putting their questions to the biblical texts. The focus of the writers is not on the economic side of the events, nor on the social or political sides; their interest is concentrated on a deeper level of meaning: God's covenant, God's coming kingdom, the religious-theocentric dimension. At this point the biblical authors leave ordinary history writing far behind, and their claims that *God* was at work for a specific purpose, say

---

20. Albrektson, *History and the Gods*, 118.

21. Woudstra, "Event and Interpretation in the OT," 54. Cf. Bright, who notes that the Old Testament presents history "in terms of theology—of certain convictions and affirmations regarding the purposes of God, his relationship to his people, his demands and his promises" (*Authority of the OT*, 147).

in the fall of Jerusalem or the crucifixion, are "beyond the realm of verification by historians";[22] these claims can be accepted only by faith.[23]

Authoritative Interpretations

The biblical interpretations of events are worthy of acceptance by faith. This is so not because the authors of Scripture were such discerning people in their own right, but, as 2 Pet 1:21 puts it, because "no prophecy ever came by the impulse of man, but men moved by the Holy Spirit spoke from God." Since the Holy Spirit inspired the authors of Scripture, their interpretations of past events are authoritative. The words they wrote are worthy of acceptance by faith because they are the word of God.

A. B. Mickelsen elucidates this point in terms of divine revelation: "Interpretation is not by human inference but rather by God's disclosure to particular servants concerning what he has done, is doing, and in some cases of what he will do. . . . God grants to his selected men an understanding of what he did. . . . This kind of interpreted event is revelation." The fact that these interpretations are authoritative revelation has immediate implications for contemporary interpreters and preachers. "The goal of interpreters (i.e., those who set forth by exegesis and exposition *an* interpretation of *the* interpretation), is to say neither more nor less than the Spirit of God conveyed to those to whom he first disclosed the meaning."[24]

The inspired biblical authors did not, of course, write their interpretations of events according to the standards of modern, Western exactitude. To require such precise accuracy and objectivity is to impose on the authors of the Bible the limitations and fallacies of nineteenth-century standards of history writing. If the term *organic inspiration* means anything at all, it is that God used the authors of Scripture in the framework of their own times.[25]

Ancient Standards

The standards according to which biblical writers wrote history are, as a study of their writings will show, ancient rather than modern. For example, from their writings we notice that they did not credit their sources as meticulously as we do today. The Gospel writers, of course, do quote the prophets frequently and even identify them from time to time, but

22. Wenham, "History and the OT," 29. Cf. de Vaux, *Bible and the Ancient Near East*, 59-61.

23. Hence Olthuis, *Hermeneutics*, 25, speaks of "certitudinal texts," for "it was an overriding concern to generate and strengthen the certitudes of faith which guided authors, redactors and communities in the canonical process."

24. Mickelsen, *Interpreting the Bible*, 65.

25. According to Van Elderen: "The doctrine of organic inspiration maintains that God used these authors in their settings and environment with their knowledge, culture, cosmology, view of reality" (*CTJ* 1/2 [1966] 174).

sometimes their identification seems to be wrong. For example, Mark 1:2 quotes Malachi and Isaiah but attributes both quotations to Isaiah. Bernard Ramm explains, however, that "the Jewish custom in citing two or three prophets in a brief catena of Scripture was to name only the leading prophet." Further, "in Matthew 27:9 a verse from Zechariah is cited as coming from Jeremiah. The Jewish tradition was that the spirit of Jeremiah was in Zechariah and such a method of citation would not offend their historical sense."[26]

We also notice that the authors of Scripture display remarkable freedom in recording conversations, sermons, and the like. Matthew apparently joined together many of Jesus' sayings and presented them as one sermon, the Sermon on the Mount. The Gospel writers, as a comparison of the Synoptics will show, felt free to change even the very words of Jesus (compare, e.g., the Lord's Prayer in Matt 6:9-13 with that in Luke 11:2-4).[27] In Acts, Luke records many sermons which obviously were abbreviated, though Luke does not bother so to inform us. But then, do we not stumble over these things because of our modern sensitivities and standards? By contrast, "a first-century audience would not have expected the brief accounts of the various sermons in Acts to be *verbatim* accounts of what was actually said, any more than we would expect the same of brief newspaper reports of parliamentary speeches (as opposed to detailed reports in *Hansard*)."[28]

We have already noted the complexity of history and the choices history writers must make in recording events. In contrast to contemporary standards, however, ancient standards allowed for much more freedom and flexibility, as a comparison of Chronicles with Samuel-Kings and Matthew with Mark, Luke, and John will readily demonstrate. For example, the Chronicler, in contrast to Samuel, feels free to omit the sins of David and to present him as the ideal king. Similarly, in the New Testament, Matthew feels free to change the order of events considerably as compared to Mark (see Chapter 11 below). From a literary angle one can speak of the artistic freedom of biblical authors. Von Rad observes that "a great part of even the historical traditions of Israel has to be regarded as poetry, that is, as the product of explicit artistic intentions. But poetry—especially with peoples of antiquity—is much more than an aesthetic pastime. . . . Historical poetry was the form in which Israel, like other peoples, made sure of historical facts, that is, of their location and their significance. In those times poetry was, as a rule, the one possible form for

26. Ramm, *Protestant Biblical Interpretation*, 203.
27. For more examples, see Chapter 11 below; see also Ladd, *NT and Criticism*, 120.
28. Marshall, "Historical Criticism," 131-32.

expressing special basic insights."[29] It is not surprising, then, to find that the authors of Scripture feel free to select some facts and to ignore others, to present a great amount of detail here and to summarize there, to rearrange the chronological order, and in general to shape and mold the material to suit their thematic (prophetic, kerygmatic) purposes.

The Purpose of the Author

Although we shall discuss the purpose of the author/redactor in more detail below in Chapter 5, we need to touch on it here also. One of the questions asked in historical interpretation is, Why did the author write this document? Was his purpose to record past events as accurately as possible, detail by detail, all in chronological sequence—a photograph of the past? Or was his purpose other and more than that? Only a detailed study of the documents can answer those questions, of course, but for now we can hint at the answers with some more general evidence. It is instructive that the first five historical books of the Old Testament are not called histories but *Torah,* instruction, while the next four—Joshua, Judges, Samuel, and Kings—are included in the division of the Prophets. Childs remarks concerning the latter classification: "The significance of this classification lies in the canon's assessment of the nature of these historical records. The object of this biblical witness is not to record history *per se*—whatever that might be—but to bear testimony to the working out of the prophetic word in the life of the nation."[30] Similarly, the first four historical books of the New Testament are not called histories or biographies but Gospels, alerting us to the fact that the Gospel writers are interested not merely in producing a photograph of the past but in proclaiming the good news of Jesus Christ in such a way that it will elicit from the readers/hearers a response of faith (see John 20:31).

Today it is generally recognized that each of the Gospel writers is a "theologian" in his own right—theologian in the sense of a person who shapes the material in order to bring a particular "theological" message. The same may be said of the Old Testament authors. Like all proclamation, these biblical messages sought to evoke a desired response from the hearers: faith, trust, obedience, and so on. Hence one ought not to approach their writings as precise, objective accounts; one ought not to approach these documents with the primary question, What happened precisely? Rather, if one wishes to do justice to these documents for what they are—Torah, Prophecy, Gospel—the interpreter's primary question

29. Von Rad, *OT Theology,* I, 109.
30. Childs, *Introduction,* 236. Cf. LaSor, Hubbard, and Bush, *OT Survey,* 191: "Throughout the Former Prophets, the religious viewpoint dominates. This, then, is not history as modern historians might write it. Rather, to oversimplify considerably, it is history from a prophetic point of view."

will have to be: What message was the author trying to get across? And what response was he seeking from his hearers?[31]

Historical Reliability

FROM the above discussion one should not draw the conclusion, however, that the historical reliability of these documents is a secondary issue. Norman Perrin plainly posits a false contrast when he writes, "None of the gospel writers is concerned to give us what we would call historical information; they are evangelists, not historians."[32] On our understanding of biblical history writing, there need be no contradiction between Evangelists and history writers;[33] moreover, the statement that "none of the gospel writers is concerned to give us what we would call historical information" is obviously false (see, e.g., Luke 1:1-4).[34] Besides, it is contrary to the whole tenor of Scripture to make light of what actually happened. We noted earlier that the authors of Scripture present interpretations of meaningful historical events. If these events did not take place, then their interpretations are floating in the air, without foundations. Thus the historical reliability of the biblical authors is indeed a crucial issue.

Historical Accuracy

We must be careful, however, not to get sidetracked with twentieth-century standards of historical accuracy. The biblical documents need not measure up to *our* standards to be authoritative. Moreover, the biblical message does not stand or fall with historical details. Whether Israel took possession of the promised land in a short time or after a long time, the point of the message stands: *that* God gave them the land of promise— however long it took. As far as the message is concerned, it makes little difference whether there were one or two blind men at Jericho, for the

---

31. Cf. Longman, *JETS* 28/4 (1985) 395: "It must be admitted that Genesis, for example, is not attempting to be as close as possible to a dispassionate reporting of events. Rather, we have proclamation—with the result that the history is shaped to differing degrees. The point is that the Biblical narrators are concerned not only to tell us the facts but also to guide our perspective of and responses to those events."

32. Perrin, *Resurrection*, 81.

33. See, e.g., Marshall, *Luke: Historian and Theologian.* Cf. Ellis, *The Yahwist: The Bible's First Theologian,* 90: "Theological interpretation, important as it was, did not blind the biblical writers to the facts. Indeed, it is true to say that the biblical historians achieved standards of reliability and excellence which were, in their day, considerably higher than the standards of historical writing in other contemporary cultures."

34. Cf. Leaney, "Historicity in the Gospels," 114: "The *intention* of the gospels . . . is to present the Lord of Salvation as historical. It is an indispensable part of their message to insist that he is to be identified with a certain known craftsman who was registered in the Roman census."

message is *that* Jesus gave sight to the blind. As far as the message is concerned, it makes little difference whether Jesus was crucified before or after the Passover meal, for the message is *that* Jesus was crucified. The point to be noted is that a message of the Bible cannot be disqualified because it fails to measure up to contemporary standards of precision. The biblical authors, either because of ancient standards of history writing or because of authorial freedom (or likely for both reasons), felt free to present their messages the way they did, and historical imprecision as far as the details are concerned cannot detract from the point of their messages. Questions of how, when, and where are unable to undermine the veracity of the kerygma; the only thing that could undermine the kerygma is the refutation of the historical event itself.

Historical Foundations

The kerygma, we can say, is the proclamation of God's acts in history; if those acts did not take place in history, then the kerygma has lost its footing. Roland de Vaux asserts pointedly, "Once we admit that the kerygma is not founded on fact and that the historical confession of Israel's faith does not have its roots in history, then we empty our faith of its content."[35] The reason for this dependence of the Christian faith on historical events is simply that Christianity, in distinction from some other religions, is a historical religion in the sense that it proclaims that our salvation depends on what God in Christ accomplished in history: "If Christ has not been raised, your faith is futile and you are still in your sins" (1 Cor 15:17). Our Christian faith, therefore, stands or falls with the reality, the historicity, of Christ's resurrection. Although one ought not to play historicity off against kerygma, Nigel Scotland makes a valid point when he claims that "central to the New Testament is the fact that it is not the message itself which saves men and women but the historical events of Jesus' life, death, and resurrection."[36] Without the historical foundation, the gospel message could not save; in fact, without the historical foundation there would be no gospel.

Similar observations can be made with respect to the Old Testament: if the message that God made covenant with his people Israel has no historical foundation, then that message loses its point and evaporates. The Old Testament messages that God acted in Israel's history—redeeming, judging, restoring, guiding—lose their very essence unless they are as historical as they claim they are. Meir Sternberg shows strikingly what is at stake from a Jewish perspective: "Were the narrative written or read as fiction, then God would turn from the lord of history into a creature of the imagination, with the most disastrous results. The shape of time, the ra-

---

35. De Vaux, *Bible and the Ancient Near East*, 59.
36. Scotland, *Can We Trust the Gospels?* 48.

tionale of monotheism, the foundations of conduct, the national sense of identity, the very right to the land of Israel and the hope of deliverance to come: all hang in the generic balance."[37]

History Writing and Parable

James Barr claims, however, that it makes little difference whether a narrative is fact or fiction. He observes quite rightly that "there was no Good Samaritan or Prodigal Son, and it makes no difference whether there was or not. The message of the parable is something other than the story which it itself tells." But this observation does not hold, as Barr suggests, for "the story of Jesus' birth, or the story of his resurrection, or that of the exodus of the Israelites from Egypt." Barr asks, "Do not all of these stories work upon us in the same way as general literature does? And do they not exercise their power upon us quite apart from the question whether things happened as they are narrated in the external world?"[38] The stories may work and exercise their power, but Barr overlooks the obvious point that historical narratives are not parables and that the message of a historical narrative is *not* "something other than the story which it itself tells." On the contrary, the story related in historical narrative is part and parcel of the message. If the Exodus and Jesus' birth and resurrection are fiction, then there is no kerygma, for the kerygma is precisely the proclamation of the occurrence of these redemptive events.

History Writing and Story

Unfortunately, matters are more complex than making a fairly straightforward distinction between parables and historical narratives. We must also acknowledge that not all historical narratives are of the same order. Some, such as those relating Jesus' resurrection, are obviously more central and foundational for the kerygma than others. Again, some narratives stand or fall with their historicity because it is the key component in their message, while for other narratives their historicity may be secondary. As John Goldingay observes: "If . . . we conclude that there is little historical truth behind Job, this will not have serious consequences for our estimate of its theological validity. On the other hand, with Kings, or with the other Old Testament history-works, the converse will be the case, because they do appeal to history, to actual events which they base their teaching on, for their validation. It is of great importance that they should be historically trustworthy."[39]

Edmund Clowney astutely points out the utter necessity of historicity when it comes to the writing of covenant history: "The brief historical

---

37. Sternberg, *Poetics*, 32.
38. Barr, *Bible in the Modern World*, 56-57.
39. Goldingay, *TynBul* 23 (1972) 81.

prologue of the covenant at Sinai is the key to understanding the whole preceding history of Exodus and the books of generations in Genesis as well. The history of the Pentateuch is not political or cultural in aim, nor is it a chronicle of stirring events. It is covenantal history: the record of God's dealings with the fathers, his covenant with Abraham and its renewal at Sinai. The force of covenant history lies in its actuality, its 'historicity.'"[40] The point is that when one turns covenant history into mere story, as is often done today, one loses the very covenant. But there is no need at all to turn covenant history into mere story, as a comparison with the ancient Hittite covenants demonstrates. "The Hittite covenants did not present stylized generalities in the historical prologue, but recorded specific instances of the sovereign's gracious dealing with the vassal."[41] Similarly, covenant history narrated in the Bible, patterned probably after contemporary international Hittite treaty forms,[42] records actual instances of God's gracious dealings with Israel.

On the one hand, therefore, the issue of historical reliability is a crucial concern. On the other hand, in interpreting narratives, one ought not to pay undue attention to this question of historicity, for ironically it may result in a distorted interpretation—as when one views the text as a clear window through which to look at what actually happened. For the text is much more like a stained glass window, and the preacher ought to focus on the author's prophetic *interpretation* of the event rather than on the (bare) event. The question of historicity, it must be remembered, was placed on the agenda by the Enlightenment and the historical-critical method; although that rationalistic mind-set needs to be answered in a prolegomena, one must be careful not to adopt this mind-set and allow it to guide subsequent interpretation. The preacher's responsibility is to hear the message of a passage as intended by its author. Sometimes, as we can see in Job, for example, that intention has little or nothing to do with giving a historical account. Frequently, however, the intention is precisely to proclaim the significance of the event narrated. It will not do, therefore, simply to bracket out the historical referent. In holistic historical interpretation one must also do justice to the historical referent and the way it functions in the text.

THE HISTORY OF GOD'S KINGDOM

A holistic interpretation of biblical texts demands further that the inter-

---

40. Clowney, *Preaching and Biblical Theology*, 41.
41. Ibid.
42. See, e.g., Bright, *Covenant and Promise*, 36-43; Kline, *Treaty of the Great King*, 28-44; Weinfeld, *TDOT*, II, 265-79; Zimmerli, *Law and the Prophets*, 52-60.

preter see the message of the text not only in its immediate historical-cultural context but also in its broadest possible context, that is, Scripture's teaching regarding history as a whole. Frequently, this universal historical context is overlooked. There is no doubt, however, that Scripture teaches one universal kingdom history that encompasses all of created reality: past, present, and future.

Creation to New Creation

The Biblical Vision

The first verse of the Bible refers to the beginning ("In the beginning God created . . .") and the next-to-last verse refers to the future consummation ("Come quickly, Lord Jesus"). Though the Bible itself was written over a span of little more than a thousand years, its vision of history extends backward all the way to the beginning of time and forward all the way to the last day. In contrast to the time frame of its own composition, therefore, the biblical vision of history spans time from the first creation to the new creation, encompassing all of created reality. Church fathers such as Irenaeus and Augustine caught this vision and, in opposition to the Gnostics, the church clearly taught that "the history of salvation embraces not only the history of mankind, but the whole of cosmic history."[43]

The Vision Lost

Hans Frei acknowledges that before the rise of historical criticism, "Christian preachers and theological commentators, Augustine the most notable among them, had envisioned the real world as formed by the sequence told by the biblical stories. That temporal world covered the span of ages from creation to the final consummation to come, and included the governance both of man's natural environment and of that secondary environment which we often think of as provided for man by himself and call 'history' or 'culture.'"[44] Frei then proceeds to show how this conception of a universal history disintegrated with the rise of critical thinking in the eighteenth century. He attributes this disintegration to a growing awareness of "a logical distinction and a reflective distance between the stories and the 'reality' they depict," and the resultant "breakup of the cohesion between the literal meaning of the biblical narratives and their reference to actual events."[45] But, as we have seen in Chapter 2 above, one might equally well point out that the very presuppositions of the historical-critical method eliminated God as Lord of and agent in history and that this elimination naturally led to the elimination of a universal history

43. Danielou, Lord of History, 28.
44. Frei, Eclipse of Biblical Narrative, 1.
45. Ibid., 5 and 4.

under God. Frei's conclusion does not necessarily follow, therefore, that in a critical or post-critical age one cannot recapture the holistic perspective of a "pre-critical" time.[46] It all depends on one's worldview and whether it can do justice to all of reality.

Recovery of the Vision

Even in a critical or post-critical age, a valid requirement of the hermeneutical circle is that, in the interest of a genuine hearing of the biblical text, one must be willing to risk one's presuppositions in dialogue with the text. Graham Stanton, for one, insists properly: "In order to avoid sheer prejudice, it is necessary to allow the text or evidence to reshape one's pre-understanding. Unless this is done quite deliberately, there is always the risk that one's starting point, instead of acting as a window to the evidence, will become a filter through which the text is always read—and distorted."[47] When interpreters are in tune with Scripture, however, not even a post-critical age can shut them off from the holistic view of a universal kingdom history which includes all of creation (nature) as well as human history. Claus Westermann exhibits this perspective when he writes: " 'The Old Testament tells a story' (von Rad); but the story which the Old Testament tells can be equated neither with the concept of history, which has developed from the Enlightenment and which received its decisive form in the nineteenth century, nor with a religious or salvation history, as opposed to profane history. We have to go back behind these alternatives to a broader concept of history, in which both have not yet been separated, one which is able to embrace historical as well as religious events, and which would be in this respect more appropriate to the way in which the Old Testament talks about history."[48] Some have called this broader concept of history "redemptive history" or "salvation history," and others "universal history." Since these terms have acquired many improper connotations, however, we shall use the term *kingdom history*.[49]

The Biblical View of History

The Old Testament

The Bible as a whole teaches one, all-encompassing history of the kingdom of God. The Old Testament contains two major historical narratives, both of which begin at the beginning and hence overlap to some extent.

46. See Sternberg's critique of Frei's analysis in *Poetics*, 81-82.
47. Stanton, *Ex Auditu* 1 (1985) 68. Cf. idem, "Presuppositions in NT Criticism," 68-70.
48. Westermann, *What Does the OT Say about God?* 25. See also idem, "Interpretation of the OT," 44-49.
49. For drawbacks in using the term *redemptive history*, see my *Sola Scriptura*, 20-21. For drawbacks of the term *universal history*, see Buss, "Meaning of History," 136.

The first, Genesis through 2 Kings, relates this kingdom history from the creation to the exile of Judah in 587 B.C. The second narrative, Chronicles and Ezra-Nehemiah, relates this history from Adam to around 445 B.C. when the remnant has returned to Palestine. As already indicated, the authors/editors are not primarily interested in writing an economic or political history of Israel; in fact, readers interested in such things are frequently referred to other books such as the Chronicles of the Kings of Israel (1 Kgs 14:19), the Chronicles of the Kings of Judah (14:29), etc.[50] Rather, the authors of these books present *kingdom* history, that is, they not only assume but clearly teach this universal history under God which, beginning with God's creation of the cosmos, runs through the human fall into sin, to God's acts of redemption and judgment in the nation of Israel, to the future when the promised Messiah will surely come. Yet the Old Testament picture is not complete: the messianic kingdom did not arrive. John Bright speaks of the Old Testament presentation as "a truncated *Heilsgeschichte*. The Old Testament is a book that is theologically incomplete; it points beyond itself and ends in a posture of waiting."[51]

The New Testament

"It is just this fulfillment of unfulfilled promise, this completion of incomplete history, that the New Testament is principally concerned to affirm."[52] The New Testament contains four Gospels which link their narratives of Jesus Christ to this truncated history of God's kingdom. In fact, two Gospel writers anchor their Gospels in "the beginning": John with "In the beginning was the Word," and Luke with Jesus' genealogy going back to "Adam, the son of God." Luke in particular presents Jesus Christ as the midpoint of this kingdom history—a history which continues after Christ's resurrection until his second coming.

Kingdom History

Thus kingdom history, as presented in the Bible, runs from creation to consummation. Genesis relates that God, in the beginning, created a kingdom (realm) and peopled it with creatures who were able to acknowledge him as King. It also relates, however, that these people rebelled against God the King and allied themselves with Satan, later known as "the ruler of the world." But God determined to reestablish his kingdom on earth; he broke the alliance between Satan and his people (Gen 3:15) and bound his people to himself in a covenant in which he promised redemption and required his people to obey the covenant stipulations or laws of the king-

50. Also, e.g., the Book of the Wars of the Lord (Num 21:14), the Book of Jashar (Josh 10:13), and the Book of the Acts of Solomon (1 Kgs 11:41).

51. Bright, *Authority of the OT*, 138.

52. Ibid.

dom. Hence all subsequent Old Testament history can be seen as the history of the coming kingdom of God. In the fullness of time Christ came proclaiming the kingdom of God, demonstrating its presence in his healing of sick and demon-possessed people, and revealing, by his resurrection, its complete victory over death and Satan. Christ the King then ascended to his heavenly throne, but he promised to come again, on the last day, to inaugurate on earth God's perfect kingdom. Hence New Testament history also can be seen as part of the history of God's coming kingdom. In other words, in both Testaments, the biblical vision of kingdom history is the vision of the *coming* kingdom of God.[53]

We can picture this kingdom history as follows:[54]

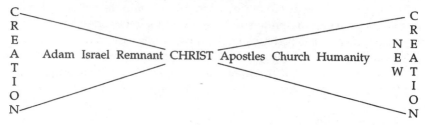

As can be seen in the sketch, one must not identify kingdom history and world history. The kingdom history pictured in the Bible is identical with world history only at the beginning (Gen 1–11) and at the end (Rev 21–22). God is certainly active in the whole world and concerned with the whole world and will in the end redeem the whole world, but starting with Gen 12 the focus of God's redemptive activity narrows primarily to one family (Abraham's) and one nation (Israel) and finally to one Person, Jesus Christ. After Christ's resurrection and with the outpouring of the Holy Spirit, all the nations of the world come into view again, and the promise is given that on the last day the entire creation will be renewed (Rom 8:21; Rev 21–22).

Creation-Fall-Redemption

GIVEN this biblical presentation of a universal kingdom history which begins with creation and ends, or rather finds a new beginning, with a new creation, we can say that a central, all-encompassing theme of Scripture is Creation-Fall-Redemption.[55]

---

53. For a development of this theme in greater detail, see my "Human Rights in Biblical Perspective," *CTJ* 19 (1984) 5-31.

54. See Cullmann, *Christ and Time*, 178. For a similar but vertical diagram, see Rhodes, *Mighty Acts of God*, 19.

55. For a detailed elaboration of this theme, see VanderGoot, *Interpreting the Bible;* see also Albert M. Wolters, *Creation Regained: Biblical Basics for a Reformational Worldview* (Grand Rapids: Eerdmans, 1985).

The Restoration of Creation

The New Testament writers go out of their way to proclaim that Jesus Christ is more than a savior of souls, more than a mediator between God and humankind; Christ is mediator between God and the cosmos, both in creating the cosmos (1 Cor 8:6; Col 1:16; John 1:3; Heb 1:2, 10) and in restoring the cosmos (Col 1:20; John 3:16). In noting this New Testament emphasis on the mediatorial activity of Christ in creation, Oscar Cullmann remarks: "This in itself is sufficient to prove that Primitive Christianity, in spite of all its concentration upon the redemptive line in the narrower sense, or rather on the basis of this concentration, has in view the *entire world process*."[56]

Holism vs. Various Forms of Dualism

The vision of the restoration of creation offers a holistic vision that opposes various kinds of dualism. Cullmann asserts correctly that "all dualism between creation and redemption is here excluded. . . . For Primitive Christianity, there is only the one line of divine activity; it is that one of which it is said from beginning to end: everything *from* God and *to* God, and everything *through* Christ."[57]

In the light of the restoration of creation, the tenacious dualism between nature and grace also loses its hold, for it turns out that grace does not stand over against nature but permeates it in order to redeem it so that it becomes what it was intended to be. Similarly, Bultmann's dualism between nature and history[58] loses its footing, for all of nature is swept up in this stream of kingdom history that leads to the complete restoration of all things. Also, any dualism between sacred history and secular history, between redemptive history and profane history, is out of the question, for sacred history becomes as broad as creation and, as J. Langmead Casserley observes, "at a deeper analysis all secular history is salvation history, for it is the history of what salvation saves."[59]

---

56. See Cullmann, *Christ and Time*, 177-78.

57. Ibid., 178.

58. See Thiselton, *Two Horizons*, 245-49.

59. Casserley, *Toward a Theology of History*, 97. See also n. 1: "The Bible . . . makes a real distinction between the history of the chosen people and that of other nations, but nevertheless insists that God is Lord of both strands of history alike." Pannenberg, *Basic Questions in Theology*, 38-42, also opposes "any attempt to delimit redemptive history as a realm of a different kind from the rest of history. . . . It belongs to the full meaning of the Incarnation that God's redemptive deed took place within the universal correlative connections of human history and not in a ghetto of redemptive history, or in a primal history belonging to a dimension which is 'oblique' to ordinary history" (p. 41). Cf. idem, "Response to the Discussion," 247-48 n. 46. For a similar emphasis in Schilder, see my *Sola Scriptura*, 122. For an excellent popular presentation of the Creation-Fall-Redemption theme and its opposition to contemporary forms of dualism,

Kingdom History and Interpretation

THE hermeneutical implication of the biblical view of history is that every biblical passage must be understood in the context of this grand sweep of kingdom history.

Historical Exposition

The interpreter must, of course, understand the author of a passage in the context of the author's particular place in history; it makes a great deal of difference whether a message is addressed to Israel before Christ or to the early church after Christ. But the message must also be related to the whole of kingdom history. A key hermeneutical principle holds that a part can be fully understood only in the light of the whole.[60] Fee and Stuart make the worthwhile suggestion that Old Testament narratives be understood at three levels: "Every individual Old Testament narrative (bottom level) is at least a part of the greater narrative of Israel's history in the world (the middle level), which in turn is a part of the ultimate narrative of God's creation and His redemption of it (the top level). This ultimate narrative goes beyond the Old Testament through the New Testament. You will not fully do justice to any individual narrative without recognizing its part within the other two."[61]

Although preachers should not display their exegetical tools on the pulpit, sermons should bring out very clearly that texts are being understood in the context of the scope of this universal kingdom history. Stuart advises: "In general, you want to avoid talking to your congregation about the passage in isolation, as if there were no Scripture or history surrounding it. To do so is to be unfair to the sweep of the historical revelation; it suggests to your congregation that the Bible is a collection of atomistic fragments not well connected one to another and without much relationship to the passage of time."[62]

Historical Application

Holistic interpretation in terms of this universal kingdom history is also crucial for relevant contemporary application. For it is the holistic interpretation that makes us aware of the fact that we today live—albeit at a different stage—in the *same* history as did the Israelites of old. Hence there is not an unbridgeable gap between then and now but a definite continuity: the ancient Israelites were involved in the same struggle for

see Brian J. Walsh and J. R. Middleton, *The Transforming Vision: Shaping a Christian World View* (Downers Grove: IVP, 1984).

60. For example, Pannenberg, "Response," 242: "Each individual entity has its meaning only in relation to the whole to which it belongs."

61. Fee and Stuart, *How to Read the Bible*, 74-75.

62. Stuart, *OT Exegesis*, 65.

the coming of God's kingdom as we are today; their needs and obligations were very similar to ours. Most importantly, of course, the same God who worked in their history then is working in our history today for the final perfection of his kingdom. Consequently, as 1 Cor 10:11 puts it, these stories of the past can be instructive for us "upon whom the end of the ages has come" (see Chapter 8 below).

CHAPTER 5

Theological Interpretation

IDEALLY, all aspects of holistic interpretation can be covered adequately by literary and historical interpretation. As the history of interpretation testifies, however, the prophetic, kerygmatic character of biblical passages has often received short shrift in historical and literary interpretation. For the sake of analysis as well as emphasis, therefore, we shall discuss separately this dimension of biblical interpretation which is usually called "theological interpretation" or "theological exegesis."

THE NATURE OF THEOLOGICAL INTERPRETATION

The Idea of Theological Interpretation

THEOLOGICAL interpretation raises such questions as, Why was this text preserved in the canon? What does God reveal in this text about himself and his will? And what does this message mean in the context of the whole Bible?

The Term and Concept

The term *theological interpretation* is problematic because the word *theological* might suggest that the biblical authors were scientific theologians or that one must be a theologian today to understand their writings. Some have suggested the following alternatives: "formulating the meaning," "religious or theological explication," "interpretation," and "theological-critical interpretation."[1] I shall use the term *theological interpretation* be-

---

1. Respectively, Reumann, Doty, Stuhlmacher, and Smitmans, as listed by Krentz, *Historical-Critical Method*, 52. L. Berkhof settles for "theological interpretation" after considering Kuyper's "mystical factor," Sikkel's "scriptural interpretation," and

cause it has been generally accepted, but I use it only with the clear understanding that "theological" refers not to theory or the discipline of theology but to *God*, specifically, the revelation *of* God and the revelation *about* God. Theological interpretation seeks to hear *God's* voice in the Scriptures; it seeks to probe beyond mere historical reconstruction and verbal meanings to a discernment of the message of God in the Scriptures; it concentrates on the prophetic, kerygmatic dimension and the theocentric focus.

Scientific and Unscientific

Rolf Knierim remarks that "there was a time . . . when the inclusion of the theology of a text into its exegesis was considered unscientific speculation. Only 'philological' and 'historical' data were admissible, as if the theology—or the content and intention of a text . . . —is not at least as much a part of its historicality as its philological phenomena and its historical context!"[2]

One of the more dramatic results of the perceived dichotomy between scientific interpretation and theological interpretation occurred in 1882 when Julius Wellhausen transferred from a theological faculty to a department of Semitic languages with the following explanation: "I became a theologian because I was interested in the scientific treatment of the Bible; it has only gradually dawned upon me that a professor of theology likewise has the practical task of preparing students for service in the Evangelical Church, and that I was not fulfilling this practical task, but rather . . . was incapacitating my hearers for their office."[3] While one may admire Wellhausen's integrity of action, one must at the same time be dismayed at the erroneous thinking that propelled it. For theological interpretation of a kerygmatic, theocentric book is not at all unscientific; on the contrary, it is unscientific to slight the Bible's unique nature and focus.

A Necessary Dimension

Wellhausen's action demonstrates that it is possible to study the Bible without any interest whatever in its theocentric focus—a reductionistic approach which can still be observed in historical as well as in literary criticism. "Just as historical criticism *can* be theologically mute if its only interest is historical reconstruction as an end in itself, so literary criticism

---

Bavinck's insistence that the Bible be read "theologically" (*Principles of Biblical Interpretation*, 133-34). Müller opts for "theological exegesis": "Exegesis which busies itself with investigation and interpreting this 'profound sense,' will therefore be a 'theological exegesis,' which takes into account the reality of the living God of all times" ("Exegesis and Kerygma," 233). Olthuis argues for "certitudinal exegesis" (*Hermeneutics*, 11-52). See p. 52 n. 48 for his objections to "theological."

2. Knierim, "Criticism of Literary Features," 125.

3. Quoted by Jepsen, "Scientific Study of the OT," 247.

can be theologically mute if its sole interest is aesthetics and/or comparative literature as ends in themselves."[4] As Wellhausen discovered, this reductionism does indeed incapacitate future ministers of the Word for their office. When interpretation stops short of the theological intention of the text, John Bright comments, "the sermon, because it lacks theological depth, tends to degenerate into a shallow moralizing."[5] Consequently, it needs to be stressed that theological interpretation is a necessary dimension of biblical interpretation, or, to put it another way, that literary and historical interpretation are incomplete as long as they have missed the text's theocentric focus.

An Integral Dimension

To avoid misunderstanding, we need to emphasize further that theological interpretation is *not* an ecclesiastical supplement to scholarly interpretation, *not* a second, "Christian" layer on top of secular, scientific interpretation. On the contrary, theological interpretation, rightly understood, is an integral part of holistic interpretation. "Any writing should be judged in the first instance in the light of the claims it makes for itself," Leon Morris asserts, and "the Bible claims to give us a message from God."[6] This biblical claim of a message from God as well as a message about God ought to be integrated in literary and historical interpretation so that theological interpretation does not become a later addition but functions from the outset as part of the interpretative process.

Reasons for Theological Interpretation

God's Word

The main reason for theological interpretation as an integral part of biblical interpretation is that the Bible claims to be God's word. If "all scripture is inspired by God" (2 Tim 3:16), divine inspiration ought to be taken into account when interpreting the Scriptures—not by discounting the human authors of the Scriptures but rather by seeing God as the divine Author working in and through these human authors. The mystery of divine inspiration is that the Bible is 100% divine while it is 100% human—a mystery which must not be resolved into a dualism which splits the Bible into divine elements and human elements, or divine factors and human factors, or divine aspects and human aspects. Hermeneutically, the mystery of inspiration means that interpreters of the Bible acknowledge that *God* speaks his word through these writings of human authors and redactors; the mystery of inspiration calls for a holis-

---

4. Hultgren, *Dialog* 21/2 (1982) 89.
5. Bright, *Authority of the OT*, 172.
6. Morris, *I Believe in Revelation*, 104-5.

tic biblical interpretation which probes beyond historical reconstruction and verbal meanings for the message of *God*.

The Canon

A related reason for the necessity of theological interpretation is that the church accepted the Bible as its standard for faith and practice. Brevard Childs argues that "a special dynamic issues from its [the New Testament's] canonical function which is not exhausted by either literary or historical analysis, but calls for a theological description of its shape and function." Hence Childs calls for "a new vision of the biblical text which does justice not only to the demands of a thoroughly post-Enlightenment age, but also to the confessional stance of the Christian faith for which the sacred scriptures provide a true and faithful vehicle for understanding the will of God."[7]

Formulating the issue of the canon somewhat differently, I would suggest that since the Bible is the church's standard of faith and practice, its interpretation requires a theocentric focus which is able to discern the revelation of God and his will. In other words, the Bible requires theological interpretation not only because it is the word *of* God but also because it is the authoritative word *about* God—his acts, his will, his relation to his creation and to his people. If the New Testament writings "were preserved, not because of interesting historical, religious, or sociological data, but solely for their theological role in speaking of God's redemption in Jesus Christ,"[8] then this theocentric emphasis must be disclosed in their interpretation.

Faith Commitment

A third reason for the necessity of theological interpretation is that a believing interpreter cannot approach the Bible in a neutral, supposedly objective, fashion but will naturally use a method of interpretation that is informed by that faith commitment. Although everyone approaches biblical literature with presuppositions and expectations, unfortunately not everyone acknowledges them or is even aware of them. By employing theological interpretation, however, interpreters frankly acknowledge that they accept the Bible as the word of God, that, standing within the tradition of the church, they try to understand it as the authoritative canon, and that they therefore approach the Bible as people committed to its authority. Far from blunting the critical faculties of interpreters, this stance of faith allows them to hear the Bible fairly and sympathetically because they will be on the same wavelength as the Bible. Although some

---

7. Childs, *NT as Canon*, 36-37.
8. Ibid., 43.

have claimed that such commitment is unscientific, Robert Polzin argues rightly that "any literary or historical criticism modeled after the uninvolved, impersonal objectivity of the natural sciences will be seen to operate according to hermeneutical principles that are in conflict with the message and spirit of the biblical text."[9] But by acknowledging the Bible's truth-claim, interpreters are in tune with the object of their investigation. Moreover, even if one should believe that the proper stance for biblical interpretation is that of an uninvolved, "objective" investigator, one must still deal with the Bible's obvious theological intentionality. The preacher's "exegetical labors are . . . not complete," says Bright, "until he has grasped the text's theological intention."[10] We shall next explore the issue of the text's theological intention or purpose.

THE PURPOSE OF THE AUTHOR

ALTHOUGH we have had occasion to touch on the topic of the purpose of the author in the chapters on literary and historical interpretation, this is the ideal place for a more extended discussion of this topic, for we cannot consider the human authors in isolation but must also take into account the divine Author.

In order to get a sense of the purpose of the author, one asks the basic question, Why did the author write (or send) this message? This is one of the more important questions in biblical hermeneutics. Jay Adams asserts: "There are few deficiencies in preaching quite so disastrous in their effect as the all-too-frequently occurring failure to determine the *telos* (or purpose) of a preaching portion. The passage, and therefore the Word of God itself, is misrepresented, misused, and mishandled when its purpose has not been determined, with the direct result that its power and authority are lost."[11]

The Purpose of the Human Author

A Shift from Subjectivism
Asking for the author's purpose is a conscious attempt to curb subjectivism in interpretation. Polzin claims that many biblical scholars approach

9. Polzin, "Literary and Historical Criticism in the Bible," 106. Cf. Olthuis, *Hermeneutics*, p. 33: "Understanding a text depends on sharing the same sphere of meaning as that text. Thus, an economic text asks first of all to be interpreted economically, a political text politically, and a certitudinal (faith) text from the faith perspective of certitude."

10. Bright, *Authority of the OT*, 172. Smart, *Strange Silence*, 115-16, argues for "hearing the text in its full original theological context," that is, "the ongoing dialogue between God and his people."

11. Adams, *Preaching with Purpose*, 27.

the Bible in the same way readers approach certain books, "like a picnic to which the author brings the words and the reader the meaning."[12] Because of so many different, even contradictory, interpretations of Bible passages, one would suspect that many interpreters do indeed bring their own meanings to the text. Therefore, a fundamental question for biblical hermeneutics is whether the authors shall be allowed to present *their* meaning or whether the readers shall bring their own meanings to the text. To ask the question is to answer it, for rank subjectivism is the death of biblical interpretation. As E. D. Hirsch points out, "To banish the original author as the determiner of meaning . . . [is] to reject the only compelling normative principle that could lend validity to an interpretation."[13] For the sake of a normative principle of interpretation, if for nothing else, one must ask for the author's purpose.

Preachers are especially prone to impose their own subjective purposes on a text. Because of their training and experience, they have a good idea of what the text will say before they exegete it. Moreover, they have selected the text to fulfill a particular purpose in next Sunday's service. Hence the danger is very real that the purpose of preachers will overrule the purpose of the text and in effect silence the text. But James Daane contends rightly that "as long as the preacher preaches, listening to Scripture is obligatory. In approaching a text preachers must allow the Scriptures to challenge and question their understanding of it." Daane points to "another subtle temptation to be avoided," and that is the concern for application: "Eager to discover relevance, the minister never takes time to hear what the text really says. . . . Application dominates interpretation. Students are particularly prone to this folly—and folly it is, for how can one apply what one has not yet heard or understood?"[14]

A major reason for seeking the purpose of the author is, therefore, consciously to shift attention away from ourselves to the Scriptures, away from our concerns to the author's concerns, away from our own purposes to the author's purpose. In other words, asking for the author's purpose is an attempt at genuine listening by cutting out all subjective interference.

Author or Redactor

The question of the author's purpose is complicated by the fact that some biblical books are thought to be the product not of one author but of one or more redactors. Today, however, the perceived gap between authors and redactors has narrowed considerably in that redactors are no longer

12. Polzin, *Moses and the Deuteronomist*, 3, quoting Northrop Frye.
13. Hirsch, *Validity in Interpretation*, 5. Cf. Craddock, *Gospels*, 22: "To go to the extreme of disregarding intention . . . is to turn interpretation into ink-blot tests."
14. Daane, *Preaching with Confidence*, 61.

considered to be "scissors-and-paste men" but creative authors in their own right. Consequently, we are justified in using the word *author* in a broad sense so that asking for the author's purpose is the same as asking for the purpose of the last major redactor.[15]

Another complication raised in connection with inquiring about the author's purpose is that we know very little about the authors of many biblical books. This lack of knowledge ought not to be considered a handicap for establishing the author's purpose, however, for that purpose ought to be established not on the basis of their psychological makeup but primarily on the basis of their writings. Searching for the author's purpose in anything but the text would introduce into the interpretation not only a hypothetical element but also a very subjective notion. "Ultimately all argument about meaning or the author's intention must be rooted in the text if it is to be objective."[16]

Intentional Fallacy?

The attempt to search out the purpose of an author is often dismissed quickly with the charge of "intentional fallacy"—the contention that it is illicit to determine the meaning of a text by inquiring after the author's intention since the meaning lies in the text and not in its author. Little is gained by this charge, however, for, depending on what is meant, the charge itself is open to the charge of fallacy.[17] It stands to reason that one ought not to impose on the text a psychologically derived authorial intention that conflicts with the meaning of the text itself. But such distortion of the text is quite different from searching *the text itself* for authorial intention. "As interpreters of the Bible, our only concern is with 'embodied' or 'objectified' intention; and that forms a different business altogether, about which a wide measure of agreement has always existed."[18]

---

15. I refer to the "major redactor," since, as Gunn, *Fate of King Saul*, 15, points out, "the last redactor may not have been the last substantial redactor."

16. Payne, *JETS* 20/3 (1977) 251.

17. Ironically, the 1946 essay "The Intentional Fallacy" by W. K. Wimsatt and M. C. Beardsley raised many questions about the *intention* of the above authors. Their intention in writing their article was naturally and rightly taken seriously, and, when Wimsatt later realized that they had not quite said what they intended, he corrected the words to fit their intention (see Barton, *Reading the OT*, 148-49, and 231 n. 19). Barton affirms that Wimsatt and Beardsley "were not so much concerned to outlaw the author's meaning as the normative meaning, as to rule out certain illicit ways of *establishing* that meaning. It is, on their terms, acceptable to say that the text means what its author meant, provided that 'what the author meant' is understood to be discoverable from the text and only from the text—not from diaries, letters or remarks overheard on the telephone" (ibid., 149-50). Cf. p. 168: "Surely questions about intention need not be so crudely psychologistic as to lead automatically to speculations about the author's 'inner life.'"

18. Sternberg, *Poetics*, 9.

Unfortunately, the question of the intention of the author is more complex than simply reading it off the text. This complication surfaces in the statement that "We can understand a text only when we have understood the question to which it is an answer."[19] There is more to a text than literally meets the eye: it is a response to a certain question or need in a particular historical situation. "It is not enough to ask for the intention of the original author," remarks Karlfried Froehlich. "Language always involves a speaker and a listener. The process of reception, language as it is *heard*, must be part of the investigation."[20] Bernard Lonergan arrives at the same conclusion with an arresting switch to the common hermeneutical rule that a text must be understood in its context: "Heuristically . . . the context of the word is the sentence. The context of the sentence is the paragraph. The context of the paragraph is the chapter. The context of the chapter is the book. The context of the book is the author's *opera omnia*, his life and times, the state of the question in his day, his problems, prospective readers, scope and aim."[21]

Whatever complex procedures are required for establishing the intention of the author with the text, Krister Stendahl maintains rightly that "the normative nature of the Bible requires . . . a serious attention to original intentions of texts." The reason for this serious attention is that "the original intentions . . . constitute the baseline of any interpretation."[22]

Determining the Purpose

Discovering the purpose of an author may be quite complicated because the author may have had more than one reason for writing the book or letter; moreover, the author may have had subsidiary purposes for including specific paragraphs or statements.[23]

In spite of this complexity, the task of determining the author's purpose is made easier by the fact that authors frequently include in their books a statement of purpose. For example, John states the purpose for writing his Gospel in unmistakable terms: "These [signs] are written that you may believe that Jesus is the Christ, the Son of God, and that believ-

19. Collingwood as quoted by Keifert in *Word and World*, 1/2 (1981) 166. Cf. Palmer, *Hermeneutics*, 250: "To understand a text . . . is to understand the question behind the text, the question that called the text into being."

20. Froehlich, *Word and World* 1/2 (1981) 142. Cf. Wardlaw, "Shaping Sermons by Context," 64: "Recent thinking by such literary critics as Jay Schleusener or John Sherwood promotes a commonsense view of interpretation that sees the author's intent, hearers' mind-set, and text integrally related and therefore necessary dimensions of understanding the text."

21. Lonergan, *Method in Theology*, 163.

22. Stendahl, *JBL* 103/1 (1984) 9-10. Cf. Sternberg, *Poetics*, 10, on the choice "between reconstructing the author's intention and licensing the reader's invention."

23. See Payne, *JETS* 20/3 (1977) 244-45.

ing you may have life in his name" (John 20:31). Similarly, Luke informs Theophilus that he intends "to write an orderly account for you, most excellent Theophilus, that you may know the truth concerning the things of which you have been informed" (Luke 1:3-4). The book of Proverbs also begins with a statement of purpose (1:2-6), while Jude (v. 3) indicates that he ended up writing for a different purpose than he originally had in mind. Even where an overall statement of purpose is lacking, authors like Paul and John at various points state the purpose of sections of their letters (e.g., Phil 1:3, 12; 2:2, 25; and 1 John 1:3-4; 2:1, 12; 5:13). Wherever these obvious statements are lacking, interpreters will have to search the text carefully for other clues to the author's purpose.

In seeking to determine the author's purpose, redaction criticism can lend a helping hand. As noted in Chapter 3, redaction criticism tries to discover the author's purpose by studying the composition as a whole, the vocabulary and comments of the author especially in introduction and conclusion, and the author's changes in sources and interpretative comments in the "seams" between sources. Rhetorical criticism can also help discover the author's purpose. As we saw in Chapter 3, rhetorical criticism concentrates on the structural patterns of the text. By exposing climactic lines, repetition (the keyword technique), chiasm, and *inclusio*, rhetorical criticism can disclose literary motifs which provide clues for discovering the overall purpose of the author.

Walter Kaiser suggests "four ways to ascertain the intention of the writer as far as his general scope and plan are concerned." The first way is "to see if the writer himself clearly sets forth his purpose in the preface, conclusion, or body of the text." Second, "study the parenetical sections . . . , particularly of the New Testament Epistles. . . . Usually an author's exhortations will flow out of his special purpose for writing his book." Third, for historical narrative, "observe what details he [the writer] *selected* for inclusion and how he *arranged* them." And finally, study "how the topic sentences of individual paragraphs work together to explicate the theme of a given section" and how the themes of all the sections relate to one another.[24] By such analyses one should get a fair idea why the book or letter was written, what questions it sought to answer, and thus what was its original intention.

God's Ultimate Purpose

HAVING gained insight into the immediate purpose of a book or passage, with biblical literature one must proceed a step further by inquiring after the ultimate purpose of a passage. We may call this ultimate purpose

24. Kaiser, *Toward an Exegetical Theology*, 79. Cf. H. Robinson, *Biblical Preaching*, 92-93.

"God's purpose," as long as we remember that the inspired human author's immediate purpose was also God's purpose. But God's ultimate purpose can be much broader and farther reaching than the relatively limited, immediate purpose of the human author. This broader, all-encompassing purpose becomes evident especially when a book or letter is interpreted in the context of the whole canon.

The Fuller Sense

Even at the human level, the meaning of literature is not exclusively limited to the intention of the author; that is, a book may mean more than its author originally intended. Barton maintains that "as a matter of fact, texts may go beyond their authors' intentions in a number of ways."[25] If this is true for literature in general, how much more will it be true for biblical literature. Biblical literature, having been united in one canon, is bound to reveal meanings that go beyond the intentions of their human authors. As Philip Payne says, "In spite of the crucial role the human author's intention has for the meaning of a text his conscious intention does not necessarily *exhaust* the meanings of his statements, especially in more poetic and predictive writings. Ultimately God is the author of Scripture, and it is his intention alone that exhaustively determines its meaning."[26]

In the history of interpretation this phenomenon of meanings beyond the author's original intention has been called the *sensus plenior*, the fuller sense. As we noted in Chapter 3, Raymond Brown defines the *sensus plenior* as "that additional, deeper meaning, intended by God but not clearly intended by the human author, which is seen to exist in the words of a Biblical text (or group of texts, or even a whole book) when they are studied in the light of further revelation or development in the understanding of revelation."[27]

Although Protestant interpreters may fear that the way of *sensus plenior* leads straight into allegorical interpretation, such is not necessarily the outcome. William LaSor explains that *sensus plenior* is "not a reading into the text of theological doctrines and theories, but a reading from the text of the fullness of meaning required by God's complete revelation." For example, Gen 3:15, "I will put enmity between you and the woman, and between your seed and her seed; he shall bruise your head, and you

---

25. Barton, *Reading the OT*, 170.
26. See Payne, *JETS* 20/3 (1977) 243.
27. Brown, "'Sensus Plenior' of Sacred Scripture," 92. Cf. the different definitions listed by Brown on pp. 151-53. On the history and development of the theory of *sensus plenior*, see Brown, *CBQ* 15 (1953) 141-62; idem, *CBQ* 25 (1963) 262-85. For a critique of the concept, see Julius Muthengi, "A Critical Analysis of Sensus Plenior," *East African Journal of Evangelical Theology* 3 (1984) 63-73. Cf. the various positions set forth by Richard, *BSac* 143 (1986) 124-26.

shall bruise his heel," has a fuller sense, in the light of New Testament revelation, than the author of Genesis would ever have realized. Similarly, the Old Testament designation "son of David" receives a fuller meaning already in the Old Testament but especially in the light of New Testament revelation.[28] Or take Abraham's words to Isaac in Gen 22:8, "God will provide himself the lamb for a burnt offering, my son," or Psalms 16, 22, and 110 as the New Testament applies them to Christ.[29] Surely, in the light of subsequent developments and revelation, these texts reveal to us a more profound meaning than that intended by their human authors.

When interpreters go beyond the safe guideline of original intentionality, the possibility of reading subjective opinions into the text becomes very real, of course. The only safeguard against eisegesis at this point is not to deny the reality of the fuller sense but to insist that that fuller sense be established only as an extension of the original sense and solely on the basis of subsequent biblical revelation.

Comparing Scripture with Scripture

The idea of the fuller sense is related to the Reformation's principle of comparing Scripture with Scripture. Both the idea of the *sensus plenior* and that of *analogia Scriptura* are grounded in the conviction that the Old Testament and the New Testament belong together and are basically one book because they are written by the same primary Author on the same topic. From this unity of the Bible and the rule that a text must be understood in its context, it follows that a biblical text must be interpreted in the context of the whole Bible. And this is exactly what the principle of comparing Scripture with Scripture requires: after establishing the original intent and meaning of the text, interpreters must verify or, if necessary, expand the meaning of the text in the light of the whole canon. Thus comparing Scripture with Scripture nudges interpreters beyond the immediate purpose of human authors to the overall purpose of the primary Author.

Progressive Revelation

In this connection, we must return briefly to the idea of progressive revelation. This idea entails that God's revelation was not given all at once but over the course of many centuries as redemptive history unfolded. During that course of history, revelation progressed from the beginnings of the Old Testament to the fullness of the New Testament. Contrary to some opinions, the idea of progressive revelation does not mean that one can trace in

---

28. LaSor, "*Sensus Plenior* and Biblical Interpretation," 275 and 272-73. Note that Brown also seeks to avoid allegorizing; see *CBQ* 25 (1963) 274 n. 64.

29. These examples are given by Payne, *JETS* 20/3 (1977) 248-49. Cf. the examples in Brown, " 'Sensus Plenior' of Sacred Scripture," 140-45.

history the minute developments of redemptive events from the fall into sin till the last day.[30] Nor does it signify a development of *ideas* about God or ethics which makes the Old Testament outdated and irrelevant for the New Testament church.[31] Rather, progressive revelation refers to the fact that "the later revelation often builds on and fills out the earlier."[32] This relation does not make the earlier revelation obsolete, for it is the foundation of later revelation and, as part of the canon, remains authoritative for the church. It does mean, however, that on the one hand the earlier (Old Testament) revelation must be compared with later revelation for its fuller sense and possibly its divergence from later (New Testament) revelation. On the other hand, New Testament revelation can be properly understood only against the background of Old Testament revelation. Consequently, the idea of progressive revelation affirms the indispensability of both Old and New Testament revelation while at the same time it underscores the necessity to interpret Old Testament revelation in the light of New Testament revelation. This broader context for understanding a biblical text inevitably broadens the scope of interpretation from the immediate purpose of human authors to the ultimate purpose of God.

Determining God's Ultimate Purpose
All of these complications—the fuller sense, comparing Scripture with Scripture, and progressive revelation—may seem to make the determination of God's ultimate purpose in a particular text an extremely difficult task. Yet it is not as complicated as it sounds. As we have seen, the key to understanding God's purpose in a particular passage is to understand the passage in the context of the whole canon. Therefore the next guiding question is, What is the purpose of the canon as a whole?

THE BIBLE'S THEOCENTRIC PURPOSE

WHEN one asks about the purpose of the canon, the thrust of the Bible as a whole, the answer seems quite obvious: the canon intends to tell us about God—not God in the abstract, but God in relationship to his creation and his people, God's actions in the world, God's coming kingdom. This theocentric purpose can be attributed also to the individual authors. "The biblical authors' purposes are predominantly theological and their selection and presentation of events is dominated by their religious viewpoint. Their primary interest is God's action in human events, not the events themselves."[33] Thus the major clue we receive regarding God's

---

30. For a critique of this endeavor, see my *Sola Scriptura*, 124-30 and 181-86.
31. See Elizabeth Achtemeier, "Relevance of the OT," 3-4.
32. Morris, *I Believe in Revelation*, 139.
33. LaSor, Hubbard, and Bush, *OT Survey*, 108. Cf. Anderson, *Understanding the*

purpose in the canon as a whole as well as in its individual passages is that God intends to tell us about *himself*: his person, his actions, his will, etc. Hence one of the most important questions we can ask in interpreting a passage is, What does this passage tell us about God and his coming kingdom?

Theocentric Interpretation

Religious Literature

Fundamentally, the Bible is more than an ordinary history book, more than artistically pleasing literature; it is religious literature, that is, "It is pervaded by a consciousness of God, and human experience is constantly viewed in its religious dimension."[34] As religious literature, the Bible reveals its theocentric nature. Everything is viewed in relationship to God: the world is God's creation; human beings are image-bearers of God; salvation belongs to God—in short, all of life belongs to and is governed by God.

The sovereignty of God is pivotal in biblical thinking. According to von Rad, "The Israelites came to a historical way of thinking, and then to historical writing, by way of their belief in the sovereignty of God in history."[35] Because God is sovereign, religion is not a separate, "sacred" corner for the biblical writers but encompasses all of life. H. H. Rowley states that for the Old Testament writers "religion . . . was something that belonged to the whole of life and experience, both individual and corporate. There is, in their view, no aspect of our life from which God is excluded, or in which He is uninterested. . . . He is a participator in the drama of all our life."[36] Theocentric interpretation seeks to do justice to that all-encompassing religious thrust of biblical literature.

God-Centered Focus

"Closely related to its status as religious literature," writes Leland Ryken, "is the matter of world view in biblical literature. . . . Biblical literature consistently affirms a God-centered world view. This means that God is not only the supreme value, but that He also gives identity to all other aspects of experience."[37] This God-centered worldview also underscores the theocentric focus of the Bible.

OT, 8: "We cannot begin to understand the Old Testament so long as we regard it as merely great literature, interesting history, or the development of lofty ideas. The Old Testament is the narration of God's action: what he has done, is doing, and will do."

34. Ryken, *Literature of the Bible*, 16.
35. Von Rad, *Problem of the Hexateuch*, 170.
36. Rowley, *Re-Discovery of the OT*, 59.
37. Ryken, *Literature of the Bible*, 16.

One can confirm this God-centered focus of biblical literature by analyzing its various genres. For example, one can ask about the focus of biblical history writing. In the Old Testament, Gerhard von Rad detects three ways of writing history: "First, God acts in history in miracles. The miracle of the Red Sea (Exod. 14) is paradigmatic. . . . All activity proceeds exclusively from God; the Israelites are in no way active in their own defense. *God* will get the glory, as Exod. 14:17 says explicitly." In the second kind of history writing, no miracles take place and the author, as in the story of Joseph, seems to be sketching the actions of people. "Only at the end, after it has led the reader through a tangle of conflicts . . . does it open up its profound mystery in the words of Joseph (Gen. 50:20): 'You meant evil against me; but God meant it for good.'" God worked not in the open but in secret; he "did his work in the decisions of men." Other examples of this kind of history writing are 2 Sam 15–18, Absalom's conspiracy, and 1 Kings 12, the fall of the Davidic-Solomonic empire. These texts "move so fully in the realm of the profane that one could almost think they were actually concerned with quite profane history," writes von Rad. "Still, the attentive reader will find even there that uplifted finger that points, as in the story of Joseph, to the effective and all-directing power above the historical stage." The third kind of history writing identified by von Rad is that which is found in Kings, the perception that "the actual organizing power behind all historical events is God's word, which works itself out creatively in history both in judgment and in protecting well-being."[38] The point to be noted is that even though not all biblical history writing testifies to the same kind of divine involvement, all of it proceeds from and points to the sovereignty of God in history. Even when God's acts are "veiled" rather than "naked" (see Chapter 2 above), the Bible writers reveal that God is still at work. Despite appearances, therefore, all biblical history writing is thoroughly theocentric.[39]

The focus of other genres of biblical literature is equally theocentric. Take wisdom literature, for example. Hans Walter Wolff notes that "recent research has revealed the international connections of the schools of wisdom literature, a literature which pursues with a single mind worldly phenomena and purely human relationships, but in Israel even wisdom literature must be seen under the rubric, 'The fear of the Lord is the beginning of knowledge' (Prov. 1:7; Job 28:28)."[40]

38. Von Rad, *God at Work in Israel*, 142-47.

39. Cf. Wolff, *The OT*, 7 and 9: "No matter how we approach the Torah, the heart of the canon, all its statements center in the name 'Yahweh,' . . . From beginning to end the literary framework reveals unmistakably the real subject of all the events." "No Old Testament presentation of past history keeps us from understanding history in the biblical sense as 'the work of Yahweh' (Josh. 24:31; Ps. 44:2; Isa. 5:12)."

40. Ibid., 10.

The only apparent exception that confirms the rule of the theocentric focus of all canonical books is the book of Esther, for it never mentions God directly and consequently was included in the canon only after much debate. Yet even the book of Esther is theocentric—albeit in a unique way. It has been noted that "the structural center of the book, artistically considered," is located in Mordecai's words in 4:13-14, "If you keep silence at such a time as this, relief and deliverance will rise for the Jews from another quarter." Consequently David Clines concludes that "the whole story speaks, though always obliquely, of a hidden presence of Yahweh in the world. The storyteller 'mirrors the nature of history in his method of narration,' and as an artist makes Yahweh conspicuous by his absence."[41]

If this theocentric focus is apparent in all Old Testament books, it is even more obvious in the New Testament, where Jesus Christ is proclaimed as the ultimate act of God, "God with us." Arnold Rhodes remarks that "the Bible is not only 'the greatest story ever told'; it is the greatest drama ever enacted—and its chief Actor is God himself. The Bible centers in his mighty acts: what he has done, is doing, and will do for us . . . and our salvation through Jesus Christ."[42] Theocentric interpretation seeks to expose in every passage this God-centered focus of the entire Bible.

Contrast to Anthropocentric Interpretation

The theocentric nature of biblical literature needs to be upheld especially over against an all too facile slide into anthropocentric interpretation and preaching. This slide can be detected throughout the history of interpretation and preaching, from 1 Clement, who generally used the Old Testament as a "book of ethical models," to the Middle Ages, when preaching the Old Testament was recommended because "its stories fascinate people and mirror their lives," to present-day preachers, who preach "Bible characters" or "biographical sermons."[43] As one advocate of preaching on Bible characters puts it: "Preaching on Bible Characters gives the minister an opportunity to set forth in a clear fashion the modern counterpart to the experience of a Biblical person. . . . There is an inexhaustible supply of material in the Scriptures from which to preach biographical sermons. This is seen when we realize that there are 2,930 different Bible characters."[44] In this type of interpretation and preaching a subtle (and sometimes not so subtle) switch takes place from the centrality of God in biblical literature to the centrality of human characters in the sermon. Donald Gowan puts his finger on a real dilemma in preaching the Old

41. Clines, *Int* 34/2 (1980) 121.
42. Rhodes, *Mighty Acts of God*, 11-12.
43. See my *Sola Scriptura*, 9-16.
44. Perry, *Manual for Biblical Preaching*, 106.

Testament when he observes that "we have wanted to use the Bible as a set of moral examples, . . . but . . . most of the book presents, not models of perfect behavior, but the story of how God deals with ordinary, imperfect human beings."[45]

Moreover, as Ernest Best points out, most of the material about Bible characters "has been recorded for a purpose other than that of giving us information about the particular person." Take, for example, the character of Peter, which has often been portrayed as weak. "The incidents in which the weakness of Peter are shown are not recorded primarily to tell us about Peter's weakness but about the mercy of God who forgives him." Thus, argues Best, "the selection of incidents which we have been given about Peter has been dominated by an interest other than the character of Peter himself. It is foolish of us therefore to use these incidents to build up a picture of the character of Peter and then to go on and apply it to men generally. We ought to use the incidents of Peter's weakness instead to argue for God's mercy and strength."[46]

Tragically, a moralistic use of the Bible undercuts the Bible's own purpose and replaces it with the preacher's agenda. Carl Kromminga rightly maintains that "despite its venerableness and its immediate utility, the traditional moralistic use of Old Testament narrative, even at its best, slowly works to reduce the dimensions of full-orbed biblical faith and obedience. . . . Moralism easily overlooks the author's intention and the divine intention in narrating a given event, or it allows that intention to play only a subsidiary role in the application of the message to life. The *revelational* scope of the text is narrowed to fit the preacher's easy exploitation of the apparent surface 'lesson' of the text."[47]

We do, of course, meet human characters in the Bible, but never in isolation, never as independent characters in their own right. Human characters in the Bible are always part of the larger story, which is theocentric. Unfortunately, preachers are easily tempted to begin at the wrong end: "We often begin by immediately concentrating on the people and are busy drawing a line from these people to the application before we know it. Naturally we may not neglect the people in the text; every detail—this too—requires our attention. Nevertheless, we must always see these human deeds as a reaction to God's action."[48] In contrast to anthropocentric interpretation, therefore, theocentric interpretation would emphasize that the Bible's purpose is first of all to tell the story of God. In relating that

45. Gowan, *Reclaiming the OT*, 3. Cf. Karl Barth, *Word of God*, 39: "In it [the Bible] the chief consideration is not the doings of man but the doings of God." For a detailed discussion of the many issues involved, see my *Sola Scriptura*.

46. Best, *From Text to Sermon*, 90-91.

47. Kromminga, *CTJ* 18/1 (1983) 38.

48. B. Holwerda, *Begonnen*, 104, as translated in my *Sola Scriptura*, 146.

story, the Bible naturally also depicts many human characters—not, however, for their own sake but for the sake of showing what God is doing for, in, and through them.[49] Hence, when preachers pass on the biblical story, they ought to employ biblical characters the way the Bible employs them, not as ethical models, not as heroes for emulation or examples for warning, but as people whose story has been taken up into the Bible in order to reveal what *God* is doing for and through them (see further Chapter 9 below).

Christocentric Preaching

IN connection with the Bible's theocentric purpose, we should also consider the demand for Christocentric preaching. Christocentric preaching, of course, like theocentric interpretation, is opposed to anthropocentric interpretation and preaching, for it requires of a sermon that neither the people in the Bible nor the people in the pew but Christ be central. Unfortunately, the legitimate demand for Christocentric preaching often results in very questionable methods of interpretation in order to have the text speak of Christ. Pitfalls like allegorizing and arbitrary typologizing can be avoided, however, if we relate Christocentric preaching to theocentric interpretation.

Christocentric and Theocentric

Often Christocentric preaching is misunderstood as "Jesucentric" preaching, that is, every sermon must somehow make reference to Jesus of Nazareth, his birth, life, death, or resurrection. That endeavor itself is not wrong, but its imposition as a methodological principle on every text is wrong, for it leads to forcing parallels between the text and Jesus. Moreover, it shortchanges Jesus, for the New Testament testifies that he is the eternal Logos, one with the Father and the Holy Spirit (e.g., John 1; 1 Cor 8:6; Col 1:15-19; Heb 1-2). It will not do, therefore, "to speak of Christ only at some fixed point part way along the line, as though previously one could speak only of God, without reference to Christ."[50] According to the New Testament, Christ acts from the very beginning—"all things were made through him" (John 1:3). From the New Testament perspective, therefore, theocentric interpretation without any further additions is already Christocentric, for Christ is God.

Yet Christocentric preaching is more than theocentric preaching. But

49. See my *Sola Scriptura*, 147, 215.
50. Cullmann, *Christ and Time*, 108. Cf. the similar thoughts of Schilder, Holwerda, et al. in my *Sola Scriptura*, 142-46. Cf. Pitt-Watson, *Primer*, 30: "We must preach the Old Testament not just as a curtain raiser to the story that begins in Bethlehem, but as part of the Christ story that begins in the beginning."

what is this "more"? It comes to expression, I think, in the deceptively simple assertion: "The Christian proclamation of an Old Testament text is not the preaching of an Old Testament sermon."[51] Christocentric preaching is the preaching of God's acts *from the perspective of the New Testament*. In other words, Christocentric preaching requires that a passage receive a theocentric interpretation not only in its own (Old Testament) horizon but also in the broader horizon of the whole canon. In this way one can do justice to two sets of biblical testimonies: on the one hand, Christ as the eternal Logos is present and active in Old Testament times, and, on the other hand, Christ is the fulfillment of the Old Testament.

Christocentric Interpretation

The New Testament teaches throughout that Jesus Christ is the fulfillment of Old Testament history, promises, and prophecies. This fact has implications for our reading and preaching of the Old Testament; it means that we must now move beyond strictly historical interpretation and interpret the Old Testament in the light of its fulfillment in the New Testament. One can argue this point both from a literary standpoint, that the Old Testament needs to be interpreted in the context of the whole canon, and also from a historical standpoint, that previous revelation needs to be interpreted in the light of later revelation. John Stek makes the latter argument when he writes: "The fact of progression in salvation history demands an ever new hearing of the word of the Lord spoken at an earlier moment in salvation history. The hearing must be new because it is a hearing in the context of the later events and circumstances in salvation history, and in the light of the word of the Lord spoken later in salvation history."[52]

Consequently Christocentric interpretation moves from the fullness of revelation in the New Testament to a new understanding of God's revelation in the Old Testament. In preaching an Old Testament passage, one may indeed be able to move from the Old Testament to the New Testament by way of promise-fulfillment, typology, development, or parallels, but the essence of Christocentric preaching lies not in the lines drawn from the Old Testament to the New Testament but in the prior move in the opposite direction—the move from the fullness of New Testament revelation to a new understanding of the Old Testament passage.

---

51. Clowney, *Preaching and Biblical Theology*, 75. On Christocentric preaching, see also Barth, *Preaching of the Gospel*, 17-20. Cf. p. 48: "The Old Testament witnesses to Christ before Christ (but not apart from Christ)."

52. Stek, *CTJ* 4/1 (1969) 47-48. Cf. E. Achtemeier and P. Achtemeier, *The OT*, 163: "The valid use of the OT in the Christian pulpit is built upon the historical fact that Jesus Christ . . . is the completion and fulfillment of the word of God witnessed to in the OT. . . . Jesus Christ is the final reinterpretation of every major tradition in the OT."

THE PURPOSE OF PREACHERS TODAY

THEOLOGICAL interpretation emphasizes various facets of biblical interpretation that might be neglected in historical and literary interpretation, particularly that the biblical message is a word *from* God and a word *about* God. In concluding our discussion of theological interpretation, we shall touch on two other areas that benefit from theological interpretation: the first concerns the purpose of the sermon and the second sermonic application.

The Purpose of the Sermon

HOMILETICIANS today insist increasingly that preachers be clear not only about the message but also about the purpose of each sermon: why it is being preached, what it tries to accomplish. Haddon Robinson suggests that preachers can determine the purpose of each sermon by "discovering the purpose behind the passage" that is being preached. Preachers should ask: "Why did the author write this? What effect did he expect it to have on his readers? . . . An expository sermon, therefore, finds its purpose in line with the biblical purposes. The expositor must first figure out why a particular passage was included in the Bible, and with this in mind decide what God desires to accomplish through the sermon in his hearers today."[53] Since theological interpretation, as we have seen, is very much interested in the author's purpose, it can render valuable service for the preacher in delineating not only the message of a passage but also its purpose. "True 'biblical preaching,'" writes David Buttrick, "will want to be faithful not only to a message, but to an *intention*. The question, 'What is the passage trying to do?' may well mark the beginning of homiletical obedience."[54] We shall return to this issue particularly in the next chapter.

Application

HANS-GEORG Gadamer and others have pointed out that application is part of the interpretative process; "understanding always involves something like the application of the text to be understood to the present situation of the interpreter." This is true especially for religious literature, for "a religious proclamation is not there to be understood as a merely historical document, but to be taken in a way in which it exercises its saving effect. . . . Understanding here is always application."[55]

The question we wish to explore briefly is how theological interpreta-

---

53. Robinson, *Biblical Preaching,* 109.
54. Buttrick, *Int* 35/1 (1981) 58.
55. Gadamer, *Truth and Method,* 274-75.

tion contributes to application. We have already seen that Christocentric interpretation is a new understanding of an Old Testament text—this new understanding, which one might call a new application, has definite implications for sermonic applications to today. Moreover, the notion of progressive revelation implies that one may not simply draw a historical equation mark between God's revelation in the Old Testament and God's message for today. In other words, God's revelation for the past is not necessarily his final word for people today. We see this point most clearly with Old Testament ceremonial and civil laws but also with such central commandments as the command to circumcise all males, "Any uncircumcised male . . . shall be cut off from his people; he has broken my covenant" (Gen 17:14), and the sabbath commandment, "the seventh day is a sabbath to the Lord your God; in it you shall not do any work" (Exod 20:10). Progressive revelation implies that one must interpret past revelation in the light of the most recent revelation. This means that one must compare Scripture with Scripture or, more precisely, that one must trace the message of the text through the Old Testament and into the New Testament. Application for today can be made only in the light of and guided by the full sweep of God's revelation in the Scriptures.

It may seem that the discontinuity inherent in progressive revelation hinders meaningful application to today. While progressive revelation undoubtedly complicates proper application, it must also be recognized that theological interpretation focuses attention on the overarching continuity which alone makes meaningful application possible. That overarching continuity, of course, is given in the triune God who is the same yesterday, today, and forever. Because God is forever the same God, application of his word to today is not only possible but mandatory. Thus theological interpretation contributes to meaningful application today, for it focuses on the one word of God about the one God.

CHAPTER 6

Textual-Thematic Preaching

THE term *thematic preaching* is sometimes used in the sense of "topical preaching" or "motto preaching" in order to contrast this type of non-biblical preaching with its biblical counterpart, which is called "textual preaching." "Thematic preaching" is not an antonym of "textual preaching," however, for these terms characterize preaching according to different categories: the first answers the question whether a sermon develops a specific theme and the other whether the sermon is based on a text. Since these are different categories, the terms *thematic preaching* and *textual preaching* are not mutually exclusive but can be meaningfully combined into "textual-thematic preaching." By the term *textual-thematic preaching* I mean preaching in which the theme of the sermon is rooted in the text.

It may be helpful at the outset of this chapter dealing with texts and themes to expand the diagram developed for Chapter 1. The diagram classifies sermons according to the following criteria: biblical content, use of text, length of text, and theme, and shows contrasts along the horizontal lines.

CATEGORIES	TYPES OF SERMONS			
Biblical content	Biblical Sermon			Nonbiblical Sermon
Use of text	Textual or Expository Sermon		Topical-biblical	Topical Sermon
Length of text	Textual Unit	Verse or Clause	Nontextual	Nontextual
Theme	Textual-thematic	Textual-multipoint	Biblical-thematic	Topical-thematic

In Chapter 1 this diagram served to portray that the term *expository preaching* cannot truly be contrasted with *textual preaching* or preaching on a single verse, since these terms describe preaching from different angles. Instead of contrasting these terms, therefore, one can easily combine them, as, for example, in an expository sermon that is based on a biblical text of one verse. For the present chapter the diagram should clarify similarly that "thematic preaching" cannot truly be contrasted with "textual preaching" since these terms, too, describe preaching from different angles. Therefore the combination of "textual preaching" and "thematic preaching" is not only a live option but, as we shall see, the preferred option. We shall first discuss textual preaching and then proceed to textual-thematic preaching.

TEXTUAL PREACHING

TEXTUAL preaching is preaching that is based on a biblical text and expounds the message of that text. This definition implies that all textual preaching requires not only a text but also *exposition* of that text. All textual preaching is therefore understood as expository preaching.

The Necessity of a Preaching-Text

ALTHOUGH it is theoretically possible to preach a biblical sermon without a specific biblical text (a "topical-biblical sermon"), there are good reasons for insisting on a preaching-text. The following three reasons stand out.

Authority of the Sermon

The major reason for insisting on a biblical preaching-text is related to the question of the authority of the sermon. Preachers are called to be ministers of the word of God. This means that the sermon should be much more than "one man's opinion"; the sermon should be the word of God. In Chapter 1 we saw, however, that a sermon is the word of God only to the extent that it faithfully proclaims the word of God in the Bible. The question is, therefore, how preachers can faithfully give voice to the word of God in the Bible. The history of preaching shows that nontextual, topical preaching all too easily derails into the quagmire of personal opinions. But a preaching-text provides the basis for keeping a sermon on track so that textual preaching is indeed the word of God.

The mere selection of a preaching-text does not, of course, guarantee that the sermon is the word of God; textual preaching, too, can derail at many points. All too often the preaching-text functions merely as a pretext for the preacher's personal opinions. Leander Keck points out that often a phrase or metaphor in the text "simply serves as a catalyst; the actual content of the sermon is derived elsewhere and frequently could have been suggested just as well by a fortune cookie."[1] Obviously, true textual preaching requires more than merely reading a preaching-text; textual preaching can claim divine authority only when it entails faithful exposition of the text.

Guideline for Preachers

A second reason for using a preaching-text is that it guides preachers in developing their sermons. Jean-Jacques von Allmen speaks of this aspect in terms of protection for preachers: the text "protects us from our imagination by setting it limits, and from lack of imagination by stimulating what we have; it protects us from heresy by bringing us back to the heart of the Gospel, and from ossified orthodoxy by forcing us to see the diversity of the apostolic and prophetic witness."[2] In this and the following chapters we shall investigate this point in detail.

Testing by the Congregation

A specific preaching-text also facilitates the congregation's testing of the word that is proclaimed. In Chapter 1 we saw that the hearers must test the sermon to see if it is worthy of acceptance as the word of God. But how can the average church member test a topical sermon? It is practically impossible. With textual preaching, however, the hearers receive a handle for testing the sermon; the handle is the preaching-text, for "it publicly gives preaching a reference which allows it to be checked—but which also allows it to be defended."[3]

The Selection of a Preaching-Text

IF it is agreed that preachers normally require a preaching-text, the next question is how such a text is to be selected. Although text selection may seem like a trivial issue, it is precisely at this point that many sermons get on the wrong track because preachers select texts that are too brief, or too long, or incomplete, or peripheral. Unfortunately, once improper text selection has sidetracked a sermon, it is extremely difficult, if not impossible, to get back on course. It is worthwhile, therefore, to consider how to start off on the right track by selecting a proper preaching-text. The following are some factors that must be taken into account.

The Church's Needs

Since the purpose of preaching is to build up the church (1 Cor 14:3; Eph 4:11-12), preachers will naturally wish to select preaching-texts with an

---

1. Keck, *Bible in the Pulpit*, 101.
2. Von Allmen, *Preaching and the Congregation*, 26.
3. Ibid.

eye to the needs of the church.[4] Such needs can cover a wide variety of areas. For the church as a whole there is the formal, liturgical need on specified Sundays to select a text in keeping with the church calendar (e.g., Advent or Easter). Preachers may also detect in their congregations specific needs or shortcomings (e.g., lack of love or joy) which should be addressed and which will thus guide them in their text selection. Moreover, personal needs of individual members, such as sorrow or unemployment, may guide preachers to texts which will address those needs. One must be careful, of course, not to diagnose needs superficially or to respond with a sermon to every perceived "need"; but as long as the needs are discerned communally (e.g., with the elders) and in the light of the Scriptures, they are a legitimate consideration in selecting preaching-texts.

The requirement that preaching-texts be selected with the needs of the church in mind discloses that text selection is not a rather formal procedure *prior* to preaching but that it is part of the very application of the sermon. The danger, of course, is that the needs of the congregation may distort subsequent interpretation of the chosen text. But the danger of misinterpretation is even greater when a text has been chosen apart from the needs of the congregation and must belatedly serve the function of meeting those needs. Therefore, preaching-texts ought to be chosen with an eye to the needs of the congregation; once chosen, however, the texts must be allowed to speak for themselves lest present needs distort the actual meaning of the texts.

The Preacher's Predilection

Another factor that undoubtedly enters into text selection is the preacher's predilection. The danger with following one's predilection is that one may concentrate one's preaching on a narrow band of texts and thus fail to preach the whole counsel of God. In order to avoid this danger, one might consciously seek to select texts from the full range of biblical texts, or one might preach a series of sermons on a whole book or epistle, or follow the texts assigned in a lectionary. In spite of the danger of one-sided preaching, however, the positive side of the preacher's predilection should not be overlooked. Texts that grab hold of preachers and speak to them will naturally be preached with more conviction and enthusiasm than texts that do not involve them at that moment. "Without doubt the best sermons we ever preach to others are those we have first preached to ourselves," writes John Stott. "When God himself speaks to us through a text

4. "Otherwise, as John A. Hutton used to declare, the man in the pulpit may keep answering questions that no one in the pew ever dreams of asking" (Blackwood, *Preaching from Prophetic Books*, 194-95). Stott discusses "liturgical," "external," and "pastoral" factors (*Between Two Worlds*, 214-18).

of Scripture, and it becomes luminous or phosphorescent to us, it is then that it continues to glow with divine glory when we seek to open it up to others."[5]

A Significant Text

Dwight Stevenson asserts that "a text, to merit the attention of a minister for a week and of a whole congregation for a half hour, should be central to the biblical revelation."[6] Although "all scripture is inspired by God and profitable for teaching" (2 Tim 3:16), some texts (e.g., the resurrection narratives) are obviously more central than others (e.g., civil laws). In view of the large amount of time required to prepare sermons and the limited opportunities to present sermons, it stands to reason that in text selection one should generally give preference to the more significant texts. Moreover, a sermon on a text about a rather obscure incident or a peripheral civil or ceremonial law may draw more attention to the preacher's ingenuity than to the word of God. Furthermore, it should be kept in mind that although every verse in the Bible is meaningful in the total complex of revelation, not every verse in the Bible makes a good preaching-text. For example, preachers who select as a preaching-text Gen 22:5 (Abraham's words to his young men) are majoring in minors. Not even Eph 1:1a, "Paul, an apostle of Christ Jesus by the will of God," makes for an appropriate preaching-text. Although the statement as such is meaningful and some preachers might use it as an occasion to say many worthwhile things, one usually does not look for messages in the caption of a letter but in the letter itself.

A Literary Unit

The question whether a preaching-text ought to be short or long can be answered in only one way: whether short or long, a preaching-text ought to be a literary unit. Perry Yoder argues cogently: "In the study of the Bible we need to begin with the assumption that the Bible writers were attempting to communicate to their audience by writing in organized units. These compositional units or paragraphs are the smallest unit of communication in the text. It is on these units that inductive study needs to focus. To take less than this is to chop up the ideas of the author and perhaps misunderstand them as a result of studying them out of context. . . . To take a larger bite is to include too much for a properly focussed study."[7]

---

5. Stott, *Between Two Worlds*, 219. On "using the self as a communicative tool," see Nichols, *Restoring Word*, 111-26.

6. Stevenson, *In the Biblical Preacher's Workshop*, 149-50.

7. Yoder, *From Word to Life*, 56. Cf. Blackwood, *Preaching from the Bible*, 94: "In the Bible the unit of composition is the paragraph. Except in certain sections—notably large parts of Proverbs—the unit of thought is the paragraph."

Although the advice to focus on paragraphs is a good general rule, it ought not to be applied too rigidly, for the Bible contains both smaller and larger thought units than paragraphs. As a matter of fact, the "smallest unit of communication" is not the paragraph but the sentence in prose and the line in poetry. On the one hand, therefore, one ought to keep an open mind to the possibility that a sentence may be such a concise summary or may be so rich in meaning that it may well form a preaching-text in its own right. On the other hand, a paragraph may well prove to be too small a unit, particularly in preaching narratives, so that one is forced to select a larger unit of several paragraphs. As Fee and Stuart point out, "Narratives cannot be interpreted atomistically, as if every statement, every event, every description could, independently of the others, have a special message for the reader. In fact, even in fairly lengthy narratives all the component parts of the narrative can work together to impress upon the reader a single major point."[8] For example, in preaching the narrative of the Lord delivering his people through Ehud, one would probably select as text all the paragraphs (4 in the RSV, 7 in the NIV) contained in Judg 3:12-30. With many narratives, such as 2 Sam 11–12 (David's adultery with Bathsheba), "the expositor would violate the story were he to preach it a paragraph at a time."[9] The point is that in all instances the selected preaching-text must be a complete unit, whether it is a sentence, a paragraph, or several paragraphs.

"Fuzziness at the edges of one's biblical text prophesies fuzziness at the edges of one's sermon," predicts Fred Craddock.[10] A poorly chosen text will haunt the preacher throughout the sermonizing process and will, in all likelihood, result in a defective sermon. It is crucial, therefore, to select a proper textual unit.

Fortunately, the biblical authors provide clues to help us discern the textual units. In Chapter 3 above, particularly in the section on rhetorical criticism, we noted that biblical authors frequently use literary devices to tip off their hearers/readers concerning the units and subunits in their work. Common literary devices marking literary units are repetition (the keyword technique), chiasm, and inclusion. Other literary clues indicating the beginning of a new unit may be "brief introductions to the material (Jer. 11:1), or notations as to time (Mark 1:32), place (Matt. 8:28), or occasion (John 5:1). It is also common for units to be rounded off with summary statements (Acts 16:5) or with a comment on the response to the preceding event (Mark 1:28)."[11]

---

8. Fee and Stuart, *How to Read the Bible*, 77.

9. Haddon Robinson, *Biblical Preaching*, 55.

10. Craddock, *Preaching*, 110.

11. Ibid., 112. See also Kaiser, *Toward an Exegetical Theology*, 95-96; and Yoder, *From Word to Life*, 57-58.

In addition to the literary devices, the content provides the most obvious clue to a textual unit: a change in content indicates a new unit of thought. Asking the following questions may be helpful in discerning the unit: "Is the goal of the unit reached? Is the story finished, the tension resolved, or the topic completed?"[12] Since a literary unit is a unit of thought, one could also say that a preaching-text ought to be a thought unit or a thematic unit. From another angle, some have insisted on a "purpose unit."[13] Whatever words or concepts are used, the point is that a preaching-text must be a unit.

The Purpose of Text and Sermon

THE question of the purpose of the text and sermon is intimately related to the process of selecting a preaching-text, for a preaching-text, we have seen, ought to be chosen to meet the needs of the congregation. In other words, preaching-texts are selected with a specific purpose in mind. In general, the purpose of sermons is to build up the congregation, to encourage and console (1 Cor 14:3), to equip its members for service (Eph 4:11-12), to teach, reprove, correct, and train in righteousness (2 Tim 3:16). What the more specific purpose of the sermon ought to be on any given Sunday can only be decided within and for each local congregation. Whenever a preaching-text is chosen to fulfill a certain purpose, however, the preacher will confront the question of the purpose of the preaching-text itself, for the purpose of the sermon may not contradict the original purpose of the text. As Donald Miller rightly maintains, "To use biblical passages for purposes not in harmony with those which prompted the writing of them is to misuse them."[14] In the process of selecting a preaching-text, therefore, one must inquire about the text's purpose.

Purpose and Theme

It is sometimes difficult to distinguish clearly between a text's purpose and its theme. Often the two will overlap, as in Jer 9:23-24, where the purpose to have Israel glory in knowing the Lord is expressed in the theme "Glory in knowing the Lord." Similarly, in 1 Tim 4:7b-8 the purpose that Timothy train himself in godliness is matched by the theme "Train yourself in godliness." It appears that where the purpose is to command some-

12. Yoder, *From Word to Life,* 57.
13. Adams, *Preaching with Purpose,* 25-26.
14. Miller, *Way to Biblical Preaching,* 126; see further pp. 130-41. Cf. Adams, *Preaching with Purpose,* 27: "When you have grasped His [the Holy Spirit's] purpose, what He intended to do to the recipient of His message, then—and then only—do you have the purpose for your sermon." Cf. Bettler, "Application," 339: "This is . . . the most critical point of applicatory preaching. The application must be that of the text. . . . If I do not know the purposes of a text, I cannot apply it."

thing or other, the formulation of this purpose may be very similar to the formulation of the theme. Still, it is useful to distinguish between purpose and theme.

Donald Miller tries to delineate the difference between theme and purpose by stating that "the theme involves the particular truth to be set forth in a sermon; the aim consists in what we desire that truth to do to the hearer. . . . The theme is the subject; the aim is the object." The theme, we can say, is the word, the message; the purpose is that which we hope to accomplish with the message. Miller demonstrates the difference particularly well with an illustration: "The purpose . . . differs from the theme as the surgeon's instrument differs from the outcome of his operation. He uses the instrument not merely to cut; he cuts in order to heal."[15] Or, to use another effective image, "A purpose differs from the sermon idea as a target differs from the arrow."[16] The clearest example of the difference between theme and purpose is presented by the prophets who announce impending destruction (*theme:* "The Lord will destroy his people") in order that Israel might repent (*purpose:* Israel's repentance and salvation).

Fred Craddock differentiates between "what the text is saying" and "what the text is doing." The question "What is the text doing?" helps identify the "nature and function of the text." "As things are being said, persons [and texts] are informing, correcting, encouraging, confessing, celebrating, covenanting, punishing, confirming, debating, or persuading."[17] Thus the question of what the text is doing or is supposed to do— whether it be informing, correcting, or whatever—gets at the text's purpose.

Discovering the Purpose of the Text

Since much of Chapter 5 above deals with the author's purpose and hence with the text's purpose, just a few comments here will suffice. In order to discover the text's purpose, one ought to ask basically *why* the author wrote the text in the way he did. This question can be answered only by studying the text in its literary and historical contexts. Biblical authors frequently answer this question themselves with a statement of purpose for either the whole book or a section (see Chapter 5 above). Where such a direct statement is lacking, detailed redactional and rhetorical studies may provide clues to the overall purpose of the author. In the light of that overall purpose in the original historical setting, one can subsequently seek to narrow down the purpose of the specific preaching-text.

15. Miller, *Way to Biblical Preaching*, 114, 115.
16. Haddon Robinson, *Biblical Preaching*, 108.
17. Craddock, *Preaching*, 123 and 122.

The Purpose of the Sermon

"Every sermon should have a specific purpose," says Miller, and "clear aim should be taken to achieve that goal. Otherwise he [the preacher] will fall into the habit of doing what the oft-quoted Archbishop Whately described as aiming at nothing, and hitting it!"[18]

The purpose of the sermon, as noted above, must be in harmony with the original purpose of the preaching-text. I use the word *harmony* advisedly in order to indicate, on the one hand, that the purpose of the sermon cannot always be exactly the same as that of the text because we live in different times and circumstances than the original recipients of the text. On the other hand, one may not change or contradict a text's purpose simply because biblical authors did not know about modern democracy, labor unions, space exploration, and artificial insemination, for example. One must always honor the original purpose of the text by remaining in harmony with it, but one may *extend* that purpose from its original Old Testament setting to its New Testament setting and from its New Testament setting to its contemporary setting. Since biblical texts were set in a new context when they were incorporated into the canon, their purpose may also take on a new focus. Moreover, since biblical texts thus became part of God's progressive revelation, rigid identity of their purpose may subvert the fact of God's *progressive* revelation. For example, if the specific purpose of Gen 17:9-14 was to have God's people circumcise all males as a sign of God's covenant, in the light of Acts 15 that can no longer be the purpose for the New Testament congregation. Similarly, if, in the context of prevailing customs, the specific purpose of 1 Cor 11:2-16 was that praying and prophesying women wear a veil, in the light of contemporary customs that original, specific purpose no longer holds. This complexity does not mean that these texts can now be set aside as antiquated; rather it means that their original purpose of acknowledging the covenant in the one case, and propriety in worship in the other, ought to be extended in a manner appropriate for this day and age. Such extension of purpose to our day naturally brings with it an element of uncertainty and the subtle temptation to impose one's own purpose on the text. "That is why the deepening or expansion of the purpose of any biblical passage must be rigorously controlled by a wrestling with the *real* aim of the original writer—an aim which may have been deeper and more profound even than the specific end toward which it was directed at any one moment."[19]

---

18. Miller, *Way to Biblical Preaching*, 113.

19. Ibid., 138. Cf. Kromminga, *CTJ* 18/1 (1983) 44: "Here we proceed with courage and caution: with courage because we must dare to take the message not beyond its basic intent but beyond the horizon of the Bible's formative age; with caution because in doing this we must be careful to be true to God's intention with this Bible narrative for our own time." Cf. Pitt-Watson, *Primer*, 38.

TEXTUAL-THEMATIC PREACHING

IF proper text selection places the sermon on the right track, proper theme formulation is intended to *keep* the sermon on the right track. In distinction from topical preaching, textual-thematic preaching obtains its theme not from the classics or the news media but from the preaching-text as understood in its context. "Any sermon worthy of the name should have a theme," asserts Miller. "Ideally, any single sermon should have just one major idea. . . . Two or three or four points which are not parts of one great idea do not make a sermon—they are two or three or four sermons all preached on one occasion."[20]

Unfortunately, preachers frequently neglect this elementary homiletical rule. As a result, their sermons derail. Miller documents many such derailments and suggests that the cause may be "a fault in ministerial training," or that "the average minister prefers to take the easy way of allegedly preaching on texts whose central meaning he has not taken the trouble to discover." It may also be, however, that theme formulation is more difficult than appears on the surface. Miller asserts that "every sermon should have a theme, and that theme should be the theme of the portion of Scripture on which it is based."[21] But the question is, Will the sermon's theme always be identical with the text's theme? In the light of the progression of revelation as well as history, should not the theme of some sermons be quite different from that of their texts? I suggest that preachers need to distinguish the text's theme from the sermon's theme. The reasons for this distinction will become clear as we discuss first the theme of the text and then the theme of the sermon.

The Theme of the Text

IN homiletics, "theme" is usually thought of as the central message, the unifying thought, the major idea, the point of the text. In literary circles, "theme" is similarly defined as "the central or dominating idea in a literary work . . . the abstract concept which is made concrete through its representation in person, action, and image in the work."[22] A theme, we can say, is a summary statement of the unifying thought of the text.

Themes in Every Form of Preaching-Text
The assumption of textual-thematic preaching is that every preaching-text has a theme. As James Daane phrases it: "The assumption behind the basic sermon is that every properly selected text expresses a truth which

---

20. Miller, *Way to Biblical Preaching*, 53.
21. Ibid., 55; the documentation of derailments is given on pp. 55-70.
22. W. F. Thrall and A. Hibberd as quoted by Clines, *Theme of the Pentateuch*, 18.

can be stated in propositional form. Every text says something about something. When it is properly interpreted, its many elements, ideas, phrases, and clauses are seen to be interrelated in such a fashion as to express a particular primary affirmation."[23]

Of late, the assumption that every preaching-text has a theme is being questioned particularly by those emphasizing the *form* of the text. They see the attempt to distill a theme from, say, a narrative text as a rationalistic approach which is not in keeping with narrative and which therefore distorts the text. For example, David Buttrick suggests that from the time of the Protestant Scholastics to the present, homiletics has been using a "rational homiletic method" and that "an underlying hermeneutic is involved: namely, that single texts contain thematics—propositions, truths, or principles." The legitimate question he raises is "if a rational, objective method can cope with biblical language which is often figural, poetic, or narrative in form."[24]

In order to avoid misunderstanding, it may be well to point out first that our assumption is not that every text or verse has a theme (an assumption indeed underlying many sermons) but that every *preaching-text* has a theme—and a preaching-text we defined earlier as a complete literary unit, a thought unit, a thematic unit. If a chosen text does not have a theme, it is not because not all preaching-texts have a theme but because not all selected texts are proper preaching-texts.

The important question Buttrick raises for textual-thematic preaching, however, is whether this method can do justice to all forms of biblical texts. Since the most common form is narrative, we shall use narrative as an example. Does the attempt to distill a theme from a narrative text necessarily lead to its distortion? Buttrick thinks so and graphically sketches what happens to the text: "The preacher treats the passage as if it were a still-life picture in which some*thing* may be found, object-like, to preach on. What has been ignored? The composition of the 'picture,' the narrative structure, the movement of the story, the whole question of what in fact the *passage* may want to preach."[25] Granted, Buttrick makes a valid point against rationalistic, scholastic preaching, but one may ask, What is it that "in fact the *passage* may want to preach"? Can we articulate that point? If we can, that is its proper theme; if we cannot, the question is how one can preach something that cannot be articulated.

The literary critic Leland Ryken raises the same fundamental issue. He writes: "If every part of the Bible were an expository essay, the right question to ask about any passage would be, What is the writer's thesis and how does he develop his argument? This is how many people read

23. Daane, *Preaching with Confidence*, 61-62.
24. Buttrick, *Int* 35/1 (1981) 47.
25. Ibid., 49.

the entire Bible, including the stories. But a storyteller has no thesis to develop—he has a story to tell. The appropriate questions to ask of a story are different from those we ask of an essay or sermon." Having said that, however, and having listed some of the questions to ask of a story, Ryken acknowledges, "Eventually a literary analysis of a story will ask what themes are embodied in the story. It is important to realize, however, that the thematic question, What is the writer's message? can be answered only if we first answer the narrative question, What happens to the characters in the story."[26] The laudable concern for doing justice to the narrative form of the text need not, therefore, lead to a denial of the existence of a theme. In fact, Dan Via calls plot and theme the "two sides of the same formal principle with plot being theme in movement and theme being plot at a standstill."[27]

Describing the theme of a narrative as "plot at a standstill" clarifies not only that narrative texts indeed have themes but also that their isolation of necessity involves stopping the action. A theme, it must be admitted, is an abstraction from the "living" narrative. The question is, however, Does such abstraction necessarily distort the text? Do not all scientists constantly abstract from full reality without thereby necessarily distorting it? The important point to remember is that the theme is indeed an abstraction and that the sermon ought to make concrete what has been abstracted. William Willimon verbalizes both the danger of thematic preaching and its necessity: "The danger of this device [theme] is that it may encourage me to treat my text as an abstract, generalized idea that has been distilled from the text—such as 'the real meaning behind the story of the prodigal son.' . . . My congregation listens to ideas about a story rather than experiencing *the* story. In spite of this pitfall, I don't know where I'm going in writing the sermon until I can clearly state a theme."[28]

Discovering the Theme

In Chapter 3 above we noted how rhetorical criticism, in particular, has brought to light ancient structural patterns that aid contemporary preachers in discerning the theme of a passage. Repetition of a word, phrase, or clause is probably the most obvious clue the ancient writers give to their themes. A chiastic structure may also provide a clue to the theme since the pivotal thought is often located at its center (A B C B′ A′). The literary structure of inclusion may also reveal the theme in its introduction and conclusion. Further, one may discover the theme "in the conclusion of

26. Ryken, "Bible as Literature," 175-76.
27. Via, *The Parables: Their Literary and Existential Dimension* (Philadelphia: Fortress, 1967), 96-97.
28. Willimon, *Preaching*, 68.

some assent-compelling argument; or in the highlight of some incident . . . ; or in the occasion which leads up to some narrative or parable."[29] However one discovers the theme of the preaching-text, it must always be formulated in the light of the larger whole, according to the
theme of the broader contexts of paragraph, section, and book.

Formulating the Theme

As we noted earlier, the theme is a summary statement of the unifying
thought of the text. In formulating the theme, therefore, one tries to lay
hold of the dominant idea that encompasses all others. The question here
is, What is the overriding thrust of the passage? What is the single point
that not only dominates all other points in this text but encompasses them
while deriving (part of) its meaning from them? "The important thing for
the sermon-maker to hear is the text's primary affirmation, and this is
heard when one understands how the secondary affirmations give content and definition to the primary affirmation."[30] Consequently, instead of
seeing the text as a number of elements recounted one after the other, one
tries to see how these various elements are combined in the chosen text,
how they are related, and what meaning they project in their specific combination.

The elements of many texts may be the same, but the specific combination of elements in each text is different and accounts for the uniqueness of each text. Chemistry provides an illuminating analogy: "When I
want to speak of the significance and characteristics of water (H_2O), I
should not speak about the merits of hydrogen (H), but rather about H as
it forms a compound in synthesis with O. And when I speak about sulfuric acid, I should not speak about H, but about that entirely different compound H_2SO_4." Similarly, "every historical text is a unit, composed,
indeed, of a variety of elements, but these elements have formed a very
specific synthesis at this point. This special synthesis gives to every text a
unique place within the totality of revelation."[31] The theme tries to capture in a few words that "special synthesis," the specific combination of
elements, the unique message of the text.

If the theme is to do justice to the fact that every preaching-text proclaims a *message*, the theme ought to be formulated as a message, an assertion. Hence the theme must contain at least a subject and a predicate. A
subject by itself, such as "gospel" or "power," does not assert anything; it
may indicate the topic the text deals with, but it does not say anything
about the topic because it is not a complete thought. But "the gospel is
powerful" is a proper theme since it says something about the subject; it

---

29. James C. Stout as quoted in Miller, *Way to Biblical Preaching*, 54.
30. Daane, *Preaching with Confidence*, 62.
31. B. Holwerda, *Begonnen*, 92, as translated in my *Sola Scriptura*, 138.

reflects the message of the text (Rom 1:16-17), albeit in skeleton form. As the homiletician H. Hoekstra wrote already in 1926: "The text *says* something; it is a communication of God, a message for us. Such a message or communication can never be couched in one concept (word) but finds expression in an assertion (a subject and a predicate) in which the one concept predicates something of the other."[32] Predication can be made by modifying the subject with an adjective (e.g., "The Powerful Gospel" predicates that the gospel is powerful), but at this stage of formulating for oneself the message of the text, it is preferable to state the theme in the form of a brief sentence.

Further, the theme of the text ought to be formulated from the author's viewpoint. This guideline seeks to ward off the common practice of formulating different themes for one and the same text by approaching it from different angles. For example, it has been suggested that 1 Sam 18:1-4 can be approached from the point of view of David, Jonathan, friendship, or God. These four different angles provide the preacher with the choice of four themes for this text: "David Honored by Jonathan," "The Crown Prince Bows before the Anointed King David," "The Friendship of Faith," and "God Paves the Way for David's Kingship."[33] Although this procedure may at first glance appear to be legitimate, what is happening in fact is that the text is isolated from its context in order to be open to these different angles of approach. Thus this practice transgresses the first rule of hermeneutics that every text ought to be understood in its context. In order to avoid this pitfall, therefore, one ought to formulate the theme of the text in the light of the theme of its larger context and ultimately the theme of the whole book. This is but another way of saying that the text's theme should be formulated from the author's viewpoint and not that of different characters in the text or that of contemporary readers.

Functions of Theme Formulation

Formulating the theme of the text is crucial for gaining a right understanding of the text. Since the author had a controlling theme which governed his selection of material and the order and manner of writing, the interpreter can gain valid understanding of the author's point only by discerning that controlling theme. In trying to distill the theme of the Pentateuch, David Clines stresses that "a quest for 'theme' is no reductionist undertaking, as if the work itself were a disposable packaging for the 'idea' that comes to realization in it. Rather, a statement of theme func-

---

32. Hoekstra, *Homiletiek*, 399, as translated in my *Sola Scriptura*, 162-63. Cf. Davis, *Design for Preaching*, 68.

33. Dijk, *De Dienst der Prediking*, 177. See further my *Sola Scriptura*, 164-66, 227. See Miller, *Way to Biblical Preaching*, 70-75, for some examples of how a subsidiary theme must be formulated and preached in the context of its broader theme.

tions, first, as an orientation to the work; it makes a proposal about how best to approach the work."[34] The same function holds for smaller segments of a work and ultimately for the unit selected as preaching-text: the theme functions as "a proposal about how best to approach" the text; that is, it serves the function of gaining the author's perspective on the text, of seeing correctly the relationship between primary and subsidiary material in the text.

Second, in the words of Clines, "a statement of theme functions as a warning or protest against large-scale misunderstanding of a work."[35] This negative function is also important at the level of the preaching-text: the formulation of a theme functions as a guard against misunderstanding, particularly as a guard against raising to dominance or isolating what is subsidiary in the text. In other words, proper theme formulation will guard the interpreter from what has been called "atomistic interpretation," that is, isolating certain "atoms" within the text from the central thrust of the text and preaching and applying those "atoms" as if they were independent units.[36]

Another function of theme formulation that is directly relevant for preaching is that "a statement of theme is the first step in formulating the message of the work within its historical context or in setting up guidelines within which future readings or interpretations of the work in different historical contexts may be considered legitimate."[37] As already indicated, the text's theme is not necessarily the same as the sermon's theme, but the text's theme certainly functions as the cornerstone for the sermon's theme; the theme of the text sets up guidelines for the subsequent understanding of the text in the context of the whole of Scripture and ultimately for articulating its message for today.

The Theme of the Sermon

THE theme of the sermon is a summary statement of the unifying thought of the *sermon*. Like the text's theme, the sermon's theme is not a subject or topic but an assertion; it seeks to articulate the message of the sermon in one short sentence. Henry Davis writes: "A well-prepared sermon is the embodiment, the development, the full statement of a significant thought. . . . But a sermon idea is more than a bare thought. It is a thought plus its overtones and its groundswell of implication and urgency." Consequently Davis prefers to speak of "the idea of a sermon."[38]

---

34. Clines, *Theme of the Pentateuch*, 18.
35. Ibid.
36. B. Holwerda, *Begonnen*, 91-92; see my *Sola Scriptura*, 63-64, 76-77.
37. Clines, *Theme of the Pentateuch*, 19.
38. Davis, *Design for Preaching*, 20.

Haddon Robinson speaks also of "the homiletical idea" and stipulates that it "be both winsome and compelling."[39] Whatever word we use, the theme or idea of the sermon ought to state as clearly and succinctly as possible the point the sermon seeks to make.

Sermon Theme and Text Theme

As proposed earlier, the sermon's theme should be distinguished from the text's theme because they are not necessarily identical. The two should never be separated, however, because textual-thematic preaching derives the sermon's theme from the preaching-text's theme as this functions in the whole of the Bible. Hence the text's theme and the sermon's theme are closely connected. As an ancient cornerstone used to serve the prospective building both as foundation and as guideline, so the text's theme ought to serve the prospective sermon both as its foundation and its guideline. Although the meaning of a text for today is not necessarily identical with its original meaning (the clearest examples being certain Old Testament laws), the meaning for today must be grounded in and be an extension of that original meaning as that becomes clear in the light of further revelation.

Accordingly, preachers must hold together past meaning and present meaning; they ought not to dissolve the tension by opting for the one or the other. "To emphasize only what the text meant, or to preach the Bible 'directly' to our generation, is to fall into a simplistic fundamentalism where one does little more than to repeat the words of the text again and again, ignoring the cultural chasm between past and present," asserts D. A. Hagner. "However, to emphasize only what the text means can in effect be to preach only our own thoughts and our own words. . . ."[40] Instead of opting for the one or the other, preachers are to take the word of God with full awareness that it was addressed first of all to the past and address it to the present. Hence they must constantly have two horizons in view, that of the text and that of the contemporary audience: "The first task of Christian preaching is to take the biblical text seriously. The second major task of Christian preaching is to take the congregational context with equal seriousness."[41]

The first task, "to take the biblical text seriously," means that its message, as it is precisely summarized in the theme, is the starting point and guideline in the formulation of the sermon's theme. In formulating the

39. Robinson, *Biblical Preaching*, 99.

40. Hagner, *ExpTim* 96 (1985) 138. Cf. Stott, *Between Two Worlds*, 221: "To search for its [the text's] contemporary message without first wrestling with its original meaning is to attempt a forbidden short cut." On the problematics of relating what the text meant in the past to what it means today (recontextualization), see, e.g., Thiselton, "Reader-Response Hermeneutics," 109-13.

41. Willimon, *Preaching*, 69.

sermon's theme, one ought not to tone down the point of the text by harmonizing it first with other texts or rounding it off in conversation with
church doctrine. The text's message ought to stand—sharp, clear, and
pointed—as a word of God to a specific people in the past. "Preaching the
content of the Bible faithfully requires one to respect the peculiarities of a
given text or writer, even if . . . this means that the emphasis of this Sunday's sermon from Romans will have certain tensions with last Sunday's
from Matthew."[42] Preachers must do justice to their preaching-texts by allowing Matthew to make his point differently from Mark, John from
Luke, James from Paul, the Chronicler from the author of Samuel-Kings.

Before formulating the sermon theme, however, preachers need also
to consider the horizon of their congregations: these are not Old Testament congregations but people living in the (late) New Testament age,
after Good Friday and Easter, after Pentecost. It would be anachronistic to
address these people as if they lived before the coming of Christ and the
Holy Spirit. Consequently, when the preaching-text is from the Old Testament, the theme of the text must be traced through God's progressive revelation from the Old Testament to the New Testament. This understanding of the preaching-text in the totality of Scripture is required not
only because of the horizon of the contemporary church but also because
the preaching-text now functions as part of the canon. Having earlier formulated the *text's* theme in the light of the book's theme, the preacher
now needs to formulate the *sermon's* theme in the light of the whole of
Scripture. In the process, the text's theme may need to be changed,
broadened, or extended before it can become the sermon's theme. On a reduced scale, the same holds true for the theme of New Testament texts.
Although both the early Christian church and the contemporary church
live in the same New Testament age, the preacher must still take into account two different horizons, that of the first century and that of the twentieth. Because of differences in the historical situation, culture, customs,
and the like, the text's theme may need to be changed or extended, before
it can become the theme of a contemporary sermon. For example, the
theme of John 13:12-17, "Followers of Christ ought to wash one another's
feet," needs to be broadened as a sermon theme to something like, "Followers of Christ ought to render humble service to each other."

Frequently, of course, the text's theme can function as the sermon's
theme without making any adjustments. The reason why no changes are
required is because the message of many texts has general validity. For example, the theme of Jer 9:23-24, "Glory in knowing the Lord," can be the
theme of a sermon any time and any place. Similarly, the theme of 1 Tim
4:7b-8, "Train yourself in godliness," can function as the sermon's theme

---

42. Keck, *Bible in the Pulpit*, 109. Cf. my *Sola Scriptura*, 227-28.

without making any adjustments. The two horizons with all their differences still exist, and the complete sermon will be different in one horizon than the other, but the themes as such are valid in both horizons. "When an idea is a universal principle applying to anyone at any time," writes Haddon Robinson, "then the statement of the homiletical idea can be identical to the exegetical idea,"[43] or, in our terminology, then the theme of the sermon can be identical to the theme of the text.

Functions of the Sermon Theme

As mentioned earlier, one of the main functions of the formulation of the sermon theme is to keep the sermon on the right track. Craddock suggests that the theme "will discipline all the content and arrangement of the sermon just as a destination disciplines a journey."[44] Elsewhere he states that "the one central idea provides a natural control over which materials are admissible into the sermon and which are not, the theme serving as a magnet to attract only the appropriate."[45] In short, constructing the sermon under the guidance of a properly formulated theme will set the direction and keep the sermon from being sidetracked.

A second, related function of the sermon theme is to ensure the sermon's unity. All homileticians seem to agree that a sermon should be a unity: in the words of Ian Pitt-Watson, "Every sermon should be ruthlessly unitary in its theme. 'This is the first and great commandment!' . . . Anything in the sermon which cannot be justified as relevant to that central theme should be ruthlessly discarded."[46] Davis offers another perspective: "Unity is a functional character of effective communication. There is no moral or religious or literary law that a sermon must embody just one idea." Instead, he claims, the demand for unity originates with the hearers: "the desire for unity is a law of the listener's mind."[47]

A third function of the sermon theme is that it promotes movement in

---

43. Robinson, *Biblical Preaching*, 97.

44. Craddock, *Int* 35 (1981) 65.

45. Craddock, *Preaching*, 156. Cf. p. 155: "What now needs to be emphasized is that the message statement be a simple rather than a compound or complex sentence in order to maintain unity and singularity of direction. Permit a few conjunctions into that sentence, a semicolon or two, perhaps an et cetera, and what happens? Fuzziness replaces focus and through the cracks between the poorly joined and disparate units of that overextended statement will creep every cause crying out for a little pulpit publicity."

46. Pitt-Watson, *Preaching*, 65, 66. Cf. Miller, *Way to Biblical Preaching*, 54: "Unity should be an outstanding characteristic of every good sermon." Cf. also Stott, *Between Two Worlds*, 225-26. See Daane, *Preaching with Confidence*, 52: "Every sermon must say one thing, and one thing only." Cf. p. 59: "The more points a sermon tries to drive home, the less it drives home. A many-pointed sermon makes no point; it only conveys confusion."

47. Davis, *Design for Preaching*, 35-36.

the sermon. Craddock argues perceptively that "unity is essential to movement. There can be no movement without unity, without singleness of theme." He contends that it is "the restraint of a single idea" that contributes to the movement. "In delivery, the limitation of the single idea is the key to forceful and effective unfolding of the message. The difference between a moving stream and a stagnant marsh is constraint. Such is the difference between sermons with and without the discipline of the controlling theme."[48]

A final function of the sermon theme is that it provides direction for the application of the sermon. Many preachers try to make their sermons relevant by spicing them with practical asides: a warning here, encouragement there, a moral here, a call for imitation there—all duly attached, usually, to various elements of the text. But the appearance of relevance and practicality is often just that, mere appearance. For we have seen that the elements of a text speak not independently but unitedly in their synthesis in that particular preaching-text, while practical asides are usually attached to isolated elements. Hence these practical asides do not really carry the authority of the text. Douglas Stuart asserts: "Rare is the passage that calls for several applications, all of equal relevance or practicability." A preacher, he says, is "not responsible to discuss all the possible ways in which the passage might strike the fancy of the reader." Rather, a preacher is "responsible to inform the reader what the passage *itself* calls for or leads to in terms of application."[49] In addition, it is well known that people are selective in their hearing and doing; they tend to pick and choose from many applications whatever suits their palate, often bypassing the kernels intended especially for them. Donald Miller reminds us that "a sermon should be a bullet, not bird shot. It ought to be designed to hit the hearer in one vital spot, rather than to spray him with scattered theological ideas unrelated to each other which touch him mildly in a dozen places."[50]

Thus both hermeneutical integrity and psychological necessity argue for a focused application. The sermon theme provides a useful function in achieving this focused application, for it can keep the sermon, also in its application, on track. If the sermon has but one point, its application cannot be anything but that same single point—driven home, possibly, in a variety of ways throughout the sermon, but nevertheless remaining one single point.

---

48. Craddock, *As One Without Authority*, 100 and 101.
49. Stuart, *OT Exegesis*, 50-51.
50. Miller, *Way to Biblical Preaching*, 53.

CHAPTER 7

The Form of the Sermon

IN Chapter 1 we already observed the significance of the form of the sermon for hearer response. If the text seeks to evoke a "wow!" or a "hallelujah!" from the hearers while the sermon manages to evoke merely intellectual assent or a yawn, the problem may well lie in the form of the sermon: a wrong form can undercut the message of the text and thus distort it, while, conversely, an appropriate form can help the message get across as originally intended. Proper formulation of the theme by itself, therefore, is not sufficient to keep the sermon on the right track; one must also consider the form in which the message will be presented. "There is no avoiding the fact that the medium is *a* message, if not *the* message."[1]

FORM AND DEVELOPMENT

Functions of Form

IN order to see the significance of sermon form, it may be well to list some of its functions. First, the sermon form reshapes the form of the text. Such reshaping is unavoidable if one does not wish simply to repeat the text. The significance of sermon form becomes evident when one realizes that this reshaping will distort the text's message unless it is done with sensitivity to the text's form.

Second, form co-determines the hearers' response, as we saw above. Some forms are more likely than others to elicit praise, or surprise, or assent, or change, or enthusiasm.

Third, form shapes the hearers' expectations. Fred Craddock points out that even the opening phrase can sometimes reveal the form and set

1. Craddock, *As One Without Authority*, 145.

the hearers' expectations—as in the familiar: "Once upon a time"; "There was a certain man"; "Dearly beloved, we are gathered here"; "There were these two Irishmen, Pat and Mike." Since the form sets the hearers' expectations, a wrong form would mislead the hearers.

Fourth, "form gains and holds interest." For maintaining interest to the end, for example, a form may use "the principle of end stress" which "withholds the point of primary interest until the end." A case in point would be inductive rather than deductive development (see below).

Fifth, "form determines the degree of participation demanded of the hearers." Overstating the case considerably, Craddock claims that "the old pattern of stating the sermon in digest at the outset, developing the sermon, and then summarizing in conclusion" makes "no demands of the listeners. . . . In contrast, the pattern, 'Not this, nor this, nor this, but this' expects the hearers to remain thoughtfully engaged to the end."

Sixth, form shapes the hearers' attitudes. Craddock asserts that, on the one hand, "ministers who, week after week, frame their sermons as arguments, syllogisms armed for debate, tend to give that form to the faith perspective of regular listeners. Being a Christian is proving you are right." On the other hand, "those who consistently use the 'before/after' pattern impress upon hearers that conversion is the normative model for becoming a believer." Similarly, a consistent "either/or" format contributes to "oversimplification" and "inflexibility," while the consistent "both/and" format contributes to broader "horizons and sympathies" but also greater indecisiveness.[2]

Although not all these functions hold for the form of each and every sermon, the list is sufficiently impressive to indicate that preachers need to weigh very carefully with each sermon what form to use. Before we discuss in some detail the didactic and narrative forms, we shall first look at the structure of a sermon in terms of deductive or inductive development.

Development within Forms

THE question of deduction or induction is the question of the direction of development in the sermon: should one move from the general to the particular or from the particular to the general? Should the sermon state the theme at the beginning and then develop it in particular points and specific applications (deduction), or should the sermon begin with the particulars and conclude with the theme (induction)? Deduction, induction, and their combination present the preacher with four major options:

2. Functions 3 to 6 are adaptations of the four functions mentioned by Craddock, *Preaching*, 172-74. On the power of long-term preaching to shape the hearers' attitudes, see Nichols, *Restoring Word*, 22-48.

- First state the general point, then particularize it (deduction).
- Present particulars first; state the point last (induction).
- First state, then particularize, then restate at the last.
- Present particulars first, next state the theme, then work out its implications.[3]

Schematically the four options look as follows:[4]

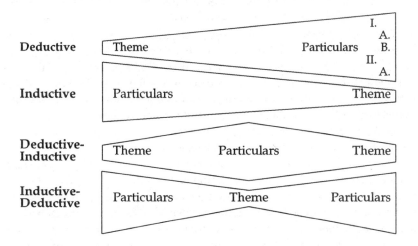

Each of these options can also be applied to subpoints in the sermon, of course, but our interest here is in the overall design of the sermon.

Deductive Development

The most prevalent design is undoubtedly that of deduction: after the introduction the theme is stated and its various aspects are developed one after the other, usually by way of "points." This is the usual design of the didactic sermon, as we shall see shortly. One advantage of deductive development is that the point of the sermon is clear from the beginning and can be reinforced throughout the sermon. It aids the understanding of the hearers since they are told the destination of the trip at the beginning and thus are better able to follow the road that leads to that destination.

---

3. Davis, *Design for Preaching*, 170. The fourth option is my formulation; cf. Davis's description on p. 176: "Roughly the first half of the sermon may be inductive, leading to a statement of the central idea somewhere about the middle; the idea is handled deductively from that point onward." This design, according to Cox, *Biblical Preaching*, 23, has also been called the "plain style" sermon: "explain the text; tell what it means; and apply it."

4. The first two adapted from Locke Bowman's diagram as found in Craddock, *As One Without Authority*, 57.

Inductive Development

In contrast to deductive development, Craddock argues forcefully for inductive development. His main argument is that "a preaching event is a sharing in the Word, a trip not just a destination, an arriving at a point for drawing conclusions and not handing over the conclusion."[5] Craddock realizes that preachers make that trip in their studies; proceeding inductively, they carefully check out the particulars before they arrive at their theme. He argues, however, that preachers ought not simply to hand their hearers that conclusion but give them the opportunity to make the trip themselves; preachers ought "to re-create imaginatively the movement" of their own thought whereby they "came to that conclusion." Inductive development thus seeks greater congregational involvement in arriving at the conclusion. Moreover, if it is done well, "one need not often make the applications of the conclusion to the lives of . . . [the] hearers," says Craddock. "If *they* have made the trip, then it is *their* conclusion, and the implication for their own situations is not only clear but personally inescapable."[6]

Craddock argues further that sermons developed by way of induction ought not to have points; rather, he suggests, one ought to think in terms of "transitions, turns in the road, or of signs offering direction toward the destination." "Sermons that move inductively sustaining interest and engaging the listener do not have points any more than a narrative, a story, a parable, or even a joke has points. But there is a point, and the discipline of this one idea is creative in preparation, in delivery, and in reception of the message."[7] From these comments, it will be apparent that inductive development is particularly appropriate for the narrative form, though it can certainly be utilized in the didactic form as well. A major advantage of inductive over deductive development is that "inductive sermons produce a sense of discovery in listeners, as though they arrived at the idea on their own."[8]

THE DIDACTIC FORM

THE didactic form of a sermon is usually, though not necessarily, developed deductively; that is, the theme is stated near the beginning and is subsequently developed in logical subpoints. In a textual-thematic sermon, in contrast to a topical sermon, the theme and its subpoints are

5. Craddock, *As One Without Authority*, 146.
6. Ibid., 57.
7. Ibid., 105 and 100. Buttrick deliberately changes the terminology from "points" to "moves" (*Homiletic*, 23). Cf. ibid., pp. 69-70.
8. Haddon Robinson, *Biblical Preaching*, 125.

derived from the text in its biblical context. Even with this specification, the category "didactic form" consists of various models.

A Model of the Didactic Form

WE shall use as representative of this form the model presented by James Daane in *Preaching with Confidence*. Although Daane is open to "several types of sermons," he holds that "the wise student will not begin with the more complex forms of sermon structures" but with "the simplest and most basic sermon structure."[9] That structure turns out to be a rather sophisticated model of the didactic form. Contrary to some caricatures of the didactic form, Daane maintains that "the sermon proper is not an attempt to prove or even argue for the truth of the proposition. It rather explicates, exhibits, spells out what the proposition declares. The components of this part of the sermon, therefore, must come from the text and not from anywhere else inside or outside the Bible. . . . Thus the whole structure of the sermon outline is determined solely by the text."[10]

Daane offers some instructive model outlines.[11] For example, a sermon outline on John 3:16 is constructed as follows:

Proposition: The Greatness of God's Love (God's love is great.)
  I. Its Costly Expression
  II. Its Unworthy Object
  III. Its Saving Purpose

A sermon on the narrative text of Gen 22:1-14 is constructed as follows:

Proposition: The Testing of Abraham's Faith (Abraham's faith is tested.)
  I. Its Provocative Antecedents
  II. Its Religious Nature
  III. Its Painful Execution
  IV. Its Unexpected Outcome

Note that in the examples each of the points begins with "Its." Although the didactic form does not necessarily require these possessive pronouns, Daane insists on them since they make for a tight, logical form. "The use of this possessive pronoun indicates that what is asserted belongs to the divine love [or to Abraham's faith] and is an aspect of its greatness [or of the testing]." As far as the adjectives are concerned, "just as the predicate in the sermon's propositional statement specifies precisely what the text is judged to say about the subject, so these adjectives define each aspect of the subject more precisely." Daane's justification for these logical outlines

9. Daane, *Preaching with Confidence,* 57.
10. Ibid., 65-66.
11. Ibid., 69-72.

is that "the Word of God is not irrational. Although we cannot wholly comprehend the Word, we can have valid knowledge of it. A logical structuring of the Word, whether as done in systematic theology, in propositional statement, and in sermon outlines, is valid, indeed necessary."[12]

Advantages of the Didactic Form

THE advantages of the didactic form are obvious. It is biblical to the extent that the theme summarizes the message of the text and the supporting points are taken from the text. It also enables the listeners to follow and to check the exposition of the text. Further, it makes for a clear, coherent structure that provides the hearers with a solid, logical framework for understanding the sermon. The didactic form does not suit every preaching-text, however, and various objections have been raised against it.

Objections to the Didactic Form

DON Wardlaw argues that the didactic form is more Greek than biblical. The original "controlling structure of Christian preaching was narrative, the recollection of what God in Christ had done, was doing, would do to intervene graciously in human affairs," but when Christianity spread into the Hellenistic world, the structure of "discursive rhetoric" was adopted. "In contrast to first-century narrative preaching, reflection became the basic sermon framework in the second century. Narration was confined to pauses for illustrations or allusions in the line of argument." According to Wardlaw, this "discursive style" or "reflective shape of the sermon" has remained the dominant form of preaching right to the present. "Preaching, per se, has meant marshaling an argument in logical sequence, coordinating and subordinating points by the canons of logic, all in a careful appeal to the reasonable hearer." Wardlaw phrases his major objection to this form of preaching as follows: "When preachers feel they have not preached a passage of Scripture unless they have dissected and rearranged that Word into a lawyer's brief, they in reality make the Word of God subservient to one particular, technical kind of reason."[13]

Another objection to the didactic form is that it "ignores movement."[14] In fairness, it must be said that proponents of the didactic form undoubtedly aim at movement; "the progression, and the advance, and the development of the argument . . . is absolutely vital."[15] In fact, the

---

12. Ibid., 66, 69. Daane here explicates a method first taught at Calvin Seminary by S. Volbeda.
13. Wardlaw, "Need for New Shapes," 11-12.
14. Buttrick, *Int* 35/1 (1981) 55.
15. Lloyd-Jones, *Preaching and Preachers*, 77.

"points" have been described as "markers of movement, highlighters of progression in the unfolding of the theme."[16] In the didactic form, however, the movement is not so much along a story line as logical: the theme is stated as the central issue and the congregation is invited to walk around it and view it from various sides, such as "its religious nature" and "its painful execution." One may grant that these logical points may sometimes be able to catch the forward momentum in the text, but the logical structuring will frequently change the movement from linear to circular, with the result that there is no sense of progression. Then the words of Andrew Blackwood are apropos: "If the sweep of a work resembled a merry-go-round, the sermon as a whole would lead to no sense of arrival."[17] Moreover, the combination of the early announcement of the theme and the lack of forward movement usually results in diminishing the elements of surprise and discovery and thus tends to reduce the level of audience interest and involvement.

The most serious objection to the didactic form, however, is that in reshaping the form of the text, it may unintentionally distort the message of the text. For passages whose aim is specifically to teach doctrine, the didactic form may work well, but for passages whose aim is to proclaim, to surprise, to encourage, to seek praise, etc., the didactic form is not very appropriate because the message "becomes transformed into an intellectual topic"; for example, "the profound song announcing God's love for our world (John 3:16) becomes in the preacher's hands the abstracted topic 'The Sacrificial Love of God.'"[18] Donald Gowan asks, "Should a sermon based on a lament be didactic in form? Hasn't something of the biblical message itself been lost if the power of the biblical language cannot be echoed in the sermon?"[19] In Chapters 1 and 3 we have already seen the close relationship between form and content; because of that intrinsic relationship, one cannot simply take the content of a biblical form, like milk in a container, and pour it indiscriminately into a different form. In literature, form and content are so intimately related that preachers must carefully select the appropriate form for the sermon if they would not distort the message of the text.

16. Kromminga, *CTJ* 18/1 (1983) 44.
17. Blackwood, *Preparation of Sermons*, 145.
18. Carl Zylstra, "God-Centered Preaching," 143-44.
19. Gowan, *Reclaiming the OT*, 13. Ronald Allen views the reshaping of the various biblical forms into the didactic form as a lack of appreciation for biblical forms: "The preacher takes the passage (story, poem, letter, command), runs it through the mill of discursive logic, often in categories supplied by systematic theology, and boils down the residue like so much sorghum. The sludge of the form is thrown away" ("Shaping Sermons by Language," 31).

THE NARRATIVE FORM

THE major alternative to the didactic form is the narrative form. The narrative form seems to be coming into its own today; according to George Bass, "preaching began to turn 'the narrative corner' at the beginning of the 1970s."[20] The narrative form is not entirely new, of course; witness the fact that Henry Davis in 1957 included in his listing of forms "a story told" and explained it as follows: "A sermon idea may take the form of a narrative of events, persons, actions, and words. The distinguishing feature of this form is that the idea is embodied in a structure of events and persons, rather than in a structure of verbal generalizations." Davis also observed that "nine-tenths of our preaching is verbal exposition and argument, but not one tenth of the gospel is exposition. Its ideas are mainly in the form of a story told."[21]

Today, however, some homileticians view the narrative form not merely as one sermon form among many but as *the* sermon form. For example, Eugene Lowry writes: "A sermon is not a doctrinal lecture. It is an *event-in-time*, a narrative art form more akin to a play or novel in shape than to a book. . . . I propose that we begin by regarding the sermon as a homiletical plot, a narrative art form, a sacred story."[22] But other homileticians argue for the narrative form only when the text is a biblical narrative. For example, Richard Jensen writes: "If the text 'makes its point' in story form then we ought to seriously consider constructing a sermon that is faithful to the content and the form of the biblical text. . . . Why should we de-story these stories in our sermons and simply pass on the point of the story to our listeners? Why should we rip the content out of the form as our normal homiletical process?"[23]

A Model of the Narrative Form

LIKE the didactic form, the narrative form allows for a great variety of options in sermon construction: it can present the biblical narrative, a contemporary narrative, or both; it can be with or without a theme; it can be

20. Bass, *The Song and the Story*, 83; see pp. 83-87 for a recent history of "the story sermon."

21. Davis, *Design for Preaching*, 157. Cf. p. 158: "We overestimate the power of assertion, and we underestimate the power of narrative to communicate meaning and influence the lives of our people."

22. Lowry, *Homiletical Plot*, 6. Cf. pp. 24-25: "This is the discrepancy that is the central question in every sermon. How can the gospel intersect the specifics of the human mystery and come out on the other side in resolution? This question *is* the form of the sermonic plot."

23. Jensen, *Telling the Story*, 128. Still other homileticians (see Riegert, *Consensus* 8/2 [1982] 17) understand "narrative preaching" in such broad senses ("the use of expressive language," elaboration of meanings "by such forms as stories") that it loses its specific focus.

developed inductively or deductively; it can follow the story line of the text or use another line of development. Preachers must choose from the many possibilities.

For those committed to textual-thematic preaching, some of these choices have already been made, of course. For preachers committed to *textual* preaching, the exposition of a biblical text, in this case the exposition of a biblical narrative, is a sine qua non for all preaching. That commitment rules out Jensen's proposal of "imaginative recasting," that is, that "we can . . . create and tell our own stories which elicit responses in the hearer similar to the responses to the original story."[24] Textual preaching cannot dispense with the biblical narrative as soon as "the responses to the original story" have been uncovered; on the contrary, the biblical narrative itself is the story to be proclaimed. That commitment still allows for options of telling the story first in its original setting and then retelling it in modern form, or first setting a problem with a contemporary story and following it with the biblical story as a solution, or some other variation[25]—as long as the biblical story remains the foundation of the sermon.

Similarly, for those committed to *thematic* preaching, the use of the narrative form does not at all imply the loss of a sermon theme. Jensen would, ideally, dispense with a theme because "the story is itself the preaching. At the end of the story the preacher is not required to come 'on stage' and tell the congregation, 'Now the point of this story was. . . .'" Jensen views the narrative sermon as a work of art like a play or painting which leaves the interpretation up to the audience. "The story, the novel, the play, the film, the painting etc. is the preaching itself. In its most developed form a story sermon is also the preaching itself!"[26]

Whatever helpful analogies one may draw with certain forms of art, however, one ought not to overlook that a *sermon* is not identical with a play or a novel or a painting: a sermon specifically seeks to proclaim God's past word in the present. That word as inscripturated had a normative point (theme), and that point ought to be transferred to today. It will not do, then, simply to tell a story and leave the interpretation to the hearers.[27] A sermon ought to be much more than an aesthetic experience; as a message from God, a sermon ought to leave no doubt as to its specific point. David would have missed the point of Nathan's story completely had not Nathan added the words, "You are the man" (2 Sam 12:7). Bass

24. Jensen, *Telling the Story*, 129.
25. See Wardlaw, "Eventful Sermon Shapes," 44.
26. Jensen, *Telling the Story*, 132, 130. For a similar view by Gadamer, cf. Thiselton, *Two Horizons*, 298-300.
27. See Stendahl, *JBL* 103/1 (1984) 9: "To ask poets (or artists) what they actually meant or intended with a piece of art is often an insult. . . . The more meanings the merrier. The normative nature of the Bible requires, however, a serious attention to original intentions of texts."

asserts that "the theme or thought of the sermon, as distilled from the pericope, is necessary if the sermon is to edify, as well as interest, the people who hear it." He suggests further that "development of the theme gives relevance to the message by suggesting concrete applications to life today, thereby eliminating any abstractions that might make The Story seem remote to the current-day congregation."[28] In the narrative form, too, a theme will help keep the sermon on the right track, ensure the unity of the sermon, promote movement, and focus the application.

It is an open question whether a narrative sermon should develop its theme deductively or inductively. On the one hand, inductive development is native to the narrative form and should not be changed unless one has good reasons for changing to deductive development. Moreover, withholding the theme to the very end certainly can add to the interest, involvement, and surprise of the hearers and to the effectiveness of the sermon. On the other hand, depending on text and congregation, one may well decide that the hearers will be able to appreciate the trip more if the destination is known from the beginning. At the cost of surprise but in the interest of clarity and meaningful involvement, therefore, one may well decide to develop a narrative sermon deductively.

Finally, with respect to the structure or outline of a narrative sermon, it is advantageous to follow the line of development in the text, the story line, the plot. Bass suggests that preachers ask: "'What is this incident all about?' 'What's the encounter, the conflict in it?' and . . . 'How will it turn out?' By asking such questions of the text and its plot, the preacher uncovers the story line which becomes the outline, or plan, of the story sermon. The plot offers and controls the shape that the biblical sermon will assume."[29] One can also say that "the sermon can simply unfold in the same scenes and development as the drama"[30] (see Chapters 9 and 11 below). This does not mean, however, that the sermon becomes a kind of homily where the preacher follows the order of the text and explains the verses and phrases seriatim. "Unlike the running commentary type of sermon, the biblical story sermon . . . does not give 'equal time' to each verse or every part of the biblical text; plot and theme suggest to the preacher what should be eliminated as well as what should be emphasized or highlighted."[31]

28. Bass, *The Song and the Story,* 109. Richard Lischer warns that "preachers who would be storytellers . . . should examine their sermons in light of the correlation that exists between form and goal. How many of our sermons end either in an intellectual 'understanding of' or an aesthetic 'wonder at' without echoing the ringing call to change so characteristic of New Testament and classical preaching?" (*Int* 38 [1984] 36).

29. Bass, *The Song and the Story,* 108.

30. Allen and Herin, "Moving from the Story to Our Story," 159.

31. Bass, *The Song and the Story,* 110. Cf. Achtemeier, *Creative Preaching,* 72: "Running commentary sermons often fail because they lack unity—meaning that the preacher has not seen the unity in the text."

Advantages of the Narrative Form

USING a narrative sermon form for a narrative text has several advantages. First, by using the same form as the text, one acknowledges the significance of the biblical form and is less likely to distort the text. "A holistic exegesis must be directed at both form and content. It is not enough to get the meaning *out of* the text and into the sermon. We must pay attention to the total configuration of textual form/content."[32]

Another advantage of the narrative form is that it provides the sermon almost automatically with forward movement and thus creates interest. "The sermon itself . . . moves structurally like a story. It is not static. It goes somewhere. It wrestles with a passage creating tension and dialogue, allowing the congregation's thoughts and feelings to emerge in places."[33]

A third advantage of narrative form is that it allows the hearers to be involved more holistically, to live *into* the message with their imagination rather than merely to reflect on it intellectually. The contrast between understanding intellectually and understanding holistically has to do with different modes of perception. Jensen asserts that "we have linear, rational modes of perception and we have nonrational and intuitive modes of perception." These different modes of perception are related, apparently, to the different brain hemispheres, the left hemisphere controlling "our rational, logical, sequential thought processes" and the right hemisphere controlling "our intuitive, holistic, imagistic thought processes."[34] The narrative form thus enables the hearers to be involved more holistically, not merely logically but also intuitively, not only intellectually but also emotionally.[35] As Ronald Allen elucidates graphically, "Story can cause unfelt feelings to be felt. It can bring to life, or connect forgotten thoughts. It can cause radically new perspectives on situations as stale as the air in the attic." He further observes that "the ancient listener or reader encountered the text not by having it 'explained' but by entering its world."[36] Because of the historical-cultural gap, however, contemporary readers of ancient stories experience difficulty in letting "the text speak directly to the senses." This is where preachers can provide valuable service. According to Allen, "The purpose of exegesis is to open the door to the world of the text so that we can enter it in ways that are historically, aesthetically, and otherwise appropriate. . . . Preaching, guided by re-

32. Jensen, *Telling the Story*, 129.
33. Carl, "Shaping Sermons by Structure," 124.
34. Jensen, *Telling the Story*, 123, 125.
35. Cf. Wardlaw, "Shaping Sermons by Context," 70: "Contextual sermon shapes do not so much banish reflection as they relocate pondering within the flow of narration."
36. Allen, "Shaping Sermons by Language," 39.

sponsible exegesis, hopes to place the text and the listeners in such a relationship that the import of the text comes alive in discursive and intuitive
dimensions analogous to those in which the text was alive for its ancient
recipients."[37]

A fourth, related advantage is that narrative form communicates implicitly rather than explicitly, obliquely rather than directly. Stories "work
by *indirection*," says Jensen. "The word from the text is *overheard* in
another context."[38] Craddock explains how narrative is the most effective
form for "overhearing": "A narrative is told with distance and sustains it
in that the story unfolds on its own, seemingly only casually aware of the
hearer, and yet all the while the narrative is inviting and beckoning the
listener to participation in its anticipation, struggle, and resolution."[39] By
communicating indirectly, the narrative form not only addresses the
whole person but is also able to get around defenses and communicate
where the didactic form would fail.

Pitfalls of the Narrative Form

THE narrative form has not only advantages, however; it also presents
some major pitfalls. The first pitfall is that preachers become so enchanted
by the narrative form that they adopt this as their one and only sermon
form. We have already noted that the narrative form cannot be used
successfully with every type of text; if the imposition of the didactic form
on all texts leads to the distortion of some texts, so also the imposition of
the narrative form on all texts would lead to distortion. Davis already
warned that "the story is not for everyday use as the form of the entire
sermon. It is not suitable for every kind of text or theme."[40] From another
angle, Craddock insists that narrative should never "replace rational argument in Christian discourse. Rational argument serves to keep the communication self-critical, athletically trim, and free of a sloppy sentimental-
ity that can take over in the absence of critical activity. We need always to
be warned against the use of narratives and stories to avoid the issues of
doctrine, history, and theological reflection."[41]

A second frequent pitfall in using the narrative form is that preachers

---

37. Ibid., 34-35.

38. Jensen, *Telling the Story*, 144; see pp. 142-47.

39. Craddock, *Overhearing the Gospel*, 135. Cf. Cox, *Biblical Preaching*, 23: "The text
comes alive in the sympathies, identifications, and tensions that take hold of the
hearer. . . . You can make application by a mere subtle suggestion. There is no need for
heavy-handed application on every point or for a moral tacked on at the end."

40. Davis, *Design for Preaching*, 161-62.

41. Craddock, *Overhearing the Gospel*, 135. In addition, Buttrick, *Int* 35/1 (1981) 56,
suggests that "form can be deceptive. . . . In preaching, deep structures and performa-
tive purposes take precedence over form."

isolate a story from its larger literary context in the Bible. Lischer charges: "By isolating stories from their contexts in canon, theology, church, and history, the aesthetic approach does more than ignore the historical dimension in interpretation; it atomizes the community's experience of the gospel—of which texts are organic parts."[42] Since stories are part and parcel of the Law and the Prophets, the Gospels and the Apocalypse, preachers must beware of isolating stories from their contexts in a particular book and in the Bible.

A third problem lies in the very advantage that narrative form communicates indirectly, obliquely. Since the story "speaks by suggestion rather than in direct and explicit statement," Davis observes that "it cannot rely on direct and definite assertion. A little too much 'preaching' quickly destroys the inherent force of the narrative."[43] Preachers appear to be caught here between a rock and a hard place: making the point too explicit destroys the force of the narrative, while leaving the point implicit makes the sermon vulnerable to widely divergent interpretations.

A fourth pitfall of the narrative form is that one may think that more substance is being communicated than is in fact the case. R. T. Brooks calls the story "a dangerous instrument" because "it does not always communicate the conviction intended by the story-teller, and it can delude both the teller and the hearer into believing that much has been communicated when very little in fact has."[44] Davis makes the surprising yet valid statement that a narrative sermon requires "a more active listening than that required to follow the thought of an assertive sermon," and if hearers fail in this active listening (as in our modern, Western culture they are apt to do), they will "hear nothing but the more superficial action of the story."[45] Others have pointed out that there are "some things that story cannot do": "The Gospel can indeed be told as story, but it raises further questions which cannot be answered simply by more stories"—questions such as "Is it truth or illusion?"[46]

And finally, a poorly structured or an "open-ended"[47] story can easily fail to make its point. William Carl observes: "I have discovered that sophisticated story systems and homiletical plots can obstruct the com-

42. Lischer, *Int* 38 (1984) 27.

43. Davis, *Design for Preaching*, 161.

44. Brooks, *Communicating Conviction*, 49.

45. Davis, *Design for Preaching*, 161.

46. Pennington, *Iliff Review* 37 (1980) 64. Cf. Cox, *Preaching*, 162: "People need a systematic view of the Christian faith, that is, a way of putting together all the fragmentary and fleeting insights and feelings, engendered by stories, so that they make a more or less consistent whole."

47. Jensen, *Telling the Story*, 146-47, argues for the possibility of a "radically open-ended sermon," that is, a story sermon without explanation, allowing the hearers to complete the story.

munication of the gospel if not handled in a disciplined manner. Without clear logic and theo-logic between various parts of the 'narrative' sermon, the preacher can appear to be meandering in a swamp."[48] The obvious way to avoid this pitfall is by clearly formulating a sermon theme and carefully constructing the sermon along the track laid out by the theme and story line.

TEXTUAL FORMS

FOR all their popularity, the didactic and narrative forms are not sufficient to cover all biblical texts: exclusive use of only these two forms would force an inappropriate form on some texts. In order to avoid forcing a form on a text, it is better not to bring a ready-made form to the text but to shift the initiative for the proper form of the sermon to the *text*— hence our heading "textual forms." "If the minister wants the sermon to do what the text does," says Craddock, "then he or she will want to hold on to the form, since form captures and conveys function, not only during the interpretation of the text but during the designing of the sermon as well."[49] If the text is a narrative, then the sermon ought to exhibit the characteristics of narrative; if the text is a lament, then the sermon ought to set the tone and mood conveyed by a lament; if it is teaching, then the sermon ought to be didactic in character. The point here is not, of course, slavish imitation of the form of the text, but such respect for the textual form that its spirit is not violated by the sermonic form; such respect for the textual form that its characteristic way of conveying its message becomes a mark of the sermon.[50]

The Textual Outline

INSTEAD of imposing our own (logical) order on the text, respect for the text demands that priority be given to its structure and order and that changes in that structure and order be introduced only for good reason. John Stott states that "the golden rule for sermon outlines is that each text

48. Carl, "Shaping Sermons by Structure," 125. Cf. Wardlaw, "Shaping Sermons by Context," 70: "While some preachers show sufficient skill with narrative sermons to need little or no reflective passages to aid the sermon's impact, many other preachers who attempt narrative-only sermons too often leave their hearers stranded in the story line for lack of clarity about the sermon's intent." Cf. Davis, *Design for Preaching*, 176.

49. Craddock, *Preaching*, 123.

50. Cf. Davis, *Design for Preaching*, 9: "A right form can never be imposed on any sermon. If it has to be imposed it is not right. The right form derives from the substance of the message itself, is inseparable from the content, becomes one with the content, and gives a feeling of finality to the sermon." Cf. also Allen, "Shaping Sermons by Language," 35-36.

must be allowed to supply its own structure. The skilful expositor opens up his text, or rather permits it to open itself up before our eyes."[51] Dividing the text into its component parts has been likened to splitting a precious stone along its natural lines: the preacher "touched it [the text] with a silver hammer, and it immediately broke up into natural and memorable divisions."[52] In Chapter 3 we saw how the ancient authors provided their hearers with literary clues to discern these divisions. Preachers today can use these structural patterns for outlining the structure of the text. For example, chiasm clearly reveals the natural structure of the text, its points of development, and its focal point. Repetition of a word or phrase may also mark a new subdivision. Scenes in narratives also form natural divisions. Perry Yoder provides further hints for discerning the structure of the preaching-text:

> Read the unit to see how many major parts or segments there are in it; where are the 'breaks' or 'joints' in the unit? . . .
> Search to see if there are phrases or words which may indicate subsections. . . .
> Look for breaks or changes in the style. . . .
> Look for changes in the type or function of the material. . . .
> Finally, . . . find the different story units or scenes in a narrative, or topical points in an argument which represent subdivisions.[53]

The Sermon Outline

THE sermon outline should honor the outline of the text, that is, it should seek to retain the focus, emphases, and order of the text. Frequently, however, the sermon outline will need to be quite different from the outline of the text, for the *sermon* outline seeks to structure the text's message in the context of the whole Bible as it applies to the church today. In other words, the composing of a sermon outline is guided not only by the outline of the text but also by the theme and purpose of the sermon. Moreover, contemporary sermons cannot simply copy ancient chiastic structures, for example, but ought to use structures that can communicate in this day and age.

Craddock lists various forms that "have demonstrated repeatedly that

---

51. Stott, *Between Two Worlds*, 229. Cf. Barth, *Preaching of the Gospel*, 81-82. Cf. also Blackwood, *Preaching from the Bible*, 37: "The textual sermon, in the technical sense, is one in which the structure follows the order of the ideas in the text."

52. Stott, *Between Two Worlds*, 230, quoting Wm. R. Nicoll regarding Alexander McLaren. Cf. Stuart, *OT Exegesis*, 35, 36: "The outline should be a natural, not artificial, outgrowth of the passage. . . . Any biblical passage whose limits have been properly identified will have a self-consistent logic made up of meaningful thought patterns."

53. Yoder, *From Word to Life*, 60-61.

they can carry the burden of truth with clarity, thoroughness, and interest, and, therefore, have come to be regarded as standard":

> What is it? What is it worth? How does one get it?
> Explore, explain, apply
> The problem, the solution
> What it is not, what it is
> Either/or
> Both/and
> Promise/fulfillment
> Ambiguity, clarity
> Major premise, minor premise, conclusion
> Not this, nor this, nor this, nor this, but this
> The flashback (from present to past to present)
> From the lesser, to the greater.[54]

Since most of these forms are found in the Bible,[55] chances are that one of them is particularly suited for the selected preaching-text. If not, another form may need to be devised, for the object is to present the sermon in a form that will do justice to the text as well as to the purpose and theme of the sermon.

Whatever form is chosen, all sermons ought to aim at the clarity, pointedness, and coherence of the didactic form and the vividness, movement, and total listener involvement of the narrative form. In practice this requirement means that within the overall form of the sermon, preachers may wish to incorporate other forms: narrative portions in a didactic sermon and discreet teaching in a narrative sermon. For no matter what form is used, the sermon ought to address the whole person; the sermon ought to be "life-size in the sense of touching all the keys on the board rather than only intellectual or emotional or volitional."[56]

---

54. Craddock, *Preaching*, 176-77. See Stott, *Between Two Worlds*, 230-31, for the five sermon forms suggested by Sangster and ten by Luccock.

55. Craddock, *Preaching*, 176-80, identifies 1 Cor 11:17-34 as problem/solution, Hebrews as constantly arguing from the lesser to the greater, as does Luke 16:10-12; Josh 24:14-15, Matt 7:13-14, and Luke 16:10-12 as either/or.

56. Craddock, *Overhearing the Gospel*, 137. Allen and Herin, "Moving from the Story," 159, suggest that for textual forms such as law codes, prophetic oracles, and wisdom sayings, "it is sometimes vivid and useful to sketch the story out of which the saying grew rather than to plunk it down in the pulpit like a chicken without feathers."

CHAPTER 8

The Relevance of the Sermon

WITHOUT genuine relevance there is no sermon. Relevance for the church here and now is the final goal of sermon preparation, yet sermons that have remained on the right track through the process of text selection, theme formulation, and form selection often derail at the point where the message for Israel or the early church must be transformed into a relevant sermon for contemporary congregations. In this chapter we shall seek to discern where and why sermons derail in applying the message and how we can keep the sermon on track right to its final destination.

In discussing the relevance of the sermon, we shift our focus toward the congregation. We cannot, of course, shift our attention exclusively to the congregation because the sermon must hold the horizons of text and congregation together. The sermon has been described as "an ellipse with two foci: the text of the Bible and the situation of the hearers. . . . Preparing and delivering a sermon means that these two foci have to be interrelated in a process of continual reciprocity."[1] Therefore, as one cannot select a text, formulate a sermon theme, and select a sermon form without an eye to the congregation, so one cannot reflect on the relevance of the sermon without an eye to the text—it is, after all, the relevance of the *text* that must lend relevance to the sermon.

Lest the question of relevance start off on the wrong foot, it is important to recognize further that preachers are not called to *make* a text relevant. To formulate the issue in terms of making the text relevant is "self-

---

1. Runia, *TynBul* 29 (1978) 41. Ian Pitt-Watson makes a similar point with the vivid imagery of a bowstring: "Every sermon is stretched like a bowstring between the text of the Bible on the one hand and the problems of contemporary human life on the other. If the string is insecurely tethered to either end, the bow is useless" (*Preaching*, 57); cf. idem, *Primer*, 46-55, on "exegesis of the text of life."

defeating from the start." If the preaching-text is not relevant, "no technique, however conscientiously and enthusiastically applied, will *make* it so," says Lawrence Toombs. If the text *is* relevant, however, the task of preachers is not to make the text relevant but to *show* "the relevance already inherent in the passage."[2] The key issue here is that preachers see the Bible for what it is, kerygma, proclamation, address, and that they therefore approach the Bible as the relevant word of God—spoken originally, to be sure, to people worlds removed from us, but nevertheless as a relevant word for that situation. The task of preachers, then, is to search "deeply enough into the text and its original situation and intentions to *find* its relevance."[3] The resulting problem facing preachers with respect to relevance is not that of *making* the text relevant but that of transferring a relevant message from the past to the present.

Even though recognizing the text's past relevance puts a different face on the problem of preparing a relevant sermon, the actual problem should not be underestimated. For in transferring a relevant message from the past to the present, preachers will need to cross the historical-cultural gap that separates the world of the text from our contemporary world. James Smart calls it a "perilous road from then to now, perilous because there are so many ways in which he [the preacher] can lose the essential content of his text (or can lose his listeners) in the course of the journey. The broad gap between then and now is the region in which so many students and preachers get lost. Their training in seminary was much more concentrated on the 'then' than on how to get from then to now."[4] Consequently, it will be worthwhile to discuss in some detail both improper and proper ways of bridging the historical-cultural gap.

THE HISTORICAL-CULTURAL GAP

The Challenge of the Gap

CRADDOCK describes the historical-cultural gap as "the geographical, linguistic, psychological, cosmological and chronological gulf between the ancient Near East and modern America."[5] Usually this gap is perceived as an obstacle to relevant preaching—and that it is—but one can also view the gap much more positively. Morna Hooker remarks that "the gospel must be expressed in our own language and culture and situation if it is to be relevant. Its expression will naturally vary from century to century, country to country, person to person."[6] These different historical-cultural

---

2. Toombs, *Int* 23 (1969) 303.
3. Stendahl, "Preaching from the Pauline Epistles," 307.
4. Smart, *Strange Silence of the Bible*, 34.
5. Craddock, *As One Without Authority*, 117.
6. Hooker, *Epworth Review* 3/1 (1976) 54.

expressions can be observed in the Bible itself, as a comparison between the Old and the New Testaments or between the Gospels will show. Consequently, the historical-cultural gap is not merely an obstacle for understanding the message today but evidence of the fact that the biblical text was *relevant* in the past—it addressed a specific people's needs in a historical-cultural form which was immediately understood. In other words, the historical-cultural gap we perceive from our vantage point is accounted for by the fact that the word of God indeed entered history in a relevant way. If preachers today wish to address their contemporary hearers with the word of God in an equally relevant way, they have no choice but to carry the message across the gap to the present historical-cultural situation. Instead of an obstacle to relevant preaching, therefore, the historical-cultural gap can be viewed as a challenge to preach the message just as relevantly today as it was in the past. The challenge is to let the word of God address people today just as explicitly and concretely as it did in biblical times. As John Stott puts it: "It is across this broad and deep divide of two thousand years of changing culture (more still in the case of the Old Testament) that Christian communicators have to throw bridges. Our task is to enable God's revealed truth to flow out of the Scriptures into the lives of the men and women of today."[7]

Unfortunately, in the laudable attempt to be relevant, many sermons fail to bridge the gap properly and as a result come to ruin. It will be instructive first to examine some of these faulty efforts.

Improper Ways of Bridging the Gap

Allegorizing
Probably the oldest way of trying to bridge the historical-cultural gap is the way of allegorizing. This method of interpretation "arose among the pagan Greeks, [was] copied by the Alexandrian Jews, was next adopted by the Christian church and largely dominated exegesis until the Reformation."[8] The allegorical method searches beneath the literal meaning of a passage for the "real" meaning. For example, the Song of Solomon may be understood as expressing not the love between a man and a woman but the love between Christ and the church. Or the parable of the Good Samaritan may be interpreted in the fashion of Origen: the traveler (Adam) journeys from Jerusalem (heaven) to Jericho (the world) and is assaulted by robbers (the devil and his helpers). The priest (the law) and the Levite (the prophets) pass by without aiding the fallen Adam, but the Samaritan (Christ) stops to help him, sets him on his beast (Christ's body)

---

7. Stott, *Between Two Worlds*, 138.
8. Ramm, *Protestant Biblical Interpretation*, 28. Cf. pp. 24-45.

and brings him to an inn (the church), giving the innkeeper two denarii (the Father and the Son), and promising to come back (Christ's second coming).[9]

Although the method is largely discredited today, preachers desperately trying to cross the gap with a worthwhile contemporary message are still known to fall back on it—not in a flagrant way, usually, but by allegorizing a few elements of a passage. For example, what is a preacher to do with the narrative of the wedding at Cana (John 2:1-11)? It has been suggested that the point of this narrative for today is, "Where we are at the end of our resources, where we have no wine, where we cannot rescue ourselves from our predicament, Jesus manifests his glory (i.e. the saving presence and action of God)."[10] Most will agree that allegorizing is a bridge from then to now that fails to bear the weight of the text: it fails to bring across the plain meaning of a passage in its historical context and thus falsifies the message.

Spiritualizing

A bridge very similar to allegorizing but apparently much more acceptable is spiritualizing. Spiritualizing takes place when the preacher discards the earthly, physical, historical reality the text speaks about and crosses the gap with a spiritual analogy of that historical reality. For example, Gen 37:24 is interpreted as follows: "Joseph is thrown by his brothers into a pit—a dreadful physical fact. But morally and spiritually, too, it may often seem that the soul of man is in a pit."[11] The problem with being thrown into a pit, apparently, is that that "dreadful physical fact" will not cross the gap because the preacher's hearers have not been thrown into a pit by their brothers. But by spiritualizing that experience, at least that element will transfer for instant application because contemporary hearers, being depressed sometimes, can relate to being spiritually or mentally in a pit. Or take the narrative of Jesus stilling the storm (Mark 4:35-41): since not too many of the hearers will find themselves threatened by a destructive, roaring storm on a foaming, raging sea, for the sake of instant application the storm and the sea are spiritualized to "storms" on the "sea of life": "Jesus whose trust in God was not deceived is still present amid the storms and stresses of life."[12] Other examples of spiritualiz-

9. Stanton, "Presuppositions in NT Criticism," 63.

10. Fuller, *Interpreting the Miracles*, 117-18. Note that with allegorizing the historicity of the event no longer plays a role; cf. p. 118: "The changing of water into wine is not something that happened long ago: it is something that happens in our midst, as we become new creatures in Christ."

11. W. R. Bowie in *IB*, I, 754.

12. C. E. Johnson, *Verbum Vocale*, 239, referring to V. Taylor, *The Gospel According to St. Mark*, 2nd ed. (repr. Grand Rapids: Baker, 1981), 273; and H. E. Luccock in *IB*, 7, 708-11.

ing abound. "Jacob's physical struggle at Peniel becomes our spiritual struggle; the physical blindness of the two men in Matthew 9 becomes our spiritual blindness; the woman's reaching to touch the border of Jesus' garment becomes our spiritual reaching to touch the spiritual Jesus; and the Cana wedding invitation to the earthly Jesus becomes our invitation to the heavenly Jesus."[13]

Like allegorizing, spiritualizing is also a bridge that fails to bear the weight of the text as is evident both in the discarding of the physical reality and in the transfer of only one or two elements of the text (why only the pit and not the brothers, the stripping, the robe, etc.?). In not doing justice to the text in its historical context, spiritualizing does not preach the message of the text but deforms it. Moreover, the elements that are spiritualized and the parallels that are drawn to the hearers today are subjective and rather arbitrary choices. On several counts, therefore, spiritualizing fails to do justice to the text, and its use undermines the authority of the sermon.

Imitating Bible Characters

A very popular way across the historical-cultural gap is that of imitating the characters in the Bible passage. We are not dealing here with the question of using Bible characters for illustrative purposes but with the question of using the characters in the preaching-text as examples or models for imitation. This way of crossing the gap also has credentials going back as far as the ancient Greeks, and it is still found today in sermons,[14] Bible introductions, and commentaries. For instance, one commonly hears today that the patriarchs are "examples of universal human attitudes toward life": "Abraham exemplifies the man of faith, even though his faith fails on one occasion; Isaac exemplifies the patient and accepting man; Jacob exemplifies the man of steadfast hope, who at first tries to realize his expectations in all too human fashion, but is later portrayed as the man who hopes and trusts in God. The Joseph novella shows even more clearly Joseph's spiritual development from pride to humility. In this way the narratives . . . apply to man in every age."[15]

Christian preachers realize, of course, that the biblical characters are presented not as ideal persons and examples but as sinful creatures with warts and all. This realistic biblical portrayal forces preachers who insist on imitating biblical "examples" to make a judgment whether a particular action is good or bad. But to make this judgment is more difficult than

13. See my *Sola Scriptura*, 77.

14. See Toombs, *Int* 23 (1969) 307: "Many preachers deal with the great figures of the Bible in a manner thoroughly Greek, holding them up as timeless exemplars and practitioners of eternally valid moral principles." See also my *Sola Scriptura*, 8-18.

15. Fohrer, *Introduction to the OT*, 95.

may appear at first sight. If the author does not make this judgment for his hearers, is one still on the right track in trying to make such a moral judgment? And by what standards does one judge an action to be good or bad? Old Testament standards? New Testament standards? Contemporary standards? Suppose that one comes to the conclusion that a specific action was good at that time, does that mean that one can recommend imitation of that action today? Should one recommend that the poor today deposit their last pennies in the collection plate (Luke 21:2)? That Christians today have their possessions "in common" (Acts 2:44-45)? That all must have an eye-blinding conversion experience (Acts 9:3-9)? That women must be veiled when praying (1 Cor 11:6)? Clowney observes: "Those who find only collected moral tales in the Bible are constantly embarrassed by the *good* deeds of patriarchs, judges, and kings. Surely we cannot pattern our daily conduct on that of Samuel as he hews Agag to pieces, or Samson as he commits suicide, or Jeremiah as he preaches treason. Judged by our usual ethics, Michal was quite right in despising David's performance before the ark, and Judas in criticizing the extravagance of Mary's use of perfume in Bethany."[16]

In spite of these difficulties, imitating Bible characters remains a popular way of trying to *make* the text relevant. "The life experiences of Bible people," Faris Whitesell claims, "illustrate certain timeless and universal truths which preachers can apply to life today."[17] Andrew Blackwood recommends that young ministers prepare once a month a "biographical sermon": "The biographical sermon is one which grows out of the facts concerning a biblical character, as these facts throw light upon the problems of the man in the pew. For instance, on Mother's Day one can preach about the way in which God watched over Baby Moses, and used his mother in sparing him for his life work. . . . In the resulting sermon . . . one can hold aloft the biblical ideal of motherhood."[18]

Unfortunately, this popular way to relevance is strewn with problems. As commonly used, this method has not even begun to ask the question of how to bridge the gap; it simply ignores the gap by drawing a historical equation mark between then and now, between Moses' mother and mothers today, between Jacob and us, between Thomas and us: we are Thomas, we are Mary, we are Peter. In the process of this simple identification, the forward movement of history and revelation is ignored, the lit-

16. Clowney, *Preaching and Biblical Theology*, 80.
17. Whitesell, *Preaching on Bible Characters*, 15. Countless books have appeared on preaching on Bible characters; see the bibliography in Perry, *Manual for Biblical Preaching*, 107. According to Stuart, *OT Exegesis*, 73, "This monkey-see-monkey-do sort of approach to applying the Scriptures is very widely followed, largely because of the dearth of good pulpit teaching to the contrary."
18. Blackwood, *Preaching from the Bible*, 52-53.

erary context in which the Bible characters function is largely disregarded, and the uniqueness of each of the Bible characters, their actions and attitudes, is overlooked.[19]

Another problem with imitating Bible characters is that it tends to transform the biblical author's *description* into *prescription* for today. Should not the question be raised if this was the author's intention? Did he *describe* these characters in order to *prescribe* a certain behavior to his readers? Donald Gowan observes correctly that "most of the Bible quite clearly does not present other human beings to us as models of behavior, although there are some exceptions to that."[20]

Moreover, biographical preaching, character preaching, and the use of human "examples" for imitation tends to shift the theocentric focus of the Bible to an anthropocentric focus in the sermon. "The major function of the OT story is to relate how God has acted, despite the acts of men as much as through them," asserts John Goldingay. "To concentrate on the human deed, then, is often to miss the point of it. Indeed, it is not merely to misuse it: it is to bring a message that is its opposite."[21]

Imitating Bible characters, though popular and superficially easy, is a dead-end road for true biblical preaching. It is a homiletical shortcut that results in a hermeneutical short circuit (see Chapter 9 below). "A legitimate 're-presentation,'" Martin Noth writes, "cannot use the individual human figures of biblical history as its subjects, either as ethical 'models,' which they in fact never are, or as exemplary 'heroes of faith' since in the biblical narratives they are never so presented, or as representatives of true humanity whose experiences . . . are to be imitated."[22]

Moralizing

Another popular bridge across the historical-cultural gap is moralizing. "Moralizing means drawing moral inferences, usually things to do or become."[23] Preachers who use moralizing as a way to relevance are often guided by a genuine desire to set forth the legitimate ethical demands of the Bible. Unfortunately, in overemphasizing virtues and vices, dos and don'ts, and in not properly grounding these ethical demands in the Scrip-

---

19. Goldingay, *Approaches to OT Interpretation*, 40, writes: "The particular decisions that OT characters had to make were unique to them, as every man's decisions are, so their action cannot be directly relevant to another situation." Cf. Clowney, "Preaching Christ," 187: "We dare not preach David's encounter with Goliath as an example of bravery to be emulated in our conflicts with the 'giants' that assault us. Such an approach trivializes the Old Testament revelation." For an extensive analysis and critique of this method, see my *Sola Scriptura*, 56-120.

20. Gowan, *Reclaiming the OT*, 17.

21. Goldingay, *Approaches to OT Interpretation*, 39.

22. Noth, "'Re-presentation' of the OT in Proclamation," 86.

23. Keck, *Bible in the Pulpit*, 101.

tures, they trivialize them and turn them into caricatures. William Willimon claims that "perhaps the most frequent modern interpretive pitfall is moralizing. . . . The pastor, in an attempt to be relevant . . . , turns every text into some simplistic, moralistic program."[24]

Moralizing is often associated with biographical or character preaching. For instance, Whitesell suggests that in biographical preaching "the preacher can discuss the evil effects of worldliness in the life of Lot, of carnality in the career of Esau, of stubbornness in Moses, of sensuality in David, and be hitting at the same sins in his own congregation without seeming to do so intentionally."[25] A clear example of moralizing is the insistence of one preacher to use 2 Sam 18:31-33, David weeping over his son Absalom, as an occasion for "relevant" remarks about parenting: "The example of this lamenting father is a warning call to all Christian parents to take the upbringing of their children seriously as long as they have the opportunity, lest they too must cry out their despair in a similar bitter lament when the grave of their children is being dug and it is too late."[26] Anyone who is the least bit sensitive to this moving story will experience such a "moral" as a foreign intrusion which is tacked on to an element in the text but misses and detracts from the point of the story.

Moralizing usually fails to bring across the actual point and intention of the text. We saw in Chapter 6 that, though many of the elements of one text may be the same as those of another, each text is unique in the way the elements are combined—the one may be H_2O (water) and the other H_2SO_4 (sulfuric acid). Moralizing tends to draw the moral inferences from isolated elements, such as H or O, without much concern for the specific combination which makes the point of the text. For example, a sermon on John 21:15-19 has three points based on three elements in the text, and each element is carried across the gap by moralizing:

   I. Jesus' Question: "Do you love me . . . ?" → Do we love him?
   II. Peter's Answer: "Yes, Lord . . ."   → This should be our answer!
   III. Jesus' Command: "Feed my sheep."   → We have a task.

Another sermon, on Acts 3:1-12, is even more selective in picking some and not other textual elements in order to present a few imperatives for today:

   v. 4: "Peter directed his gaze at   →   We must give full attention to
   him" (the lame man).   people in need.
   vv. 9-10: People saw change in   →   Do people see change in us?
   the healed man.

---

24. Willimon, *Preaching*, 71.
25. Whitesell, *Preaching on Bible Characters*, 21.
26. Ph. J. Huyser, *Gereformeerd Theologisch Tijdschrift* 50 (1950) 216, as translated in my *Sola Scriptura*, 80.

v. 12: Peter preached.   →   We must preach![27]

Moralizing not only misses the point of the text by transferring mere elements but also by transforming the *de*scription of past people into *pre*scription for people today. Surely the question must be raised: Is this indeed the intention of the text? Was this the author's purpose for his original audience? Moreover, like character preaching, moralizing tends to transform the theocentric focus of the Bible into anthropocentric sermons. In doing so, it can easily turn grace into law by presenting imperatives without the divine indicative. Moralizing, writes Leander Keck, "has the effect of transforming the Bible into an assortment of moral precepts and examples. The Bible's own agenda is replaced. . . . The Bible's own way of thinking is sidetracked."[28]

And yet, the Bible makes ethical demands which sermons should undoubtedly pass on. How can one tell whether one is passing on legitimate ethical demands or merely moralizing? Carl Kromminga makes some helpful distinctions between moralizing and proclaiming the legitimate ethical demands of a passage:

> First, moralism easily overlooks the author's intention and the divine intention in narrating a given event, or it allows that intention to play only a subsidiary role in the application of the message to life. The *revelational* scope of the text is narrowed to fit the preacher's easy exploitation of the apparent surface "lesson" of the text. The larger themes of revelation which shape the story in its context are for the most part ignored. Second, the *ethical* scope of the text is consequently also narrowed. The broad structures of covenant, theocracy, and holy office, and the ethical responsibilities which they imply, are usually sacrificed to the interpreter's urgent desire to find a limited exemplary moral lesson in the narrative. Third, by narrowing both the revelational and ethical dimensions of the text, the moralistic approach feeds religious individualism and tends to diminish the church's sense of corporate responsibility for God's cause and work in the world and in history.[29]

Moralizing, too, is a bridge that cannot bear the weight of the text. In carrying only a few moral demands across the gap, it is reductionistic;

---

27. Both sermons heard in Grand Rapids, Michigan, in 1979. Cf., e.g., the exposition of H. E. Luccock, *IB*, 7, 708-11, on Mark 4:35-41:

[35] Let Us Go Across to the Other Side. . . . Have we kept the lure which the horizon had for Jesus? . . .

[36] And Leaving the Crowd. . . . Are we able to leave a crowd in our personal life? . . .

[37] And They . . . Said to Him, 'Teacher, Do You Not Care if We Perish?' . . . Instead of rushing to communicate our panic to him, we should allow him to communicate his calm to us. . . .

[39] And There Was a Great Calm. . . . If Christ is on the ship, . . . there can come calm instead of storm.

28. Keck, *Bible in the Pulpit*, 102-3.
29. Kromminga, *CTJ* 18/1 (1983) 38.

what is worse, in presenting those morals as the relevance of the text, it distorts the message of the text. According to Keck, "Moralizing has got to go! It ruins the preacher, it obscures the gospel, it distorts the history of biblical groups and communities, and it inhibits the Bible from coming through on its own terms. There has got to be a better way."[30]

CONSIDERATIONS FOR PROPERLY BRIDGING THE GAP

Concentrate on the Original Message

OUR discussion of improper ways of bridging the historical-cultural gap shows that one of the major pitfalls of application is that preachers transfer isolated elements of the text rather than its specific message. Although this practice creates the impression of relevance, it is only pseudo-relevance, for historically the relevance of the text inhered not in the separate elements but in the combination of elements as these formed the specific message which was proclaimed to the original hearers/readers. In order to retain that original relevance and authority, preachers ought to adhere to that original message also in their application.

Concentration on the original message will keep the sermon from being sidetracked by all kinds of "practical" remarks that may be related to elements in the text but have nothing to do with the intended message. For example, concentration on the original message will show that the story of Joseph being thrown into a pit was not intended to be linked to our "pits" of depression, that the information about Moses' mother was not given to teach us about the ideals of motherhood, and that David's lamenting the death of Absalom was not recorded to teach us a lesson on parenting. Douglas Stuart rightly insists: "Unless you are convinced that it is the *intention* of the Scripture that it be applied in a certain way, no suggestion as to application can be confidently advanced."[31]

Concentration on the original message is the only way toward valid application. Before one can determine the meaning of a text for today, one must know what the writer intended to convey to his original hearers/readers. Kromminga writes that "this is crucial to the matter of application. The application to our times will take a different shape, but the original hearers, as they were addressed in the text, are the initial recipients of the revelation and its claims. If I am not to distort the Scriptures, I must reach my hearers today with the message of the text *by way of* its meaning directed to and (to the extent the Bible discloses this) grasped by the first hearers."[32] In order to determine responsible applica-

30. Keck, *Bible in the Pulpit*, 105.
31. Stuart, *OT Exegesis*, 73.
32. Kromminga, *CTJ* 18/1 (1983) 41. Cf. Richard, *BSac* 143 (1986) 207.

tion for today, therefore, the questions that beg to be answered first are: What issues did the author seek to address? What questions did he seek to answer? What is the specific message he proclaimed? That relevant message, as summarized in a thematic statement, should be transferred to today. As we saw in Chapter 6, this procedure does not imply that the text's theme necessarily becomes the sermon's theme, but the text's theme (message) is the unit that is to be confronted with the question, So what? What does this mean for today?

Before we look at further steps, it may be helpful to sketch the contrast between transferring *elements* of the text across the historical-cultural gap and my proposal of transferring only the original *message*. Transferring elements can be visualized as elements being carried across apart from their specific combination in a particular text:

Text   Today
Element H → → → → → → → → → → H′
Element H → → → → → → → → → → H′
Element O → → → → → → → → → → O′

Transferring the *message*, by contrast, may be visualized as carrying across the gap the historical, relevant point of the text:

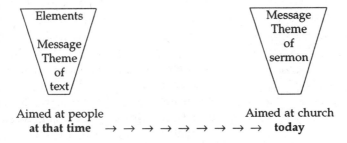

Aimed at people   Aimed at church
at that time → → → → → → → → → **today**

Recognize the Discontinuity

IN transferring the message of the text to the church today, the message needs to pass through various levels of discontinuity that may necessitate changes in the message. We can distinguish at least three levels where discontinuity may make a difference: the levels of revelation, kingdom history, and culture.

Progressive Revelation

First, the original message of the text will have to be traced throughout the Scriptures. Since revelation progresses within the Testaments and especially from the Old to the New Testament, and since preachers must aim the message at New Testament congregations in the twentieth century, the theme of the text must be traced from Genesis 1 to Revelation 22 before one can confidently assert that this is God's word for today. In comparing Scripture with Scripture, some original messages need not be changed appreciably while others will need to be changed considerably. Jesus himself compared Scripture with Scripture when, being questioned about divorce (Matt 19:3-9), he contrasted the teaching of Deuteronomy 24 with that of Genesis 1 and 2 and changed the teaching in the process. A sermon on Gen 17:9-14 would have to change the original message drastically because of progressive revelation. In this passage God demands covenant keeping in terms of circumcising all males: "Any uncircumcised male . . . shall be cut off from his people; he has broken my covenant." The New Testament, especially Acts 15, changes this message in an astonishing way. Another central Old Testament passage that undergoes an amazing, albeit gradual, change in the New Testament is the commandment to rest on the *seventh* day (Exod 20:8-11; see Col 2:16; Rom 14:5). One can think further of all the laws regarding animal sacrifices—laws which are fulfilled in Christ's supreme sacrifice but which may not on that account be discarded, since they also point forward to our obligation to sacrifice ourselves (Rom 12:1; 1 Pet 2:5). Until one has understood the message of the text in the context of the whole canon, one cannot claim to have heard the word of God for the church today.

Stages of Kingdom History

Discontinuity also takes place at the level of the different stages of kingdom history at which the text and the sermon are aimed. The message of the text was addressed to people living either before Christ or shortly after his death and resurrection. By contrast, preachers today aim their sermons neither at an Old Testament congregation nor at the early church but at the church in the twentieth century. The largest amount of discontinuity will be present, of course, when the text is originally aimed at people in Old Testament times and the sermon needs to address people in the twentieth century; one must then do justice both to the progression of revelation into the New Testament and the fact that the hearers live twenty centuries after Easter and Pentecost. But discontinuity exists even when the text is addressed to the early New Testament church and the sermon must be proclaimed to the church today. For example, a sermon on Rom 13:1-7 will have to take into account that the church today does not live in the time of the Roman empire but in a modern democracy or a fickle dictatorship waiting for the next coup. And a sermon on Paul's instructions to slaves and masters (e.g., Eph 6:5-9), though applicable to employers and employees today, will have to take into account that church and society today no longer accept slavery as an economic fact.

In extending biblical lines from first-century issues to contemporary issues such as nuclear warfare, ecology, population explosion, the role of women, etc., one may have to follow the trajectory of biblical teaching beyond the New Testament, so that the message today will be as current and relevant as when it was first given. Perry Yoder warns that if we do not take seriously "that all words are given in a specific context and are shaped to that context . . . , our application may be more a repeating of an earlier culture and its own limitations than a realization of God's will for us today in a different setting."[33] Of course, the further one extends the trajectory of biblical teaching beyond the New Testament, the more careful one must be that one indeed follows the direction of Scripture and not private or public current opinion.

Cultural changes

A final area of discontinuity is that of cultural changes. At this level also, discontinuity will be most pronounced between the ancient, Near Eastern, agricultural society of the Old Testament and modern, Western, post-industrial societies. But one should not overlook the discontinuity between the first-century, Near Eastern, agricultural society of the New Testament and modern societies. For example, the essence of Jesus' command that we "ought to wash one another's feet" (John 13:14) is missed today when we literally wash one another's feet on Maundy Thursday. Because of the change in customs, roads, transportation, and footwear, one cannot simply proclaim the same message Jesus proclaimed but must transform it into twentieth-century deeds of humble service if one wishes to make the same point in our culture. Similarly, Paul's instruction in 1 Cor 11:5 that women ought to wear a veil runs into cultural discontinuity, as does his admonition to "greet one another with a holy kiss" (2 Cor 13:12). Cultural changes do not negate the original message but make transformation in the light of our present culture mandatory.

Recognize the Overarching Continuity

DISCONTINUITY by itself would stop relevant biblical preaching dead in its tracks. Happily, discontinuity functions not by itself but within an overarching continuity. We can observe this continuity in at least two areas.

One Faithful God

The God who introduced himself to Moses as "I am who I am" is the source of all continuity we experience on earth. Yahweh is the faithful covenant God who guarantees the continuity of the seasons, "seedtime and harvest, cold and heat" (Gen 8:22). When Yahweh later makes

33. Yoder, *From Word to Life*, 39.

covenant with Abraham, he again proves himself to be faithful to his promises and constant in his covenant demands. In contrast to the many pagan gods, differing from one country to another and from land to river to sea, Deut 6:4 proclaims: "Hear, O Israel: Yahweh our God, Yahweh is one." And because Yahweh is one, he can demand our undivided devotion wherever we are in the world and at whatever stage of history we live: "You shall love Yahweh your God with all your heart, and with all your soul, and with all your might" (v. 5). God is faithful and dependable, then as well as now. As James puts it in the New Testament, "The Father of the heavenly lights . . . does not change like shifting shadows" (1:17, NIV). Hebrews 13:8 makes a similar confession concerning Jesus Christ: "Jesus Christ is the same yesterday and today and for ever."

The continuity between the message for the first hearers and that for the church today will be readily apparent when we consider that it is the same God who upholds the world now as well as then, the same God who provides seedtime and harvest, the same God who acts in history in redemption and judgment, the same God who desires to save his people and demands their loyalty. In other words, once we have caught the theocentric focus of the text—what it reveals about *God's* acts, *God's* promises, *God's* will (see Chapter 5 above)—we have caught hold of the continuity that allows for meaningful application today in spite of discontinuity, for the triune God is constant, steadfast, faithful, the same today as he was in the distant past.

One should not allow continuity to minimize the obvious discontinuity, of course. There is indeed discontinuity between the way the kingdom of God manifested itself in the theocracy of Israel and the way in which it manifests itself today, but this discontinuity takes place within the continuity of the one coming kingdom of God. There is indeed discontinuity in history between B.C. and A.D., but this discontinuity consists of stages in the universal kingdom history (see Chapter 4 above). There is indeed discontinuity between the old covenant and the new covenant, but this discontinuity functions within the continuity of the one covenant of grace. There is indeed discontinuity between the covenant stipulations of the old covenant and those of the new covenant, but this discontinuity comes to expression in the context of the continuity of God's law: "You shall love the Lord your God with all your heart, and with all your soul, and with all your mind. . . . And . . . you shall love your neighbor as yourself. On these two commandments *depend all the law and the prophets*" (Matt 22:37-40).

In his constancy and faithfulness, therefore, God provides continuity with his unchanging redemptive purposes: in bringing in his kingdom, in establishing his covenant, in promising salvation, and in demanding obedience. Because of that continuity, God's word to people in a bygone age can be meaningfully transferred and proclaimed to people today.

One Covenant People

In addition to the continuity provided by God's faithfulness throughout the ages, one should also recognize the continuity between the ancient recipients of God's word and the church today. Note that at this point we are *not* comparing, as is customary, Bible characters with people today, for that comparison is a homiletical shortcut that leads to imitating Bible characters, moralizing, and the construction of other flimsy bridges between then and now. If we wish to take seriously the proposal that we can discover the relevance of the text for today only by way of its original relevance, then we ought not to begin by comparing Bible characters with people today and arrive at an application before the process of interpretation has even begun. The prior question is, How did the *original recipients* understand this passage? How was it relevant for preexilic Israel or postexilic Israel? How did it speak to Christians in Rome or Ephesus? It may be helpful to think of every Bible book as a letter written to a specific people: 1 Corinthians is a letter, but so is Matthew, and Isaiah, and Genesis—a letter at least in the sense that each is a document addressed to specific people. Accordingly, one ought to begin not by comparing Bible characters with people today but by comparing those who first heard or read the letter (message) with those who hear the letter today. In other words, the comparison should be made between the original recipients of the book and contemporary recipients.

In spite of the discontinuity between God's people in the past and God's people today, we are all God's people—covenant people. This continuity between Israel and Christians today is established in Christ. Paul writes to the Ephesians: "Remember that you were at that time separated from Christ, alienated from the commonwealth of Israel, and strangers to the covenants of promise, having no hope and without God in the world. But now in Christ Jesus you who once were far off have been brought near in the blood of Christ" (2:12-13). Faith in Jesus Christ makes people today covenant people of God just like Israel of old. For "if you are Christ's, then you are Abraham's offspring, heirs according to promise" (Gal 3:29; cf. 1 Pet 2:9-10).

In spite of various discontinuities, therefore, God's word addressed to Israel is meaningful for the church today because recipients then as well as now are people of the same covenant of grace. In a very real sense we are the same people, created and redeemed by the same God, sharing the same faith, living in the same hope, seeking to demonstrate the same love. Because of this common denominator of covenant people, one can draw analogies between the recipients of God's word in the past and congregations today and thus discover the relevance of the Old Testament word for the contemporary church. Elizabeth and Paul Achtemeier emphasize rightly that "this correspondence, this analogy between Old Israel and the new, has as its sole basis the salvation history, in which the church is understood as the realization of that new people of God, created in Christ, which was promised in the Old Testament. . . . They cannot be compared on the grounds that men are the same in every age and that therefore Israel's experience is instructive for the church." Because the church today is also God's covenant people, however, "we are not spectators of the salvation history, but participants in it, and Israel in the Old Testament is not a strange people to be observed, but the congregation of God of which we also have become members through Christ."[34]

It follows, therefore, that a message which told the ancient Israelites about God's dealings with their fathers may be heard by the church today as God's dealings with *its* fathers, and a message which told the ancient Israelites about their history may be heard by the church today as a message about *its* history, for the church was grafted on to Israel, as Paul puts it, "to share the richness of the olive tree" (Rom 11:17). Since the ancient Israelites and we are one covenant people through Christ, their God is our God, their forefathers are our forefathers, their history is our history, and their hope is our hope. Likewise, their books are our books, for the books God had intended first of all for them are "profitable" also for us (2 Tim 3:16).

Given the unity of God's people throughout the ages, preachers legitimately seek to "identify what today's hearers share with the authors' original hearers so that the text confronts them both. When this happens," writes Keck, "the event of the text repeats itself; just as I Corinthians confronted the Christians in Corinth with Paul's word . . . , so the sermon becomes the vehicle through which Paul's words confront today's congregation."[35] Krister Stendahl aptly reminds us that "analogies are only analogies, they are never one hundred percent identical with the original. But their power and helpfulness depend exactly on the depth of understanding of the specificity of the *then* and the specificity of the *now*."[36]

Accordingly, preachers ought to look carefully for analogies between the first recipients and the congregation today. Whenever such analogies can be established, the message addressed to God's people in the past can easily be shifted to God's people today—assuming, of course, that the context of the canon does not change that message. In fact, for interpreting the Epistles, Fee and Stuart have formulated the rule: "Whenever we share comparable particulars (i.e., similar specific life situations) with the first-century setting, God's Word to us is the same as His Word to them."

34. Elizabeth Achtemeier and Paul Achtemeier, *OT and Proclamation*, 122, 158; cf. 150-53.
35. Keck, *Bible in the Pulpit*, 116.
36. Stendahl, "Preaching from the Pauline Epistles," 307; cf. p. 308: "The power of biblical preaching lies in the specifics at both ends."

They explain that this rule gives "twentieth-century Christians a sense of immediacy with the first century. It is still true that 'all have sinned' and that 'by grace we are saved through faith.' Clothing ourselves with 'compassion, kindness, humility, gentleness and patience' (Col. 3:12) is still God's Word to those who are believers."[37] That same sense of immediacy can be obtained with the Old Testament when we discover genuine analogies between ancient Israel and the church today—again assuming that the context of the canon does not change the message. The distance between then and now can be bridged with genuine parallels because the people who first heard the word and the people who hear it today are one covenant people. "Preaching that emerges from the awareness of these continuities will not 'apply' the text to life today; rather, it will communicate the discovery of its pertinence because today's church is already addressed along with the original readers."[38]

Focus on the Goal of the Text

"TO understand a text," writes Richard Palmer, "is to understand the question behind the text, the question that called the text into being."[39] If preachers wish to pass on the message in its original relevance, they ought to focus on that question behind the text, on the reason why the text was written—its goal or purpose (see Chapter 6 above). Every properly selected preaching-text seeks to accomplish a specific goal among the original hearers: answer a question, comfort, encourage, correct, teach, motivate to obedience, praise, trust, etc. If preachers can delineate that specific goal, state the question to which the text is a focused response, they are halfway in conceiving a relevant sermon. The other half, of course, is discovering a genuine analogy among contemporary hearers so that the text is an authentic response to *their* question, sorrow, discouragement, sin, ignorance, lack of praise, trust, obedience, etc. "The key to proper application of a passage is *comparing life issues*," explains Stuart. "To apply a passage you must try to decide what is the central issue . . . with which the passage is concerned. . . . Then you must try to decide whether such issues are still active in the lives of persons or groups today."[40] When no genuine parallel to the contemporary hearers is discovered, one will need to go through the following more complicated procedures.

Redefine the Specific Issue
If the issue is so culturally specific that no analogy can be found in any

---

37. Fee and Stuart, *How to Read the Bible*, 60.
38. Keck, *Bible in the Pulpit*, 116.
39. Palmer, *Hermeneutics*, 250.
40. Stuart, *OT Exegesis*, 47.

other age, it may help to free the issue from its immediate historical-cultural referents, being careful not to generalize the issue to such an extent that the point is lost. For example, when one preaches on Paul's warning against the Judaizers, it may seem that a genuine parallel with today's church is impossible because there are no Judaizers in contemporary churches as there were in Galatia. But if one can free the issue at stake from the specific historical-cultural referents of Judaizers and circumcision, then the parallel becomes more apparent. What was it precisely that the Judaizers insisted upon with their demand for circumcision? Keck suggests that "the Judaizers were demanding that gentile Christian men be circumcised if they wanted to be first-class, bona fide Christians," and therefore "'circumcision' is any required act that is supposed to supplement trust in Jesus as the sole requirement for a right relation to God and to God's people." When one deduces that this was the crux of the issue, "one can see how often 'Galatianism' appears in our churches, and Paul's word will be as pungent a confrontation with the gospel today as it was then."[41]

Search for the Underlying Principle

Another procedure that may be helpful in transferring the message to today is searching for the underlying principle. When no immediate analogy is apparent, one can search behind the historical-cultural form of an instruction for the principle of which it is an expression. Why did the author write this? Of what principle is this a culturally conditioned expression? When one has discovered the underlying principle, it is easier to perceive a genuine analogy between the hearers then and now. "Since principles are more general, less tied to specifics, they usually have a wider range or scope of application. This means that the same principles can take on a variety of forms in different cultures and thereby help us transcend cultural relativity."[42]

For example, if the preaching-text contains the words, "You shall not boil a kid in its mother's milk" (e.g., Exod 23:19), it seems impossible at first sight to find an analogous situation today to which the text speaks meaningfully. Certainly the Jewish custom of not mixing meat and dairy products either in a meal or in the refrigerator seems to miss the point. Why was this directive given to Israel at that time? What was the significance of boiling a young goat in its mother's milk? It has been suggested that this strange custom was a Canaanite fertility rite.[43] If that is the case,

41. Keck, *Bible in the Pulpit*, 118.
42. Yoder, *From Word to Life*, 40.
43. See Childs, *Book of Exodus*, 485-86. Cf. J. Philip Hyatt, *Exodus*, NCBC (Grand Rapids: Eerdmans, 1980), 249-50. However, see also more recent theories in Jacob Milgrom, "'You Shall Not Boil a Kid in Its Mother's Milk,'" *Bible Review* 1/3 (1985) 48-55.

the principle behind this command is that God's people must avoid the pagan fertility cult and its rites. That principle can then, via analogy, be reapplied for God's people in our contemporary culture with its many "fertility" cults and rites. Fee and Stuart aptly caution, however, that "the 'principle' does not now become timeless to be applied at random or whim to any and every kind of situation. . . . It must be applied to *genuinely comparable situations.*"[44]

The Question of Identifying with Bible Characters

HAVING discussed at some length the analogies that can and ought to be recognized between the original hearers and the church today, we are now in a position to reflect on the question whether one may also discover analogies between Bible characters and hearers today in order to draw parallels between then and now. This question, it will be clear, relates specifically to narrative texts and comes perilously close to the imitating of Bible characters and moralizing we rejected earlier. With the contemporary shift to narrative sermons, however, the question of identifying with Bible characters has been raised in a new way. William Thompson tries to put his finger on the difference: "The easiest mistake to make in identifying one's self with the text is to see it as a model for morality rather than a mirror for identity."[45]

The Issue

Proponents of narrative preaching wish to use the text as "a mirror for identity"; that is, contemporary hearers must recognize themselves in the *text.* "Without the factor of recognition of our common lot," writes Fred Craddock, "the preacher cannot build enough bridges between text and listener; with the factor of recognition, those structures are unnecessary."[46] It is a question, then, of recognizing oneself and enabling the hearers to recognize themselves in the text. The way this recognition can come about, it is commonly argued, is by identifying with the characters portrayed in the Bible.

The best case for identification is probably made by Craddock when he argues for the method of "overhearing": "The parables of Jesus were told to be overheard. 'There was a certain man': anonymous, past tense, somewhere else—nothing here addressed to me. Relax and enjoy the

---

Milgrom himself (p. 54) opts for Philo's interpretation: "A substance that sustains the life of a creature (milk) should not be fused or confused with a process associated with its death (cooking)."

44. Fee and Stuart, *How to Read the Bible,* 63.

45. Thompson, *Preaching Biblically,* 70.

46. Craddock, *Preaching,* 134-35.

story. And then it happens; I am inside the story, and the door closes behind me." Craddock claims that "overhearing Scripture, as with music or drama or a good book, owes most of its power to these two factors: distance (I am an anonymous listener, reader, viewer, unrelated to the event) and participation (I am drawn in by identification with persons and conditions within the event)."[47] Our interest here is primarily the second factor, participation which comes about by identification with persons and conditions within the event. Craddock elucidates this point further when he notes: "Participation means that the listener overcomes the distance, not because the speaker 'applied' everything, but because the listener identified with experiences and thoughts related in the message that were analogous to his own."[48]

One of the pioneers of the "narrative school" is Amos Wilder. He addresses the issue of identification as follows:

> The myriads of men taught by the Bible know that the children of God in his family are all different, and each has his own history, and his own gifts, and his own guilt and his own blessing. Nevertheless our various plots and histories overlap in various wonderful ways, and especially perhaps our moral histories. Therefore we can see ourselves in the stories of Adam, Noah, Abraham, Moses, David, etc.; or in the persons of this or that disciple of Christ or this or that person confronting his death or Resurrection, not to mention Christians of later times or the figures in the *Divine Comedy*, or *Paradise Lost*.[49]

If one can identify equally with later Christians or characters in *Paradise Lost*, one faces the preliminary question whether the method of identifying with Bible characters does full justice to the fact that these narratives function in the Bible and not in *Paradise Lost* or, for that matter, in the Koran. Employing this method, could one select a preaching-text from the Koran just as well as from the Bible? Ernest Best charges that "identification runs the danger of neglecting the situational and cultural embedding of each biblical story,"[50] but a more critical issue is that identification runs the danger of neglecting the canonical embedding of each biblical story. Can a story simply be lifted out of its literary context of the Bible so that we can identify with its characters the way we do with characters in any other story? And should not the fact that these stories are part and parcel of the *canon* make any difference in our approach? Moreover, can the overhearing of parables, as is frequently proposed, serve as paradigm for listening to historical narratives without losing the very purpose of these narratives?

47. Craddock, *Overhearing the Gospel*, 112, 115.
48. Ibid., 123.
49. Wilder, *Early Christian Rhetoric*, 58.
50. Best, *From Text to Sermon*, 92.

Bypassing these preliminary but fundamental questions at this point (see Chapters 1–4 above), let us look at some concrete proposals for identifying with Bible characters. In a chapter on "Preaching on the Patriarchs," Henry Mitchell recommends: "Take special care to preselect the lesson to be taught, and to identify the character who learns it. Then be sure so to present that person that the audience will be drawn to identify with her or him and so experience its way through that saving truth. . . . For instance, the tale of Jacob wrestling with God is a gold mine for teaching folks who have unresolved interpersonal conflicts and guilt. But they will presume that the message is given to 'somebody else,' unless Jacob is so introduced that they like him and identify with him, so as to live out his lesson and go through his change from cheater to chosen vessel."[51] Notice that the purpose of identification is that we learn the same "lesson" as the Bible character learned but, so to speak, from the inside of the story.

Since biblical narratives usually have more than one character, however, a valid question is, Whose "lesson" do we need to learn? With which Bible character should we identify? And does not the message of the text change when we shift our target for identification from one character to another? James Sanders admits frankly that the message changes but recommends it nevertheless: "Dynamic analogy means we can read a text in different ways by identifying with different people in it." The example he uses is Luke 4, the narrative about Jesus preaching in the synagogue at Nazareth, where we can "identify with Jesus" and get one reading, then again we can identify with "the good folk in the synagogue, Jesus' relatives and friends of his hometown," and get other readings.[52] But if the meaning of the narrative changes—as it does—with every change of identification, not only are the possibilities for identification endless but the possibilities for abuse of the text are endless. If preachers create one message by having the listeners identify with Jesus and another message by having them identify with "the good folk in the synagogue," then the method of identification has led them to break the first rule of hermeneutics—that every text must be understood in its context according to the author's intent and not according to the preacher's predilection.

A further question may be raised: Who decides with which character the congregation should identify? Take a model sermon on Acts 10:9-29,

51. Mitchell, "Preaching on the Patriarchs," 41. Cf. Ryken, *How to Read the Bible as Literature*, 44: "Every sermon based on a biblical narrative assumes that what happens to the characters in the story is somehow a model of the enduring human situation."

52. Sanders, *God Has a Story Too*, 20. William Thompson asserts similarly: "A . . . traditional way of working with identification is to choose one person in a narrative with whom to ask the congregation to identify. . . . One might even identify with each of the three characters in a series of sermons, or even within one sermon. The possibilities are endless" (*Preaching Biblically*, 72).

Peter's vision and visit to Cornelius. The congregation is being asked to identify with Peter in Joppa: "You, a latter-day Simon Peter. . . . You keep finding yourself at table with people who seem unclean." The sermon finishes with the climax, "It didn't come easily, did it, Peter? It rarely does come easily, such basic change. You always did resent those unclean folk, mainly because you never felt you were that clean. At bottom the real issue has been *your* uncleanness, hasn't it, Peter?"[53] But is that really the issue in Acts 10, Peter's and our uncleanness which God declares clean? Has not the method of identification here led to an anthropocentric sermon which misinterprets the passage and fails to pass on the very point of the text, namely, that it was *God* who broke down the dividing wall between Jew and Gentile and drove the exclusive church out among the Gentiles? Moreover, since most of our hearers, like Luke's hearers, are Gentiles, it seems that if there is to be any identification, it should be with the Gentiles and not with Peter. Who decides with which character the congregation identifies?

Objections

In many instances, it seems fair to say, the method of identifying with Bible characters raises more problems than it solves. In fact, many of the pitfalls of imitating Bible characters and of moralizing return in this modern attempt of identifying with Bible characters. If it is the preacher's choice to select out of several characters in the text the one with whom the congregation should identify, then the method is completely subjective and, depending on the preacher, may be arbitrary. If, as we see in the examples above, the method of identifying with Bible characters leads to anthropocentric sermons, then the theocentric character of the Bible is shortchanged. If, as is being advocated, the preacher preaches a text one Sunday from the perspective of one character and the next Sunday from the perspective of another character, thus achieving two different messages from one and the same text, the inevitable result will be that one or both sermons ride roughshod over the author's intention and distort the text's message. In short, the method of identifying with Bible characters can easily lead to rank subjectivism, slighting of authorial intention, and distortion of the text.

In dealing with the narrative of Jesus healing a paralytic, Best notes all the many different characters—the paralytic, the four friends, the householder, and many more—and the typical question that is often asked, "With whom do you identify?" Best calls it "a false assumption" that "each one of us must identify with some person or group in the story."

53. Wardlaw, "Shaping Sermons by Context," 77, 80.

"We can be sure," he writes pointedly, "that in this story Jesus did not heal the man so that we should mirror ourselves in the attitude of one of those standing around nor did Mark record it for that purpose; there is no justification for using it in that way at all."[54]

Controlled Use of Identification

In spite of the objections raised above, the matter of identification with Bible characters is too important simply to dismiss as being without justification. The problems of this method revolve around the lack of control (subjective, arbitrary) and the slighting of authorial intention. Both problems can be solved, however, by going back to the original relevance of the passage: How did the original hearers understand the passage? Did the author intend his hearers to identify with a certain character? By going back to the passage's original relevance, one both honors the author's intention and acquires the needed control for responsible understanding and transmission.

One question to ask, therefore, is whether the author intended his original hearers to identify with a certain character. While this question will drastically reduce the number of identifications, it will leave the way open for discerning intended models for self-recognition. It is clear, I think, that in the Old Testament the patriarchs Abraham, Isaac, and Jacob are presented as figures in which Israel was to recognize itself; these forefathers represented Israel.[55] As the ancient Israelites heard the stories of Abraham, Isaac, and Jacob, they were completely involved because this was *their* story; what God did for the patriarchs, he did for *them*; if God had not given Abraham and Sarah a child in their old age, Israel would never have come into existence. As the ancient Israelites listened to these stories, however, I cannot imagine that they were learning lessons on resolving interpersonal conflict or on lying about your wife, or any other such lessons which Abraham, Isaac, or Jacob might have learned. The object was rather that the Israelites should learn their identity and their obligation: who they were in relationship to the covenanting God, who God was, and what they owed the God who had created and redeemed them. Since God's people today are one covenant people with ancient Israel, these narratives may be used also today for learning our identity and our obligation—provided, of course, we take into account that today we live after the coming of Christ.

Another, less likely, model for Israel's self-recognition was the judge

---

54. Best, *From Text to Sermon*, 90.

55. Cf. von Rad, *Biblical Interpretations in Preaching*, 27: "Now there is no doubt that in reading this ancient story ancient Israel recognized itself in Abraham as believing community, as people of God (and not primarily as individuals)."

Samson. By noting many parallels between Samson and Israel, John Stek establishes the plausibility that the Samson story "confronted Israel with a mirror image of herself":

> As Samson was given birth by a special act of Yahweh (out of barrenness), so Israel herself was the product of Yahweh's special intervention in history (remember Isaac, Jacob, and the Exodus). As Samson was consecrated to Yahweh (as a Nazirite) from birth, so Israel was to be wholly consecrated to Yahweh (circumcision). As Samson was constantly drawn to the blandishments of Philistine women, so Israel was constantly drawn to the blandishments of the peoples around her (she "made love" to the gods of the neighboring peoples—as the prophets charged). As Samson called on Yahweh only when in a life crisis, so Israel called on Yahweh . . . only when she was in deep crisis.[56]

If Samson is a model for Israel's self-recognition, the question becomes: What did the author intend Israel to learn from this model? It will be clear that the author's intention was not to have Israel learn some lessons that Samson learned about fraternizing with the enemy, about keeping a secret, about promiscuity, suicide, and the like. Rather, by identifying with Samson, the people of Israel would learn to see themselves as God saw them: flawed, yet by God's grace called to advance his kingdom. Stek fleshes out Samson's relevance for Israel as follows: "As Yahweh used even flawed Samson in his warfare against the Philistines, so he had used and would use flawed Israel in his struggle to establish his kingdom in the earth. As Yahweh graciously responded to Samson's cries for help in his moments of crisis, so Yahweh had heard and would hear Israel's cries for help when threatened by the powers of this world. As Samson was invincible against his foes, far surpassing mere human strength, when acting in the power of Yahweh, so Israel was and would be invincible in the strength of Yahweh. As Yahweh ultimately triumphed over Dagon through his flawed servant Samson, so he would triumph over the gods through his flawed servant Israel."[57] Notice that all these parallels are theocentric and that they apply not directly to individuals but to God's covenant people Israel. Being one covenant people with Israel, the church today may also recognize itself in Samson; not, however, for learning some easy lessons or drawing out some cheap morals for individuals, but in order, like Israel, to see itself and its responsibilities in the light of God's covenant and his coming kingdom.

The prophet Jonah is another instructive figure. "There is no reason to doubt that, in Jonah's attitude toward the Assyrians, all Israel would identify itself with him and would know itself to be rebuked in him," writes

56. Stek, *Former Prophets*, 32. Cf. Webb, *Book of the Judges*, 179.
57. Stek, *Former Prophets*, 32.

Stek. "And there is equally no reason to doubt that this is exactly what the writer intended."[58] In transmitting the message of Jonah to the church today, there is no reason why that original intention of the author should not be utilized by having the church recognize itself in Jonah—provided, of course, that the parallel between Israel and the church today be properly drawn and that the kingdom-historical distance between Israel and the church be taken into account (after Pentecost there is even less excuse for lack of concern for the nations).

A more general question one ought to ask in this connection is, From what perspective did the author expect his hearers to understand the story? James Kugel observes that modern reading tends to be "hero" reading: "In the hero-reading, we are Moses, and the subject of the book [of Exodus] is Moses' (i.e., our) adventures with God, in which the people function as a stiff-necked foil to ideal piety. But there is nothing *natural* in such a reading." In fact, in response to the question, "Where is the ancient Israelite listener?" Kugel suggests that that listener was to identify not with Moses but with "the people."[59] Thus identification here is not so much a question of self-recognition as it is a question of entering the story from the right angle, understanding it from its intended perspective. Roland Allen illustrates this point well with the parable of the Good Samaritan. In preaching this parable in its context of the lawyer testing Jesus (Luke 10:25-37), "we need to enter the context as one of Luke's listeners. Luke's listeners would probably have identified with the lawyer (who was an expert in Torah), inasmuch as he was a respected member of the religious community. In preaching, I want to hear the parable, therefore, in ways analogous to the ways in which the lawyer might have heard."[60] In short, the angle of entry into a text makes a difference to the understanding and preaching of that text.

Hence, the question of identification is not merely a question of bridging the historical-cultural gap; it is also a question of gaining the right entry into a text. By hearing the passage as the original audience heard it, we not only gain entry into the text from the intended angle but we also gain the control that can keep in check arbitrary, subjective, and other irresponsible ways of handling the text.

RELEVANT PROCLAMATION TODAY

BECAUSE of the sharp division in some sermons between the explication and the application, congregations often experience only the application as relevant. Although the stark contrast may be alleviated somewhat by

---

58. Stek, *CTJ* 4/1 (1969) 39.
59. Kugel, *Prooftexts* 1/3 (1981) 229-30.
60. Allen, "Shaping Sermons by Language," 41.

attaching applications to each of the points of the sermon, this procedure does not solve the problem of irrelevance but only spreads it in smaller sections over the entire sermon. The ideal, of course, is to construct sermons that will be experienced as relevant from beginning to end. Although there are no easy steps to attain this ideal, the following comments may be able to clarify the issues and point the way.

The Sermon as Relevant Communication

The Bible as Proclamation

The reason why sermons often break into irrelevant and relevant parts is that the Bible is perceived to contain objective revelation, either doctrine or historical events, which the preacher must describe and apply to the congregation. The emphasis in this approach is, therefore, on *making* relevant what is perceived to be objective, distant, irrelevant. We have seen, however, that the Bible is kerygma, proclamation, relevant address, appeal. New Testament scholars have highlighted this trait of the Bible with the striking statement, "in the beginning was the sermon," that is, "the New Testament texts were the product of preaching, teaching, exhortation, and comforting, and . . . in turn they preach, teach, exhort, and comfort."[61] A similar case can be made for Old Testament texts: being the product of a long history of preaching, teaching, exhorting, and comforting, they now preach, teach, exhort, and comfort. As Paul's letter to the Romans is proclamation to the church in Rome, and Luke's "letter" to Theophilus is proclamation to the Greeks, so Genesis as well as Amos, Psalms as well as Proverbs, is proclamation to ancient Israel. The point is that biblical texts are God's word *addressed* to his people and, therefore, already applied and relevant. Hence preachers today need not transform an objective entity into a relevant word but need only transmit a relevant message from the past to the present.

Moreover, one must have an eye for the way a passage transcends its own historical horizon. "God caused the Word spoken in those days to be put in writing with a view to us and our salvation. . . . A respect for the true nature of the Bible opens the way for applied explanation in preaching, and raises us above the level of an objectivistic explanation which has to be amplified and compensated by application."[62] Thus the whole sermon, like the passage on which it is based, ought to be relevant communication.

The Explication/Application Problem

In view of the relevance of the Bible for us today, some have suggested

61. Perrin, *Introduction*, 19.
62. Trimp, *WTJ* 36 (1973) 27.

that we drop the traditional distinction between explication and application and speak instead of "applicatory explication," or passing on the
"message in its 'applicatory' character," or "making the content of the text
concrete for the church here and now," or embodying "the explanation . . .
in the application."[63] Although these reformulations rightly try to avoid
the dualism of objective explication plus directed application, they do not
thereby solve the actual problem of producing sermons which are relevant from beginning to end. For the fact remains that the written message
was originally addressed to a different church than the one addressed by
the preacher today, and the only responsible way to understand the message for today is to do full justice to its meaning in that original historical-
cultural setting. To put the issue succinctly: since the message was first
addressed to an ancient church, it requires explication; since that message
now needs to be addressed to a contemporary church, it requires application. The problem preachers face is how to integrate explication and application so that the whole sermon comes across as relevant communication.

Working toward a Solution

Although the problem of proper integration will have to be solved for
each sermon individually, a few general suggestions may be helpful. As
we saw in Chapter 6 above, the message of some texts is so universal that
the theme of the text can become the theme of the sermon. If the message
is, in addition, relatively free of historical-cultural discontinuity, it can be
immediately transmitted to the church today.

Moreover, "the move from understanding what the text meant to
what it may mean, from historical, descriptive exegesis to proclamation,
need not be made in the pulpit. . . . That interpretative move must be
made, but in many cases it must be made in the study rather than in the
pulpit."[64] Nevertheless, preachers need not be apologetic about providing
their congregations with some of the results of their exegetical study. The
presence of explication in the sermon does not automatically lead to a dualistic sermon of which only the second half is relevant, for explication
forms the foundation for application. As the basis for application, explication of how a passage was originally understood is not at all irrelevant; on
the contrary, explication provides the reasons for the particular application. As such, explication provides the congregation with the tools to test
the message. Stuart suggests that the listeners "need to be shown how the

---

63. Respectively Van Dijk, Veenhof, Holwerda (see my *Sola Scriptura*, 157) and
von Allmen, *Preaching and the Congregation*, 54. Cf. Bettler, "Application," 332:
"Preaching is application. . . . Application, no matter how skillfully structured or
helpfully delivered must never be viewed as an 'add-on.'"

64. Keck, *Bible in the Pulpit*, 114.

application is based on a proper comprehension of the passage's meaning, and they will probably not take the application to heart unless this is clear to them."[65] As an opening of the Scriptures, as a searching with the congregation for the contemporary point of the passage, explication not only leads to relevant application but is itself inherently relevant.

Further, one need not follow the basic pattern of explication/application, past meaning/present meaning, in every sermon. Although that is the basic exegetical pattern in one's study, the sermon can usually be constructed in a more direct, unified way. One can begin with today's question, to which the text gives the answer, or with the original question and relate it to the present situation. One can develop the sermon or any of its points deductively or inductively and use any of a variety of forms (see Chapter 7 above). Moreover, textual-thematic preaching seeks to follow the theme in explication as well as application, thus enhancing the unity of the sermon (see Chapter 6 above). Since the theme is an assertion, a summary statement of the proclamation, following the theme throughout the sermon will also promote the relevance of the sermon from beginning to end.

Congregational Involvement

Addressing Needs

Congregational involvement can be further heightened by aiming the sermon at specific needs in the congregation, by addressing the sermon, as the text before it, to specific questions. "There seems to be a lot of difference in the quality of the attention accorded when the preacher begins by giving the impression that he is going to try and answer a question which is real and important in the lives of the people in the pews."[66] But how can one meet the many, varied needs of a large group of people? Donald Miller compares preaching to shooting quail: "If you aim for all the birds, you hit none, but if you aim for one, you are likely to get several." He suggests that this holds true for preaching because "the basic spiritual needs of men are quite the same" and because "ofttimes the needs of individuals are best met in crowds."[67] In any event, aiming the sermon at specific needs of individuals will promote congregational involvement in the sermon.

Addressing the Whole Person

One must further address the whole person. In the past, sermons have been aimed all too frequently at either the intellect or the will. Ian Pitt-Watson argues for emotional as well as intellectual and volitional involvement: "Unless there is some measure of emotional involvement on the

65. Stuart, *OT Exegesis*, 77.
66. Brooks, *Communicating Conviction*, 87.
67. Miller, *Way to Biblical Preaching*, 119.

part of the preacher and on the part of his hearers the *kerygma* cannot be heard in its fullness for the *kerygma* speaks to the whole man, emotions and all, and simply does not make sense to the intellect and the will alone."[68] Today the case for addressing the whole person is frequently made in terms of the imagination and addressing the brain's right hemisphere. Certainly narration, whether it be of the biblical passage or of an illustration, tends to involve the whole person. Craddock lists several characteristics of narration that are able to involve people:

> The human condition is presented with genuine insight. . . .
> Primary attention is given to the specific and particular rather than the general. . . .
> Sermon materials are realistic rather than contrived. . . .
> Narration and description are with emotional restraint and an economy of words. . . . Too many adjectives in effect tell listeners what to see and hear and how they are to respond to what is described. . . .
> Events are viewed from a single perspective unless the hearer is instructed otherwise.[69]

Whatever strategies are used, the passage which in biblical times was directed at the "heart" ought today also to be directed at the whole person.

Using Dialogue

Although most sermons are in the form of a monologue, the monologue ought to be a dialogue with the hearers, that is, it ought to respond to the reactions of the hearers as these might come up during the sermon. This requirement does not mean that one should interrupt the flow of the sermon with the odd, "But I hear you saying. . . ." It means, rather, that one ought to consider what major objections and questions the audience might raise and try to address these issues in the sermon. Edmund Steimle suggests that "the key to authentic dialogue rests largely on the sensitivity of the person in the pulpit, along with the possibility of lay participation in the preparation of the sermon to help insure the presence of genuine dialogue in the sermon."[70] Responding in the sermon to the anticipated reactions of the hearers will, when done sensitively, promote their involvement. In fact, since dialogue incorporates into the sermon the

68. Pitt-Watson, *Preaching*, 47-48. Cf. Wardlaw, "Need for New Shapes," 20: "If sermons are to move people significantly, today preachers need to understand that people are moved to action not by reason alone, and to seek new sermon forms compatible with that understanding."

69. Craddock, *Preaching*, 162-165. On the research and pros and cons of "indirect suggestion" versus "direct application" see Freeman, *SWJT* 27/2 (1985) 35-36.

70. Steimle, "Fabric of the Sermon," 170. Cf. Stott, *Between Two Worlds*, 61: "One of the greatest gifts a preacher needs is such a sensitive understanding of people and their problems that he can anticipate their reactions to each part of his sermon and respond to them." Cf. Barth, *Preaching of the Gospel*, 74.

possible reactions of people, the hearers will sense themselves to be very much a part of the sermon.

Using Concrete, Vivid Language

Finally, the hearers become involved in the message through the use of concrete, vivid language. Henry Davis recommends using "as few words as possible": "The chief quality of personal communication is that it says a great deal, and suggests more, in a very few words. Excess words therefore destroy its chief quality." He further advocates the use of "short, strong, clear, familiar words," and "sensuous rather than abstract, and specific rather than general words." He explains that "sensuous words are words that are close to the five senses, suggesting pictures the mind can see, sounds it can hear, things it can touch, taste, smell."[71]

Since pictorial language in the nature of the case stimulates the senses, figures of speech also invite involvement. "Like an artist or novelist a minister must learn to think in pictures," suggests Haddon Robinson. "Metaphors and similes produce sensations in the listener or cause him to recall images of previous experiences."[72] Like good illustrations, figures of speech often function for the hearers as lights that illumine and clarify obscure concepts in the sermon.

Preachers must also learn to think in terms of specifics in order to avoid abstractions and generalizations. "When for example they call for their congregations to 'witness to the world in the home, in the office, at school, or in the street,' preachers . . . [ought to] ask themselves, 'What, specifically, do you have in mind?'"[73] Abstractions communicate little and generalizations even less. By pushing beyond generalizations to particulars, however, preachers will make their language concrete and specific and clarify their proposals so that their hearers can visualize what is demanded and become meaningfully involved. Thus even the choice of words contributes to the relevance of the sermon.[74]

We have now worked our way through all the major steps of sermon preparation, from awareness of the necessity of expository preaching to

71. Davis, *Design for Preaching*, 268-71. Craddock elucidates this point in his typical "sensuous" style: "If the sermon revives the memory of the odor of burped milk on a blouse, it evokes more meaning than the most thorough analysis of 'motherhood'" (*As One Without Authority*, 93).

72. Robinson, *Biblical Preaching*, 186, 187. Cf. Buttrick, *Homiletic*, 27: "Good preaching involves the imaging of ideas—the shaping of every conceptual notion by metaphor and image and syntax."

73. Steimle, "Fabric of the Sermon," 174.

74. See Cox, *Preaching*, 179-92, on other "factors of attention and interest." He deals with matters of vital interest, the familiar, the unusual, mystery, suspense, conflict, humor, and the concrete.

the employment of a holistic historical-critical method, and from holistic interpretation to proper text selection, theme formulation, form determination, and relevant communication. So far we have discussed the various issues in a more or less general way, that is, as they apply to all or most genres of biblical literature. In the final chapters the foregoing discussions will be focused on specific biblical genres. We shall examine in turn issues in preaching Hebrew narrative, prophecy, gospel, and epistle.

CHAPTER 9

Preaching Hebrew Narratives

OF all the biblical genres of literature, narrative may be described as the central, foundational, and all-encompassing genre of the Bible.[1] The prominence of the narrative genre in the Bible is related to the Bible's central message that God acts in *history*. No other genre can express that message as well as narrative. G. W. Stroup observes that "history necessarily assumes narrative form in its recounting and interpreting of what happened. . . . The reference to historical events explains why the genre of narrative is of such overwhelming importance to Israel, why the Pentateuch is built on a narrative frame rather than that of a law code or a collection of wisdom sayings."[2]

In fact, the Old Testament as a whole (as well as the New Testament) is built on a narrative frame; it contains two major history works: Genesis to 2 Kings, covering the period from the creation to the exile of Judah; and Chronicles to Nehemiah, spanning the period from Adam to the return from the exile. Moreover, narrative is found in all three Hebrew divisions: in the Torah, primarily in Genesis, Exodus, and Numbers; in the Prophets, primarily in Joshua, Judges, Samuel, Kings, and Jonah; and in the Writ-

---

1. The Bible has often been called a storybook. There is more truth to this description than a person, skeptical of children's story Bibles, might suspect. Louis Bloede, *Iliff Review* 37 (1980) 55, explains: "The Bible is really a storybook — the story of God's involvement in the universe, in human history, in inter-personal relations, and in the inner life of individuals." Cf. Stroup, *Promise of Narrative Theology*, 136: "The core of Scripture is a set of narratives which serve as the common denominator for the whole of Scripture."

2. Stroup, *Promise of Narrative Theology*, 149; cf. Ryken, *Literature of the Bible*, 77: "Historical narrative is the inevitable mode for writing about the God who acts in history."

ings, primarily in Chronicles, Ezra, Nehemiah, Ruth, Esther, and Daniel. Narrative sections are also found in all other genres of Old Testament literature: in prophecy (e.g., Isaiah and Jeremiah), in wisdom (e.g., Job), and in the Psalms. When one considers the length of some narratives as well as their distribution throughout the Old Testament, it is evident that narrative is the supporting frame and the predominant genre of the Old Testament.

A peculiarity of narrative is that it, more than any other genre, contains other forms of literature, such as law, psalm, wisdom, and prophecy. The reason for this peculiarity is not difficult to detect, for in narrative, "speeches are made, letters are written, laws quoted, prophetic messages delivered, and the like."[3]

A definition of "narrative" can be either narrow (historical narrative only) or broad (all narrative). Since we are dealing with the narrative genre in general, we can adopt the broader definition proposed by Gabriel Fackre: "Narrative, in its encompassing sense, is an account of events and participants moving over time and space, a recital with beginning and ending patterned by the narrator's principle of selection."[4]

We shall first reflect on the historical and literary dimensions of Hebrew narrative and then focus specifically on its interpretation and preaching.

HEBREW HISTORY WRITING

The Question of Historicity

SINCE Chapters 2 and 4 above deal quite extensively with the questions of historicity, the historical-critical method, and biblical history writing, we can here focus specifically on Hebrew narrative.

While history is necessarily written in the narrative genre, this does not mean, of course, that every narrative in the Bible is therefore history writing—as the existence of parable readily shows. The narrative genre encompasses different forms, ranging from factual history writing to fictional parables.

History and Fiction

In order to avoid misunderstanding, it may be well to state at the outset that fiction is not necessarily false. Yet "one of the persistent misconceptions of textual hermeneutics is the correlation of the truth-falsity distinction with the history-fiction distinction. What is historical and actual is taken to be truthful, and therefore what is fictional and imagined is

---

3. Wilcoxen, "Narrative," 95.
4. Fackre, *Int* 37 (1983) 341.

thought to be false." As should be evident from biblical parables, "a fictional work can assert a truth by the telling of a story even though it does not give us factual references."[5]

Form-critical Classifications

Since there are different narrative forms, form critics try to delineate the various forms more precisely. For example, George Coats divides "the principal narrative genres in the Old Testament" into saga, tale, novella, legend, history, report, fable, etiology, and myth.[6] One of the dangers of such classification is that the class of "history" would lead one to suspect that all the other classes are nonhistorical and that, contrary to the actual content of Scripture, nonhistorical rather than historical narrative is predominant. Donald Gowan remarks aptly that "the judgment about facticity must be made equally about materials written in the form of history and those in the form of saga or legend or short story, and should not be prejudged in accordance with the form-critical label which is attached to them."[7] That being the case, form criticism is less than helpful in resolving the question of historicity.

Moreover, Coats's description of "history" in contrast to "tale" and "novella" sets up a contrast between objective reporting and artistic narrating that sounds more modern than ancient: "History as a genre of literature represents that kind of writing designed to record the events of the past as they actually occurred. Its structure is controlled, then, not by the concerns of aesthetics, nor by the symbolic nature of a plot, but by the chronological stages or cause-effect sequences of events as the author(s) understood them. It is not structured to maintain interest or to provoke anticipation for a resolution of tension. It is designed simply to record. . . . As an example of history, see the Deuteronomistic History or the Chronicles."[8] This restrictive description (little concern for aesthetics, plot, audience interest, resolution of tension) does not even fit the suggested examples of Deuteronomistic History and Chronicles. In the light of various kinds of modern classifications of texts and their implied hermeneutics, it would be well to keep in mind Amos Wilder's observation that "the earliest narratives took no account of such distinctions."[9] Instead of allowing classifications to prejudge the issues of historicity, aesthetics, plot, tension, etc., it is better to approach the text with an open mind on these issues.

---

5. Clarence Walhout, "Texts and Actions," 74 and 77.
6. Coats, *Genesis*, 5-10.
7. Gowan, *Reclaiming the OT*, 15.
8. Coats, *Genesis*, 9.
9. Wilder, *Int* 37 (1983) 359.

History Writing

The Complexity of History Writing

It is well-known that Hebrew history writing is quite different from the nineteenth-century ideal of "accurate, objective history." History writing is much more complex than Positivism ever suspected. According to Robert Alter, "it is quite possible that the writer faithfully represents the historical data without addition or substantive embellishment. The organization of the narrative [Judges 3], however, its lexical and syntactic choices, its small shifts in point of view, its brief but strategic uses of dialogue, produce an imaginative reenactment of the historical event, conferring upon it a strong attitudinal definition and discovering in it a pattern of meaning."[10] Concerning Samuel and Kings, Ronald Clements observes that "it becomes evident upon examination that the purpose of the stories was not simply to report events in an impartial and objective fashion, such as the critical historian would do."[11] Since impartial, objective reporting is not the purpose of biblical history writing, it should not be judged and disqualified by that nineteenth-century standard.

Prophetic History Writing

As pointed out in Chapter 4, like all history writing, biblical history writing consists of the presentation of an interpretation of certain selected events. In distinction from secular history writing, however, biblical authors wrote history in a theocentric manner: "The way in which the stories have been told has been more surely controlled by questions of a theological and religious nature than by purely historical concerns."[12] As such, biblical history writing may be called prophetic history writing. Moreover, compared to contemporary standards, ancient standards allowed biblical authors much more freedom and flexibility to mold and shape the material in order to drive home their specific messages. Whenever necessary, they freely rearranged the chronological order, selected some facts while ignoring others, summarized here while detailing there. However, neither the distinctive prophetic perspective nor the artistic freedom of biblical authors is a reason for approaching these texts with the skepticism that has become the hallmark of the historical-critical method. On the contrary, there is good reason to approach biblical historical narratives with confidence in their historical reliability. In reading biblical narratives, our assumption, like that of the original hearers, is that we

10. Alter, *Art of Biblical Narrative*, 41; cf. p. 35.
11. Clements, *HorBT* 4 (1982-83) 54. Cf. Jennings, "Interpreting the Historical Books," 46: "History is not just history. History is three-dimensional: (a) what happened; (b) the writer's understanding of what happened; and (c) the message the writer wants to get across."
12. Clements, *HorBT* 4 (1982-83) 56.

can read them as historical narratives unless there are valid reasons for not doing so (see Chapter 2 above).

Historical and Nonhistorical Narratives

THE question of historicity is more complex, however, than affirming in general the historical reliability of Hebrew historical narratives. The problem lies more specifically in discerning which narrative is historical, which is not, and what *difference* this distinction makes for interpretation.

Parables

Parables are a clear form of nonhistorical narrative. Since "the message of a parable is something other than the story which it itself tells,"[13] the question of historicity makes no difference at all to its interpretation. Nathan's parable about the rich man who slaughtered a poor man's pet lamb for his guest (2 Sam 12:1-4) carries its message whether or not the story actually happened. Until fairly recently the New Testament story about the rich man and Lazarus was thought to be historical, but today most would call it a parable; since its message is something other than the story, however, its historicity makes no difference in apprehending its message. Consequently, we can conclude that some biblical narratives make their point irrespective of their historicity.

Story and History

We noted in Chapter 4, however, that the contemporary emphasis on story tends to extend this feature of parables to *all* narratives. For example, Robert Roth writes: "We are not asking now if this story is true or fictional. Stories are told regardless of that question." And again: "We are not concerned to prove historical details. We would no more reject the detail of a miraculous healing than we would delete dragons or elves from fairy stories."[14] David Clines would like to read the Pentateuch as story, "story and not history being the primary mode of communication of religious truth. . . . What is offered in a story is a 'world'—make-believe or real. . . . Within the story there is no distinction between the real and the unreal. . . . No awkward historical questions about the material of the Pentateuch stand in the way of its efficacy in creating 'world'

---

13. Barr, *Bible in the Modern World*, 56.

14. Roth, *Story and Reality*, 12, 31. Cf. James Barr, *JR* 56 (1976) 5: "The long narrative corpus of the Old Testament seems to me, as a body of literature, to merit the title of story rather than that of history." Note how Barr reveals his presuppositions in describing the difference between "story" and "history": "The story contains within itself large elements which no one seriously considers as history and which belong rather to the area of myth and legend. . . . The story moves back and forward, quite without embarrassment, between human causation and divine causation" (ibid., p. 7).

or in drawing its readers into participation in its world."[15] Concerning the historical nature of Israel's conquest of Canaan, Clines remarks elsewhere that it makes little difference to the *interpretation* of these narratives "since these narratives would continue to be tales about Israel's success when obedient to God, about Israel's unity, about leadership, about conflicts within and without a group, about religious war, and so on."[16] The question may be raised, however: Is it indeed the case that historicity makes little or no difference in interpreting *all* biblical narratives, or is this assumption a contemporary evasion of the problems brought about by a destructive historical-critical method?

The Importance of Historicity

ALTHOUGH there is much to be said for the power of story and how it works apart from the question of historicity, it must also be said that treating all biblical narratives like parables is a gross oversimplification, for not all biblical narratives are nonhistorical. If a narrative "claims by its form and intent to be history, then it does matter whether the event recorded really happened or not," Gowan contends. "If it didn't, then we have nothing to preach about it."[17] The issue here again is the intent or purpose of the text. If the intent of a narrative entails relating historical events, then sidestepping that intent in one's interpretation fails to do full justice to that narrative's meaning.

Historical Narrative

Historical narrative has been defined as "a complete prose narrative whose basic structure and style suggests a 'telling' of events in chronological sequence (whether or not the chronology is accurate or even clearly spelled out). History takes its form not so much from aesthetic interests, such as dramatic plot and artistic expression, as from the intent to narrate and interpret events as they were presumed to have occurred, and with awareness of cause-effect relations among them."[18] History writing can quite naturally use dramatic plot and artistic expression, but the author's interest is *more* than aesthetic expression, namely, "to narrate and interpret events." Hence mere aesthetic interpretation of the story falls short of the mark. If the intent of historical narrative entails the narration of actual events, then one can no longer declare the historical referent of the narrative to be inconsequential for interpretation. In distinction from that of parables, the message of historical narrative is at least partially the story which it tells.

15. Clines, *Theme of the Pentateuch*, 102-4.
16. Clines, *Beginning OT Study*, 39.
17. Gowan, *Reclaiming the OT*, 26.
18. Long, *1 Kings*, 30; cf. pp. 3-8.

The Old Testament Testimony

The Old Testament itself witnesses to the importance of taking its historicity seriously. In the words of Stroup, "At the heart of Israel's confession of
faith (Deut. 26:5ff.) is a claim about an event in history ('and the Lord
brought us out of Egypt with a mighty hand and an outstretched
arm' . . .) and the truth of Israel's faith stands or falls with that claim."
Israel's faith "refers first and last to specific historical events in its collective past in which it believes Yahweh has been decisively and redemp-
tively at work."[19] If the historicity of these events is denied or ignored,
however, these narratives are stripped of their essence, for their purpose
is precisely to relate what God has done in Israel's history. With these historical narratives, one cannot claim that the message is "something other
than the story which it itself tells," for here the message *is* the story, the
history, which is related. A denial of historicity here not only assails "the
truth of Israel's faith" but undermines our own Christian faith as well (see
Chapter 4 above). Ultimately, our faith is founded not in "history-like"
narratives but in history itself, or rather, in the God who acts in history.

Functions of Historical Referents

THE fundamental importance of historicity should not, however, make
us lose sight of the fact that historical referents function differently in different narratives. Hermeneutically, the function of historical referents can
range all the way from being indispensable for interpretation to being inconsequential.

Hermeneutically Indispensable

The historical referent of the Exodus narrative, for example, the fact that
God rescued his people from slavery in Egypt, is indispensable in interpreting and preaching this narrative, for in this case the history itself is the
message. A denial of historicity here is a denial of the message. Most historical narratives in the Old Testament would fit into this category.

Validation of Teaching

In some historical narratives, however, historical referents are not directly
the point of the narrative but function as validation of its teaching. For example, Kings "claims to explain why the exile came about, and in doing
so to explain the ways of God, and the two explanations depend on each
other." Hence John Goldingay concludes that "the theology is dependent

19. Stroup, *Promise of Narrative Theology,* 137 and 149. Cf. Elizabeth Achtemeier
and Paul Achtemeier, *OT and Proclamation,* 164: "The Scriptures are the testimony to
what God has actually done, and if the actions of God in Israel and his Son Jesus are
reduced to ideas or symbols or 'eternal truths,' there is no basis for our faith."

on the events, their veracity is a *sine qua non* of the validity of the theology."[20] In this case, the message is a teaching drawn from history; although the message is other than the history itself, the historical referent is nevertheless indispensable to validate the teaching.

Hermeneutically Inconsequential

In yet other narratives, the historical referent is *hermeneutically* inconsequential. Take, for example, the book of Job. Does the historicity of Job, his family, and his friends make any difference for the interpretation of the book? One might ask, What is the purpose of the author of Job? Is it to teach people about certain historical events or is it to give people insight into the problem of suffering? To ask the question is to answer it. Thus, in the case of Job, the question of historicity is *hermeneutically* of no consequence.[21] The same point may be made with respect to the book of Jonah. As we noted in Chapter 8, the purpose of the author of Jonah is to have Israel identify itself with the figure of Jonah so that it may learn about its disobedience, its mandate in the world, and its compassionate creator God. The point of the story is made whether Jonah is a historical figure or not.[22]

Essential for Most Narratives

The question may be asked, however, if this nuanced way of dealing with the historicity of narrative might not lead to the wholesale abandonment of historicity in interpretation. Does the "domino theory"—when one falls, all fall—necessarily hold true for the historicity of biblical narratives? For example, if the question of historicity makes no difference to the interpretation of Jonah, can the same be said with respect to Abraham, who also, as we saw in Chapter 8, is a figure who represents Israel? But in the case of Abraham, the message itself requires the historical referent because the point of the story, God's covenant faithfulness, is dependent on the historicity of God making covenant with Abraham. Moreover, as we noted in Chapter 4, the historical prologue to a covenant needs to list genuine historical occurrences or it defeats its own purpose of placing the vassal in a position of obligation. Or consider Genesis 1: as historical nar-

20. Goldingay, *TynBul* 23 (1972) 80.

21. See ibid., 81: "If then we conclude that there is little historical truth behind Job, this will not have serious consequences for our estimate of its theological validity."

22. Childs, *Introduction*, 426, calls Jonah a "parable-like story" and writes, "Because the book serves canonically in the role of an analogy, it is as theologically irrelevant to know its historicity as it is with the Parable of the Good Samaritan." Cf. von Rad, *OT Theology*, II, 289: "Quite obviously, it is a story with a strong didactic content, and should not be read as an historical account." Cf. LaSor, Hubbard, and Bush, *OT Survey*, 350-53. For arguments that "the author of Jonah intended his work to be read as didactic history," see Alexander, *TynBul* 36 (1985) 36-59.

rative, the creation account is unique because it could not possibly be an eyewitness account. Moreover, its highly stylized structure (eight creative acts spread in parallel fashion over two sets of three days; see Chapter 3 above) has led interpreters to identify this narrative as wisdom literature and/or poetry and to deny or ignore its historical referent. However, this narrative, too, requires its historical referent for the validity of its message. One of the purposes of Genesis 1 is to teach Israel that their God Yahweh is the Creator of the entire universe and that therefore they ought not to worship, like their pagan neighbors, the "two great lights" and the stars (see Deut 17:2-7). In order for that message to be valid, one needs to accept as historical *that* God created the sun, moon, and stars. When and how God created them is a secondary issue which the author does not intend to answer, if he indeed sought to fit eight creative acts into the literary framework of the Israelite week. But the actuality of the historical referent of God creating sun, moon, and stars is demanded by the narrative if it is to retain its original validity as proclamation of the greatness of Israel's God and as polemic against pagan idolatry.

Preaching Texts, Not Bare Facts

HAVING seen, on the one hand, the crucial importance of acknowledging historicity and the difference it usually makes in interpreting historical narratives, we also need to appreciate, on the other hand, that preachers are to preach texts and not bare facts. The attempt to preach "the facts" behind the narrative inevitably leads to various problems.

First, preachers may be tempted to counter the doubt sown by the historical-critical method and raise all kinds of arguments to "prove" the historicity of the account. The pulpit, however, is not the place for extended argumentation for (or against) historicity, for such argumentation distracts from a genuine, realistic hearing of the text.

Second, by concentrating on "the facts," the interpreter looks right through the text as if it were a transparent windowpane. Both those using the historical-critical method and those trying to counter it by proving the historicity of the Bible are thus in danger of ignoring the text. But this procedure fails to do justice to the text, for no historical narrative is a transparent windowpane for viewing the facts beyond; historical narratives are more like stained-glass windows which artistically reveal the significance of certain facts from a specific faith perspective.[23] One must do justice to the text.

Third, preachers who try preaching facts run into the problem that they present "objective facts" and then have difficulty making an applica-

23. Cf. Stek, "Bee and the Mountain Goat," 59: "The author has presented not a flat photograph but a hologram to be viewed from various angles."

tion that does not appear to be tacked on. The problem is self-made, of course, because the text offers only interpreted facts; moreover, these interpreted facts are addressed to a specific people and thus already applied. Historical narratives take up the facts of the past and project them forward pertinently to future generations. "Even before they are 'used' for preaching," writes Kurt Frör, "the Old Testament texts themselves are already proclamation and appeal to the church."[24] Thus preachers can avoid many problems if they see their task not as preaching the facts behind the texts but as preaching texts which have already applied the interpreted facts (see further Chapter 8 above). Since these texts come to us in the form of Hebrew narratives, however, we need to consider carefully the literary dimension of Hebrew narratives.

LITERARY CHARACTERISTICS OF HEBREW NARRATIVE

IN discussing rhetorical criticism in Chapter 3, we have already seen the value of literary analysis for determining a textual unit, its theme, and its meaning in its larger literary context. Contemporary emphasis on literary analysis is leading increasingly to the realization that Hebrew narratives are artistic productions.[25] Robert Alter argues that literary art plays a crucial role "in the shaping of biblical narrative . . . , determining in most cases the minute choice of words and reported details, the pace of narration, the small movements of dialogue, and a whole network of ramified interconnections in the text."[26]

In reading Hebrew narratives as literary art, we must be careful not to read them in the light of Greek (Aristotle's *Poetics*) and modern Western literary conventions.[27] Although there are many similarities, to read Hebrew narrative through glasses colored by Western conventions could easily lead to a lack of understanding or distortion of the text. John Welch reminds us that "ancient art forms developed in accordance with the

24. Frör, *Biblische Hermeneutik*, 123.

25. Gerhard von Rad states, "Many of these narratives are . . . products of a determined intent at art and were in those days certainly evaluated as works of art" (*God at Work in Israel*, 12). David Gunn sees the purpose of the story of King David as "*serious* entertainment," that is, "entertainment which demands the active engagement of those being entertained, which challenges their intellect, their emotions, their understanding of people, of society and of themselves" (*Story of King David*, 61).

26. Alter, *Art of Biblical Narrative*, 3.

27. Alter contends that "the characteristic presentation of such narrative events in the Bible is notably different from that of the Greek epics and romances and of much later Western narrative literature" (ibid., 64). Cf. Miscall, *Workings of OT Narrative*, 142: "In my research, I have found that all the notions of narrative and the related issues— plot, character, theme, etc.—which are derived from some part of Western literature are of limited value in the analysis of biblical narrative." Cf. Kugel, *Idea of Biblical Poetry*, 304; and Sternberg, *Poetics*, 56.

needs of oral tradition." This fact partially accounts for the contrast with modern prose. "Modern style demands, for example, that an author write more or less linearly, following a line of syllogistic or dialectic reasoning, or developing a continuous flow of ideas. Circuitousness and repetitiveness are shunned in most circumstances. In many ancient contexts, however, repetition and even redundancy appear to represent the rule rather than the exception. Parallelism thrived."[28] Edward Greenstein helpfully pinpoints some further differences between Hebrew narrative style and that of Western literature:

> Because the Bible's stories are so familiar, we are prone to underestimate the considerable differences in narrative style between biblical storytelling and that of most Western literature. For example—and at the risk of oversimplifying—the Western narrative in which we are steeped is meant to be read by leaps and bounds, passage after passage. The biblical text, by contrast, is intricate and intensive, demanding slow-paced attentiveness to detail. . . . Biblical literature is geared toward the ear, and meant to be listened to at a sitting. In a "live" setting the storyteller negotiates each phrase with his audience. A nuance, an allusion hangs on nearly every word. Indeed, wordplay *per se* is a regular feature of the Bible's art.[29]

From the fact that Hebrew narratives follow other conventions than are familiar to most of us, one should not deduce that one needs to be an expert to understand these narratives but only that awareness of the Hebrew conventions will enable a sharper, clearer understanding of them. "One might imagine the Bible as a rich and variegated landscape, perfectly accessible to the observer's eye, but from which we now stand almost three millennia distant. Through the warp of all those intervening centuries, lines become blurred, contours are distorted, colors fade; for not only have we lost the precise shadings of implication of the original Hebrew words but we have also acquired quite different habits and expectations as readers, have forgotten the very conventions around which the biblical tales were shaped."[30]

In order to draw Hebrew narratives into focus, therefore, we need to place ourselves in the position of the original hearers and become aware of the specific ancient Hebrew conventions of communication which they simply assumed.[31] We shall take a closer look at the following aspects of

---

28. Welch, "Introduction," 12. Cf. Kugel, *Idea of Biblical Poetry*, 59: "Biblical parallelism . . . while . . . concentrated in the so-called 'poetic' books, . . . is to be found almost everywhere."

29. Greenstein, *Prooftexts* 1 (1981) 202.

30. Alter, *Art of Biblical Narrative*, 185.

31. See ibid., 47: "An elaborate set of tacit agreements between artist and audience about the ordering of the art work is at all times the enabling context in which the complex communication of art occurs." See the questions Barry Webb brings to the text in his literary study of Judges: *Book of the Judges*, 39-40.

Hebrew narratives: scene, characterization, dialogue, plot, narrator, and rhetorical structures.

The Scene

"IN Old Testament prose," says J. P. Fokkelman, "the scene is about the most important unit in the architecture of the narrative."[32] Although there are various modes of narration (straight narrative, description, comment, and scenic), the predominant mode of narrating is the "scenic," that is, "the action is broken up into a sequence of scenes. Each scene presents the happenings of a particular place and time, concentrating the attention of the audience on the deeds and the words spoken."[33]

Adele Berlin likens Hebrew narratives to "the frames from which films are made. Each one exists separately, and they are combined in a certain order to make the greater narrative, but an individual frame has no life of its own outside of the film as a whole."[34] Thus the scenic mode of most Hebrew narrative underscores the importance of understanding the theme of the scene (frame) in the context of the whole narrative (just as the narrative needs to be understood in the context of the whole book).

Number of Characters

A notable feature of scenes is that each scene usually has no more than two characters.[35] When there are more than two characters, the twofold division usually still obtains with one individual character and a group which functions as a collective character.

God's Presence

Another notable feature of these scenes—a feature generally overlooked in contemporary discussions—is the pervasive presence of God. Frequently God is one of the two "characters" in a scene: for example, God and Adam (Gen 3), God and Cain (Gen 4), God and Noah (Gen 6), God and Abraham (Gen 12), God and Samuel (1 Sam 16), etc. God appears also in the person of the angel of Yahweh with, e.g., Hagar (Gen 16), Moses (Exod 3), and Gideon (Judg 6), and as "the commander of the army of Yahweh" with Joshua (Josh 5). Prophets also function as the voice of God. Even in scenes where God, in a particular frame, is not one of the "characters" or is not represented by one of the characters, the scene as a whole will undoubtedly reveal the presence of God, for the human characters act out the scene against the backdrop of God's promises, God's enabling power, God's demands, God's providence.

32. Fokkelman, *Narrative Art in Genesis*, 9.
33. Licht, *Storytelling in the Bible*, 31 and 29.
34. Berlin, *Poetics*, 125.
35. See Alter, *Art of Biblical Narrative*, 72; Cf. Long, *1 Kings*, 149.

Characterization

Character Description

In contrast to Western prose, Hebrew narratives do not describe their characters in great detail. We may be told that Saul was tall and that David was handsome, but that is about the extent of direct description. Berlin observes that "what is lacking in the Bible is the kind of detailed physical or physiological description of characters that creates a visual image for the reader."[36] Whenever such physical details are given, however, they are usually significant. Alter advises, "When a particular descriptive detail is mentioned—Esau's ruddiness and hairiness, Rachel's beauty, King Eglon's obesity—we should be alert for consequences, immediate or eventual, either in plot or theme."[37]

Characters, of course, can be described in other than physical ways. Berlin reminds us that "descriptive terms may be based on status (king, widow, wise man, wealthy, old, etc.), profession (prophet, prostitute, shepherd, etc.), gentilic designation (Hittite, Amalekite, etc.)." She suggests that "the purpose of character description in the Bible is not to enable the reader to visualize the character, but to enable him to situate the character in terms of his place in society, his own particular situation, and his outstanding traits—in other words, to tell what kind of a person he is."[38]

Contrasted Characters

Another way in which Hebrew narrative portrays characters is by contrasting one character with another: Abraham and Lot, Sarah and Hagar, Jacob and Esau, Rachel and Leah, Ruth and Orpah, etc. One should also be aware that characters are contrasted not only side by side in relatively small literary units but also, at some distance, in the large literary units and in varying degrees of complexity. For example, Rahab and Achan are contrasted, as are Samuel and the sons of Eli, David and Saul, David, Nabal, and Abigail, and David, Uriah, and Bathsheba.[39] Consequently these characters must be interpreted in relation to each other. Sometimes one character is a foil for another; at other times "the one in the shadow makes the one in the spotlight shine all the more brightly by contrast."[40]

Parallel Characters

In addition to contrasting characters, biblical authors will sometimes par-

---

36. Berlin, *Poetics*, 34.

37. Alter, *Art of Biblical Narrative*, 180.

38. Berlin, *Poetics*, 35-36. See also Sternberg, *Poetics*, 325-28 on characterization, and pp. 329-33 on the use of names.

39. Some of these examples were suggested to me by J. H. Stek.

40. Berlin, *Poetics*, 136.

allel one character with another so that the former takes on the stature of its counterpart. For example, the author of Joshua deliberately draws parallels between Joshua and Moses (e.g., Josh 1:5, 17; 3:5, 7, 17; 4:14, 23; 5:15) so that Joshua comes to possess "the attributes of a 'second' Moses." The author of Kings similarly draws parallels between Elijah and Moses so that Elijah is presented as "a new Moses, acting like the mediator of a covenant between Yahweh and his people from a mount, destroying his enemies with a curse, actually seeing God pass by, handing his work to a successor, and being actually taken up by God."[41] This narrative technique of "parallel characters" (my phrase), sometimes called "historical recurrence," "re-enactment," or "narrative analogy,"[42] may also occur in more complex forms such as parallels between pairs of characters. For example, the author of Samuel-Kings first presents Samuel and David, and later Elijah and Elisha, as figures comparable to Moses and Joshua.[43] The significance of parallel characters is that, according to the author's intention, one character must be understood in the light of its counterpart.

Words and Actions

The predominant way of characterization in Hebrew narrative is not by description but by the words and actions of the characters. Samuel Sandmel points out that "we are told concrete things, that is, that Peninnah vexed Hannah, not that Hannah was a vexed woman; we are not told that Eli was a condescending person, but instead we see him acting in condescension. We must notice this preference for the concrete, since it permeates all of Hebrew narration."[44]

Another peculiarity to keep in mind with respect to the actions of characters is that Hebrew narratives "do not, as a rule, tell about the ordinary, everyday behaviour of the characters, but about their unusual and singular exploits."[45]

Dialogue

IN Hebrew narrative, dialogue is one of the main methods of characterization. According to Alter, dialogue is so preponderant that "everything in the world of biblical narrative ultimately gravitates toward dialogue. . . . Quantitatively, a remarkably large part of the narrative burden

41. Trompf, *VTSup* 30 (1979) 214 and 215.
42. "Re-enactment" is Trompf's term (ibid., 214); "narrative analogy" is Berlin's (*Poetics*, 136).
43. See Stek, *Former Prophets*, 48-49, 106-7. Cf. Savran, "1 and 2 Kings," 162-63, on the Elijah/Elisha-Moses/Joshua parallel.
44. Sandmel, *Enjoyment of Scripture*, 16-17.
45. Bar-Efrat, *Immanuel* 8 (1978) 24.

is carried by dialogue, the transactions between characters typically un-folding through the words they exchange, with only the most minimal in-tervention of the narrator." Indeed, narration is often "relegated to the role of confirming assertions made in dialogue."[46]

Narration and Dialogue

Alter suggests that there is a "special rhythm with which the Hebrew writers tell their tales: beginning with narration, they move into dialogue, drawing back momentarily or at length to narrate again, but always cen-tering on the sharply salient verbal intercourse of the characters." He con-siders the first words in dialogue so important that he proposes the fol-lowing rule: "In any given narrative event, and especially at the beginning of any new story, the point at which dialogue first emerges will be wor-thy of special attention, and in most instances, the initial words spoken by a personage will be revelatory, perhaps more in manner than in matter, constituting an important moment in the exposition of character."[47] The initial words may also reveal the plot. For example, the initial words of Naomi to her daughters-in-law—"The Lord grant that you may find a home" (Ruth 1:9)—set the stage for the plot of this narrative: Will Ruth find a home in Israel?

Contrastive Dialogue

Since scenes are generally limited to two characters, Hebrew writers are able to use contrastive dialogue to contrast and portray different characters. Compare, for example, "Esau's inarticulate outbursts over against Jacob's calculated legalisms in the selling of the birthright (Gen. 25); Joseph's long-winded statement of morally aghast refusal over against the two-word sexual bluntness of Potiphar's wife (Gen. 39); Saul's choked cry after David's impassioned speech outside the cave at Ein Gedi (1 Sam. 24)."[48]

Stylized Speech

Another feature of dialogue is stylized speech, which is especially notice-able when one character repeats in whole or in part the speech of another character. Alter advises that we "watch for the small differences that emerge in the general pattern of verbatim repetition. . . . Frequently enough, the small alterations, the reversals of order, the elaborations or deletions undergone by the statements as they are restated and sometimes restated again, will be revelations of character, moral, social, or political

---

46. Alter, *Art of Biblical Narrative*, 182 and 165. Webb calls dialogue "the primary carrier of the theme" (*Book of the Judges*, 75).
47. Alter, *Art of Biblical Narrative*, 75, 74.
48. Ibid., 72.

stance, and even plot."[49] Notice, for example, the serpent's blatant alteration of God's speech. According to Gen 2:16-17, God had said, "You may
freely eat of every tree of the garden; but of the tree of the knowledge of
good and evil you shall not eat." The serpent, however, asked the woman,
"Did God say, 'You shall not eat of any tree of the garden'?" The woman's
subsequent alteration of God's speech makes God's demand appear quite
unreasonable: "We may eat of the fruit of the trees of the garden; but God
said, 'You shall not eat of the fruit of the tree which is in the midst of the
garden, *neither shall you touch it . . .'"* (Gen 3:1-3).

Summarized Speech

Sometimes, instead of quoting speech verbatim, the narrator will summarize it. This change from quoting to summarizing may also be significant. "The reasons for such divergence," Alter suggests, "would range
from a felt need for rapid movement at a particular point in the narration,
a desire to avoid excessive repetition . . . , some consideration of conceal-
ment or decorousness, or a devaluation of what is said."[50]

Plot

THE plot of narrative consists of the arrangement and interrelationship of
the narrated events. A narrative "must have a 'plot,'" claims Jay Wilcoxen,
that is, a "beginning, middle, and end which contribute to the buildup
and release of dramatic tension."[51] According to Tremper Longman, plot
is usually "thrust forward by conflict. The conflict generates interest in its
resolution. The beginning of a story, with its introduction of conflict, thus
pushes us through the middle toward the end, when the conflict is resolved." The diagram on page 204 is helpful for visualizing the role of
plot in narrative.[52]

Single Plots

Plots can be either single or complex—single plots being the most common in biblical narrative. Shimon Bar-Efrat explains that single plots "ex-

49. Ibid., 183; cf. p. 91: "If the requirements of oral delivery and a time-honored
tradition of storytelling may have prescribed a mode of narration in which frequent
verbatim repetition was expected, the authors of the biblical narratives astutely discovered how the slightest strategic variations in the pattern of repetitions could serve
the purposes of commentary, analysis, foreshadowing, thematic assertion, with a
wonderful combination of subtle understatement and dramatic force."
    50. Ibid., 78.
    51. Wilcoxen, "Narrative," 93. For various views of plot, see Matera, *CBQ* 49
(1987) 235-36.
    52. The diagram is taken from Tremper Longman III, *Literary Approaches to Bibli-
cal Interpretation* (Grand Rapids: Zondervan, 1987), p. 92, and is used by permission.

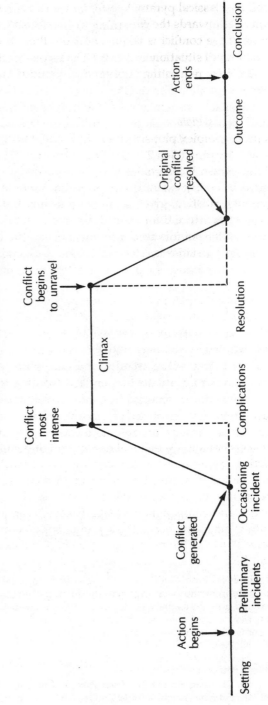

The Structure of Biblical Narrative

hibit the classical pyramid pattern. From a peaceful initial situation the action rises towards the climax where the decisive step determining the outcome of the conflict is taken, and from there it drops again to a more or less tranquil situation at the end." Examples of this kind of plot are Genesis 22 (God requesting Abraham to sacrifice Isaac) and the book of Esther.[53]

Complex Plots

A more complex plot structure shows up, for example, in the narrative of Isaac's blessing (Gen 27). Bar-Efrat explains: "The narrative . . . reaches its climax when Jacob comes very close to the suspicious Isaac and is subjected to bodily examination. A resting point is reached when Isaac, apparently satisfied, gives Jacob his blessing. But when immediately after Jacob's departure Esau enters his father's tent the story flares up again. A new resting point is reached only after Jacob departs from his home and a physical distance is created between the hostile brothers."[54]

Pace

Generally, the plot in Hebrew narrative moves at a faster pace than that of modern narration. This rapid pace is the result of short sentences, a lack of detail, and the absence of extended character description. Sandmel points out that "there is a concomitant directness in the narration, with the result that the impact of the events, coupled with the perception and the insight, can be far stronger than a leisurely, extended account would be."[55]

The narrator can, however, slow down the action in various ways. We saw above that direct speech, in contrast to summary, slows down the action. Other devices for slowing down the pace are the verbatim repetition of speeches and exceptional description of detail.[56] The significance of detecting "retardation" in the narrative is not only that it helps one perceive the built-in suspense but, more importantly for preachers today, that it helps one understand "the structure of the narrative, its culminating points and consequently its significance." For, as Bar-Efrat points out, an author may slow down the action in order to dwell at length on what he considers to be the more important point. For example, "the story of David and Bathsheba (2 Sam. 11) reveals that the author lingers on the passages concerning Uriah, whereas the passages on Bathsheba are hurried over quickly in summary. This may be taken as hinting that David's sins against Uriah are of greater weight than those against Bathsheba"[57]—or rather,

---

53. Bar-Efrat, *VT* 30 (1980) 165.
54. Ibid., 166-67.
55. Sandmel, *Enjoyment of Scripture,* 16.
56. See Alter, *Art of Biblical Narrative,* 53.
57. Bar-Efrat, *Immanuel* 8 (1978) 25-26.

that the author considered David's premeditated murder of Uriah more ominous than his impulsive adultery with Bathsheba.

The Narrator

BESIDES characters and events (plot), the narrator is "an integral part of the narrative, one of its structural constituents—even a most important one," writes Bar-Efrat. "His voice is heard continually, along with the voices of the acting characters, through his eyes we see and through his ears we hear whatever is happening in the narrative world. He also interprets for us the events of this world."[58] Although the narrator usually remains inconspicuous, we become aware of his presence when we look for telltale signs exposing the distance between the narrator and the narrated events, e.g., "the pillar of Rachel's tomb, which is there to this day" (Gen 35:20), the "twelve stones . . . are there to this day" (Josh 4:9), "in those days there was no king in Israel" (Judg 17:6). We also become aware of the narrator when we pay attention to how he "introduces the characters, informs us who is talking to whom and sometimes also defines the nature of the talk ('he said,' 'he called,' 'he commanded,' etc.)."[59] Most important for us, of course, is to discern how the narrator evaluates events, for this will enable us to determine the thrust of a passage. In order to detect the narrator's evaluation, we will have to be aware of his omniscience and point of view.

Omniscience
The narrator is almost always omniscient, that is, "he knows everything and is present everywhere." Bar-Efrat demonstrates the omniscience of the narrator in 2 Sam 10–20 as follows:

> He [our narrator] enters into the innermost chambers, he hears the intimate conversation between Amnon and Jonadab, he witnesses Amnon overpowering the resisting Tamar and he is aware that the old David did not 'know' the fair Abishag. From time to time he informs the reader, by means of direct inside views, of the thoughts, feelings and intentions of the characters. . . .
> The most notable evidence of the narrator's omniscience is to be found in what he tells us about God, His judgment ("But the thing that David had done displeased the Lord"), His feelings ("and the Lord loved him") and

57. Bar-Efrat, *Immanuel* 8 (1978): 25-26.
58. Ibid., 20.
59. Ibid., 22. For a listing of fourteen "varieties of the narrator's own discourse," see Sternberg, *Poetics*, 120-21. Sternberg also notes the threefold distinction in English literature between "the actual writer, the implied author, and the narrator," but contends that in biblical narrative "the implied author and the narrator . . . practically merge into each other" (pp. 74-75). Cf. Longman, *Literary Approaches*, 84, 87.

His intentions ("For the Lord had appointed to defeat the good counsel of Ahithophel, to the intent that the Lord might bring evil upon Absalom") (2 Sam. 11:27; 12:24; 17:14).[60]

Even though the narrator is omniscient, he does not share all he knows with the reader. Alter suggests that "the reticence of the biblical narrator, his general refusal to comment on or explain what he reports, is purposefully selective."[61] This purposeful selection becomes another clue to understanding the purpose of a particular narrative. Why does the narrator evaluate certain characters and actions but not others? What is the narrator's point of view?

Point of View

In literary criticism, "point of view" designates "the position or perspective from which a story is told."[62] For example, in disclosing his omniscience in the words "but the thing that David had done displeased the Lord" (2 Sam 11:27b), the narrator presents an evaluation of David's sins of adultery and murder. "This [is] the narrator's conceptual point of view," says Berlin, "the perspective of his attitude towards the story he is telling. He disapproves of David's actions."[63] More significant than the narrator's attitude, however, is the fact that the narrator tells us that it "displeased the Lord." Thus the narrator presents not just his own human point of view but the point of view of the Lord.[64]

Only occasionally will the narrator disclose God's point of view to his readers, sometimes directly (Abram "believed the Lord; and he reckoned it to him as righteousness," Gen 15:6) and sometimes by way of one of the characters ("As for you, you meant evil against me; but God meant it for good, to bring it about that many people should be kept alive," Gen 50:20). But on the whole the narrator does not provide many direct evaluative comments. Accordingly, one needs to raise the question, Why no evaluation? Are we today perhaps too moralistically inclined in expecting

60. Bar-Efrat, *Immanuel* 8 (1978) 20. On the narrator's omniscience, see also Sternberg, *Poetics*, 84-99.

61. Alter, *Art of Biblical Narrative*, 184. On "narrative reticence" or "gapping," see especially Sternberg, *Poetics*, 186-263.

62. Berlin, *Poetics*, 46. Following Boris Uspensky, Longman distinguishes point of view in four different planes: spatial, temporal, psychological, and ideological. Spatial refers to whether the narrator is omnipresent, temporal to whether he transcends time, psychological to whether he is omniscient, and ideological to the narrator's evaluation (*Literary Approaches*, 87-88).

63. Berlin, *Poetics*, 47.

64. Berlin states rather cautiously that "one often gets the impression that the narrator is reflecting the way God would evaluate events if he had been the one telling the story" (ibid., 148 n. 28), but the matter can be stated more unequivocally: the narrator tells the story from God's point of view because he is a spokesman for God; see Chapter 1 above.

constant evaluations? For what purpose did the author relate this narra-tive? Von Rad suggests that the lack of evaluation on the part of the nar-rator "is intended to show him [the reader] not to be so hasty in judging the characters in these stories. Rather, he is to pay attention to what God has let happen to them."[65] More precisely, the lack of character evaluation exhibits the narrator's purposeful attempt not to close off the narrative at the human level but to keep the narrative open to God: What is the covenant God doing in and through and in spite of these human characters? Thus the narrator not only narrates from God's point of view but manages to turn our attention to God even when the narrative is about human characters.

Rhetorical Structures

IN Chapter 3 we already explained some of the typical structural patterns that are used in prose as well as in poetry: repetition, parallelism, chiasm, and inclusion.[66] All of these patterns and more can be found in Hebrew narratives. We shall examine some of the more common structures.

Repetition

Repetition is a favored device in Hebrew narrative. It ranges from the re-petition of words to the repetition of whole speeches (see the discussion of dialogue above). Martin Buber describes the repetition of words and its significance as follows: "A *Leitwort* is a word or a word-root that recurs significantly in a text, in a continuum of texts, or in a configuration of texts: by following these repetitions, one is able to decipher or grasp a meaning of the text, or at any rate, the meaning will be revealed more strikingly."[67]

Alter calls attention to the range of repetition by observing that repeti-tion takes place not only in key words but also in motifs, in themes, and in a sequence of actions such as "the three captains and their companies threatened with fiery destruction in 2 Kings 1."[68] Divergence from ex-

---

65. Von Rad, *God at Work in Israel*, 12.
66. Though mostly prose, Hebrew narrative will soar into poetry at times (e.g., Gen 1:27; 2:23; 8:22; 12:1-3; 25:23). According to Fokkelman, "Genesis," 36, "The body of prose functions as a setting in which, repeatedly, the gem of a poem sparkles." As to the function of these poems, "by serving as crystallization points, they create mo-ments of reflection. In a powerful and compact formula they summarize what is rele-vant; they condense the chief idea and lift it above the incidental" (p. 44). In Chap-ter 10 below we shall deal with poetry in greater detail.
67. Buber, *Werke*, vol. 2: *Schriften zur Bibel* (Munich, 1964), 1131, as translated by Alter, *Art of Biblical Narrative*, 93.
68. Alter, *Art of Biblical Narrative*, 95-96: on motifs—"A concrete image, sensory quality, action, or object recurs through a particular narrative"; on themes—"An idea

pected repetition may also be significant: "Where the narration so abundantly encourages us to expect this sort of repetition, on occasion the avoidance of repetition, whether through substitution of a synonym or of a wholly divergent word or phrase for the anticipated reference, may also be particularly revealing."[69]

Repetition can also serve a different purpose than guiding the hearer to the meaning of the narrative. With the narration of events which take place simultaneously, the technique of resumptive repetition serves to return the audience to the original point of the story after it has followed a branch for a while. For example, according to 1 Sam 19:12, "Michal lowered David from the window and 'he fled and escaped. . . .' The reader remains with Michal and the encounter between her and Saul's men. But meanwhile David has been making his escape, as we are told in 19:18 . . . 'And . . . David fled and escaped.'"[70]

Inclusion

Inclusion is a special form of repetition found also in Hebrew narrative, for example, Deut 1:1 and 29:1 (MT 28:69). As explained in Chapter 3 above, inclusion marks primarily the limits of a literary unit by repeating at the end words and phrases from the beginning. For an audience which received this narration aurally, inclusion signaled the end of the narration and may have reiterated the message by reminding the audience of the opening statement.

Chiasm

Welch calls chiasm "a significant ordering principle within, not only verses and sentences, but also within and throughout whole books."[71] Since chiasm is a sophisticated form of repetition, the clue to identifying chiasm is repetition. "Where repetition is frequent, . . . the analyst must at least ask if the narrative has been constructed with a chiastic architecture; if the narrative shows repetition, does it also show the necessary inversion, balance, and climactic centrality?"[72]

Chiastic patterns can be found in dialogue as well as in scenes. Bar-Efrat provides a good example of chiasm in dialogue in his analysis of the

---

which is part of the value-system of the narrative . . . is made evident in some recurring pattern." For a detailed analysis of repetition, see Sternberg, *Poetics*, 365-440.

69. Alter, *Art of Biblical Narrative*, 180.

70. Berlin, *Poetics*, 126-27. For more examples of resumptive repetition, see Talmon, "Ezra and Nehemiah," 360. For other possible uses of resumptive repetition, see Burke O. Long, "Framing Repetitions in Biblical Historiography," *JBL* 106/3 (1987) 385-99.

71. Welch, "Introduction," 11.

72. Dillard, *JSOT* 30 (1984) 86.

speech of Hushai (2 Sam 17:8-13).[73] Notice the chiastic structure for each half of the speech, the two halves being linked at the center (X):

A You *know your father* and his men, that they are *powerful* and embittered,
B *Like a bear* robbed of her cubs in the field.
C And your father is skilled in war and he will not pass the night with *the people.*
X Behold, even now he is hidden in one of the pits or IN ONE OF THE PLACES.
C' And it will be when some of them will fall at the beginning, whoever hears it will say: "There has been a slaughter among *the people* who follow Absalom."
B' Then even the brave man, whose heart is *like* the heart of *a lion,* will utterly melt.
A' For all Israel *knows* that *your father* is *powerful* and brave men are those who are with him.
D Let *all Israel* be completely *gathered* to you, from Dan to Beersheba,
E *As the sand by the sea* for multitude; and you in person go to battle.
X' And we shall come upon him IN ONE OF THE PLACES where he is to be found,
E' And we shall light upon him *as the dew falls on the ground;* and of him and all the men that are with him not even one will be left.
D' And if he be *gathered* into a city, *all Israel* will carry ropes to that city, and we shall drag it into the brook, until not even a small stone is to be found there.

Fokkelman provides a good example of chiasm in a scene in his analysis of Gen 25:20-26, the first scene of the *toledoth* of Isaac.

A Isaac was forty years old when he took to wife Rebekah		v. 20
B Rebekah was barren; prayer for children answered		vv. 20/21
C his wife Rebekah conceived		v. 21
the children struggle together within her		v. 22
D Rebekah asks for ⎫ an ORACLE		v. 22
D' Yahweh grants her ⎭		v. 23
C' her days to be delivered were fulfilled		v. 24
and behold, there were twins in her womb		v. 24
B' birth and appearance of Jacob and Esau		vv. 25, 26a
A' Isaac was sixty years old when she bore them		v. 26b

Fokkelman admits that although the chiastic structure here is "not everywhere compelling, . . . nevertheless the structure of this passage betrays what is the heart of the matter in Gen. 25.19-26, that which is the centre of the symmetrical composition, D + D'. The oracle is central."[74] Preachers might be tempted to use this passage for a sermon on "Answered Prayer,"

---

73. Bar-Efrat, *VT* 30 (1980) 170-71.
74. Fokkelman, *Narrative Art in Genesis,* 93.

or "The Patience of Isaac," or "Motherhood." But the structure of this scene focuses on the Lord's words: "Two nations are in your womb, and two peoples, born of you, shall be divided; the one shall be stronger than the other, the elder shall serve the younger." The structure, therefore, shows that "it is not Isaac's trial of waiting and the answering of his prayer which constitute the plot, but that the ins and outs of the children's birth [and the implications of the oracle] are the main point."[75]

This last example especially shows the significance of recognizing chiastic structures. It not only provides a greater appreciation of Hebrew narrative as literature, but it also helps delineate the literary unit to be used as preaching text and prevents misinterpretation by centering on the theme of the passage.

Stereotyped Patterns

Sometimes the structure of Old Testament books consists of a stereotyped pattern, such as the well-known pattern in the book of Judges:

    A. Israel does evil in the sight of Yahweh
    B. Yahweh hands them over to an oppressor
    C. Israel cries to Yahweh
    C'. Yahweh raises up a deliverer for Israel
    B'. Yahweh hands the oppressor over to the deliverer
    A'. The land has rest

The author of Kings uses the following "stereotyped framework . . . to introduce and conclude the material presented for a particular king's reign."

    A. *Introductory framework*
       1. Royal name and accession date . . .
       2. King's age at accession (Judah only)
       3. Length and place of reign
       4. Name of queen mother (Judah only)
       5. Theological appraisal
    B. *Events during the reign* . . .
    C. *Concluding framework*
       1. Formula citing other sources of regnal information
       2. Notices of death and burial
       3. Notice of a successor[76]

---

75. Ibid.; for the chiastic structure of scene 2 (Gen 25:29-34), see pp. 95-97. For three chiastic structures supporting the "development of plot and theme" in Judg 4–5, see Stek, "Bee and the Mountain Goat," 55-57. Other examples of chiasm in Judges may be found in Webb, *Book of the Judges*, 83, 90, 108, 114, etc.

76. Long, *1 Kings*, 22. For "type-scenes," see, e.g., Alter, *Art of Biblical Narrative*, 51-52; James G. Williams, "The Beautiful and the Barren: Conventions in Biblical Type-Scenes," *JSOT* 17 (1980) 107-19; and Buss, "Understanding Communication," 96-99. The suggestion that biblical authors used type-scenes is based on only a few repeti-

Structural Levels

Bar-Efrat suggests that structures can be detected at four different levels: "(1) the verbal level; (2) the level of narrative technique; (3) the level of the narrative world; and (4) the level of the conceptual content."[77]

At the *verbal* level, for example, the repetition of the words "And there was evening and there was morning" divides the first creation account into seven clearly marked sections.

At the level of *narrative technique*, "the analysis of structure . . . is based on variations in narrative method, such as narrator's account as opposed to character's speech (dialogue), scenic presentation versus summary, narration as against description, explanation, comment, etc." For example, the narrative of Samuel's birth (1 Sam 1:1–2:11) alternates between summary and scene as follows:

Summary (i 1-3)
    Scene (verses 4-18)
Summary (verses 19-20)
    Scene (verses 21-23a)
Summary (verse 23b)
    Scene (i 24–ii 10)
Summary (verse 11)[78]

At the level of *narrative world*, the analysis of structure is related primarily to the characters and the plot but also to setting, clothes, etc. For example, the narrative of Amnon and Tamar (2 Sam 13) provides "a striking illustration of structure based upon identity of characters." After the opening section introducing the main characters, the narrative is constructed as a chain with seven links, each link being made up of two characters, the second of which is first in the next link.

Jonadab-Amnon (verses 3-5)
    Amnon-David (verse 6)
        David-Tamar (verse 7)
            Tamar-Amnon (verses 8-16)
                Amnon-servant (verse 17)
                    servant-Tamar (verse 18)
                        Tamar-Absalom (verses 19-20)

"It should be observed," says Bar-Efrat, "that Amnon is found in the first two links, whereas Tamar is found in the last two. . . . In the middle link, which is much larger in size than any of the other ones (9 verses), Amnon and Tamar meet and here the climax of the story is reached."[79]

---

tions and is therefore rather hypothetical; the phenomena might just as plausibly be explained as actual repetitions of and/or allusions to earlier events.

77. Bar-Efrat, *VT* 30 (1980) 157-70.

78. Ibid., 158-59.

79. Ibid., 162.

Finally, on the level of *conceptual content*, "the analysis of structure is based on the themes of the narrative units." For example, one of the themes of 1 Samuel is "the transference of leadership—from Eli to Samuel, from Samuel to Saul and from Saul to David." This theme divides the book into three parts, chapters 1–7 dealing with Eli and Samuel, chapters 8–15 with Samuel and Saul, and chapters 16–31 with Saul and David."[80] Hence structural patterns may be found at various levels and can be very significant indicators of the intended meaning of a passage.

HOLISTIC INTERPRETATION

In interpreting Hebrew narrative, one needs to take into account all dimensions relevant to its interpretation. Since Chapters 3 to 5 treat holistic interpretation at length, the discussion here can be relatively brief as we look specifically at holistic interpretation of Hebrew narratives. We shall consider in turn literary, historical, and theological interpretation.

Literary Interpretation

Understanding in Total Context
Since Hebrew narrative is a distinct genre of literature, it requires a distinct hermeneutical approach. Haddon Robinson puts his finger on a major difference between interpreting narrative and some other genres of literature: "When working in narrative literature, an expositor will seldom have to work through a maze of complex grammatical relationships, but instead will have to derive the author's meaning from the broad study of many paragraphs."[81] Especially when the narrative consists of a series of scenes, the meaning of each scene (frame) will have to be established in the context of the whole act (film). Although understanding in context is important for all genres of literature, it is more crucial for narrative to be understood in its literary context than it is for, say, wisdom literature.

In Chapters 3 and 7 we noted the tendency, in interpretation as well as preaching, to isolate narratives from their literary contexts. In view of this tendency toward atomism, we need to underscore that one can determine and proclaim the meaning of a specific narrative only in the context of the whole book (and ultimately of the whole Bible), for each part finds its specific meaning only in the context of the whole.

Attention to Detail
Even while one searches the total context for clues to the meaning of a

80. Ibid., 168-69. See Savran, "1 and 2 Kings," 148, for a seven-part chiastic structure marking all of 1 and 2 Kings.
81. Robinson, *Biblical Preaching*, 69.

specific Hebrew narrative, one must also pay attention to the details of the text. As we saw in the section on literary characteristics (above), details in the narrative often provide valuable clues to the intended meaning. For example, while physical description of characters is rare, when it does occur it is usually a significant detail for understanding the narrative. It is important to note when a character's words or deeds are contrasted with those of another character. The first words of a character may be highly significant, as are changes in a speech that is otherwise repeated verbatim. Attention should be paid to the plot, how the tension is built up and eventually resolved. When the narrator slows the pace by lengthy quotations, stylized speech, or detailed description, he may be providing a clue as to what he considered important. Attention should further be paid to the point of view of the narrator, his stance, his evaluation of events or his neglect of evaluation. And, of course, one should have an eye for repetition, a sudden change in expected repetition, chiasm, and other literary structures at the different levels where they may occur since any and all of these may be clues to the intended meaning. Finally, wherever possible, one should compare the selected passage with parallel passages elsewhere (e.g., a passage from Chronicles with Samuel-Kings), for such a comparison will often reveal the author's changes, emphases, point of view, and purpose.

Questions to Put to Narrative

Because Hebrew narrative is different from other genres of literature, one must put questions to narrative that are suited to bring out the meaning of this specific genre. Some of these questions are the following: How many "scenes" are in this "act," and how does each "scene" (frame) fit into the "act" (film)? What other structures can be detected in the narrative, and do they set its limits and concentrate its focus? Who are the main characters and how are they described? Are the characters contrasted with each other, and does one (or both) parallel earlier figures (or prefigure later figures)? Does the dialogue of the characters reveal character, plot, evaluation of conduct? What is the plot, the tension that needs to be resolved? Does pace retardation suggest the narrator's emphasis? Where is the narrator and what is his point of view? Does he evaluate the characters and, if not, why not? What is the specific point of the narrative, and how does this point fit into the theme of the book? Questions like these seek to elicit the specific meaning of the narrative.

Historical Interpretation

Hear as the Original Audience

Historical interpretation is interested in discovering the meaning of the text in its own historical-cultural context. For the interpretation of narrative, the historical questions concerning the author, the original audience, the time, setting, and purpose of writing are important, for they provide further clues to the purpose and meaning of a passage. Historical interpretation forces one to zero in on the author and the original audience in order to hear the narrative in the same way the original audience heard it. Because of the historical, cultural distance between a contemporary interpreter and the original audience, it should come as no surprise that historical interpretation brings to the surface elements of *discontinuity*, that is, customs, practices, laws, etc., that no longer hold today.

The Context of Kingdom History

Historical interpretation can also bring out the *continuity* that exists between then and now by understanding the historical referents of historical narrative in the context of the universal kingdom history that stretches from creation to the new creation. Most biblical scholars agree that biblical historical narratives are not biographies that can be isolated from their larger context, as occurs in biographical, character preaching.[82] The historical referents of these narratives are, in the nature of the case, parts of a larger history. One way to do justice to this larger framework is to see each narrative in the context of the overall theme of biblical history writing. That theme may be designated as the coming kingdom of God. It is first stated in the book of Genesis. "Gen. 3:15 places all subsequent events in the light of the tremendous battle between the Seed of the woman and the seed of the serpent, between Christ coming into the world and Satan the ruler of this world, and it places all events in the light of the complete victory which the Seed of the woman shall attain. In view of this, it is imperative that not one single person be isolated from this history and set apart from this great battle. . . . From this point of view the facts are selected and recorded."[83]

Moreover, since the ultimate narrative of God's coming kingdom reaches beyond the Old Testament and beyond the New Testament to the future new creation, relating an individual Old Testament narrative to this ultimate narrative will link it directly to modern times, for the past as well as the present form part of that one history. Recognizing the connection

---

82. Cf. Long, *1 Kings*, 8: "The OT offers no examples of genuine biography, although scholars from time to time have incorrectly used the word."

83. M. B. Van 't Veer, "Christologische Prediking," *Van den Dienst des Woords* (Goes: Oosterbaan & LeCointre, 1944), 149, as translated in my *Sola Scriptura*, 135. Cf. Fee and Stuart, *How to Read the Bible*, 74: "The Old Testament narratives . . . have plots that are part of a special overall plot. . . . The *top level* is that of the whole universal plan of God worked out through His creation. Key aspects of the plot at this top level are the initial creation itself; the fall of humanity; the power and ubiquity of sin; the need for redemption; and Christ's incarnation and sacrifice." Cf. Miller, *Word and World* 3/3 (1983) 289.

between these ancient narratives and kingdom history thus opens the door to their contemporary relevance.

Theological Interpretation

MORE crucial for narrative than for any other genre is the question, What does *God* here reveal about himself? The reason why this question is so crucial for narrative should be plain: in no other genre does the attention so easily drift from the theocentric focus of Scripture to human beings.

The Slide into Anthropocentric Preaching

Reasons for anthropocentric preaching are not hard to find. In biblical narrative the human characters frequently appear to be center stage. Moreover, it is so easy in preaching simply to relate the story of Joseph and his brothers, of Ehud and Eglon, of David and Bathsheba, and draw a few "lessons" for the contemporary congregation. It is somewhat understandable that busy preachers fall into the trap of preaching anthropocentric sermons from time to time; what is less understandable is that homileticians, presumably after giving it some thought, would advocate this approach. A quotation from two homileticians will clarify the point at issue:

> Another effective type of expository preaching is that of preaching on Bible characters. Faris D. Whitesell, in his excellent book on this subject [*Preaching on Bible Characters*], gives many reasons for placing this type of preaching in high priority. He points out that this is perhaps the easiest way to preach the Bible, the most likely to appeal to people and to hold their attention, . . . and the most likely to be remembered. And, for freshness and variety, there are approximately four hundred Bible characters from which to choose.[84]

> For permanent collection of Biblical material, buy two cheap Bibles and clip out all the passages related to this character. Paste them together in chronological sequence. . . . The keyword for the sermon will be "characteristics," "traits," or some such word. . . . In the sermon, be sure to take the character off the pedestal by finding those traits that are relevant and most practical for the listener. . . .

> [Example:] Sermon from the life of Jonathan.

---

84. C. W. Koller, *Expository Preaching without Notes* (Grand Rapids: Baker, 1969) 32. See further p. 25 on the two approaches for a "biographical sermon": "(1) Under the first main point, tell the story of that life, preferably in chronological order; and under the second main point, draw out the lessons; or (2) tell the life story, and indicate each phase by a main point, followed by the lessons derived."

  I. Courage—I Sam. 14:6
  II. Humility—I Sam. 18:4
  III. Loyalty—I Sam. 19:2[85]

Similar advice can be found in many homiletics texts. The question is, however, if such an anthropocentric approach does justice to the Scriptures. Marten Woudstra, for one, observes that "the aim of biblical historiography is not to focus on the human agents of the redemptive drama, or to exploit their good and evil deeds for purposes of moral example or deterrent." Woudstra points to Joshua 24 as an illustration of "how sacred history must be viewed": "Throughout this summary the emphasis is on what God, the covenant Lord, has done. It is this emphasis, not that of moral example, that causes the people to respond with an expression of loyalty to their Lord and demonstrate their willingness to serve only him."[86]

Sometimes preachers, sensing the deficiency of straight anthropocentric preaching, will try to do justice to both God and human characters as two distinct factors in the text. This procedure often leads to a curious split in the sermon between a theocentric explication and an anthropocentric application. In historical narrative, however, it is not a question of two opposite factors which must each receive their due, but rather one "factor," God, who works for, with, through, and sometimes in spite of people. God, after all, is the God who makes covenant with people. In the covenant history narrated in the Bible, the human characters appear not for their own sake but for the sake of showing what God is doing for, with, and through them. As von Rad puts it in connection with Genesis 16 (Hagar and Ishmael), "There can be no doubt that the story in no way intends to provide us with examples. . . . The sermon must be careful . . . to treat not of human affairs but of *God's* gracious ways of dealing with men."[87]

Theocentric Narratives

We noticed the theocentric focus of Hebrew narrative earlier by observing how frequently God or his representative is one of the "characters" in a scene and also how the narrator relates the story from God's "point of view." Even where God appears to be absent from a scene, we noted, the "film" as a whole will reveal the presence of God because the human characters act out the scene against the backdrop of God's promises, God's enabling power, God's covenant demands, God's providence. A few examples will make this point clear. The narratives about Joseph in Egypt appear to center on human characters and, taken in isolation, might

---

85. Perry, *Manual for Biblical Preaching*, 108.
86. Woudstra, *Book of Joshua*, 3-4.
87. Von Rad, *Biblical Interpretations in Preaching*, 32.

easily be preached in an anthropocentric fashion. When understood in their context, however, these narratives cannot be interpreted anthropocentrically, for the context contains two of Joseph's speeches that "unlock the whole narrative," as von Rad puts it. The first speech is in the scene of recognition: "And now do not be distressed . . . because you sold me here; for God sent me before you to preserve life. . . . So it was not you who sent me here, but God" (Gen 45:4-8). Von Rad comments: "Here Joseph at last speaks openly of God, and here the last veil is lifted; for here, finally, is manifested what in truth is the primary subject of the whole story: God's will to turn all the chaos of human guilt to a gracious purpose. God, not the brothers, 'sent' Joseph to Egypt."[88] Joseph's second revealing speech takes place at the end of the book and functions as the key to interpreting the whole Joseph story: "As for you, you meant evil against me, but God meant it for good, to bring it about that many people should be kept alive, as they are today"(Gen 50:20).

Or take, for example, the gruesome story in Judges 3 of Ehud stabbing and killing Eglon. Because of all the blood and gore, few preachers may feel comfortable preaching this narrative today, but those who do preach it may easily do so in an anthropocentric manner. For instance, W. Vischer understands Ehud's action as a "cogent contribution of the Bible to the right of killing a tyrant"[89]—in other words, given similar circumstances, a positive example. In opposing Vischer, D. F. Baumgärtel stresses that Eglon is a negative example: "This murder becomes immediately relevant for our faith, when we . . . begin to realize that we desire to act just like the brave Ehud. . . . Indeed, we are Ehud."[90] But the author of Judges 3 intends to provide neither a positive example for killing tyrants nor a negative example of how bad we are; on the contrary, the author has cast this narrative in a theocentric framework: "the Lord strengthened Eglon" (v. 12), and "the Lord raised up for them a deliverer, Ehud" (v. 15). Moreover, structural analysis discloses a chiastic structure centered on Ehud saying "I have a message of God for you" and thrusting his sword into Eglon's belly.[91] Consequently, the author's purpose is not to give moral examples but to reveal that God is at work in history, first in judging his people through Eglon, but now especially in redeeming his people through Ehud. Therefore, the author's message to the original hearers is in no way anthropocentric; it is a message for Israel to recognize the hand

---

88. Von Rad, God at Work in Israel, 31-32.

89. W. Vischer, Das Christuszeugnis des Alten Testaments (Munich: Kaiser, 1935), II, 89.

90. D. F. Baumgärtel, Verheissung: Zur Frage des evangelischen Verständnisses des Alten Testaments (Gütersloh: Bertelsmann, 1952), 94.

91. See Stek, Former Prophets, 20.

of the Lord in judgment and in redemption, together with the implied admonition (vv. 7 and 12): Do not forget the Lord your God!

As a final example of the theocentric character of Old Testament narrative (see also Chapter 5 above), we turn to 2 Samuel. In 2 Samuel the history of David appears to be narrated strictly from a human point of view—except, as we noted earlier, that the omniscient narrator lets us in on God's evaluation of David's adultery and murder: "But the thing that David had done displeased the Lord" (11:27b). Von Rad comments: "If he [the reader] has taken note of the brief and quite unemotional warning at *II Sam.* xi.27, and then read of the succession of blows which befall the house of David, the reader will know where to look for the explanation of all this piling up of disasters: God is using them to punish the King's sin." At a later juncture the author provides another glimpse of God's evaluation—one which we might easily overlook: "And the Lord loved him [the baby Solomon]" (2 Sam 12:24). Von Rad remarks that "at the end of the long story when Solomon is left in command of the field after untold complications, the reader will recall this sentence and understand that it is not human merit and virtue which have made the throne secure, but a paradoxical act of election on the part of God." The author of Samuel makes a third comment of this nature in 2 Sam 17:14: "For the Lord had ordained to defeat the good counsel of Ahithophel, so that the Lord might bring evil upon Absalom." According to von Rad, "This was the turning-point in the rebellion, and the change in the situation was the work of God himself, who had heard the prayer of the King in his profound humiliation."[92] Summing up, von Rad opines that "the deuteronomist shows, by a wholly valid process, just what redemptive history is within the context of the Old Testament: it is a course of events shaped by the word of Yahweh, continually intervening to direct and to deliver, and so steadily pressing these events towards their fulfilment in history."[93]

A Theocentric Purpose

In general, it may be said that biblical historical narratives are told for a theocentric purpose: "Their purpose is to show God at work in His creation and among His people. The narratives glorify Him, help us to understand and appreciate Him, and give us a picture of His providence and protection."[94] This theocentric purpose can be detected in all the historical books of the Old Testament. The following summary will suffice to make the point in a general way: "A striking feature of all the historical books proper is that they emphasize the activity of the Lord in bringing about

---

92. Von Rad, *Problem of the Hexateuch*, 199-200.
93. Ibid., 221.
94. Fee and Stuart, *How to Read the Bible*, 74.

His divine purpose: He punishes those who disobey Him and blesses those who worship Him (Deut.), if people pray to Him and trust in Him their enemies are virtually impotent (Chronicles, Ezra-Nehemiah), what the prophets preach, happens (Kings) and what Yahweh promises (to the patriarchs or David) is fulfilled (Genesis-Joshua and Samuel)."[95]

Other Purposes

The overall theocentric purpose of historical narrative does not invalidate other purposes. One obvious purpose of the theocentric narratives is to stimulate faith in and obedience to Yahweh. That purpose is attained, however, not by holding up people as examples of faith and obedience but by showing in the actions of the covenant God that he is worthy of our trust and obedience. John Goldingay compares the purposes of Old Testament narratives with those of the New Testament: "Three of the five New Testament narratives explicitly inform us of their purpose in writing: it is to tell us about Jesus in order to encourage in us a securely based faith in him (see Luke 1:1-4; John 20:31; Acts 1:1-5 . . .). It is a fair inference that the aim of the major Old Testament narratives . . . is comparable: it is to encourage faith and hope, repentance and commitment, in relation to Yahweh the God of Israel."[96] Only the particular passage itself, of course, can reveal its specific purpose, whether that be to call to faith, or hope, or love, or repentance, or commitment, or whatever.

Christocentric Interpretation

A genuine theocentric interpretation will take the pressure off attempts to force "lines to Christ," for from the New Testament perspective theocentric interpretation is already Christocentric since Christ is the eternal Logos (see Chapter 5 above). Nevertheless, one ought not to overlook the fact that a Christian sermon on an Old Testament passage ought to be different from a sermon preached by a Jewish rabbi, for the Christian sermon will need to take as its context the New Testament as well as the Old Testament. In other words, Christian preachers take their stand in New Testament times, after the coming of the Messiah, and hence they will read an Old Testament passage in the light of the New Testament. From that New Testament standpoint, it is indeed possible to discover prophecies that are fulfilled in Christ, types of which Christ is the antitype, offices which point forward to our Prophet, Priest, and King. But those messianic and typological lines are not the essence of Christocentric interpretation and preaching. Fee and Stuart point out that when Jesus said "the scriptures . . . bear witness to me" (John 5:39), he was not speak-

95. I. H. Eybers, "Some Remarks," 45.
96. Goldingay, *Anvil* 1 (1984) 265.

ing about every individual Old Testament passage but "of the ultimate, top level of the narrative, in which His atonement was the central act, and the subjection of all creation to Him was the climax of its plot."[97] Genuine Christocentric interpretation of Hebrew narrative is not dependent on a typological line here and a fulfilled messianic prophecy there but on understanding the passage in the context of the universal kingdom history which finds its goal and climax in Christ.

GUIDELINES FOR PREACHING HEBREW NARRATIVES

THOSE who suggest that "narrative material . . . is probably the easiest to preach"[98] are probably not aware of the problems of interpreting narratives, the pitfalls in transferring narratives relevantly from the past to the present, and the difficulties of good narrating today. In this and the preceding chapters, we have noted many of the problems and pitfalls. The difficulties, however, ought not to paralyze the efforts of preachers or lead them to avoid these rich passages. To chart a course through this difficult terrain, we need to focus our discussion on the problem areas in preaching these narratives and look for some concrete homiletical guidelines.

Text Selection

WE noted in Chapter 6 that texts are easily distorted by the wrong selection. The question is not whether texts should be long or short; the only requirement is that a preaching-text be a complete unit. This requirement holds for all genres of literature but needs to be emphasized especially for preaching narratives. The reason for this special emphasis is that narratives are particularly susceptible to the abuse of isolating a detail which appears to fit a particular preaching occasion. For example, the words spoken to Elijah in 1 Kgs 19:7b, "Arise and eat, else the journey will be too great for you," have been isolated as a text for a communion service; "Jesus also was invited to the marriage" (John 2:2a) for a wedding service; "they saw no one but Jesus only" (Matt 17:8b) for the ordination service of a new preacher—each with all-too-predictable applications.[99] Tempting though it may be to cut up a narrative to fit the occasion, one can counter this temptation effectively by the requirement that every preaching-text be a unit. Fee and Stuart aptly remind us:

> Narratives cannot be interpreted atomistically, as if every statement, every event, every description could, independently of the others, have a special

97. Fee and Stuart, How to Read the Bible, 75.
98. For example, Thompson, Preaching Biblically, 106.
99. See my Sola Scriptura, 169.

message for the reader. In fact, even in fairly lengthy narratives all the component parts of the narrative can work together to impress upon the reader a single major point. . . .

In this way, narratives are analogous to parables . . . in that the whole unit gives the message, not the separate individual parts. The punch, the effect, the impact, the persuasiveness—all come from the entire sequence of the events related.[100]

The requirement that a preaching-text be a unit does not mean that in church one must read the whole unit prior to preaching. If the unit is lengthy, one can read key sections, as long as these sections are understood and preached in terms of the whole unit. Or if one thinks it advantageous to focus the attention of the congregation on a verse or two, one can do so as long as the verse is the key verse, say, the heart of a chiasm, and it is understood and preached in terms of the whole unit. The requirement of selecting a textual unit thus seeks to prevent the isolation of mere textual fragments for the sake of instant application.

The requirement of selecting a textual unit also argues against the common practice of combining a few verses from one book with a few verses from another. True, one ought to compare Scripture with Scripture and be aware of contrasts, parallels, and fulfillments. Yet in the selection of a preaching-text, it is best to confine oneself to a unit that is addressed to *one* historical situation. This suggestion is not intended to block the tracing of the textual theme from the Old Testament to the New Testament or the interpretation of one text against the background of another, but to avoid the confusion that results when one combines units that are directed at different historical situations.

Because of the interrelated scenes, Hebrew narratives are ideal material for series of sermons. A series of sermons on a narrative is able to show development as no single, twenty-minute sermon can. Another advantage of a sermon series is that one need explain the historical-cultural background only once and can then assume it as a given. A further advantage is that continual exposure to the ancient narrative will tend to narrow for the congregation the historical-cultural gap between then and now.

Holistic Interpretation

ONCE the text has been selected, it needs to be interpreted holistically; that is, it needs to be understood in its literary, historical, and theological dimensions. It may be helpful to think of historical narratives as "proclamations of God's acts in history."[101] That simple definition highlights three important dimensions of historical narratives: their unique keryg-

100. Fee and Stuart, *How to Read the Bible*, 77.
101. See my *Sola Scriptura*, 214-15.

matic nature, their theocentric focus, and their historical referents. The preacher's task today is to reproclaim these past proclamations for the church today.

Even the briefest statements, we noticed above, can provide the key that will unlock the meaning of a narrative. It is imperative, however, that we hear the narrative the way the original listeners heard it. This requirement means that we have to be acquainted with their world—their language, geography, history, politics, commerce, culture, mores, customs— in order to catch the meaning, nuances, and allusions of words and phrases. Although such historical listening is bound to make preachers aware of the historical gap between then and now, it will also make them aware of the concrete relevance of the passage for Israel. The word of God is indeed historically conditioned—how else could it be relevant?—but it is not historically *bound;* the ancient narrative can therefore become relevant again in the new historical situation preachers address today. John Watts points out the value of realizing that "these stories are told to convey a meaning, to teach something, not just to relay information. . . . One is likely to discover that the same pastoral and pedagogical concerns that motivated the teller and writer millennia ago are relevant to our needs today."[102] Hence past relevance forms a bridge to relevant preaching of these narratives today.

Preachers need to ask, therefore, What was the purpose for which this particular narrative was told to Israel? What did the author seek to accomplish? In general one can say that he desired to acquaint his audience with what God had done for Israel. But one can ask further questions: For what purpose did he seek to tell Israel about God's acts? Was it to motivate Israel to faith, or trust, or hope, or obedience, or repentance, or what specifically? What kind of response did he seek from Israel? "The more the interpreter's reason for using the story coincides with the original reason for telling it, the stronger will be the effect. The sermon gains in credibility to the extent that it is obviously pressing the same claims to truth which the text is doing."[103]

Theme Formulation

THE theme of a narrative work may . . . be regarded as a conceptualization of its plot," writes Clines. "In conceptualizing plot, theme tends to focus its significance and state its implications."[104] This definition of a narrative's theme is more specific than our general definition that theme is "a

---

102. Watts, "Preaching," 74.
103. Ibid.
104. Clines, *Theme of the Pentateuch,* 17-18.

summary statement of the unifying thought of the text" (see Chapter 6 above). Both definitions seek to block preachers from isolating and preaching textual fragments by insisting that elements of the narrative not be treated independently but as parts of the overall thrust of the text. In addition, both definitions seek to keep preachers from distorting the application by transferring mere elements (such as H and O) when the text has united those elements into a very specific combination that is quite different from the elements themselves (say, H_2O).

Hence the question in theme formulation is, What is the point of this narrative? In the context of the book, what is the central thrust of this narrative? Since the point of the narrative is a message to Israel, the theme should be formulated as an assertion (subject and predicate). Moreover, it should be formulated from the "point of view" of the author (narrator) and not of any character, unless the author uses one of the characters to present his own point of view.

Once the theme of the narrative is formulated, it ought to be tested in the context of the canon, for the message for that particular historical situation is not necessarily the message for the church today. Before formulating the sermon's theme, therefore, preachers ought to check if the text's theme needs revision in the light of the fuller revelation given in the New Testament.[105] In view of the rather general purposes of Old Testament narrative to acquaint Israel with God's acts in history and to call the Israelites to faith and obedience, the theme of a narrative text can usually function as the theme of the sermon.

The Form of the Sermon

THE most appropriate form for a sermon on a narrative text is, not surprisingly, the narrative form. The logical teaching form tends to circle around a subject so that the narrative loses both its forward momentum as well as its total, experiential impact. By contrast, the narrative form can retain both the original movement and impact. There is great merit in following the structure and development of the text itself. Watts advances the following reasons: it assures close "identity with the original," and "it prevents us from imposing an alien, arbitrary outline on the classic."[106]

---

105. Th. C. Vriezen, *Outline of OT Theology*, 115, advises: "The preacher will . . . fulfil his task best, if, instead of looking upon Old Testament and New Testament as two different entities, he considers the Bible as a unity, historical and organic, the parts of which, however different in date of origin, in form and in life-setting, are one because of the eschatological perspective they offer on the Kingdom of God, and because of the fact that in them the same Spirit speaks of the same God, however widely they may differ in their manner and in the character of their authors."

106. Watts, "Preaching," 74.

Moreover, developing the sermon in the same form as the text will enable the congregation all the better to follow the exposition of the text and to test and remember the sermon.

The distinguishing feature of the narrative form is that "the idea is embodied in a structure of events and persons, rather than in a structure of verbal generalizations."[107] This characteristic makes for a delicate form whose impact can easily be disturbed. As we saw in Chapter 7, the story conveys meaning indirectly, by suggestion rather than by assertion, and thus the sermon based on a narrative should also be more suggestive than assertive. At the same time, however, the sermon must clearly reveal the theme so that the listeners cannot misunderstand its message. Thus the narrative form has to strike a delicate balance between simply narrating the story and providing explicit statements for right understanding. As Donald Gowan puts it, "Preaching from these biblical stories presents us with the challenge of saying something *about* them, not just retelling the story without helping people to recognize what it has to say to them, but to present that interpretation without becoming completely discursive and losing the effectiveness of the story form."[108]

In this connection, Haddon Robinson opines that a narrative sermon should still have a theme and subpoints: "As in any other sermon, a major idea continues to be supported by other ideas, but the content supporting the points is drawn directly from the incidents in the story." The question is whether one should state the theme and subpoints explicitly. Robinson recognizes that "narratives seem most effective when the audience hears the story and arrives at the speaker's ideas without his stating them directly." But "whether the points are stated or only implied depends on the skill of the preacher, the purpose of the sermon, and the awareness of the audience."[109]

The narrative form allows for much variety. One can construct the sermon deductively or inductively or select some form that employs both. One can take a cue from the plot conflict in the narrative and construct the sermon in the form of a problem/solution model or follow another pattern. If one uses the problem/solution model, one can begin with the problem faced by the character in the text or by the original audience, or one can begin with a contemporary problem to which the text provides an answer.

---

107. Davis, *Design for Preaching*, 157.

108. Gowan, *Reclaiming the OT*, 56. Buttrick, *Homiletic*, 335, recommends a form used in telling stories to children and in black narrative preaching: "The skilled Black preacher will tell a biblical story as present-tense narrative, but move in and out of the story with analogues, explanations, and interpretations as the plot line of the story moves along."

109. Robinson, *Biblical Preaching*, 124.

Whatever form is used, preachers today cannot simply retell the story they find in the text, for, in order to make it intelligible to a contemporary audience, they will have to provide the historical background as well as the cultural milieu. Sometimes preachers try to overcome the historical-cultural distance by retelling the story in modern dress. R. T. Brooks makes the valid point, however, that it is easier for us to get back into ancient times than to "update" the story for modern times. "It should be possible, for instance, to describe the Old Testament character of Naaman the Syrian in such a way that in spite of his alien culture and his leprosy we feel for ourselves the naturalness of his disappointment when the prophet Elisha merely sends a messenger to tell him to wash in the river Jordan." We should not have to "substitute the Thames and the Mersey for the original rivers of his derisive comparison. . . . Modernize the story too much and it loses its plausibility. . . . It is easier to get back to Naaman's time (or rather, that of his narrator)."[110]

The Relevance of the Sermon

FOR establishing the relevance of a narrative passage, the major point of comparison ought to be sought not between characters in the text and people today but between the people addressed by the author and the people addressed by the preacher today. Brooks states that although "telling a story so that its intrinsic paradigmatic value is revealed in the narrative can be difficult, . . . it is achieved by listening for the intention of the original story-teller and then serving that intention so faithfully that it stirs up resonances in the world today."[111] Consequently, the question is, How much is the church today like the original audience and in need of the same message?

It will be clear that, in spite of differences, the church today is basically the same as the Old Testament church: God's covenant partner, called to faith and obedience. For example, as Israel heard the stories of Abraham, Isaac, and Jacob as stories about itself, namely, its origin, so the New Testament church may hear these stories as stories about itself, its origin; in a very real sense these are our stories, our history, and therefore directly relevant to the church today. Similarly, as the Old Testament church was called to faith and obedience through these narratives, so the church today can be called to faith and obedience through these ancient narratives. When the message becomes more specific than calls to faith or obedience, the historical-cultural distance will become more pronounced, but the thrust of the message will still hold. For example, the narrative of

110. Brooks, *Communicating Conviction*, 57.
111. Ibid.

the creation of sun, moon, and stars (Gen 1:14-19) contains a polemic against the veneration of these heavenly bodies because they were worshiped as gods by Israel's pagan neighbors. In our secular culture today we are generally not tempted to worship sun, moon, and stars because we conceive them to be mere things. But a little reflection will show that these "things" turn out to be just as autonomous and independent of the Creator God as the sun, moon, and stars were in the pagan view. Thus the polemical thrust of the passage may shift somewhat, but it still maintains its relevant edge today: Do not be tempted by the pagan worldview today which regards the universe as a closed continuum and thus ignores the Creator God.

Edmund Steimle advises that the sermon should be as "lean and spare as the fabric of the Bible. The fact that the Bible is often studied as great literature is due in no small part to the way in which the biblical stories are told: no wordiness, no superfluity of adjectives, but lean and spare, the narrative making its point briefly and sharply."[112] The reason why sermons should be lean and to the point is not because this is the way the Bible is written but rather because a few strokes will allow the audience to become actively engaged in filling in the rest. The authors of Hebrew narrative frequently used this technique themselves. "With a few deft strokes the biblical author, together with the imagination of his reader, constructs a picture that is more 'real' than if he had drawn it in detail. . . . Minimal representation can give maximum illusion."[113]

If one uses the narrative form for preaching Hebrew narratives, few illustrations will be required to clarify and carry the message since the narrative form itself performs that function. Clarifications may be required, however, with respect to ancient customs, laws, geography, etc.

Finally, as the Old Testament narrator is almost inconspicuous in narrating the events, so contemporary preachers should not get in the way of the narrative but allow it to carry its own message. In preparing the sermon, one would do well to remember that people are edified neither by an oratorical performance nor by information about certain Bible characters; rather, people are built up as they hear God's word about the covenant God who makes history with people, now as well as then.

---

112. Steimle, "Fabric of the Sermon," 173.
113. Berlin, *Poetics*, 137.

CHAPTER 10

Preaching Prophetic Literature

IN contrast to Hebrew narrative, which tends to camouflage the fact that it is relevant address, prophetic literature openly declares its immediate relevance by presenting itself as preaching. Hans Walter Wolff states that, "beginning with Amos, we have purely and simply *collections of sayings* from the classical prophets. Only seldom do narrative elements appear. They have the sole function of making individual sayings understandable (e.g., Amos 7:10-17)."[1] Although Wolff overstates the case somewhat, he does bring out the significant fact that the origin of prophetic literature lies in the actual preaching of the classical prophets. In spite of naming these prophets the "writing prophets," therefore, we must keep in mind that many prophecies were *spoken* before they eventually became the literature we have in the Bible today.

When we think of prophetic literature, we usually think of the collection of books designated in the Hebrew Bible as "the Latter Prophets." Although these prophetic books will be our main concern in this chapter, our focus is both narrower and broader. On the one hand, it is narrower because the Latter Prophets contain also genres other than the prophetic—genres such as narrative (e.g., Isa 36–39 taken from 2 Kgs 18–20; Jer 26–29; 32–45), song (e.g., Isa 5:1-7; 42:10-13; 44:23; 49:13), wisdom (e.g., Amos 3:3-6; Isa 28:23-29; Ezek 18:2), and apocalyptic literature (e.g., Isa 24–27; Joel; Zech 12–14). On the other hand, our focus is broader than the Latter Prophets because prophetic literature is found also in other genres—in genres such as Hebrew narrative (e.g., 1 Kgs 17), gospel (e.g., Matt 24), and apocalyptic literature (e.g., Rev 2–3). Thus, while this chap-

---

1. Wolff, "Prophecy," 15.

ter will treat primarily the Latter Prophets, the discussion relates to the prophetic genre wherever it is found in the Bible.

We shall first examine the essence of biblical prophecy and its literary features, and subsequently combine these insights with those of Chapters 1–8 above in order to derive practical guidelines for preaching prophetic literature.

THE ESSENCE OF BIBLICAL PROPHECY

A Message from God about God

BIBLICAL scholars generally agree that prophets were messengers of God, heralds who delivered a communication from God. They spoke "in the name of Yahweh" (Jer 26:16). As their name *nabi* implies, they were "called" by God to speak for him.[2] Thus they spoke the very "words of Yahweh" (Jer 43:1). The prophets themselves underscored that they brought a message from God by their frequent pronouncements: "Thus says Yahweh," and "for the mouth of Yahweh has spoken" (see Chapter 1 above).

The message of the prophets was not only a message *from* God, however, but also a message *about* God, his covenant, his will, his judgment, his redemption, his coming kingdom. The prophet Amos relayed the essence of biblical prophecy when he proclaimed (4:12), "Prepare to meet your God, O Israel!" A. B. Mickelsen comments perceptively, "Whether he is discussing the past, present, or future, the prophet is seeking to make God the most genuine reality that men can know and experience."[3] Hence an important mark of biblical prophecy is its theocentric character.

A Message for the Present

A second mark of biblical prophecy is that it was addressed by the prophets to their contemporaries. This mark may seem self-evident, but it requires emphasis today when dictionaries define prophecy as "a foretelling or declaration of something to come," and people study prophecy for the sake of acquiring a blueprint of the future. As we have our weather prophets and our market prophets, so we have our "religious" prophets

---

2. The original meaning may have been passive, "the one called (by God)," but subsequent usage may have given the word an active connotation, "the one calling out (for God)." See Johannes Schildenberger, "Prophet," in *Encyclopedia of Biblical Theology*, ed. J. B. Bauer (New York: Crossroad, 1981), 716. Cf. LaSor, Hubbard, and Bush, *OT Survey*, pp. 298-99.

3. Mickelsen, *Interpreting the Bible*, 287.

who approach biblical prophecy as a "jigsaw puzzle"[4] which will forecast future events when the various pieces are put in their proper places. Preachers can undoubtedly preach sensational sermons and draw a good crowd by using prophecy to predict the future, but the question is, Does such a message carry the authority of the Scriptures?

Dated Prophecies

Although biblical prophets did indeed speak about the future, the first biblical given is that they addressed their contemporaries. Though their messages frequently referred to the future, the words of the prophets were addressed to the present. It is striking how often the prophecies are preceded by precise dates: "The words of Amos . . . which he saw concerning Israel in the days of Uzziah king of Judah and in the days of Jeroboam . . . king of Israel, two years before the earthquake" (Amos 1:1). "In the year that King Uzziah died I saw . . ." (Isa 6:1). In Jeremiah we find the exact year of the different prophecies listed many times, for example, in 1:2-3; 3:6; 21:1; 25:1; 28:1; 32:1; 33:1; 34:1; 35:1; 36:1; 40:1; 42:7; and 45:1. Ezekiel similarly lists precise dates no less than fourteen times. Surely we cannot ignore the dates and read these prophecies as if they were addressed directly to us today.

Historical Exposés

Moreover, the prophecies themselves reveal the Lord's concern to speak first of all to his people then and there. The Lord said to Ezekiel, for example: "Son of man, I have made you a watchman for the house of Israel; whenever you hear a word from my mouth, you shall give them warning from me" (3:17). As a reminder of the prophets' concern with the present, it has been suggested that they should be thought of as *forth*tellers rather than as *fore*tellers. Although this distinction is open to criticism for setting up a false contrast between present and future, to think of the prophets first of all as *forth*tellers is helpful in acquiring a proper approach to biblical prophecy. For it is clear that the prophets first of all address themselves to the state of the nation, to God's covenant people. They uncover and point out the idolatry, the corruption, the injustice that exists under the veneer of religiosity, and they call for a radical change. "Prophecy is essentially a ministry of disclosure, a stripping bare," says Wolff. "Israel's great prophets do not merely lift the veil of the future in order to destroy false expectations; at the same time, they expose the conduct of their contemporaries. . . . Prophets tear the masks away and show the true face of the people behind them."[5]

---

4. See Boersma, *Is the Bible a Jigsaw Puzzle . . . : An Evaluation of Hal Lindsey's Writings.*

5. Wolff, *Confrontations*, 35.

The Need for Historical Interpretation
In view of the specific dates given with biblical prophecies as well as their focus on the people then and there, it is evident that *historical* interpretation of biblical prophecy is a requisite for valid interpretation. The necessity of historical interpretation can be seen even when we look next at prophecy as foretelling the future.

A Message about the Future

THERE is no doubt that foretelling the future is another mark of biblical prophecy. This is not to say that every prophecy necessarily speaks of the future but that, in general, biblical prophecy frequently foretells events that are to take place in the future. Unfortunately, this aspect of prophecy is often misused by interpreters who join together bits and pieces in order to acquire a coherent picture of the last days.

No History of the Future
Biblical prophecy, however, is not a type of "forecastive" history writing. Mickelsen points out that "prophecy never gives as complete a picture of an event as does an historian's account. The historian must provide some account of the antecedents to an event, of the event itself, and of its consequences."[6] But prophecy does not provide all these particulars. On that account alone, prophecy is not a type of history writing about the future.

Moreover, the prophets spoke about the future from a specific, restricted viewpoint. Delitzsch called this viewpoint "the foreshortening of the prophet's horizon," while others prefer to speak of "prophetic telescoping."[7] This "prophetic perspective" is often likened to a traveler viewing a mountain range from some distance. "He fancies that one mountaintop rises up right behind the other, when in reality they are miles apart," as, for example, in prophecies concerning "the Day of the Lord and the twofold coming of Christ."[8] This prophetic perspective, though eyeing the future, is hardly a three-dimensional historical perspective.

Furthermore, the prophets naturally cast their predictions in a historically and culturally conditioned form. The prophet "speaks to his people in their language, in their thought patterns. He makes use of the customs which they know. When he refers to transportation, he talks about horses, chariots, camels, small ships, larger grain boats. When he speaks about armaments, he mentions spears, shields, swords, etc. When he discusses the

---

6. Mickelsen, *Interpreting the Bible*, 289. Cf. p. 292: "Prophecy cannot be history written beforehand because God does not disclose major and minor elements that are essential for even an incomplete historical picture."

7. See J. B. Payne, *Encyclopedia of Biblical Prophecy*, 137.

8. Berkhof, *Principles of Biblical Interpretation*, 150.

means and manner of worship, he may refer to the temple and sacrifices."[9] This historically and culturally conditioned form is completely overlooked when people in all seriousness propose that the prophets predict for our time a rebuilding of the temple in Jerusalem and reinstitution of animal sacrifices and a final battle fought with horses and chariots and spears and swords. The very form of biblical predictions indicates that the prophets' concern was not to write in advance a history for the twentieth or twenty-first century after Christ (see Heb 5–10).

The Future for a Contemporary Response

Yet the prophets did foretell events that were to take place in the future. However, they foretold these events not so much for the sake of the future as for the present, and not for satisfying the curiosity of their contemporaries but for their repentance or encouragement. Mickelsen aptly warns, "To lose sight of the original hearers and to focus our attention on what may tickle the fancy of the curious-minded in the present day is to lose sight of the very reason for the message."[10] The message of the future, whether of judgment or of salvation, was proclaimed to effect change in the original hearers. Bernhard Anderson illustrates vividly how the future can impact on the present: "Just as a doctor's prediction that a patient has only a short time to live makes the patient's present moments more precious and serious, so the prophet's announcement of what God was about to do accented the urgency of the present. The prophet was primarily concerned with the present. His task was to communicate God's message for now, and to summon the people to respond today."[11] If people continued in their apostasy, they would undoubtedly undergo the judgment foretold; however, if they repented by turning to the Lord and walking in his ways, the Lord would stay the judgment and instead shower his people with the blessings of salvation (Jer 7:5-7; cf. Amos 5:1-17).

Conditional Announcements

If God would indeed avert the foretold judgment in response to his people's repentance, the implication is that the prophets' announcements of impending judgment were conditional: the judgment would come only if the people continued in their evil ways. That condition need not be expressed with every prophecy; it could simply be assumed (see Jer 26:17-19; Jonah 3:4, 10).

---

9. Mickelsen, *Interpreting the Bible*, 295.

10. Ibid., 288; cf. p. 287: "The prediction of God's doings was given to a particular historical people, to awaken and stir them. They might not grasp all the meaning of the message, but the message—with the disclosure of future things—was given to influence the present action."

11. Anderson, *Understanding the OT*, 227.

Some interpreters have suggested, however, that the message of the prophets was unconditional. In fact, Gene Tucker favors changing Gunkel's form-critical label of "threat" to "announcement of judgment" because "the term *threat* is not strong enough for the prophet's bad news concerning the future. It is too weak primarily because it implies a conditional element."[12] Donald Gowan also argues for unconditional announcements, though it forces him to make a distinction between the earlier prophets (see 2 Kgs 17:13) and the Latter Prophets: "What distinguished them [the latter] from the rest was this unconditional threat of coming doom. . . . The prophets did not call for reform, for they knew it was too late; the end of the present order was near and could not be averted."[13]

But the question may be asked, Why did the prophets preach to Israel if they knew it was too late? And why did God send them to preach if it could not make a difference anyway? Wolff answers rather lamely that "the prophets' criticism of their own time had . . . the function of giving the basis for punishment."[14] Tucker suggests another reason: "The future has already been decided. The purpose of the announcement of judgment was to set that future into motion." Here we come upon an odd notion espoused by some form critics. According to Tucker, the prophets believed that the word of God they spoke had "the power to create history. . . . 'By their threatening word they believed they were making the future disaster inevitable.' . . . Because it was felt that the prophetic word was a powerful force, those who disagreed with the prophets did not simply ignore them, but tried to hush them up."[15] In other words, the spoken word of God was supposedly conceived of as a "piece of the deity"[16] which, once released, was no longer under God's control but accomplished its prediction automatically.

Regrettably, these form critics are reading some decidedly pagan and fatalistic notions back into the biblical forms. It is one thing to say that God's word is powerful—it is quite another to say that it has its own inherent power; it is one thing to say that God's word accomplishes its purposes—it is quite another to say that, once spoken, God no longer controls

12. Tucker, *Form Criticism of the OT*, 62.

13. Gowan, *Reclaiming the OT*, 125 and 126. Wolff asserts similarly: "Nowhere at all can it be perceived that the prophet expects an alteration of circumstances through repentance of the people on the basis of his indictments. The contrary is the case" ("Prophecy," 22).

14. Wolff, "Prophecy," 22. Cf. Tucker, *Form Criticism of the OT*, 64.

15. Tucker, *Form Criticism of the OT*, 62, quoting G. Fohrer, *JBL* 80 (1961) 318.

16. L. Dürr, quoted in Schmidt, *TDOT*, III, 120-21: "There appears already in the OT at the end of its development the concept of the 'divine word' which proceeds from the deity but operates independently, moving silently and surely in its course, a piece of the deity, the bearer of divine power, clearly distinguished from it and yet belonging to it, a hypostasis in the real sense of the word."

that word or the future. Certainly the Bible offers no evidence that the word of God is ever thought to be an entity which has its own inherent power to bring about what has been announced, irrespective of human response or of God's concern.[17] This idea flies in the face of the central biblical notion of the sovereignty of God, who remains in charge of his word and who is able to change the outcome in response to human repentance.

One need not search far in the classical prophets to discover that they presented a God who interacts dynamically with his people. Jeremiah proclaims in the Lord's name: "If at any time I declare concerning a nation or a kingdom, that I will pluck up and break down and destroy it, and if that nation, concerning which I have spoken, turns from its evil, I will repent of the evil that I intended to do to it" (18:7-8; cf. 26:13-19). Joel (2:13-14) encourages the people: "Return to the Lord, your God, for he is gracious and merciful, slow to anger, and abounding in steadfast love, and repents of evil. Who knows whether he will not turn and repent . . . ?" And Jonah, angry that God did not follow through on his announcement, "Yet forty days, and Nineveh shall be overthrown," blurts out: "That is why I made haste to flee to Tarshish; for I knew that thou art a gracious God and merciful, slow to anger, and abounding in steadfast love, and repentest of evil" (3:4 and 4:2; cf. 3:10). God's word of judgment does not cast the future in iron, predetermining its very outcome, for God remains in control of his word and is free to respond to human repentance and prayer (Isa 38:1-6).

Even Amos, the gloomiest of prophets, does not simply announce the judgment in order that people may know the reasons for it when it comes. Nor does he set loose a word that cannot be stopped. In the very chapter where Amos announces the fall of "the virgin Israel," he entreats the people repeatedly: "Seek me and live," "Seek the Lord and live," and "Seek good, and not evil, that you may live" (5:4, 6, 14). That same chapter also articulates what may be considered the theme of the whole book: "Let justice roll down like waters, and righteousness like an ever-flowing stream" (5:24). Even if one concludes, in spite of these pleas, that the evidence in Amos points to the inevitability of God's judgment, one must remember that that inevitability is rooted not in God's word of judgment but in the obstinacy of the people who fail to mend their ways. Thus, even when the judgment appears inevitable, its announcement as such is still conditional. "This is the mysterious paradox of Hebrew faith," writes Abraham Heschel: "The All-wise and Almighty may change a word that He proclaims. Man has the power to modify His design."[18]

---

17. Cf. Schmidt, *TDOT*, III, 121: "In the OT . . . *dabhar* does not represent a personified force which exists more or less independently of God, a 'natural, tangible substance' [Dürr]."

18. Heschel, *Prophets*, II, 66. Cf. I, 174: "Sin is not a *cul de sac*, nor is guilt a final

The Purpose of the Announcements

The distinction made earlier (see Chapter 6 above) between theme and purpose is also helpful in interpreting prophecy. For some of the confusion about conditional announcements of judgment is partially caused by the failure to distinguish the message from its purpose. Sometimes the message and purpose are the same, but frequently they differ. For example, the message in announcements of judgment is impending doom, but the *purpose* is to bring Israel to repentance in order thus to avert the very content of the message. "Have I any pleasure in the death of the wicked, says the Lord God, and not rather that he should turn from his way and live?" (Ezek 18:23). Since God is what he is, his purpose in announcing judgment is to have Israel "return" to him. "The eighth century prophets . . . looked toward God's tomorrow for the purpose of accentuating the urgency of today. Each in his own way sounded the call that was heard in authentic services of worship: 'O that *today* you would hearken to his voice!' (Ps. 95:7b; echoed in Heb. 3:7; 4:7). In the crises of their times they announced that people were being given a last chance to amend their ways."[19]

The prophets also announced events that were to take place in the distant future, far beyond the lifetime of their hearers. Although these announcements, in the nature of the case, were not conditional upon the response of contemporary hearers, they were not given merely to satisfy their curiosity about the future but to guide and encourage them. "Such eschatological expressions as 'behold, the days are coming,' 'and it will happen in that day,' 'at that time,' 'in those days' are . . . intended . . . to show that God's program will move forward according to his schedule. He is going to act, and what he will do affects what the hearers are doing now. If they will take into account his future activity, they will live differently from those who ignore the reality of God."[20] These distant future events, then, are announced to serve as beacons for God's people—beacons which will help them get their bearings and set their course in life, beacons which will give direction, hope, and encouragement, even in the darkest hour.

A Message about the Coming Kingdom

THE message of the prophets is ultimately a message about the coming King and the coming kingdom.

---

trap. Sin may be washed away by repentance and return, and beyond guilt is the dawn of forgiveness. The door is never locked, the threat of doom is not the last word."

19. Anderson, *Eighth Century Prophets*, 23.
20. Mickelsen, *Interpreting the Bible*, 288.

A Universal Kingdom

Isaiah, in particular, sketches the universal dimension of this kingdom, for we see it spread to the ends of the earth and embracing people from all tribes and nations. "It shall come to pass in the latter days that the mountain of the house of the Lord shall be established as the highest of the mountains . . . ; and all the nations shall flow to it, and many peoples shall come, and say: 'Come, let us go up to the mountain of the Lord, to the house of the God of Jacob; that he may teach us his ways and that we may walk in his paths'" (2:2-3). The invitation to join is given to all peoples: "Turn to me and be saved, all the ends of the earth! For I am God, and there is no other. By myself I have sworn . . . : 'To me every knee shall bow, every tongue shall swear'" (Isa 45:22-23).

Continuity with the Past

The future universal kingdom is portrayed in pictures of the past. The prophets speak of a new creation (Isa 65:17; 66:22), a new exodus (Hos 2:14-15; Isa 40:3; 41:17-19; 43:16-17; 48:21; 52:12; Jer 23:7-8; 31:2-3), a new covenant (Jer 31:31-34), a new David (Isa 11:1; Jer 23:5; Ezek 34:23-24; 37:24-25), and a new Jerusalem (Isa 62; 65:18-25). The homiletical significance of this portrayal is that there is continuity between God's acts in the past and his acts in the future. The future kingdom is coming not into some supra-historical realm but into our history and on our earth. "The prophets envisaged the establishment of the kingdom of God on earth— although upon the earth transformed by the power of God. There would be continuity between 'the new thing' and 'the former things' which God had done here on earth."[21] Hence these announcements about the distant future hold immediate relevance for God's people, then as well as now. For it is within the human horizon that God will work out his redemption—a distant horizon, perhaps, but still *our* horizon.

The Coming King

A central figure in the coming kingdom is the coming King. Frequently God is the one who comes with judgment and salvation. But the prophets also depict another figure who will establish this universal kingdom: "He [my servant] will not fail or be discouraged till he has established justice in the earth; and the coastlands wait for his law" (Isa 42:4). Although the prophets seem to avoid the title "King" for this figure—probably because the kings in Jerusalem "were now emancipated from Jahweh and behaving as independent rulers"[22]—there is no doubt that they look for an anointed One, a Messiah, a ruler like King David, only greater.

---

21. Winward, *Guide to the Prophets,* 33.
22. Von Rad, *OT Theology,* II, 172.

Prophecies which point to the coming Messiah are usually classified as "messianic." Many prophecies, of course, refer indirectly to the coming King: prophecies announcing the coming kingdom, future salvation, the messianic age, and the day of the Lord. However, "only when the Messiah is clearly in view, or when the messianic reign is described, should prophecy be called messianic. Otherwise great confusion arises."[23] Even in that specific, narrow sense, messianic prophecy shows quite a range of motifs and details. Stephen Winward provides a succinct summary:

> There would be a new David in the coming kingdom. Like the son of Jesse, he would originate in Bethlehem, and on him the Spirit of the Lord with its manifold gifts would rest (Micah 5:2; Isaiah 11:1, 2). Bearing the noble titles "Wonderful Counsellor, Mighty God, Everlasting Father, Prince of Peace," from David's throne he would rule over a wide dominion in justice and righteousness (Isaiah 9:6, 7). Isaiah called him "God with us," and Jeremiah, "The Lord is our righteousness" (Isaiah 7:14; Jeremiah 23:6). In exilic and post-exilic oracles, he is portrayed as the good shepherd and the lowly king (Ezekiel 34:23; Zechariah 9:9). According to the anonymous prophet of the exile, the salvation within history would be achieved through the Servant of the Lord. Despised and rejected by men, led like a lamb to the slaughter, raised from the dead and highly exalted, through his vicarious sufferings he would win salvation for the nations (Isaiah 52:13 to 53:12).[24]

When preaching on a messianic passage, the tendency may be to draw a direct line from the prophecy to Jesus in the New Testament. But this shortcut does not do full justice to the history of revelation. Messianic prophecies may not be exempted from historical interpretation any more than other kinds of prophecy. Since messianic prophecies, too, were addressed first of all to specific people in the past, we must hear these prophecies first the way these people heard them. For example, a passage about the Servant of the Lord should not be read immediately as referring to Christ, for in its original setting it could refer to the nation of Israel (e.g., Isa 41:8; 44:21), or to the righteous remnant which was "to bring Jacob back" to God (e.g., Isa 49:5), or to the suffering Servant (Isa 53). Historical interpretation alone can determine how the concept is used in a particular passage and what its meaning was for Israel. Only after its past meaning has thus been determined can one legitimately and with greater understanding move to its fulfillment in the New Testament. Or take the well-known messianic passage, "Behold, a young woman shall conceive and bear a son, and shall call his name Immanuel" (Isa 7:14). Before we move from this passage to its New Testament fulfillment (Matt 1:23), we ought to seek to understand it in its own historical setting in Isaiah as a

---

23. LaSor, Hubbard, and Bush, *OT Survey,* 397-98.
24. Winward, *Guide to the Prophets,* 33.

sign for King Ahaz. Bypassing historical interpretation for the sake of immediate messianic proclamation fails to do justice to the way the Lord gave this revelation historically: first the sign to Ahaz, then to Israel, and finally *the* sign to the New Testament church. With messianic prophecy, too, we ought to try to uncover its original historical significance and from that starting point look for a filling up of the prophecy until it is completely fulfilled.

Progressive Fulfillment

The many Old and New Testament prophecies about the future and their fulfillments accustom us to expect a *gradual* filling up of a foretold event: "It must be filled up by God, as it were, to its full content."[25] Thus we can see in the Scriptures progression both in terms of the details of the prophecy—"Later revelation often discloses elements omitted from earlier revelation"[26]—and in terms of the fulfillment of the prophecy. In this connection, William LaSor makes a helpful distinction between biblical prophecy and mere prediction of future events. In contrast to mere prediction, he suggests that prophecy "is a revelation of God's purpose in the present situation and in its on-going character. . . . Prophecy, in the sense that it reveals some part of God's redemptive purpose, is capable of being filled, of achieving a fullness, so that when it is *filled full* it is *fulfilled*. If we understand prophecy in this sense, we no longer ask the question, 'Is prophecy capable of more than one fulfillment?' It is capable of more and more filling until it is entirely fulfilled."[27]

LITERARY CHARACTERISTICS OF PROPHETIC LITERATURE

THE task of preachers today, however, is more than reproclaiming the original spoken prophecies, for these prophecies are now embedded in the literary contexts of a book and of the canon. The spoken prophecies were written down by the prophets themselves (Isa 8:16; 30:8), by a secretary (Jer 36:4, 32), or by the prophets' disciples. Subsequently these written prophecies were collected and frequently combined with autobiographical, biographical, or other explanatory narratives and comments. Through a complex process which we can no longer trace, the spoken prophecies eventually became the literature we find in our Bibles today. We shall first examine the literary structure of the prophetic books and then look at some of the forms and rhetorical devices used in prophetic literature.

25. A. Szeruda, *Das Wort Jahwes*, 24, as quoted in Schmidt, *TDOT*, III, 115.
26. Mickelsen, *Interpreting the Bible*, 292.
27. LaSor, *TynBul* 29 (1978) 55.

The Structure of Prophetic Books

ANYONE reading the Latter Prophets will soon discover and be frustrated by the lack of a chronological structure. This is not to say that prophetic books have no structure at all but only that they have a different structure from what we have come to expect in Western literature, and even to some extent in Hebrew narrative.

Chronological Structure

The general lack of chronological structure is due in part to the prophetic origin of these books. Commenting on Jeremiah, Anderson writes, "We should realize at the outset that we are not dealing with a 'book' in the modern sense, but with an *anthology*. . . . Prophetic literature is highly composite and bears the traces of a complicated history."[28] Some books, like Amos and Hosea, are compilations of "oracles delivered at different times and linked together in their present arrangement either by the prophet himself or by his disciples. Consequently, the same prophetic themes are repeated over and over again, with variations from situation to situation."[29] But other books do reveal a chronological structure. According to von Rad, "Ezekiel is the first to give us the benefit of an arrangement according to a chronology based on the time at which the oracles were delivered."[30] Similarly, the books of Haggai and Zechariah show chronological development.

Topical Structure

Prophetical books also exhibit a certain amount of organizing by subject matter. This topical arranging varies from small units which contain symbolic actions (Ezek 4–5), visions (Amos 7–9), or oracles sharing "the same opening or concluding formulas" (Amos 5:19–6:7; Isa 5:8-24) to large sections which group together oracles, for example, against foreign nations (Isa 13–23; Jer 46–51; Ezek 25–32).[31] The most common compilations are oracles of judgment against Israel and oracles of salvation. In fact, the sequence of oracles—oracles of judgment followed by oracles of salvation—forms an overall pattern that structures most prophetic books. Brevard Childs notes that this pattern "extends to the three major prophets (Isaiah, Jeremiah, Ezekiel) as well as to many of the smaller books (Hosea, Amos, Micah, Zephaniah, Haggai, Zechariah). The effect is that

28. Anderson, *Understanding the OT*, 369.
29. Ibid., 284. Cf. Young, *Introduction to the OT*, 249, on the lack of structure in Jeremiah and the resultant repetition. But see the structure suggested by Rosenberg, "Jeremiah," 190-91.
30. Von Rad, *OT Theology*, II, 33; cf. p. 221.
31. West, *Introduction to the Bible*, 235.

the great variety of prophetic material has been ordered within a unified schema which functions in the end as a message of salvation."[32] This pattern of judgment and salvation can also be observed within subdivisions of certain books.[33] The obvious hermeneutical implication of this pattern is that the spoken prophecies of judgment must now be read in the literary context of promised salvation.

Forms in Prophetic Literature

Prose and Poetry

In distinction from the predominant prose of Hebrew narrative, prophetic literature is mostly poetry. Von Rad notes regarding the Latter Prophets, "While there are exceptions, the prophets' own way of speaking is, as a rule, in poetry: that is to say, it is speech characterised by rhythm and parallelism. In contrast, passages in which they are not themselves speakers but are the subjects of report, are in prose."[34] James West observes that "only five of these books (Obadiah, Micah, Nahum, Habakkuk, and Zephaniah) are cast entirely in the poetic form," while "the remainder contain some amount of prose material: prose discourses, autobiographical or biographical narratives, and historical excurses."[35] The mixture of prose and poetry in the Latter Prophets is obviously related to the mixture of narrative and speech. While narrative is written in prose,[36] the prophetic speeches account for the poetry. This is not to say that all prophetic speeches are poetry (for prose speeches see, e.g., Jer 7:1–8:3; 17:19-27; 18:1-12), nor that the distinction between prose and poetry is always apparent (compare the RSV and the NIV on Jer 11:15-16; 23:5-6; 31:31-34). In fact, since the difference between Hebrew poetry and prose is not nearly as clear as the difference between English poetry and prose, the distinction between biblical poetry and prose is the subject of intense scholarly debate and, since James Kugel's *The Idea of Biblical Poetry*, is somewhat elusive.[37] But in general we can say that prophetic speeches are mostly in the form of poetry.

---

32. Childs, *OT Theology*, 238.

33. For example, Micah shows this pattern in each of its subdivisions, irrespective of whether it is divided into two or three parts. See LaSor, Hubbard, and Bush, *OT Survey*, 359-60.

34. Von Rad, *OT Theology*, II, 33.

35. West, *Introduction to the Bible*, 234.

36. It has been suggested that "the ancient Hebrew writers generally avoided verse narrative . . . because of its associations with pagan mythology" (Alter, *Art of Biblical Poetry*, 28, referring to S. Talmon).

37. See Kugel, *Idea of Biblical Poetry*, 59-95, especially pp. 82-84. Cf. Stek, "When the Spirit Was Poetic," 75-76. Alter speaks of "the dismaying range of discussion on this topic" (*Art of Biblical Poetry*, 4).

As to the reasons why the prophets used one form rather than the other, Robert Alter observes that *prose* seems to have been preferred "in most situations where the vector of speech was God to prophet rather than God through prophet to the people."[38] *Poetry,* however, seems to have been preferred for prophetic speech to the people. It was preferred not only because it made "public address more emphatic and—both literally and figuratively—more memorable," but also because the prophet spoke for God. "Since poetry is our best human model of intricately rich communication, not only solemn, weighty, and forceful but also densely woven with complex internal connections, meanings, and implications, it makes sense that divine speech should be represented by poetry."[39] In comparison with other biblical poetry, prophetic poetry is not "markedly distinguishable" in "basic form and technique," says Norman Gottwald. What distinguishes prophetic poetry from other poetry, however, is "its formulation toward specific situations. The prophetic 'life situation' was the moment of social, political, and religious crisis when men must decide the destinies of people and nations."[40]

Accounts, Speeches, and Prayers

Since Claus Westermann's study in the 1960s, *Basic Forms of Prophetic Speech,* most form critics distinguish among three major forms in the Latter Prophets: (1) accounts or reports, usually in the form of narratives about the prophets; (2) prophetic speeches, "the words of God delivered by a messenger of God"; and (3) prayers, "utterances directed from man to God." Westermann notes that "these three major forms are confirmed as the basic elements of the tradition in the prophetic books in that they represent at the same time—and this is certainly no accident—the basic forms of the three parts of the canon: the account is the basic form of the historical books, and speech to God in the form of lament and praise is the basic form of the Psalter." Not surprisingly, prophetic speeches are "the major component of most prophetic books."[41] We might add that prophetic speeches are *typical* of the prophetic genre; without prophetic speech there is no prophetic genre. Since we have already discussed narratives ("accounts") in Chapter 9, and since prophetic *speeches* are typical of the prophetic genre, in this chapter we will concentrate on the speeches.

38. Alter, *Art of Biblical Poetry,* 138. Prose was also preferred in "the oracular vision, like those that take up a good part of Zechariah, or like the vision of the seething caldron at the beginning of Jeremiah (1:13-19)" (ibid., 137).

39. Ibid., 140, 141.

40. Gottwald, *IDB,* III, 838. Cf. Alter, *Art of Biblical Poetry,* 139-40.

41. Westermann, *Basic Forms,* 90-92. See also Tucker, *Form Criticism of the OT,* 57-59; and Gowan, *Reclaiming the OT,* 121.

Various Literary Forms

In proclaiming their messages, the prophets used a wide variety of literary forms. "There are funeral songs (Amos 5:1) and parodies of the same (Isa. 14:4-21). There are series of 'woes' (Isa. 5:8ff.) which probably also had their origin in funeral customs. There are speeches reminiscent of legal procedure (Mic. 6:1ff.). There are parables (Isa. 5:1-7), wisdom sayings (Amos 3:3ff.), and quotations of torah (Isa. 1:16-17)."[42] There are prophetic oracles, laments, dialogues, cultic hymns, and many more. We shall look more closely at some of the more prominent forms.

The prophets evidently adapted forms from many different areas of life, but one form is characteristic of prophecy: the *prophetic oracle* or *announcement*. Not only is this, as von Rad states, "the form which the prophets used more frequently than any other to deliver their messages," but also, as Wolff notes, "the prophets show that they are messengers of Yahweh when they make use of this category as the basic form of what they say."[43]

Form critics are not entirely agreed, however, on the components of this main prophetic form. Wolff claims: "In form the announcement category has two characteristics: it is introduced by the formula, 'Thus saith the Lord' (and sometimes concluded with 'the Lord has spoken'), and Yahweh always speaks in the first person."[44] But von Rad insists that before one can speak of the literary category "prophetic oracle," the messenger formula "thus says the Lord" must be preceded by a preface which gives "the first precise designation of those for whom it was intended."[45] Meanwhile, Gowan speaks of "a two-part speech, an announcement accompanied by a reason."[46]

It appears that the prophetic oracle can be identified by various elements, the major ones being: (1) a statement of the reason for Yahweh's action, (2) the messenger formula, and (3) the announcement of Yahweh's action. The order of these elements may vary. For example, Amos 1:3-5 shows the following sequence:

Thus says the Lord:	(3a)	*Messenger formula*
"For three transgressions of Damascus. . . .	(3b)	*The reason*
So I will send a fire . . ."	(4)	*The announcement of Yahweh's action*

Also, it appears that we cannot even insist on the presence of all three elements before recognizing a prophetic oracle because instances occur

---

42. Gowan, *Reclaiming the OT*, 122. Cf. von Rad, *OT Theology*, II, 38.

43. Von Rad, *OT Theology*, II, 37, regarding the "messenger formula"; Wolff, *The OT*, 76.

44. Wolff, *The OT*, 76.

45. Von Rad, *OT Theology*, II, 37.

46. Gowan, *Reclaiming the OT*, 123; cf. Achtemeier, "Preaching from Isaiah," 120.

where only two elements reveal a prophetic oracle. For example, Isa 8:6-8 omits the central messenger formula "thus says the Lord," but even with only two elements (the third is implied in v. 5), it is clearly a prophetic oracle:

"Because this people have refused . . . ;   (6) *The reason*
therefore, behold, the Lord is . . ."   (7) *The announcement of Yahweh's*
                                              action

In identifying the prophetic oracle form, therefore, we cannot insist on a specific sequence of elements or on the presence of exactly three elements. In this form, too, we must grant the prophets the flexibility we so readily grant them in their use of other forms.

The prophetic oracle consists of two basic types: the prophetic judgment speech and the prophetic salvation speech, which have each, in turn, been divided into subtypes.[47] Note also that the prophetic oracle is capable of incorporating various other forms.[48] We shall look at two of these other forms: the covenant lawsuit and the funeral dirge.

Sometimes the prophets proclaimed God's judgment by borrowing the legal language from the law court. This form, known as the *covenant lawsuit,* was ideally suited to charge the nation with its sin and announce God's verdict. For example, in Mic 6:1-2 Yahweh summons his people to court:

Hear what the Lord says:
Arise, plead your case before the mountains,
    and let the hills hear your voice.
Hear, you mountains, the controversy [lawsuit] of the Lord,
    and you enduring foundations of the earth;
for the Lord has a controversy [lawsuit] with his people,
    and he will contend with Israel.

Then follows Yahweh's charge:

"O my people, what have I done to you?
    In what have I wearied you?
    Answer me!"

This charge is followed by the defendant's plea (vv. 6-7) and the indictment (v. 8; cf. Hos 4:1-17; Isa 3:13-26).[49]

---

47. On the "prophetic judgment-speech to individuals" and "the announcement of judgment against Israel," see Westermann, *Basic Forms,* 129-210; for "salvation oracle" and "proclamation of salvation," see, e.g., Merrill, *BSac* 144 (1987) 153-55.

48. Cf. Wolff, *The OT,* 76: "With their characteristic flexibility they [the prophets] were able to incorporate into this basic form many other categories."

49. For a more detailed analysis of this lawsuit form, see, e.g., Merrill, *BSac* 144 (1987) 148-53.

Another effective form was that of the *funeral dirge*. This form was well-suited for shocking carefree Israel into an awareness of their precarious position before God and in the world. For example, Amos (5:1-2) "sang a funeral dirge over Israel. This little lamentation *(qinah)* appears in a special 3-2 qinah-meter, and imitates the dirges that mourners wailed at the scene of death:

> Fállen, no móre to ríse,
>   is the vírgin Ísrael;
> forsáken oń her lańd,
>   with nońe to upraíse her."[50]

In studying the many forms in prophetic literature, two things must be kept in mind. First, as von Rad points out, form "is never just something external, concerned with literary style alone. . . . What determined the choice of the form was primarily the subject-matter of the message."[51] Second, attention to the details of form should not blind us to the theocentric focus of prophecy and its forms. Elizabeth Achtemeier shows both the variability of form and the constancy of the prophets' theocentric focus:

> This form [of prophetic oracle] undergoes wide variations in the Major Prophets and is almost dissipated in Ezekiel, but the emphasis on God's activity remains, and is present in all the principal genres of prophetic literature. Whether the form is that of woe oracle pronounced over the dead (Isa. 5:8-10), legal procedure (Isa. 41:21-24), parable (Isa. 5:1-7), lamenting dirge (Jer. 9:17-22), prophetic torah or teaching (Isa. 1:10-17), salvation oracle (Jer. 35:18-19), priestly oracle of salvation (Isa. 41:8-13), or allegory (Ezek. 17:1-21), the principal reference is to the activity of God among his people or among the nations as a whole, and no sermon from the prophetic literature truly deals with those oracles unless it deals with that dynamic of Yahweh's activity.[52]

Rhetorical Structures

As the prophets, in their speeches, can use various forms and forms within forms, so they can use rhetorical structures and rhetorical structures within structures. Sometimes rhetorical structures such as inclusion and chiasm encompass the forms,[53] and sometimes these structures, especially repetition and parallelism, function within forms.

50. Anderson, *Understanding the OT*, 275.
51. Von Rad, *OT Theology*, II, 39.
52. Achtemeier, "Preaching from Isaiah," 120.
53. See Lundbom, *Jeremiah*, 113: "We have seen that the Jeremianic speeches are controlled not by fixed genre structures, i.e., the letter, lawsuit, hymn, lament, judg-

The discussion of Hebrew narrative (see Chapter 9 above) applies also to the narratives found in the Latter Prophets. Here, too, we find scenes, characterizations, dialogues, plots, narrators, as well as rhetorical structures.[54] We need not repeat that discussion here but shall concentrate instead on the rhetorical structures of the prophets' speeches.

As we noted earlier, the speeches of the prophets consist of both prose and poetry but primarily of poetry. We also noted that the difference between the two is not as easy to describe as the difference between English prose and poetry. This difficulty is related to the fact that Hebrew prose, because of its artistic use of rhetorical structures, tends to form a continuum with poetry, where we find these same rhetorical structures, albeit in more condensed form and greater numbers. A key difference between poetry and prose is poetry's delicately balanced, parallel half lines and lines. Alter speaks of the parallelism of meaning as "an underlying formal mode which the poet feels free to modify or occasionally to abandon altogether."[55] According to Norman Gottwald, "The fundamental formal feature of canonical poetry is the correspondence of thought in successive half lines, known as parallelism of members. The thought may be repeated, contrasted, or advanced; it may be figurative, stairlike, or inverted. The parallelism may be both within lines and between lines."[56] With the prophets' speeches, therefore, particularly those written in poetry, we ought to discern the major forms of parallelism in addition to other rhetorical structures such as repetition, inclusion, and chiasm. We shall look briefly at each in turn.

---

ment speech, or whatever, but by structures which were dictated by canons of Hebrew rhetoric in the 8th-6th cc. B.C."

54. For the frequent use of dialogue in Jeremiah, see Willis, "Dialogue between Prophet and Audience as a Rhetorical Device in the Book of Jeremiah," *JSOT* 33 (1985) 63-82. Habakkuk, of course, consists mainly of the two cycles of dialogue between the prophet and the Lord. Dialogue is further found with visions (Amos 7:7-9; Jer 1:11-14), in the dialectic of assertion-objection-rebuttal (Mal 1:2-3, 3-6; 2:10-16, 17; 3:7, 8, 13), the lawsuit form (Mic 6:1-8), etc.

55. Alter, "Characteristics of Ancient Hebrew Poetry," 612. In groping to formulate the difference between prose and poetry adequately, Alter states, "Some of these prose prophecies make use of loosely parallel semantic-syntactic structures that distantly recall the background of poetry, but without the compactness, the strong rhythmic character, and the regularity of semantic matching and development that are observable in biblical verse" (*Art of Biblical Poetry*, 137). Cf. p. 138 on "the rhythmic regularity of matching statements that we will encounter in prophetic poetry proper," and pp. 7-9 on "semantic parallelism," "syntactic parallelism," and "parallelism of stresses between the half-lines."

56. Gottwald, *IDB*, III, 829. Cf. p. 830: "The habit of the Hebrew poet of balancing thought against thought, phrase against phrase, word against word, is the persisting feature of his method of working."

Synonymous Parallelism

A common form of parallelism is synonymous parallelism, which "states the same thought in successive stichs [half lines]."[57] For example, the two half lines of Isa 45:11b say roughly the same thing:

> Will you question me about my children,
> or command me concerning the work of my hands?

Synonymous parallelism does more, however, than the name implies; it does not merely say the same thing over again but says it in a different way and hence with different meaning. Alter makes the valid observation that "literary expression abhors complete parallelism, just as language resists true synonymity, usage always introducing small wedges of difference between closely akin terms." He suggests that "the predominant pattern of biblical poetry is to move from a standard term in the first verset [half line] to a more literary or highfalutin term in the second verset." "The characteristic movement of meaning is one of heightening or intensification . . . , of focusing, specification, concretization, even what could be called dramatization. . . . The rule of thumb, then . . . is that the general term occurs in the first verset and a more specific instance of the general category in the second verset."[58] For example, Isa 45:12 twice shows this movement from the general to the specific:

> I made the earth,
> and created man upon it;
> it was my hands that stretched out the heavens,
> and I commanded all their host.

Inverted Parallelism

Inverted parallelism is similar to synonymous parallelism but reverses the elements in the second half line so that the pattern changes from *ABAB* to *ABBA*. For example, Isa 2:3c shows inverted parallelism:

> For out of Zion shall go forth the law,
> and the word of the Lord from Jerusalem.

For the relationship between inverted parallelism and chiasm, see the discussion below on chiasm.

---

57. Ibid., 831. Note that occasionally more than two "half lines" make up a full line.

58. Alter, *Art of Biblical Poetry*, 10, 13, 19; see p. 22 for a few exceptions to the rule. Cf. idem, "Characteristics of Ancient Hebrew Poetry," 615-20. Cf. also Muilenburg, *VTSup* 1 (1953) 99.

Antithetic Parallelism

"Antithetic parallelism balances the stichs [half lines] through opposition or contrast of thought."[59] It does not occur frequently in the prophets, but there are some instances, such as Isa 1:16b-17a:

Cease to do evil,
  Learn to do good.

Isa 1:3 shows an interesting combination with its four half lines:

The ox knows its owner,
  and the ass its master's crib;
but Israel does not know,
  my people does not understand.

The first two half lines as well as the last two exhibit synonymous parallelism (called "internal synonymous parallelism" because it occurs between two half lines). The relationship between the first two half lines and the last two shows antithetic parallelism (called "external antithetic parallelism"). With antithetic parallelism, observes Wolff, "the alternatives sharpen one's perception."[60]

Synthetic Parallelism

Synthetic parallelism, finally, "balances stichs [half lines] in which the second element advances the thought of the first."[61] Hos 5:14 manages to exhibit as many as three kinds of parallelism in four half lines:

For I will be like a lion to Ephraim,
  and like a young lion to the house of Judah.
I, even I, will rend and go away,
  I will carry off, and none shall rescue.

Half lines one and two are in the form of synonymous parallelism. The first two half lines and the last two form synthetic parallelism: "the figurative language in the first two lines is explained in the next two." And finally half lines three and four demonstrate "climactic parallelism: the last line resumes the thought of the third line and carries it further."[62]

Repetition

Just as repetition is the key to discovering rhetorical structures in Hebrew narrative, so it is the key in prophetic literature. As we saw in Chapter 9, repetition can function at various levels, such as key words, motifs,

---

59. Gottwald, *IDB*, III, 832.
60. Wolff, *The OT*, 71.
61. Gottwald, *IDB*, III, 832.
62. Wolff, *The OT*, 71.

themes, and a sequence of actions. In prophetic literature we find the same range of repetition. For example, Amos (1:3–2:5) precedes his oracle against Israel with seven oracles that have the same structure:

Messenger formula:	"Thus says the Lord"
The reason:	"For three transgressions . . ."
Announcement of Yahweh's action:	"So I will send a fire . . ."
Concluding messenger formula:	". . . says the Lord."

Since this is the prophetic oracle form, we can also say that this is a seven-fold repetition of that particular form, though repetition occurs also in the details within each of the seven forms. Even this detailed repetition, however, does not merely say the same thing over and over again but shows progression in the differences. For example, the oracles circle around Israel—Damascus, Gaza, Tyre—and come ever closer in terms of family ties—Edom, Ammon, Moab, Judah—until Israel itself is confronted. Also, whereas the other nations are condemned for trampling various human rights as generally perceived, Judah is condemned for rejecting "the law of the Lord." But the overall impact is that of judgment—an impression left by the sevenfold repetition of that theme before the prophet turns to Israel.

Inclusion

The example from Amos above also shows how repetition can be used for inclusion *(inclusio):* the introductory "thus says the Lord" is repeated in the "says the Lord," thus effecting closure. Inclusion here serves to mark the limits of each unit, while the repetition of the words also reiterates that this is a message from Yahweh himself. Another example of inclusion is found in the oracle against Tyre in Ezek 26:15-18:

> Thus says the Lord God to Tyre: Will not the coastlands shake at the sound of your fall? . . .

> Now the isles [coastlands, NIV] tremble on the day of your fall; yea, the isles that are in the sea are dismayed at your passing.

Here, too, inclusion marks the limits of the unit, and the repetition of the coastlands' shaking and trembling adds to the internal repetition of trembling to denote the fearful prospect of the Lord's judgment upon Tyre.

Jack Lundbom sees inclusion functioning at three levels: that of the book as a whole ("The words of Jeremiah" [1:1] and "Thus far the words of Jeremiah" [51:64]), that of speeches as a whole (poems), and that of units (stanzas) within speeches. Unfortunately, many of the inclusions are lost in the standard English translations. He also argues that "not all inclusios are the same. Most consist of repeated vocabulary or phraseology at the beginning and end of a unit. But . . . it is necessary only that the end show continuity with the beginning, and that this continuity be taken as a deliberate attempt by the author to effect closure."[63] Of course, the lack of repeated vocabulary adds greater uncertainty to the identification of inclusion.

Chiasm

In Chapters 3 and 9 we have already become acquainted with chiasm. Chiasm and inverted parallelism are often identified, but it is helpful to distinguish between them. All chiasms are forms of inverted parallelism but not every inverted parallelism is a chiasm, for in addition to showing inverted parallelism, true chiasm reveals the focus, the pivotal point, of a passage. What, for example, is the structure of Jer 2:9?

> Therefore I still contend with you, . . .
> and with your children's children I will contend.

While some label the structure of this verse "chiasm," it is more precise to call it "inverted parallelism" since it lacks "climactic centrality."[64]

Chiasms can mark the limits of either large or small units and reveal their central focus. A few examples from the prophets will suffice. Amos 5:10-13 exhibits the following chiastic structure, which focuses the passage on the judgment of the wealthy.[65]

> A   They hate him who reproves in the gate,
>   and they abhor him who speaks the truth.
> > B   Therefore because you trample upon the poor
> >   and take from him exactions of wheat,
> > > C   you have built houses of hewn stone,
> > >   but you shall not dwell in them;
> > >   you have planted pleasant vineyards,
> > >   but you shall not drink their wine.
> > >   For I know how many are your transgressions,
> > >   and how great are your sins—
> > B'   you who afflict the righteous, who take a bribe,
> >   and turn aside the needy in the gate.
> A'   Therefore he who is prudent will keep silent in such a time;
>   for it is an evil time.

Another good example of chiasm is found in the prayer of Jonah. This chiastic structure sets the limits of the literary unit (RSV 1:17–2:10; MT 2:1-11) and focuses it on Jonah's descent and Yahweh's redemption in bringing

63. Lundbom, *Jeremiah*, 16-17, with Hos 8:9-13 as example.

64. For the former view, see Lundbom, *Jeremiah*, 62; cf. Gottwald, *IDB*, III, 833. For the latter view, see, e.g., Dillard, *JSOT* 30 (1984) 86, who insists that chiasm display not only repetition, inversion, and balance, but also "climactic centrality."

65. Garrett, *JETS* 27/3 (1984) 275. See idem, *JETS* 28/3 (1985) 295-97 for the suggestion of two interlocking chiasms covering all of Joel.

him up from "the Pit." The structure also highlights the theocentric emphasis throughout:

1:17–2:1	A	Yahweh appointed a great fish to swallow Jonah
2:2	B	Jonah's prayer from Sheol: a lament
2:3-4	C	Though driven from Yahweh's presence, Jonah continued to look to his "holy temple"
2:5-6b	D	Jonah's descent to "the roots of the mountains"
2:6c	D'	Jonah's ascent "from the Pit" by Yahweh
2:7	C'	Though his "soul fainted" within him, Jonah continued to turn to Yahweh in his "holy temple"
2:8-9	B'	Jonah's prayer in Yahweh's temple: a thanksgiving
2:10	A'	At Yahweh's word the fish vomited out Jonah on dry land[66]

Repetition, inclusion, and chiasm serve various functions in prophetic speeches. Lundbom sums up concisely: "Structures alert the audience
to where the preacher is going, sometimes functioning to restore focus,
other times to give the necessary emphasis—whether in the middle or at
the end. In the case of chiasmus, variation is sometimes necessary when
the speech builds heavily upon repetition. And for the listeners, the inclusio and chiasmus are mnemonic devices aiding them in retention."[67]

GUIDELINES FOR PREACHING PROPHETIC LITERATURE

IN this final section, we shall integrate the results of our inquiry into biblical prophecy with the general chapters on interpretation and preaching.
In searching for specific guidelines for preaching prophetic literature, we
shall follow the process of sermon preparation step by step, from text
selection, to holistic interpretation, to theme formulation, to form determination, to relevant preaching.

Text Selection

FOR prophetic literature, as for any other genre, one must be careful to
select a preaching-text that is a unit. Preachers may be tempted to isolate
a pithy prophetic saying for certain occasions, but that saying functions
biblically in its own historical and literary contexts. When there is a short-
age in the church budget, for example, it will not do simply to isolate Mal
3:10a, "Bring the full tithes," in order to persuade church members to fulfill their financial obligations, for the text speaks of bringing the tithes into
the "storehouse" and of food in the temple and of people who have
completely turned away from God. Because the prophetic word was

---

66. Adapted from Christensen, *JBL* 104/2 (1985) 226. For another example, see
ibid., 230. For the delicate interweaving of chiastic structures within a large chiasm
encompassing the whole book of Jonah, see idem, *JETS* 28/2 (1985) 133-40. For a suggested chiasm structuring all of Jeremiah, see Rosenberg, "Jeremiah," 190-91.

67. Lundbom, *Jeremiah*, 114.

spoken in and for a specific situation, one should resist the temptation of isolating prophetic speech from its historical context, let alone isolating a fragment of prophetic speech from its literary context.

As we have seen, prophetic literature is distinctive in generally showing its original oral character. The prophetic oracles are frequently introduced by the dates when they were first received or given and by other historical information. Kurt Frör contends that in preaching the prophets, a fruitful preaching-text consists not of the bare prophetic oracle but of the *pericope* in which the word is united with the unique historical situation in which it was originally spoken.[68] Not all prophetic oracles have been recorded with their historical background, of course, but whenever historical dates and situations are present in the immediate literary context, it is well to include them in the preaching-text. With historical references in the preaching-text itself, historical interpretation—which is necessary in any case—will flow from and tie right in with the preaching-text.

The preaching-text must also be a literary unit. Von Rad underscores the reason for this requirement when he notes, "To add a verse from the unit which follows, or to omit one which properly belongs to the close of an oracle, can alter the whole meaning."[69] In other words, wrong text selection can derail the sermon from the start because it will lead to wrong interpretation. Consequently, it is good policy to study the passage carefully for literary forms and structures. Forms such as prophetic oracle, covenant lawsuit, and funeral dirge frequently show the original limits of the unit. Rhetorical structures such as inclusion and chiasm also signaled to the original audience the end of a unit by returning to its beginning. The termination of a series of repetitions could have the same effect. Preachers today can make good use of these original clues to detect a literary unit.

A literary unit, however, is not necessarily a complete preaching-text. As we noted above, the preaching-text should extend, if possible, beyond the literary unit of a prophetic oracle to include historical background. In a similar vein, John Willis cautions about isolating units of dialogue. "The words of the two or more speakers in a dialogue situation should not be isolated into separate pericopes, even if they contain a complete thought unit in themselves (as, e.g., the words of the people in [Jer] 3.22b-25; 14.7-9, 19-22). Rather, the pericope includes everything within the dialogue."[70] The concern here is to avoid skewing subsequent interpretation and preaching by selecting a text that has only a limited focus or a restricted angle or an unbiblical idea. The preaching-text should be of sufficient length to encompass the central, normative message. If this becomes too lengthy for adequate coverage, a smaller section can be selected as long as it is central and subsequently interpreted in its larger context.

68. Frör, *Biblische Hermeneutik*, 227.
69. Von Rad, *OT Theology*, II, 39.
70. Willis, *JSOT* 33 (1985) 76.

Literary Interpretation

ONCE the text has been selected, it must be interpreted holistically, that is, in all its aspects and dimensions. Some speak here of "grammatical-historical-contextual analysis." Mickelsen explains these three adjectives as follows: One "must understand the meaning of the words and the exact relationship the words have to each other. He should know the historical background of the prophet and the people to whom the prophet minis-ters. He should note the context that precedes the passage and the context that follows the passage."[71] Holistic interpretation seeks to do all this and more. We shall try to get an idea of the whole picture by examining in turn literary, historical, and theological interpretation as it applies specifi-cally to prophetic literature.

The Meaning of the Words

In literary interpretation our first concern is with the words and their meaning in their specific combination in the text. Since much of prophetic literature is poetry, careful note must be taken of the various kinds of par-allelism and how they are used to reinforce, sharpen, and extend the meaning of the passage.

Metaphor

Figures of speech are much in evidence in prophetic literature. The proph-ets display a particular fondness for metaphor. Metaphor has the power to make us see reality in new ways, from different and surprising angles. For example, Wolff notes that "Hosea alone, in various passages, calls Yahweh Israel's husband, lover, fiancé, father, physician, shepherd, fowler, and even lion, leopard, bear, dew, fruit tree, moth, and dry rot."[72] If that summary gives an idea of the range of prophetic metaphors, it should also be noted that the prophets frequently concentrate on one metaphor, nursing it along, extending it in various ways. "One figure, or a cluster of closely related figures, tends to govern a sequence of several lines. *Leitwörter*, key-words, are insisted on as a way of driving home the thematic emphasis of the poem. . . . A concentration of nearly synony-mous words is deployed over a whole passage."[73]

As an example of such concentration on a particular metaphor, let us consider Ezekiel's prophecies against Tyre. His first metaphor for Tyre is the figure of the "rock," which not only describes Tyre's location off the coast but is also the meaning of its name. "To call the city 'rock' is to speak

---

71. Mickelsen, *Interpreting the Bible*, 299.
72. Wolff, *The OT*, 72.
73. Alter, *Art of Biblical Poetry*, 144.

metaphorically, to claim for the identity of the city the qualities of the ground on which it was built," writes Carol Newsom. "'Rock' forms the filter through which the city's existence and character are perceived." But that sense of solidity and security is soon shattered when the Lord announces his judgment upon the "Rock": "I will scrape her soil from her, and make her a bare rock. She shall be in the midst of the sea a place for the spreading of nets" (Ezek 26:4b-5a). In the next chapter, Ezekiel changes the metaphor to a ship: Tyre is a beautiful ship, carefully constructed, wealthy because of its ability to trade. "After the long, slow description of the construction of the ship and its staffing, Ezekiel simply takes the ship to sea and sinks it in a single, sudden verse (v. 26). Immediately the sense of the fragility of the ship dominates the connotations present to the reader. The metaphoric schema through which the readers have been organizing their ideas of Tyre's wealth and power is itself reordered, so that Tyre is seen to be vulnerable to sudden destruction even at the height of its power."[74] This example demonstrates not only how the prophets used metaphor but also how literary and historical interpretation go together, even in interpreting metaphor, for someone who is not acquainted with the fact that Tyre was a rich and secure trading center built on a rocky island off the Phoenician coast could hardly catch the force of the metaphor.

Hyperbole
The prophets also make effective use of the exaggerated statement known as hyperbole. In fact, Wolff says that "hyperbole has even more impact" than metaphor because "its dramatic intensification . . . forces the hearer to recognize the verdict of guilty." For example, Amos (4:1) calls the rich women of Samaria "cows of Bashan," picturing them as "choice cattle being fattened for market, with their senseless trampling around (i.e., oppression), and their thirst for strong drink."[75]

Forms and Structures
Besides paying attention to the various figures of speech, in literary interpretation one ought to look for various forms that may give a clue to the meaning. It must be remembered, however, that the prophets sometimes use old forms to communicate new meanings (e.g., the funeral dirge as a song of derision, Isa 14:4-15). The recognition of rhetorical structures is also helpful in discerning the thrust of a passage: repetition may be a good clue to the heart of a passage, and chiastic structure will also show the central concern of a passage.

---

74. Newsom, "Maker of Metaphors," in *Interpreting the Prophets*, 192-94.
75. Wolff, *The OT*, 72.

Literary and Historical Contexts

Literary interpretation inquires further into the meaning of the passage in its present literary context. A passage must be understood first in its immediate literary context but ultimately in the context of the book and of the canon. On this point, however, scholars disagree. On the one hand, von Rad, because of his emphasis on tradition-historical understanding, de-emphasizes the present literary context of prophecy: "Each *logion* was, for those to whom it was addressed, *the* word of Jahweh. . . . All that we have are the various individual words in which, on each specific occasion, *the* word of Jahweh was proclaimed in a different guise."[76] On the other hand, Childs, because of his emphasis on canonical understanding, practically eliminates the original historical context: "To assume that the prophets can be understood only if each oracle is related to a specific historical event or located in its original cultural milieu is to introduce a major hermeneutical confusion into the discipline and to render an understanding of the canonical Scriptures virtually impossible."[77] He contends that "in the transmission process, tradition, which once arose in a particular milieu and addressed various historical situations, was shaped in such a way as to serve as a normative expression of God's will to later generations of Israel who had not shared in those original historical events. In sum, prophetic oracles which were directed to one generation were fashioned into Sacred Scripture by a canonical process to be used by another generation." Thus, for example, Childs sees the shift in Amos from judgment in chaps. 1–8 to the promise of salvation in chap. 9 not as a reason "to distinguish between genuine and non-genuine oracles," nor as an attempt to soften Amos's harsh message, but "to confirm the truth of Amos' original prophecy and to encompass it within the larger theological perspective of divine will which includes hope and final redemption."[78]

I do not think, however, that the options of either strict historical interpretation or canonical literary interpretation are a true dilemma. It seems to me that we can recognize the importance of historical interpretation of each prophetic oracle while acknowledging at the same time that the canonical literary context has added a new dimension to its interpretation. In other words, instead of seeing historical and canonical literary in-

---

76. Von Rad, *OT Theology*, II, 130. Cf. p. 299: "The message of every prophet was exactly directed to meet a specific time, and it contained an offer which was never repeated in precisely the same form as it had with the original speaker."

77. Childs, *Int* 32 (1978) 53. Cf. his *Introduction*, 337: "Specifically in terms of Second Isaiah, the final form of the literature provided a completely new and *non-historical* framework for the prophetic message which *severed* the message from its original historical moorings and rendered it accessible to all future generations" (my emphases).

78. Childs, *Int* 32 (1978) 47 and 49. For more examples, see pp. 49-53.

terpretation as opposite poles, I see the latter as an extension of the former. This escape between the horns of the dilemma does not resolve all problems, as we shall see in theme formulation below, but at least it allows us to do justice to the literary as well as the historical context of the text.

Historical Interpretation

IN historical interpretation, one attempts to hear the message the way the original recipients heard it.

Dated Prophecies

Since prophetic literature shows clearly that most of its prophecies were originally spoken in specific historical situations, one cannot bypass historical interpretation and still have valid interpretation. Stephen Winward explains: "The revelation was for the contemporaries of the prophet who received it; it was communicated in their language and thought forms, related to their needs, relevant to the situation in which they lived. That is why it is always necessary to look at a given message against the background of the historical situation in which it was delivered. Only when it is studied in its original context can any message be rightly understood, and be rightly re-applied to the changed circumstances of our own times."[79]

Some prophecies, of course, lack specific historical references, and thus their historical interpretation will need to be against a more general background, such as preexilic Israel or postexilic Israel. Other prophecies have been dated with care, however, usually in the superscription of the book (e.g., Amos 1:1) but also within the book. In fact, the four prophecies in Haggai are dated to the day: in our calendar, August 29, 520; October 17, 520; and two on December 18, 520 B.C. Such dating, as well as more general references, enables us to place the original oracle in its historical context and to understand it accordingly.

The Purpose of the Author

In historical interpretation one also makes initial inquiries about the author's purpose. Why did the prophet speak the way he did? To what problem did he respond? What question did he seek to answer for his recipients? Was his immediate purpose to teach, to reprove, to correct, to comfort, to predict future events? These questions must be kept in mind also when one subsequently considers the passage in its broader literary contexts.

79. Winward, *Guide to the Prophets*, 29.

Theological Interpretation

THEOLOGICAL interpretation reminds us that the primary concern of Scripture is to acquaint us with God, his word, his will, his acts.

Theocentric Interpretation

In prophetic literature, the theocentric emphasis is so evident that it is hard to ignore. Yet this central feature can be overlooked in the busyness of sermon preparation and attention to detail. Consequently, theological interpretation serves a useful function if it reminds preachers of the central concern of the prophets—the concern to reveal God at work in history for the purpose of reestablishing his kingdom on earth.

Sometimes this central thrust is overlooked because preachers concentrate on the person of the prophet. If biographical and character sermons are recommended for historical narrative, I suppose the prophets are fair game too. Yet prophetic literature itself opposes any such use of the prophets. Von Rad observes that reading prophetic literature with a view to "biographical detail, imports into these stories a viewpoint which is foreign to them themselves. Even the idea of 'prophetic personalities' which so readily comes to our minds is very far from being what the sources themselves offer us. . . . We can even feel that the sources are opposed to any attempt to write 'lives' of the prophets. Had the writer of Amos VII.10ff. had any intention of giving information about Amos's own life, he would never have ended his account as he does, and have failed to inform the reader whether or not the prophet complied with the deportation order."[80] The prophets are sketched only as office-bearers, as messengers of the Lord, to provide background for their messages, for the *messages* are the central focus. Even when the focus shifts occasionally to the prophet himself, for example, Jeremiah in his suffering or Hosea and his marriage, the concentration on the prophet is not for his sake but for the sake of the message that is being proclaimed through his life and trials.

Predictions and Fulfillments

The theocentric thrust of prophetic literature can also be overlooked when preachers become totally absorbed in detailed analyses of predictions and fulfillments. Of course, when prophets prophesy concerning future events, one ought to consider the question of fulfillment, but not at the cost of neglecting the relevance of this word for the prophet's immediate hearers. Some of the questions that need to be raised when the passage speaks of future events are the following: Was the prophecy conditional or unconditional? If it was conditional, was that condition met, say, by re-

---

80. Von Rad, *OT Theology*, II, 35; on Jeremiah see pp. 206-8.

pentance, so that the prophecy did not need to be fulfilled? If the condition was not met or if the prophecy was unconditional, was the prophecy fulfilled in Old Testament times?[81]

Prophecies concerning the fall of Samaria and Israel were fulfilled in 721 B.C. and concerning the fall of Jerusalem and Judah in 587 B.C. Prophecies concerning restoration to the promised land were fulfilled in the successive returns to the land from 538 B.C. on. These fulfillments do not mean that these prophecies concerning judgment and restoration are now finished and no longer speak today. On the contrary, when one sees fulfillment as a gradual filling up, then the judgments of 721 and 587 B.C. are indeed major stages in the process of fulfillment, but in the context of the New Testament we can see further stages: the judgment that fell on the suffering Servant, Jesus Christ, and ultimately the final judgment when the wicked are expelled from the earth (Rev 20:15). And the return to the promised land in 538 B.C. was indeed a major stage in filling up the prophecies regarding the restoration to the land, but in the light of the New Testament we can see further stages: the meek "shall inherit the earth," Jesus said (Matt 5:5), and Rev 21 shows the final fulfillment of the restoration to the land when we see God's people enjoy shalom on the renewed earth.[82] Thus the relevance and the eschatological perspective of ancient prophecies hold also for us today—whether these prophecies have been partially fulfilled in the past or whether, like some of the prophecies concerning the new creation (Isa 65–66), they await their total fulfillment in the future.

Messianic Prophecies

When Old Testament prophecies are seen in the context of the New Testament, many will reveal their fulfillment in Jesus Christ. The New Testament writers themselves, of course, frequently explain Jesus' person and actions as fulfillment of Old Testament prophecy. In fact, Peter (1 Pet 1:11) writes that it was the Spirit of Christ himself that enlightened the prophets: "They inquired what person or time was indicated by the Spirit of Christ within them when predicting the sufferings of Christ and the subsequent glory." And Paul writes in 2 Cor 1:20: "For all the promises of God find their Yes in him [the Son of God, Jesus Christ]." Consequently,

---

81. Cf. Ramm, *Protestant Biblical Interpretation*, 250-53.

82. Armerding, *Dreams, Visions, and Oracles*, 71, advises: "The significance intended by the author should initially control our investigation, to which may be added possible expansion in the light of parallels between the New Testament and the Old. Thus, for the New Testament Christian there is a freedom to move away from both a sort of mechanical one-to-one view that reads predictive prophecy as merely a series of newspaper reports written before the event, and also too rigid a system of interpretation that limits the imagination and freedom to recognize divinely intended correspondences and equivalencies."

interpreters will miss the heart of prophecy when they fail to link it to Jesus Christ.

Messianic prophecies by definition find their fulfillment in Jesus Christ. In Jesus' birth, Matthew sees fulfillment of Isa 7:14: "Behold, a young woman shall conceive and bear a son, and shall call his name Immanuel." In Jesus' birthplace, Matthew sees fulfillment of Mic 5:2: "But you, O Bethlehem Ephrathah, . . . from you shall come forth for me one who is to be ruler in Israel." Other prophecies, such as the Servant passages in Isaiah, are more general but can also be related directly to the birth, life, death, and resurrection of Jesus. Since messianic prophecies find their fulfillment in Jesus, this connection ought indeed to be made in the sermon.

Nevertheless, when preaching on Old Testament prophecy, one ought not to move too quickly to the New Testament. For some preachers, drawing a line to Jesus in the New Testament is the heart of Christocentric preaching, but the question must be asked, What does one accomplish by simply drawing a line to Jesus? Does this line build up the congregation? Take, for example, a sermon on a passage from Isaiah about the suffering Servant. In the interest of preaching a Christocentric sermon, many tend to move quickly from the suffering Servant in Isaiah to *the* suffering Servant in the New Testament. But what is gained by that quick shift to the New Testament? If the text is from the Old Testament, surely one must uncover the depth of Old Testament prophecy—in the light of the New Testament—before making the move to the New Testament. John Bright comments on the Servant passages:

> However the Servant is pictured, even when conceived as the coming Redeemer, the Servant mission is always laid before Israel as her calling and destiny. It is not enough to describe the Servant; the call goes out: 'Who among you fears the Lord and obeys the voice of his servant . . . ?' (50:10). Israel is to be the people of the Servant; only so will she be the people of God. As the Servant, prophetlike, proclaims the righteousness of God to the world, so must Israel; as the Servant, priestlike, mediates the salvation of God to men through his suffering, so must Israel. As the Servant gains a victory and a Kingdom through his sacrifice, so must Israel know no other royal path.[83]

With this kind of exposition, the line to Christ not only becomes much more significant, but the relevance of the passage for the church is also exposed in that the New Testament shows that the *church* today is God's Servant in the world.

---

83. Bright, *Kingdom of God*, 151.

Theme Formulation

FORMULATING the theme of prophecy in the form of an assertion will come quite naturally since prophecy so obviously asserts something. Precise formulation of the sermon theme is quite complicated, however, for with prophecy one needs to take into account several factors.

Theme, Purpose, and Literary Context

The theme of the text may be plain, say, a passage from Amos proclaiming judgment upon Israel, but the purpose of the prophet to call the nation to repentance casts quite a different light on that theme of judgment: the prophecy is conditional. This is one reason why the theme of the text cannot function directly as the theme for a contemporary sermon. A second reason lies in the fact that this conditional prophecy of judgment is now part of a book which concludes with a prophecy of salvation. Does that literary context affect the way the theme of the text ought to be formulated? Tucker claims, "When the speeches which had been delivered over the years on various and sundry occasions were collected and then written down, they were given a new and different life. . . . A speech which originally served one purpose may serve a different one in the context of the book."[84] One need not agree with Tucker's extreme formulation to realize that the new literary context may change the thrust of a passage.

Two Horizons

We can see the problem also from the side of the audience. When we desire to hear the passage as the original audience heard it, which audience do we have in mind? The one that heard the original spoken message or the one that heard or read the written message? In some cases the difference may be minor, but in the case of Isaiah, for example, it makes a difference between a preexilic audience and an exilic or postexilic audience. Consequently, before formulating the theme of the text one must take into account two horizons, that of the original audience and that of the recipients of the book.[85] As a rule, however, the difference will

84. Tucker, *Form Criticism of the OT*, 70-71.
85. Sometimes in prophetic literature one must take into account a third horizon, that of the "narratee," i.e., the group that the "narrator" addressed directly. The narratee can be distinguished from the original audience and the original recipients of the book particularly in the prophecies against the nations. For example, in Isa 14:28-32 Isaiah addresses an oracle directly to Philistia, but it is intended for the ears and later the eyes of Judah. Similarly, in Nahum the narrator addresses the Ninevites while his remarks are intended for the Judeans. For the distinction among author, implied author, and narrator, and that among reader, implied reader, and narratee, see Longman, *Literary Approaches*, 83-87.

be minor, and the theme of the passage in the context of the book will usually be no more than an extension of the original theme.

The Theme of the Sermon

Once the theme of the text has been formulated in its literary context, that theme should be traced through the Scriptures for confirmation, analogies, contrasts, fulfillments, deepening, or expansion. With that information, it should be projected onto the horizon of the contemporary audience and be altered, if necessary, to function as a sermon theme that speaks today as it did originally, but now in the context of the whole Bible and in a new situation. A sketch of the steps involved (1 to 6) might help visualize this proposal for theme formulation:

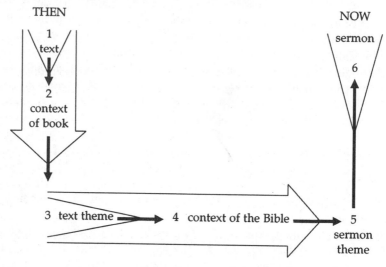

The Form of the Sermon

THE sermon's form should respect the text's form. This stipulation does not mean that sermons on passages in the form of a funeral dirge or a lawsuit need to copy these forms for contemporary audiences, but it does mean that preachers should try to convey to their contemporary audiences the mood and feelings originally evoked by these forms. In the liturgy as well as in the sermon it may be possible to capture the sadness of a funeral dirge or lament or the matter-of-fact atmosphere of a lawsuit or the joy of an oracle of salvation or hymn of joy (e.g., Isa 44:23). When the prophecy is in poetry, the sermon can emulate the prophecy's use of concrete imagery. When the prophecy spins out a metaphor, the sermon can follow suit and allow the audience to participate in this new and often surprising vision. Above all, a sermon on prophecy demands a form which, like the prophetic oracle, addresses the audience directly with the word of the

Lord, a form which leaves no doubt as to who has broken God's covenant stipulations and what its awful results will be, but also a form which is able to convey the loving-kindness of God and his ultimate redemption.

The Relevance of the Sermon

THE message of the prophets, we have seen, was intensely relevant for its original audience, often a matter of life or death. That same relevance ought to be the hallmark of sermons on prophecy today. Yet preachers may never lose sight of the fact that their congregations are neither preexilic nor postexilic Israel but the church of Jesus Christ in the twentieth century A.D. Thus the historical-cultural gap makes its presence felt.

The Historical-Cultural Gap

In pursuit of a relevant sermon, the temptation will be great to bypass the historical-cultural gap by drawing a simple historical equation mark: as Amos condemned the injustice of Israel, so the contemporary preacher condemns the injustice of contemporary nations. But one cannot simply take Amos's message of judgment, transport it across twenty-seven centuries and thousands of miles, and unload it on contemporary nations. Aside from other considerations, the fact that Israel was God's special people prevents this simple identification between then and now. In the words of Elizabeth Achtemeier, "The context of the covenant relationship militates against drawing direct parallels between Israel's life as a nation and the life of any present-day secular state."[86] Preachers must accept the consequences of historical interpretation. For example, Isaiah condemned Judah's alliance with Assyria (chap. 7) and later its alliance with Egypt (30:1-5; 31:1-3). "He opposes trust in such alliances and in military weapons, in the strongest terms, calling instead for faith in Yahweh's protective action as the basis of Judah's defense and foreign policy (cf. Isa. 30:15-17). The preacher who wishes to apply such oracles to modern international affairs should not simply lift them out of their historical context and impose them, willy-nilly, upon the twentieth century as eternal principles. They cannot be used to give absolute divine sanction to modern pacifism or isolationism."[87]

Analogies between Then and Now

The question is, therefore, how to preach just as relevantly as the prophets did, while doing justice to their and our unique historical situations. Part of the answer lies in seeking proper analogies between then and now.

86. Achtemeier, "Preaching from Isaiah," 122.
87. Ibid., 124.

We should note first of all the analogy between the audience addressed then and the audience today: both Israel and the church today are God's covenant people. Further, God's requirements of his covenant people, then and now, are generally the same: Love the Lord your God and love your neighbor. Thus God's judgment also today "awaits those who 'sell the needy for a pair of shoes' (Amos 2:6), or who use religion as a cloak for greed and injustice (cf. Isa. 1:10-17), or who have mixed modern idolatries (such as self-justification) with the Gospel of Christ (cf. Hos. 13:2-4). These sins are sins in the New Covenant, too."[88] Since we have become a global village today, it is quite legitimate to draw analogies between the condemnation of the people in Israel who became rich at the expense of the poor and our riches today at the expense of the poor in Third World countries. The prophets exposed sin where they saw it. At the same time they announced God's forgiveness for those who repent, and that forgiveness can be proclaimed with even more conviction after Christ than before his death and resurrection.

The main connection between then and now, however, lies in the faithful covenant God who is the same yesterday, today, and forever. As we noted, the message of the prophets is fundamentally about God and his actions to restore his kingdom on earth. That message holds true for today as well. In fact, God's judgments of the past are a sobering reminder to people today that God is utterly serious about destroying the wicked, and his promises of a glorious future are as much a beacon of hope and encouragement for contemporary Christians as they were for ancient Israelites.

---

88. Fee and Stuart, *How to Read the Bible*, 163.

CHAPTER 11

Preaching the Gospels

THE Gospels proclaim the climax of God's acts in human history, the sending of his Son. They pronounce the fulfillment of Old Testament prophecy in the coming of Jesus Christ. Thus the Gospels continue where Old Testament narrative and prophecy leave off: they continue the narrative of the coming kingdom of God. Mark begins his Gospel, significantly, with the words "The beginning of the gospel of Jesus Christ, the son of God," and he characterizes the beginning of Jesus' ministry as follows: "Jesus came into Galilee, preaching the gospel of God, and saying, 'The time is fulfilled, and the kingdom of God is at hand; repent, and believe in the gospel'" (1:1, 14-15). With the arrival on earth of the King of kings, the kingdom of God has drawn near. In fact, as Jesus powerfully demonstrates in his healing words and deeds, not since God's perfect creation has the kingdom of God been so real on earth. Whereas the prophets proclaimed that the kingdom would come in the future, Jesus proclaims that it *has* come: "If it is by the Spirit of God that I cast out demons, then the kingdom of God has come upon you" (Matt 12:28; cf. John 12:31).

Since the Gospel writers stand in the Old Testament tradition, it should come as no surprise that similarities exist between the genre of gospel and that of prophecy and Hebrew narrative. Like prophecy, the Gospels confront us with the complexity of two levels of original hearers: the hearers of Jesus' words (disciples, Pharisees, etc.) and the audience of the evangelists (the churches addressed). Further, the Gospels present the same kind of history writing we find in Hebrew narrative—history writing that is informed by a "religious view of history"[1] and which can thus freely concentrate on God's acts in history. The Gospels even evidence the

---

1. Harrison, *Introduction to the NT*, 248, regarding Luke.

same kind of narrative style as Hebrew narrative, presenting, as a rule, sequences of scenes and direct rather than indirect speech.[2] Finally, like the Old Testament books of Samuel-Kings and Chronicles, the four New Testament Gospels deal with the same historical events, thus inviting comparison with each other. In the light of these similarities, many of the earlier comments on preaching Hebrew narrative and prophecy also apply to the gospel genre.

Despite these similarities, the gospel genre is distinct and requires a separate discussion. In this chapter we shall deal in turn with the gospel genre, its form of history writing, its literary characteristics, and finally its use in contemporary preaching.

THE GENRE OF GOSPEL

WE noted earlier that the genres of Hebrew narrative and prophecy contain other genres of literature; similarly, the genre of gospel does not exist in "pure" form but also contains a number of other genres. For example, apocalyptic literature is found in Mark 13 (cf. Matt 24 and Luke 21), songs or hymns in Luke 1 and 2 (the songs of Mary, Zechariah, and Simeon), in Matt 11:25-30, and in John 1 (the Prologue),[3] and prophecy is found in some of Jesus' speeches. The critical question, however, concerns the essence of the genre of gospel. The significance of this question goes far beyond obtaining a neat system of classification: genre designation sets the expectations of interpreters and determines the questions they ask of the text (see Chapter 1 above). Thus genre designation is an initial step in interpretation.

In view of this hermeneutical significance of genre designation, it is not surprising that religious/philosophical presuppositions have played an important role in determining the essence of the gospel genre. On the one hand, for example, those who for existentialist or other reasons downplay history tend to classify gospel as a unique genre *(sui generis)* which tells little about the historical Jesus. Norman Perrin says flatly that "a Gospel does not portray the history of the ministry of Jesus from A.D. 27-30 . . . , but the history of Christian experience in any and every age."[4] On

---

2. Best, *Mark*, 142-43.

3. On Matt 11:25-30, see Davies, *Invitation*, 126: "This is arranged in strophes and may be a highly finished hymn used at baptism." On John 1, see Brown, *Gospel According to John*, I, cxxxiii.

4. Perrin, *What Is Redaction Criticism?* 75. Cf. ibid.: "The Gospel of Mark . . . is a mixture of historical reminiscence, interpreted tradition, and the free creativity of prophets and the evangelist. It is, in other words, a strange mixture of history, legend, and myth. It is this fact . . . to which we have to do justice in our thinking about the significance of the 'Gospel' as the characteristic and distinctive literary product of early Christianity."

the other hand, Graham Stanton compares the Gospels with ancient biographical writing and comes to a totally different conclusion: "The wholly justifiable insistence that the gospels are not biographies has tended to hide the fact that when they are placed alongside comparable ancient writings, they are seen to tell us a surprisingly large amount about the life and character of Jesus."[5] We shall take a brief look at efforts to classify the Gospels as a genre.

Characterizations of the Gospel Genre

THE Gospel writers themselves, except for Mark (1:1), did not designate their works as gospels. The superscriptions "The Gospel According to . . ." were added by the church in the second century. The question arises if the church thereby intended to mark the Gospels as a unique type of literature and if that characterization was a valid judgment. Scholars have sought to link the Gospels to either Old Testament, early Judaic, or Greco-Roman literature.[6] This effort has led to a wide variety of characterizations and subsequent interpretations. For example, the Gospel of Mark has been characterized as history, apocalyptic literature, biography, apology, sermon, drama, passion narrative with extended introduction, and secret epiphanies.[7] Some of the more likely characterizations of the Gospels are biography, dramatic history, and the unique genre of gospel.

Biography
A fairly common designation for the gospel genre is biography. For example, Charles Talbert defends the designation of biography and summarizes it as follows: "Ancient biography is prose narration about a person's life, presenting supposedly historical facts which are selected to reveal the character or essence of the individual, often with the purpose of affecting the behavior of the reader."[8] Others disagree, however. George Ladd asserts, "The Hellenistic world knew the biographical literary form; but the Gospels do not conform to this pattern. They do not relate the outward history of a hero, nor the inner development of his character."[9]

---

5. Stanton, *Jesus of Nazareth in NT Preaching*, 135-36; cf. p. 117.
6. Aune, "Problem of the Genre of the Gospel," 10.
7. See Best, *Mark*, 140.
8. Talbert, *What Is a Gospel?* 17. Cf. Shuler, *Genre for the Gospels*, 109: "Matthew belongs to that form of laudatory biography which can be identified as the encomium biography genre, and there is no longer any need either to qualify or to apologize for the use of the word *biography*." The most recent defense of the Gospels as "a subtype of Greco-Roman biography" is found in Aune, *NT in Its Literary Environment*, 17-74. But note that Aune excludes Luke because "it belongs with Acts" (p. 77).
9. Ladd, *NT and Criticism*, 128.

Dramatic History

Other scholars prefer the designation "dramatic history." For example, Roland Frye suggests that the Gospels "partake of the character of dramatic history, in which history is not ignored and is not purposefully violated, but is transmuted into a form which can attract large numbers of people who are separated from the original events by barriers of time and culture and specialized interests."[10] Although this suggestion has merit, it is doubtful that the essence of the ancient gospel genre can be captured precisely in this category.

A Unique Genre

While granting that the Gospels have some features in common with other genres, other scholars identify gospel as a unique genre. Amos Wilder states: "This is the only wholly new genre created by the Church and the author of Mark receives the credit for it."[11] Ralph Martin observes that "the 'stories of Jesus' life' were called among Christians themselves *gospels*. . . . And in so doing they were laying claim to the appearance of a new genre of writing for which no current categories would do. Therefore they chose a new word to describe a new phenomenon, namely a type of literary composition which would not properly be called a biography of Jesus or a chronicle of his exploits or even a set of reminiscences by his friends and followers."[12] This identification of gospel as a unique genre still leaves the question, of course, about the precise nature of this genre. For our purposes, comprehending the nature of the gospel genre is more important than exact classification. We shall therefore proceed to an enumeration of the primary characteristics of the gospel genre.

Characteristics of the Gospel Genre

Kerygma

The first characteristic of gospel is linked to its original usage in the New Testament. Gospel has to do with preaching, with proclamation. Originally the gospel was that which was preached; for example, "Jesus came

10. Frye, "Jesus of the Gospels," 77. Cf. idem, "Literary Perspective for the Criticism of the Gospels," 211: "That recognition [of the Gospels as dramatic history] can help us to account for a number of problems, such as differences between the Gospels themselves. Within the genre of dramatic history, such differences are to be expected. Chronology may be rearranged, incidents diversely selected, emphases shifted, and episodes presented in distinctive lights. Such divergences are an inevitable characteristic of the genre."

11. Wilder, *Early Christian Rhetoric*, 28. Cf. p. 29: "The gospel action is not a history so much as a ritual re-enactment or mimesis. . . . Mark offers us the faith-story of Christ as a pattern of meaning or life-orientation for the believer, especially for the Roman Church in a situation of persecution."

12. Martin, *Mark*, 21.

into Galilee, preaching the gospel of God" (Mark 1:14; cf. 1 Cor 1:17; Gal 1:11). Martin remarks that "the New Testament invariably connects 'gospel' . . . with verbs of speaking and responding, and never with verbs of writing and reading. . . . 'Evangelist' in this period meant a herald, a proclaimer of good news, and not a scribe busy with his reed-pen."[13] This original usage of the word *gospel* is also reflected in the later genre of gospel, that is, the written Gospel: it is proclamation, kerygma. This characteristic indicates that the gospel genre does not merely supply information but is an earnest call to faith: "These [signs] are written that you may believe . . ." (John 20:31). The Gospels, writes Martin, are "preaching materials, designed to tell the story of God's saving action in the life, ministry, death and resurrection of Jesus of Nazareth. They were called 'gospels' because they gave the substance of 'the gospel,' declared in Romans 1:16 to be God's power to salvation to all who believe."[14]

Good News

The second characteristic of gospel is linked to the meaning of the word *gospel:* the gospel genre proclaims good news. LeRoy Lawson states: "The Gospel writers have one overriding purpose: they are announcing the good news that the reign of God has come to earth in the person of Jesus Christ, who brought with Him the possibility of forgiveness of sins and the gift of eternal life."[15] This characteristic of good news does not imply that the gospel genre may not contain messages of judgment (see, e.g., the "woes" of Matt 23), but even such messages of judgment are proclaimed for the purpose of repentance and forgiveness and thus are intended as good news.

The Centrality of Jesus and God's Kingdom

A third characteristic relates to the specific content of the gospel genre, namely, the person of Jesus Christ. The Gospels focus first and foremost on Jesus Christ; their concern, in Luke's words, is to deal "with all that Jesus began to do and teach" (Acts 1:1). Intimately intertwined with the message about Jesus Christ is the message of the kingdom of God. According to I. Howard Marshall, "There is virtually general agreement among scholars that the kernel of Jesus' message was the proclamation of the kingdom of God."[16] Jesus himself not only proclaimed the kingdom of God (Matt 4:23) but he commanded his disciples to do likewise (Matt

13. Martin, "Approaches to NT Exegesis," 230.
14. Martin, *Mark*, 21.
15. Lawson, *Matthew*, 9. Cf. Smalley, *John*, 138: "By definition a Christian Gospel is a written statement of the 'good news' *(euangelion)* proclaimed about Jesus as the Christ."
16. Marshall, *I Believe*, 222. Cf. Bright, *Kingdom of God*, 216.

10:7). The third stage of proclamation, the written Gospels themselves, may now also be characterized as proclamations of the kingdom of God. For example, the Gospel of Matthew begins with the royal genealogy of the Son of David, contains five major discourses on the kingdom (see below), and concludes with the command of King Jesus to "make disciples of all nations," for "all authority in heaven and on earth has been given to me" (28:18-20). Thus the gospel genre may be characterized as proclamation of the good news of the kingdom of God that has come in the person of Jesus Christ.

Kerygmatic History Writing

Even though the foregoing characteristics describe the essence of the gospel genre, in the light of contemporary discussions about historicity it is appropriate to name one more characteristic. While gospel may not be biography or history, it is nevertheless a form of history writing. In conformity with the kerygmatic nature of gospel, we shall call it kerygmatic history writing. That the Gospels are a form of history writing needs to be emphasized today over against redaction critics who would play theology off against history and over against literary critics who would play story off against history. Though one may grant that the Gospels do not present historical events in the precise, objective way prescribed by nineteenth-century canons of historiography, it is preposterous to argue, as some do, that the Gospels are "made-up stories" because they are narratives.[17] We have seen earlier that narrative is the ideal genre for relating history. How else would one write history? Moreover, why would the Gospel writers, who aim to testify especially to the reality of Jesus' passion and resurrection, "make up stories" when the recollection of these events was available to them in oral and possibly written traditions which had been formed by eyewitnesses? We shall have to examine further precisely how the evangelists wrote history, but it will not do simply to disregard references to eyewitnesses, historical research, and the intention to write "an orderly account . . . that you may know the truth" (Luke 1:1-4).[18]

---

17. For example, W. S. Vorster claims blatantly, "After the rise of *Redaktions-geschichte* and especially as a result of the latest literary critical studies of the gospels, it has been proved beyond doubt that the gospels are narratives, made-up stories where theology and proclamation, history and interpretation form part of the functions of the text as a process of communication. . . . The narrative character of the gospel genre calls into question both kerygma and history as distinctive characteristics of the gospel genre" (*NTS* 29 [1983] 91).

18. See Guthrie, *NT Introduction*, 87-88: "Where an author specifically states his own intention, that must always be given more weight than any scholarly conjectures. . . . Luke meant to write a historical account."

NEW TESTAMENT HISTORY WRITING

ALTHOUGH our main focus in this chapter is on the four Gospels, we must not overlook that the Gospel writer Luke continued with a second volume, Acts. The book of Acts, obviously, cannot be classified as a gospel; but the accepted designation of the gospel genre to the exclusion of Acts results in the unfortunate division of what was intended as one work, Luke-Acts. Recently the unity of Luke-Acts is being brought to the fore again. Some show this unity by way of Luke's overall theme that God continues his work of salvation especially through Jesus Christ.[19] Others seek to demonstrate the unity of Luke-Acts by reading the two volumes as one story.[20] In view of the unity of Luke-Acts and the fact that Acts, like the Gospels, consists mainly of historical narratives, we shall consider Acts along with the Gospels in the following sections.

Since Chapters 2 and 4 above present a rather extensive discussion of the historical-critical method and the complexities of history and history writing, we can confine our discussion here to a few specific aspects of New Testament history writing. In preaching the Gospels and Acts, two historical questions are foundational: First, how did the authors write history? Second, are their works reliable? In addressing these questions, we shall look in turn at the characteristics of New Testament history writing and at its reliability.

Characteristics of New Testament History Writing

Post-Resurrection Accounts

The Gospels were written after Jesus' resurrection. Unfortunately, the phrase "post-resurrection accounts" has taken on pejorative overtones because some critics have used this phrase to cast doubt on the historicity of the Gospels: presumably they narrate not history but the post-Easter faith of the early church. It is true, of course, that the Gospels would not have been written if the church had not believed that Jesus had risen from the dead. Instead of using the post-Easter situation to cast doubt on the historicity of the Gospels, however, one can use that situation more credibly

19. See, e.g., O'Toole, *The Unity of Luke's Theology: An Analysis of Luke-Acts.*

20. For example, Robert Tannehill, *Narrative Unity*, I, xiii: "Luke-Acts is a unified narrative because the chief human characters (John the Baptist, Jesus, the apostles, Paul) share in a mission which expresses a single controlling purpose—the purpose of God. The individual episodes gain their significance through their relation to this controlling purpose of God, and the narrator has made efforts to clarify this relation." See p. 2: "Luke-Acts has a unified plot because there is a unifying purpose of God behind the events which are narrated, and the mission of Jesus and his witnesses represents that purpose being carried out through human action." Cf. p. 21.

to *confirm* the essential historicity of the Gospels: the existence of the post-Easter Gospels argues *for* the historicity of Jesus' resurrection, for it was the startling news of Jesus' resurrection that gave the impetus to the oral and written traditions that ultimately culminated in the Gospels. It would be well, therefore, to set aside the ominous connotations of doubtful history when we hear of "post-resurrection accounts" and replace them with the positive connotations of good news.

We may also observe that the Gospels are not unique in being "post-. . . accounts," for that feature marks all significant historical accounts. If John F. Kennedy had not become president of the United States, for example, who would have written a history about his actions? It is only *after* certain events have taken place that history is written. Consequently, the fact that the Gospels are "post-. . . accounts" is not out of the ordinary and is by itself no reason to approach these documents with skepticism about their historicity.

Many critics are suspicious of the Gospels, however, because they suspect that the post-Easter faith *created* a history of Jesus which is not in accord with the events that actually took place. It seems fair to say that the Easter faith colored the history which the Gospels narrate: after Jesus' resurrection the authors of the Gospels were able to perceive dimensions and implications which they had been unable to see prior to that event (cf. John 16:12-15). But to say that their Easter faith *colored* the way the authors wrote pre-Easter history is quite different from saying that they *created* a new history.

Other critics contend that the authors' purpose of calling people to faith in the risen Lord made them radically alter pre-Easter history. Although the Gospel writers undoubtedly wrote for a faith response, it does not follow that this purpose caused them to lose sight of the historical Jesus. Herman Ridderbos acknowledges that they desired "to summon all men to faith in the resurrected and living Lord" but continues:

> It may not be deduced from this that those who set down the apostolic tradition concerning Jesus of Nazareth were no longer conscious of the border between the life of the historical Jesus and that of the exalted Lord. In the Gospels . . . they proclaim him [the living Lord] as he once became knowable in his coming to men, in his fellowship with them. . . . If they had told fanciful stories for that purpose [to evoke faith], then they would have been found to be false witnesses (see 1 Cor. 15:15). Nevertheless their purpose was not only to increase our historical knowledge, but to evoke faith. . . . This design explains the construction, selection, and forming of the materials; it also explains the freedom with which they used their available material.[21]

21. Ridderbos, "Tradition and Editorship in the Synoptic Gospels," 258-59.

Selection of Material

As we noted in Chapter 4, all history writers are necessarily selective in choosing which events and which aspects of these events they will write about. For the Gospel writers it was no different. John tells us specifically that he had to make a selection of the "signs" Jesus did "in the presence of his disciples" (20:30; cf. 21:25). A comparison of the Synoptic Gospels shows that their authors, too, had to make a selection of the material that was presumably available to them. Even Mark, who is generally considered to be the first evangelist, had to make choices as to what to include and what to exclude. The selection made is usually a pointer to the interest and purpose of the author.

In using the author's selection as a pointer to his purpose, we must keep in mind that "Mark need not have chosen every pericope in his gospel because it contained his particular theology or point of view. He may have included some simply because they were well known. Others stood in complexes that would have required him to excise them if he wanted to exclude them from his gospel, and Mark apparently was inclined to use these complexes as whole units."[22] Another reason for selection might have been "the simple concern for the preservation of what was available to them."[23] This complication should caution us not to build a case for the author's purpose exclusively on his selection of certain pericopes. In general we can say, however, that the selection made by a Gospel writer, especially when contrasted with the selection in other Gospels, is a good initial indicator of the author's purpose.[24]

Rearrangement of Material

Besides selecting their material, the Gospel writers arranged it to suit their particular purposes. We shall see many examples of this arranging when we look at Gospel structures later, but one well-known example may clarify the concept here. Matthew has arranged Jesus' sayings in five major discourses, the first of which is known as the Sermon on the Mount. Luke, by comparison, has a much smaller Sermon on the Mount (Plain) and has placed many of the other sayings in different sections of his Gospel. Ridderbos remarks that "the evangelist [Matthew] arranges his narrative under thematic, not under temporal [chronological], viewpoints and does not hesitate elsewhere—when we compare him with his fellow evangelists—to break the connections. . . . All sorts of details which ap-

22. Stein, *NovT* 13 (1971) 190.
23. Fee and Stuart, *How to Read the Bible*, 115.
24. Cf. ibid.: "The evangelists as divinely inspired authors selected those narratives and teachings that suited their purposes."

pear in Mark are either left out by Matthew or shortened; conversations are summarized, . . . amplified or changed."[25]

Modification of Material

In addition to selecting and arranging their material, the Gospel writers shaped the material according to their purposes. George Ladd observes that "it is almost universally recognized that the early church *shaped* the oral tradition to meet its particular needs; and the most recent scholarship has emphasized that the authors of the Gospels were no mere purveyors of tradition but were theologians in their own right. This means that the Gospels are not pure, 'objective' history, if 'objective' means the work of detached, disinterested authors. Each evangelist *selected* his material and to some degree *shaped* his material to suit his particular theological and ecclesiastical interests."[26]

Examples of shaping abound in the Gospels. Staying with the Sermon on the Mount, one can compare Matt 5:3 with Luke 6:20:

Blessed are the poor in spirit,
for theirs is the kingdom of heaven.

Blessed are you poor,
for yours is the kingdom of God.

Or compare the Lord's prayer in Matt 6 with that in Luke 11. One can multiply these examples many times over simply by comparing parallel passages in the Gospels. In contrast to contemporary standards of historiography, the Gospel writers show a remarkable degree of freedom to modify their sources, including even the very words of Jesus.[27]

Kerygmatic Focus of Material

The Gospel writers selected, arranged, and modified their material ultimately for only one purpose: to focus their material as relevant proclamation for their hearers. As the oral tradition they used was proclamation, so also their own work was intended to be proclamation. Proclamation, of course, always has a specific focus: a specific point it wishes to bring across to the hearers, a specific response it seeks to elicit from them. Glen Edwards writes concerning Mark, "Proclamation, not chronology or biography or portraiture, is Mark's intention. This explains the story-like character of the document. The chronological and geo-

25. Ridderbos, "Tradition and Editorship," 258.
26. Ladd, *I Believe*, 74.
27. Cf. Osborne, *JETS* 28/4 (1985) 407: "Some freedom is demanded by the data." Cf. Fee and Stuart, *How to Read the Bible*, 115: "This principle of adaptation [arrangement and modification] is also what explains most of the so-called discrepancies among the Gospels."

graphical problems that emerge in the book are resolved by remembering that Mark wrote more to make a point than to reconstruct events in precise detail or, for that matter, in exact sequence."[28]

The unmistakable freedom of the Gospel writers to select, rearrange, and modify their material for preaching purposes has raised many questions about the reliability of the Gospels. Since unreliable texts make poor sources for preaching the word of God, it is crucial for preachers to come to clarity on the issue of reliability.

Reliability of New Testament Narratives

USUALLY the question of reliability is reduced to the question of historical reliability, even though the former encompasses much more than the latter. Since the historical foundations of the Gospels are constantly under attack, however, and, moreover, are crucial to any sense of reliability, we shall concentrate on the historical dimension.

The Question of Historicity

The historical foundations of the Gospels have been attacked by form critics, redaction critics, and literary critics. It is not that these various forms of criticism necessarily undermine the Gospels, but the presuppositions of some of their adherents can easily turn a legitimate hermeneutical tool into a loose cannon. It is well-known that Rudolf Bultmann used form criticism to shoot down the "quest for the historical Jesus." Using redaction criticism, Bultmann's pupil Willi Marxsen states, "With this approach [redaction history], the question as to what really happened is excluded from the outset."[29] In employing literary criticism, W. S. Vorster claims that "story . . . is not a presentation of 'reality'; it is narrated reality. As a result it is a mistake to interpret a narrative in direct relation to the real world."[30]

Often the historicity of the Gospels is questioned because the authors are seen not as historians but as "theologians" or "preachers" who shape their messages according to their kerygmatic purposes. The question may be raised, however, if the recognition of the Gospel writers as "theologians" necessarily detracts from their historical reliability. It should be evident that the choice between historian and theologian is not a real dilemma but an outgrowth of the hardy fact-value dualism which sets in

28. Edwards, *SWJT* 21/1 (1978) 55.
29. Marxsen, *Mark the Evangelist*, 23. Norman Perrin takes this approach a fatal step further: "So far as we can tell today, there is no single pericope anywhere in the gospels, the present purpose of which is to preserve a historical reminiscence of the earthly Jesus" (*Rediscovering*, 16).
30. Vorster, *NTS* 29 (1983) 92.

opposition the historian who presumably presents facts ("bare facts") and the theologian who presents values. In actuality, of course, the historian as well as the theologian presents an *interpretation* of meaningful facts. Marshall, for one, asserts that "the basis of this general outlook, namely that the tasks of proclamation and of writing history are incompatible, is pure assumption, and baseless assumption at that. . . . There is no reason why the interests of the theologian and the historian should be mutually exclusive."[31]

The Significance of Historicity

The question of historicity is too important to ignore or sidestep. Hermeneutically, when an author intends to write historical narrative, one cannot simply "bracket out" the historical referents but must do justice to the author's intention. Doctrinally, the question of historicity is important for one's view of inspiration and of Scripture, though the data of Scripture should shape the doctrine, of course, and not the doctrine the data. But most importantly, the historicity of the Gospels in general concerns the very foundations of our faith, salvation, and preaching.

It is crucial to recognize that history is the foundation of the kerygma: history was prior to the kerygma and history gave rise to the kerygma. In other words, without the history there would have been no kerygma. As Ridderbos puts it: "The early church did not create the story; the story created the early church! . . . It was the history that brought forth the kerygma, and this sequence cannot be reversed without destroying the nature of the gospels."[32]

In Chapter 4 we noted that Christianity, in contrast to most world religions, is a historical religion, that is, it is based on God's acts in history, particularly the suffering, death, and resurrection of Jesus Christ. "This historical 'once-for-all-ness' of Christianity . . . makes the reliability of the writings which purport to record this revelation a question of first-rate importance."[33] In fact, our salvation and our message of salvation through

31. Marshall, *Luke*, 46-47. Ridderbos similarly refuses to accept the dilemma: "To play kerygma off against history short-changes the character of the synoptic tradition. . . . The kerygmatic role of the gospel traditions has not smothered interest in the life and character of Jesus" (*Studies*, 41). Cf. Hooker, "In His Own Image?" 36-37; and Turner, *GTJ* 4/2 (1983) 265-69. Cf. Fee and Stuart, *How to Read the Bible*, 115: "Being authors does *not* mean they were creators of the material; quite the opposite is true. Several factors prohibit greater creativity, including, we believe, the somewhat fixed nature of the material and the sovereign oversight of the Holy Spirit in the transmission process. Thus they were authors in the sense that with the Spirit's help they creatively structured and rewrote the material to meet the needs of their readers."

32. Ridderbos, *Studies*, 42. Cf. Childs, *NT as Canon*, 209: "The evangelists who shaped the Gospel texts in faith testify to the force of the resurrection in evoking that very faith."

33. Bruce, *NT Documents*, 8.

Jesus Christ depend on the historicity of these narrated events. Without assurance of the historicity of Jesus' suffering, death, and resurrection, there can be no assurance of salvation, and our messages of salvation will be groundless. Paul's words ring as true today as when he first articulated them: "If Christ has not been raised, then our preaching is in vain and your faith is in vain" (1 Cor 15:14). "An incarnational faith must rest on real events. The hard documentary element in the Christian story must be told for what it is—and received for what it is."[34]

Criteria for Historicity

In Chapter 2 we already set forth the major criteria developed by New Testament scholars for determining the authenticity of Jesus' words and deeds. In addition to following the path of these criteria for historicity, one can argue for the essential historicity of the Gospels in other ways. Ladd points to the following facts: "(1) the brief period of time which elapsed between the events and the record of the events, (2) the role of eyewitnesses in preserving the tradition, (3) the role of the authoritative apostolic witness, and (4) the role of the Holy Spirit."[35] Moreover, one can argue the case from the purpose of the authors. For example, aside from his kerygmatic purpose, Matthew clearly has an apologetic aim. R. T. France remarks: "To engage in apologetics at all implies that the traditions which are being explained are believed to be factual, or there would be no point in defending or explaining them. And it would hardly be wise to construct that apologetic by inventing fictional events to account for factual traditions." Similarly, Matthew is obviously concerned to show that Jesus is the fulfillment of Old Testament expectations. "It is hard to see how Matthew could make this claim, . . . if he did not believe the events [he reports concerning Jesus] to be factual."[36] Again, if the intention of John was to combat an early form of docetism, that intention could be met only by the narration of actual historical facts, not by inventions.

Another way of arriving at the essential historicity of the Gospels is by concentrating on their similarities. Although there is merit, as we shall see, in contrasting the Gospel accounts, we should not overlook their essential agreement on many historical events: Jesus' ministry, preaching, miracles, confrontations, suffering, death, burial, resurrection, and post-resurrection appearances. The case for the historicity of Jesus' words and deeds is much more firm than some critics have made it out to be.

---

34. Brooks, *Communicating Conviction*, 50. Cf. Marshall, *I Believe*, 84: "The person who has Christian faith is a believer in the historical Jesus as the one who is now alive as the risen Lord."

35. Ladd, *NT and Criticism*, 163.

36. France, "Scripture, Tradition and History," 260-61.

The Question of Reliability

As indicated, the issue of reliability is broader than that of historical reliability. Peter speaks of historical reliability when he writes, "We did not follow cleverly devised myths when we made known to you the power and coming of our Lord Jesus Christ, but we were eyewitnesses of his majesty." But he continues, "And we have the prophetic word made more sure. . . . Men moved by the Holy Spirit spoke from God" (2 Pet 1:16-21). Ultimately, the issue of reliability is a matter of faith in God's word.

Still, historical reliability is important, for it is foundational for preaching the Gospels and Acts (as well as the Epistles) with integrity and certainty. Even so, we must not claim more than we ought. We can claim reliability only in matters the inspired authors *intended* to teach. This statement cuts two ways. On the one hand, one cannot criticize the authors for failing to present the kind of "biographical precision" which "they themselves obviously did not intend."[37] On the other hand, one should not claim for these narratives greater historical precision than their authors intended to give. The question, therefore, again comes down to the intent of the author.

What can we say about the intent of the Gospel writers in general? Concerning Mark, Donald Guthrie writes: "The main interest of Mark was not biographical but evangelistic. . . . But this must not blind our eyes to the historical element within it. A Gospel, designed as it was to proclaim salvation to needy people, must be historically based to be valid." Concerning Luke, Guthrie observes that "he tells us he purposes 'to write an orderly account,' and while he may not mean by this a narrative in strict chronological order in every detail he is entitled to be taken seriously about his orderly intention. Moreover, he makes clear that his purpose is to be carried out after great care in ascertaining the facts. In short, Luke meant to write a historical account." Similarly, with Acts "we may assume that Luke intended his work to be regarded as historical, but not in the sense of a dry chronicle of events."[38] Even John, who is usually considered to be more of a "theologian" than any of the other Gospel writers, took history seriously. Stephen Smalley concludes his extensive study of

---

37. Ladd, *NT and Criticism*, 168.

38. Guthrie, *NT Introduction*, 79, 87-88, 316. Cf. Aune, *NT in Its Literary Environment*, 116: "By substituting the term 'narrative' for Mark's 'gospel,' Luke indicated his intention to write history." Cf. Marshall, *Luke*, 52 and 18: "Modern research has emphasized that he [Luke] was a theologian. The evidence which we have considered has shown that because he was a theologian he had to be a historian. His view of theology led him to write history." "Luke was concerned that his message about Jesus and the early church should be based upon reliable history." Regarding precision in Acts, cf. Fee, *NT Exegesis*, 41-42: "It is the nature of Hellenistic historians to paint vivid pictures of real events and not necessarily to offer the dry chronicle of a police report. This is history that is also story."

John with the comment, "Thus we may conclude that John is an evangelist whose Gospel concerns salvation history. As such it contains both history—which the fourth evangelist takes seriously—*and* theology; not one without the other."[39]

Summarizing, we can say that all the Gospel writers intend to write their good news about Jesus Christ in a historical way, that is, they relate actual historical events to proclaim their good news. Even though they write their accounts in a special, kerygmatic style, the evidence for their historicity is sufficient for approaching the Gospels with confidence in their historical reliability. As Marshall puts it, "Although the Gospels were not written by scientific historians, we have good reason to believe that they incorporate reliable information about Jesus. . . . To be sure, the Gospels and their sources give 'interpreted' pictures of Jesus, but these interpretations represent an understanding of Jesus based on the historical facts."[40]

As far as preaching these narratives is concerned, therefore, we can assume their historicity unless there are clear indications to the contrary (the most obvious example being parables). With that foundational issue settled, preachers ought to move beyond this historical concern and concentrate on the specific purpose for which each narrative was recorded. That purpose may indeed be to make the hearers aware of certain historical events, but it may be much more than that: to call to faith, to encourage, to comfort, to correct, to teach, etc. If the purpose is broader than historical, such questions as, What happened precisely? How did it come about? are the wrong questions because they work at cross-purposes with the text. In trying to answer these questions, we shall miss the very point of the text. Instead our questions ought to be: Why did the author relate this incident? Why did he include it in his Gospel? What did he intend to convey? What kind of response did he expect from his first hearers? A literary analysis will help answer these questions.

LITERARY CHARACTERISTICS OF THE GOSPELS

THE paradigm shift from history to literature is unmistakable in scholarly research on the Gospels. Most New Testament scholars now appear to concentrate on the Gospels as story. Redaction or composition

---

39. Smalley, *John*, 190; cf. p. 172: "Since history is indispensable to his witness, John would be less ready to corrupt than to preserve its historical basis." Cf. Ridderbos, *Studies*, 60: "It cannot be denied that John wanted to write history. The gospel as a whole, with all its historical, chronological, and topographical details, is proof of this."

40. Marshall, *I Believe*, 235. Cf. Scotland, *Can We Trust the Gospels?* 46: "The evidence for accepting the Gospels as reliable historical evidence is solid." For a view of this debate in Roman Catholic circles, see Ellis, *Matthew*, 156-65.

criticism still plays a role, but the impetus has clearly shifted to rhetorical criticism and especially literary or narrative criticism. David Rhoads observes that "biblical scholars have long practiced literary criticism, sharing source criticism and redaction criticism and form criticism in common with literature scholars . . . , but only recently have biblical scholars begun to investigate the formal features of narrative in the texts of the Gospels, features which include aspects of the story-world of the narrative and the rhetorical techniques employed to tell the story."[41] Although, as we noted earlier, this new literary criticism shortchanges the text's historical dimensions by getting locked into the "closed and self-sufficient world" of the story,[42] a positive result is a more holistic approach than is usually applied to the Gospels and to the individual narratives. "The challenge that literary criticism presents to both the academy and the church . . . is to rediscover a sense of the wholeness of each of the Gospels."[43]

The Structure of the Gospels

Similarities and Differences

The purpose of each of the Gospel writers is frequently discovered by focusing on the differences among the Gospels. While this procedure is legitimate, it should never be carried out at the cost of overlooking the similarities among the Gospels. All the Gospels, it is clear, bring a similar message in concentrating on the person of Jesus Christ and the kingdom of God he brings. Further, all the Gospels conclude with the climax of Jesus' resurrection, and yet all remain open to the future.[44] Moreover, Matthew, Mark, and Luke are called the Synoptic (common view) Gospels be-

---

41. Rhoads, *JAAR* 50/3 (1982) 411-12. On the difficulty of writing narrative without punctuation and paragraphs, and for a discussion of some of Mark's techniques, see John Drury, "Mark," in *The Literary Guide to the Bible*, ed. Robert Alter and Frank Kermode (Cambridge: Harvard University, 1987), 406-7.

42. Rhoads, *JAAR* 50/3 (1982) 414; cf. p. 413 on "the autonomy of the story-world." Cf. Matera, *CBQ* 49 (1987) 234: "For the literary critic the text is not a window through which one views another reality. The text, with the story world it creates, is the sole object of the literary critic's investigation."

43. Fowler, *Christian Century* 99 (May 26, 1982) 629.

44. See Beardslee, *Literary Criticism of the NT*, 20-21: "The movement toward the future is most clearly revealed in the way these books come to an end—the 'end' of the book does not simply bring the 'plot' to a conclusion which resolves the action, though there is a sense in which this takes place. More profoundly, however, the ending—the story of resurrection conveyed through the disciples' discovery of the empty tomb—shows that the story does not end with the ending of the book; rather the Gospel narrative is a story of how something began that is still in process and moving toward its future and conclusion."

cause they are similar in contents, order, and language. Arnold Rhodes demonstrates the similarity in order with the following outline:

THEME	MATTHEW	MARK	LUKE
Infancy Narratives	1:1–2:23		1:1–2:52
Introduction to Jesus' Work	3:1–4:11	1:1-13	3:1–4:13
Galilean Ministry	4:12–18:35	1:14–9:50	4:14–9:50
From Galilee to Jerusalem	19:1–20:34	10:1-52	9:51–19:27
Last Days in Jerusalem	21:1–27:66	11:1–15:47	19:28–23:56
Resurrection	28:1-20	16:1-8	24:1-53[45]

The similarities among the Synoptics extend to their very words, Matthew using 51 percent of Mark's words and Luke 53 percent, a fact usually explained by the theory that Matthew and Luke used Mark (or the source of Mark) as one of their sources.

Having noted some of the similarities, one also ought to observe the differences among the Gospels. If Matthew and Luke used Mark as one of their sources, they deliberately rearranged details in Mark's order—not because they thought Mark was in error but "because a topical rearrangement better suited" their purposes.[46] They also changed Mark's words in many instances. Moreover, Matthew and Luke extended Mark's narrative both at the beginning with infancy narratives and genealogies going back to Abraham and Adam, respectively, and at the end with Jesus' missionary mandate and the account of the Holy Spirit guiding the church "to the end of the earth" (Acts). We can clearly see the differences among the Gospels when we look at the overall literary structure of each Gospel.

Mark

The Gospel of Mark, being the earliest and briefest, is often thought to be the least affected by literary restructuring. Mark is the Gospel of action, passing by many of Jesus' sayings in order to narrate "immediately" (used more than 40 times) Jesus' next action. It has been noted, however, that Mark does not merely follow a chronological sequence but arranges some of his material topically. For example, he has collected a number of parables in one section (chap. 4), mission instructions in another (chap. 10), and disputes in yet another section (chap. 12). Although the overall structure of Mark is still much debated, some intriguing proposals have recently been put forward. For example, M. Philip Scott argues for an overall chiastic structure in Mark:

45. Rhodes, *Mighty Acts of God*, 265.
46. Ladd, *NT and Criticism*, 167.

A (1:2) An angel witnesses to his coming
  B (1:11) You are my Son
    C (2:7) Who can forgive sins *ei me heis ho theos*
      D (3:29) The guilt of the scribes
        E (3:33) Who is my mother . . .?
          F (3:35) The primacy of doing God's will
            G (4:40) Who is this that the winds . . . obey him?
              H (6:3) Jesus is called the son of Mary
                I (8:27) Who do you say that I am?
                  J (8:31) Prophecy of betrayal, passion, resurrection
                    K (9:7) This is my Son: listen to him
                  J' (9:30) Prophecy of betrayal, passion, resurrection
                I' (10:18) Why call me good? . . . *ei me heis ho theos*
              H'(10:47) Jesus is called Son of David
            G' (11:28) By what authority do you do these things?
          F' (12:30) The primacy of God's commandment of love
        E' (12:37) How is Christ David's Son?
      D'(12:40) A judgment on the scribes
    C' (14:61) Are you the Christ the Son of the Blessed God?
  B' (15:39) Truly, this man was the Son of God
A' (16:6) An angel witnesses to his going

The center of the chiasm is the narrative of Jesus' transfiguration. Scott observes that the transfiguration pericope is literally in the center of Mark, with 5,393 words before it and 5,447 words after it, and the words "This is my beloved Son; listen to him," are in the center of the pericope, with 100 words before them and 101 after them. Combining the chiastic structure with other telltale signs in Mark, Scott proposes an outline for Mark consisting of three main parts: 1:9–8:30; 8:31–13:37; and 14:1–15:47.[47] Many outlines for Mark have been suggested, the most basic (as sketched below) probably being that of acknowledging two main parts: 1:14–8:26,

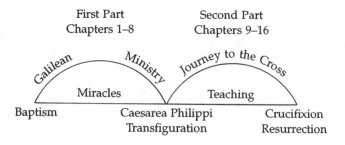

First Part — Chapters 1–8 — Galilean Ministry — Miracles — Baptism

Second Part — Chapters 9–16 — Journey to the Cross — Teaching — Caesarea Philippi — Transfiguration — Crucifixion — Resurrection

---

47. Scott, *BTB* 15 (1985) 18-19, 25; for a more detailed chart, see p. 19. Cf. the proposal of Rudolph Pesch (*Naherwartungen*), summarized by Paul Achtemeier, *Mark*, 37-38; and that of Robbins, *NovT* 23/2 (1981) 113-14.

and 8:27–16:8, the turning point being Peter's confession in 8:29, "You are the Christ."[48]

Matthew

While Matthew follows Mark's twofold structure of Jesus' ministry in Galilee (4:12–18:35) and his ministry in Judea and Jerusalem (19:1–28:15), he has clearly imposed a new structure by introducing five major teaching sections which all end with the almost identical words, "and when Jesus finished these sayings." These five teaching sections all have to do with the kingdom of heaven:

1. The law of the kingdom (5–7)
2. Preachers of the kingdom (10:5-42)
3. Parables about the kingdom (13:1-52)
4. Life in the kingdom (18:1-35)
5. The consummation of the kingdom (24:1–25:46)

Having taken note of the resultant structure of narrative alternating with discourse, D. J. Clark and J. de Waard suggest that Matthew can be divided into three "acts" of approximately equal length. This discloses an intricate pattern of three chiastic structures within an overall ABA chiastic structure:

Act 1	Narrative	chs 1–4
	Discourse	chs 5–7
	Narrative	chs 8–9
Act 2	Discourse	ch 10
	Narrative	chs 11–12
	Discourse	ch 13
	Narrative	chs 14–17
	Discourse	ch 18
Act 3	Narrative	chs 19–22
	Discourse	chs 23–25
	Narrative	chs 26–28[49]

On the basis of the five discourses and other indicators, H. Bernard Combrink similarly suggests a chiastic pattern covering the whole of Matthew's Gospel:[50]

---

48. The diagram is taken from Doris B. J. Campbell, *The Synoptic Gospels: A Commentary for Teachers and Students* (London: John Murray, 1966), p. 6, and is used by permission. For the two main parts, see also Kingsbury, *Int* 33 (1979) 364.

49. Clark and de Waard, *Scriptura*, Special 1 (1982) 5.

50. Combrink, *TynBul* 34 (1983) 71. Cf. Ellis, *Matthew*, 12-13.

A.	1:1–4:17	*Narrative:* The birth and preparation of Jesus.
B.	4:18–7:29	Introductory material, *First Speech:* Jesus teaches with authority.
C.	8:1–9:35	*Narrative:* Jesus acts with authority—ten miracles.
D.	9:36–11:1	*Second Discourse:* The Twelve commissioned with authority.
E.	11:2–12:50	*Narrative:* The invitation of Jesus rejected by "this generation."
F.	13:1-53	*Third Discourse:* The parables of the kingdom.
E'.	13:54–16:20	*Narrative:* Jesus opposed and confessed, acts in compassion to Jews and gentiles.
D'.	16:21–20:34	*Fourth Discourse within Narrative:* The impending passion of Jesus, lack of understanding of the disciples.
C'.	21:1–22:46	*Narrative:* Jesus' authority questioned in Jerusalem.
B'.	23:1–25:46	*Fifth Discourse:* Judgement on Israel and false prophets, the coming of the kingdom.
A'.	26:1–28:20	*Narrative:* The passion, death and resurrection of Jesus.

Others are of the opinion, however, that Matthew's divisional markers are not the five discourses but the phrase "From that time Jesus began to preach [to show his disciples]," which occurs in 4:17 and 16:21. This view leads to a three-part structure, which Jack Kingsbury describes as follows:

(I) The Figure of Jesus Messiah (1:1–4:16);

(II) The Ministry of Jesus Messiah to Israel and Israel's Repudiation of Jesus (4:17–16:20); and

(III) The Journey of Jesus Messiah to Jerusalem and His Suffering, Death, and Resurrection (16:21–28:20).[51]

Moreover, Kingsbury notes that Matthew brackets his story with two key passages: "Behold, a virgin shall conceive and bear a son, and his name shall be called Emmanuel (which means, God with us)" (1:23), and "Lo, I am with you always, to the close of the age" (28:20). "In combination these structural features reveal that what Matthew intends with his kerygmatic story is . . . to proclaim the truth that in the person of Jesus Messiah, God has drawn near with his end-time rule to dwell with his people, the church, until the consummation, thus inaugurating the final age of salvation."[52]

Luke

Luke, no less than Matthew, has brought major changes into the twofold

51. Kingsbury, *Matthew as Story,* 38.

52. Kingsbury, *Int* 33 (1979) 367. Ridderbos opts for a four-part structure: "In this structure four almost equal parts can be distinguished, each of about 270 verses: 1:1–9:35 (270 vss.); 9:36–16:12 (270 vss.); 16:13–23:39 (272 vss.); 24:1–28:20 (258 vss.)" ("Tradition and Editorship," 248). By contrast, Gundry concludes that "the Gospel of Matthew is structurally mixed" (*Matthew,* 11).

structure of Mark. "As with the other Synoptics, he describes first the ministry of Jesus in Galilee and concludes finally with his passion in Jerusalem. But between these two foci of the Gospel ellipse he has inserted his 'Great Interpolation' depicting the journey which lay between these two basic spheres of activity. Whereas the other Synoptics make only passing mention of this transition from the north to the south (Mt. 19:1; Mk. 10:1), Luke has expanded the last journey 'on the way to the Cross' into his most conspicuous section."[53] The result of this insertion is a structure consisting of three major parts:

Introduction: Preparation for the Ministry of Jesus (1:5–2:52)

   I. The Ministry in Galilee (4:14–9:50)
   II. The Ministry between Galilee and Jerusalem (9:51–19:27)
   III. The Ministry in Jerusalem (19:28–23:56)

Conclusion: Consummation of the Ministry of Jesus (24:1-53)

Luke introduces another major change by following up his Gospel with a second volume. He "prefaces his Gospel with an exordium, a literary device employed by Greek writers of his era," which was intended "to cover both the Gospel and the Acts."[54] Luke-Acts, therefore, seeks to tell one continuous story. Norman Perrin notes "the careful parallelism of the baptism and descent of the Spirit in each volume, the parallelism of the journey motif of Jesus to Jerusalem and Paul to Rome, and the great significance of the teaching of the risen Jesus (Luke 24:46-49; Acts 1:8)."[55]

Jesus' mandate to the disciples (Acts 1:8) also functions as the structure of Acts: "You shall be my witnesses in Jerusalem and in all Judea and Samaria and to the end of the earth." Like the Gospel of Luke, then, the book of Acts consists of three main parts marked by changes in geography:

   I. The Ministry in Jerusalem (1:12–7:60)
   II. The Ministry in Judea and Samaria (8:1-40)
   III. The Ministry to the End of the Earth (9:1–28:31)

John

The Gospel of John, of course, has quite a different structure from that of the Synoptics. As the prologue indicates, John wishes to relate Jesus' story from the perspective of the preexistent Word which became flesh. Kingsbury remarks that whereas the Synoptic evangelists "work with the horizontal time-line: there is the time of Old Testament prophecy, and there is the time of the Baptist and of Jesus, the time of eschatological fulfillment . . . , [John] adapts his story to a schema which is vertical and spa-

---

53. Hull, *RevExp* 59 (1962) 423; see the detailed outline on pp. 426-32.
54. Martin, *NT Foundations*, I, 244, with reference to Josephus, *Against Apion* 1.1; 2.1. Cf. Aune, *NT in Its Literary Environment*, 117; cf. pp. 77-80.
55. Perrin, *Introduction*, 205. Cf. Moessner, *NovT* 28/3 (1986) 220-56.

tial in character and which sets forth the descent and ascent of the cosmic savior (3:17; 4:42; 16:28)."[56] Although a case has been made recently that the book "is structured from beginning to end according to [a] chiastic pattern, A B C B' A'," most scholars identify a two-part structure: "The Book of Signs (1–12) and the Book of the Passion (13–20/21), with 13:1 as a hinge."[57] This hinge also reveals the "vertical character": "Now . . . when Jesus knew that his hour had come to depart out of this world to the Father." Smalley describes John's Gospel as a drama with two acts: "*Act 1* deals with the revelation of the Word to the world, and consists of six signs with their associated discourses and 'I am' sayings (Jn 2–12)." "*Act 2* . . . (Jn 13–20) concerns the glorification of the Word for the world, and concentrates on those who acknowledged the claims for Jesus, the Word, already set out in Act 1."[58] We see something of the intricate literary structure of this Gospel in a table which summarizes Smalley's discussion of the relationship between the seven signs, the discourses, and the "text-like sayings which expound various aspects of the theme of eternal life as that is to be found in and through Jesus the Christ."[59]

Sign	Discourse	Saying
		"I am"
1. Water into wine (2)	New life (3)	the true vine (15:1)
2. The official's son (4)	Water of life (4)	the way, and the truth, and the life (14:6)
3. The sick man (5)	Son, life-giver (6)	the door of the sheep (10:7)
4. The five thousand fed (6)	Bread of life (6) and Spirit of life (7)	the bread of life (6:35)
5. The blind man (9)	Light of life (8)	the light of the world (8:12)
6. Lazarus (11)	Shepherd, life-giver (10)	the resurrection and the life (11:25)
7. The catch of fish (21)	Disciple life (14-16)	the good shepherd (10:11)

Although scholars may not be entirely agreed on the literary structure of each of the Gospels, it is clear that all four Gospels have been carefully crafted to bring across their particular message.[60]

---

56. Kingsbury, *Int* 33 (1979) 373.

57. For the chiastic analysis, see Ellis, *Genius of John,* 14-15, with credit to John Gerhard. For the two-part structure, see Martin, *NT Foundations,* 272.

58. Smalley, *John,* 194 and 200.

59. Ibid., 91-92.

60. Cf. Frye, "Jesus of the Gospels," 78: "For the four gospels, the turning point is in each case concerned with the confession of Jesus as the Christ. In Matt. 16:16, Peter makes it; in Mark 9:7, it is the voice from the cloud declaring 'this is my beloved son;

Narrative Features

SINCE the Gospel writers as well as Jesus stood in the Old Testament tradition, it is not surprising that many narrative features in the Gospels are similar to the ones being detected in Old Testament narrative. We shall look in turn at the elements of scene, characterization, dialogue, plot, and narrator.

The Scene

"In scenic narrative . . . the action is broken up into a sequence of scenes. . . . Conflicts, direct statements of single acts, and direct speech are preeminent."[61] Scenic narrative is found in all four Gospels.

According to Robert Tannehill, many scenes in the Synoptic Gospels are "episodic," that is, they seem to stand on their own, with no causal connection to other scenes: "The total picture of Jesus and his mission is being enriched through repeated, similar episodes, each of which adds some new variation to familiar situations and themes." This comment does not imply that these scenes can be interpreted in isolation but that they should be understood in the larger context in relation to similar scenes. Tannehill suggests that "it will help us to understand the function of an individual scene if we understand how it is linked with other scenes which reinforce, enrich, and modify its implications, so that it becomes part of a larger developing portrait of Jesus and his contemporaries."[62]

Many scenes are causally related, however, and can be understood only in connection with each other. Take, for example, the scenes in John 9 of Jesus healing the man blind from birth. "These scenes succeed one another in rapid fashion . . ., their sequential unity being maintained by the dropping of one character from the scene while the other remains to continue the action with a new character in the following scene."[63] Or take the scenes in Luke 8 and 9. Clark and de Waard make a good case for an intricate, interrelated pattern:

Scene 3   3 plain healing miracles (8:1-17)
Scene 4   3 instances of reaction to Jesus (8:18-34)
Scene 5   3 causes of opposition to Jesus (9:1-17)
Scene 6   1 healing, 1 reaction, 1 opposition (9:18-34)

---

hear him;' in Luke 12:8-9, it is Jesus himself teaching about confession and denial of the Son of man; and in John 9:37-38, it is the self-identification of Jesus followed at once by the climactic affirmation of the man born blind who now sees all things clearly." Note that Frye's method of arriving at the center can stand some refinement: "I totalled the verses in each gospel (excluding the textually dubious verses in Mark 16 and John 8), then divided by two to find the numerical centers" (p. 87 n. 5).

61. Licht, *Storytelling in the Bible*, 29-30. Ernest Best remarks that "by far the largest part of the narrative of the Gospel [of Mark] is 'scenic'" (*Mark*, 143).

62. Tannehill, *Narrative Unity*, I, 4 and 172.

63. Raymond Collins, *Introduction*, 220.

In diagram form, the pattern of these four scenes becomes clear:

Scene 3	Scene 4	Scene 5	Scene 6		
3 Episodes of healing	3 Episodes of reaction	3 Episodes of opposition	1 Episode of healing	1 Episode of reaction	1 Episode of opposition

"This arrangement shows the thematic unity of the whole block, and reveals Scene 6 as thematically focal. The healing miracle it contains is in fact a raising from death, the only one in this gospel, and a fitting pinnacle to the healings in Scene 3. The 'reaction' is the blind man's recognition of Jesus as 'Son of David,' a theme suppressed by Jesus here, but accepted at the end of his ministry in 20:29–21:17. The 'opposition' is the ultimate blasphemy of attributing Jesus' power to a demonic source, a theme developed in Acts 2."[64]

Characterization

In New Testament narratives, as in the Old Testament, characterization is achieved not so much by character description as it is by narration of the character's words and actions. Here, also, groups such as the disciples or the crowds may function as a single character. In Matthew's Gospel, for example, "the principal characters . . . are Jesus, the disciples, the Jewish leaders, the crowds, and the minor characters." In addition, we should emphasize that in all four Gospels, Jesus is the leading "character"; in fact, he is in a class by himself.[65]

The Gospel writers, like the Old Testament narrators, frequently use the device of *contrasting characters*—the device in which one character serves as a foil for another. For example, in the Gospels we find contrasted Jesus and King Herod, Jesus and the Jewish leaders, the Jewish leaders and the crowds, the disciples and the crowds, Peter and the beloved disciple (John), the wise men from the East and Israel (Matt 2), Simon the Pharisee and the sinful woman (Luke 7:36-50), etc. The minor characters in particular often serve as foils for other characters.[66]

We also find in the New Testament narratives *"parallel characters,"* that

64. Clark and de Waard, *Scriptura*, Special 1 (1982) 20.

65. Kingsbury, *Matthew as Story*, 10. He also states: "The importance Matthew confers on Jesus conspicuously sets him apart from all other characters." Paul Achtemeier remarks that "there is no question that for the Gospel of Mark, Jesus is the central figure. If he is not present in every scene, he is the subject around which every narrative turns, and it is his activity and his fate that are Mark's chief concern" (*Mark*, 53). Smith writes similarly for the Gospel of John: "Other characters have significance only insofar as they stand in relation to Jesus. . . . The various characters serve either to highlight the character and significance of Jesus or to represent various possible responses to him" (*John*, 101).

66. See Rhoads, *JAAR* 50/3 (1982) 419. Cf. Kingsbury, *Matthew as Story*, 26.

is, characters who are intended to be interpreted in conjunction with each other. Some obvious parallel characters are Elizabeth and Mary (Luke 1), and John the Baptist and Jesus (Mark 1:14; 6:14-16). Some characters, because of the distance between them, do not obviously parallel one another, though they may well have been so intended: for example, Jesus and Moses (Matt 5:1; 7:29; 17:1-8; 28:16-20), and John the Baptist and Elijah (Matt 11:14; 17:10-13). In addition, Stephen in his dying prayer parallels Jesus (Acts 7:60 and Luke 23:34); "Peter and especially Paul perform the same type of healings (Luke 5:17-26—Acts 3:1-10; 14:8-18), raise people from the dead (Luke 7:11-17; 8:40-56—Acts 9:36-43; 20:7-12), preach repentance to Jew and Gentile alike (Luke 24:44-48—Acts 10; 17:16-33), and suffer shame and rejection by their own folk (Luke 22:47–23:49—Acts 4:1-22; 21:27–22:29) in imitation and in 'the name' of their master."[67]

Dialogue

Dialogue is a form of characterization, the characters being sketched by the words they speak. As in Old Testament narrative, dialogue usually follows the "rule of two," that is, it is limited "to two persons at any one time. Others on stage are either provided with exit cues or reduced to simple bystanders."[68] Dialogue can also be used for emphasis simply because it takes up more narrative space than does a brief summary. Tannehill states that "dialogue in a dramatic scene emphasizes, while summary narration of events gives them a subordinate position."[69]

Matthew, we have seen, highlights five major discourses of Jesus, thus demonstrating the value he places on discourse. John's Gospel, too, is known for its lengthy monologues as well as its dialogues. Clearly, dialogue as well as monologue is used by the Gospel writers for teaching purposes. We see this use in John's Gospel, for example, in Jesus' conversations with Nicodemus, the Samaritan woman, and Martha and Mary. "In each case, what begins as a private conversation gradually enlarges to address the reader. . . . Whatever may be the topic as the conversation begins, the ending is always a revelation of God giving life eternal to those who believe. In other words, the Johannine conversation is a proclamation form, a sermonic design."[70]

Plot

Plot is basically the story line; that is, the "beginning, middle, and end

---

67. Moessner, *NovT* 28/3 (1986) 220. Cf. Aune, *NT in Its Literary Environment*, 119. See O'Toole, *Unity of Luke's Theology*, 62-72, for an extensive listing of the parallels between Jesus and Stephen and Jesus and Paul.

68. Ellis, *Genius of John*, 8.

69. Tannehill, *JR* 57 (1977) 391.

70. Craddock, *Preaching*, 172. Cf. Aune, *NT in Its Literary Environment*, 51-52.

which contribute to the buildup and release of dramatic tension."[71] Thus plot always involves conflict, "a struggle between two opposing forces."[72]

Most New Testament scholars are convinced that each Gospel has an overall plot, primarily because each Gospel has the prerequisites of plot: conflict, and beginning, middle, and end. For example, Kingsbury tries to uncover the conflict in Matthew's Gospel but has to face the complication that Matthew presents many conflicts: conflicts between Jesus and Satan, demons, "the forces of nature and of illness, civil authorities (such as Herod and Pilate), Gentiles (including Roman soldiers), and Israel, above all its leaders," etc. Of these many conflicts, which is the overriding conflict that structures the plot in Matthew's Gospel? Kingsbury concludes that "by and large, two conflicts dominate: that between Jesus and Israel, especially the Jewish leaders; and that between Jesus and the disciples. Whereas the first conflict turns out tragically for Israel, the second ends in reconciliation for the disciples."[73] By concentrating on plot, therefore, by analyzing the story line in terms of conflict and resolution, interpreters seek to arrive at the overall thrust of each Gospel.[74]

The distinction between plotted time and narrative time may also be helpful in detecting the author's intentions. Narrative time is "the order in which events referred to in the narrative occurred"; plotted time is "the order in which the reader learns of those events." For example, "we learn that John was arrested before Jesus began his public mission ([Mark] 1:14; narrative time), but we do not learn the outcome of that arrest until much later in the narrative (6:17-28; plotted time). . . . We learn that John's public proclamation resulted in his death at the same time we learn that Jesus is now extending his proclamation. . . . In that way, the narrator can suggest to the reader that John, Jesus' forerunner in preaching (1:7-8), is also Jesus' forerunner in a martyr's death."[75]

---

71. Wilcoxen, "Narrative," 93. See the discussion of plot in Chapter 9 above.

72. Combrink, *TynBul* 34 (1983) 74.

73. Kingsbury, *Matthew as Story,* 3 and 41. For the conflicts in Mark, see Rhoads, *JAAR* 50/3 (1982) 415-17.

74. Tannehill advises: "We must pay special attention to the main story lines which unify the Gospel, for it is not only the continuing centrality of Jesus which makes Mark a single story but also the fact that certain events can be understood as the realization or frustration of goals or tasks which are suggested early in the story" (*Semeia* 16 [1979] 58). Matera ventures the following description of Matthew's plot: "In the appearance of Jesus the Messiah, God fulfills his promises to Israel. But Israel refuses to accept Jesus as the Messiah. Consequently, the Gospel passes to the nations" (*CBQ* 49 [1987] 243). Combrink proposes that "the narrative plot of Matthew consists of the following three elements: (1) Setting (1:1–4:17); (2) Complication (4:18–25:46); (3) Resolution (26:1–28:20)" (*TynBul* 34 [1983] 75).

75. Paul Achtemeier, *Mark*, 45.

The Narrator

There appears to be general agreement that in the Gospels, as in Old Testament narratives, we have "reliable narrators" so that we need not distinguish between narrator and "implied author." The narrator stands outside the story but makes his presence known by introducing the characters, by providing the readers with information which is usually not available to the characters (e.g., Matt 1:1 stating that Jesus is the Messiah), and by narrative commentary. Examples of narrative commentary in Matthew's Gospel are the genealogy, the formula-quotations indicating fulfillment of prophecy, "the explanation of terms (1:23; 27:33) or translation of foreign words (27:46); remarks that are addressed directly to the reader (24:15; 27:8; 28:15); and the many statements that apprise the reader of the thoughts (21:25-27), feelings (2:10, 22), perceptions (21:45; 22:18), and intentions (21:46) of characters."[76] Since Matthew relates the thoughts, feelings, perceptions, and intentions of characters, he is identified as an "omniscient" narrator. Mark shows similar "omniscience" by relating what his characters feel and think (5:28, 33; 6:49; 15:10), and even what Jesus thinks and feels (2:8; 5:30; 8:12).[77]

The most important question to ask about the narrator concerns his point of view. For it is according to his point of view that the narrator selects the events he relates, the aspects of the events he relates, the order in which he relates them, and the point he makes with them.[78] Although the author may have included certain pericopes for purposes other than the story line, on the whole the narrator's point of view will provide a good clue to his overall purpose.

Another question that is raised in connection with the narrator's point of view is the question of his evaluation of events and characters. This is not a simple matter because, as is generally true in the Old Testament, the narrator seldom expresses his direct approval or disapproval. Nevertheless, Tannehill contends that "values and beliefs are pervasive in narrative even when the narrator does not express them directly. We are always perceiving characters and events in the way that the narrator presents them to us, which may imply negative or positive judgments about them and will also represent judgments about what is important."[79] Understandably, Jesus especially is considered to offer true evaluative commen-

76. Kingsbury, *Matthew as Story*, 31. For Mark, see Achtemeier, *Mark*, 43.
77. Vorster, *NTS* 29 (1983) 91.
78. Cf. Tannehill, *JR* 57 (1977) 387-88: "The narrator chooses how to tell the story. This choice will reflect the narrator's selective emphasis and values. . . . The narrator chooses the way which fits his purpose . . . , and so his purposes are mirrored by his stories."
79. Tannehill, *Narrative Unity*, I, 7-8.

tary. As Kingsbury puts it, "There is only one true way in which to view things in Matthew—namely, the way established by God, and this is the way in which both Matthew as narrator and Jesus also view things."[80]

With respect to evaluation, especially that of characters, narrative criticism leaves the way wide open for a moralistic approach. It may be helpful to observe that evaluation is necessary for understanding where characters stand with respect to Jesus and his message and what they contribute to the plot which is centered in Jesus, but such character evaluation does not mean that these characters may now be isolated from the story and presented as models for the congregation to emulate. The general lack of direct evaluation by the narrator and the unity of his story are obvious indicators that his intent is not to have his Gospel read as a collection of moral tales.[81]

Rhetorical Structures

IN New Testament narratives, not surprisingly, we meet some of the same rhetorical structures we find in Old Testament narratives. We shall look at repetition, inclusion, and chiasm.

Repetition

Repetition is used throughout the Gospels and at various levels. We find repetition of words: for example, the ninefold "blessed" of the Beatitudes; repetition of phrases: for example, the fivefold "You have heard that it was said" (Matt 5), or the threefold "and your Father who sees in secret will reward you" (Matt 6); repetition of patterns of sayings: for example, in Mark 8–10; and repetition in discourses: for example, the three discourses in John 6, 8, and 10.[82] We also find repetition in scenes: for example, Peter denying Jesus three times in a single scene (Mark 14:66-72); Jesus announcing his coming suffering in a sequence of scenes (Mark 8:31; 9:31; 10:33-34); Jesus feeding the multitude in two separated scenes (Mark 6:30-52; 8:1-21); and the same character, Nicodemus, appearing in key scenes at the beginning, middle, and end of Jesus' ministry (John 3, 7, 19).

The device of repetition serves various functions. The most obvious function is emphasis, especially in oral style. Moreover, "the use of repetition for emphasis is clear from the fact that the most detailed and em-

---

80. Kingsbury, *Matthew as Story*, 33. Cf. Achtemeier, *Mark*, 44.

81. This is not to say, of course, that the Gospels have no ethical dimension. See Verhey, *Great Reversal*, 72-112.

82. See Achtemeier, *Mark*, 33; and on John, U. C. Von Wahlde, "Literary Structure and Theological Argument in Three Discourses with the Jews in the Fourth Gospel," *JBL* 103/4 (1984) 575-84.

phatic instance is [usually] placed last, that is, the series forms a climax."[83]
Repetition can function further to highlight a theme or to develop it. As
far as the reader is concerned, "repetitive pattern heightens awareness of
both similarities and differences, for it guides the reader in making comparisons."[84] In addition, repetition is used as a mnemonic device. Repetition is also the basis, of course, for the formation of more intricate patterns
such as parallelism, inclusion, and chiasm.

Inclusion

Inclusion marks units of literature by repeating the beginning at the end.
Wherever true inclusion is found, preachers can be sure they have identified a textual unit. One must be careful, however, not to identify as inclusion what is merely twofold repetition.[85] Many examples of inclusion
can be given. The Beatitudes are enclosed by "for theirs is the kingdom of
heaven" (Matt 5:3, 10). A few other units marked by inclusion are Matt
15:11-20; 18:1-4; 19:13-15; 19:30–20:16.

Inclusion marks not only relatively small units but can also enclose an
entire Gospel. Matthew uses Jesus' concluding words, "I am with you always, to the close of the age" (28:20), to remind us of his first quotation
from the Old Testament about the promised Immanuel, "God with us"
(1:23). This inclusion, like many others, not only rounds off the unit but
also highlights its message.[86]

In Mark we find a more complex form of what we might also call inclusion for its ABA pattern. Several times Mark "sandwiches" one story in
the middle of another. For example, the story about the woman with the
issue of blood is found in the middle of the story about Jairus's daughter
(5:21-43); the story about the beheading of John the Baptist is inserted in
the middle of the mission of the twelve and their return (6:7-31); and the
cleansing of the temple is placed in the middle of the story of Jesus curs-
ing the fig tree (11:12-25). "There are still some unresolved problems connected with this particular Markan structure," Paul Achtemeier admits.
But "it is clear in the account of the temple that the bracketing material is

83. Tannehill, *JR* 57 (1977) 390. For repetition, parallelism, rhythm, and tension,
see idem, *Sword*, 40-57.
84. Tannehill, *Narrative Unity*, I, 20. See pp. 170-71, 178 for a discussion of "type-
scenes."
85. This error happens rather frequently in, e.g., J. C. Fenton, *The Gospel of St Matthew* (Baltimore: Penguin, 1963).
86. See Kingsbury, *Matthew as Story*, 40: "Strategically located at the beginning
and the end of Matthew's story, these two passages 'enclose' it. In combination, they
reveal that the message the story of Matthew proclaims is that in the person of Jesus
Messiah, his Son, God has drawn near to abide to the end of time with his people, the
church, thus inaugurating the eschatological age of salvation." On inclusions in John,
see Ellis, *Genius of John*, 9-10.

meant to interpret the material that stands within. The cursed and withered fig tree makes clear that Jesus is not purging the temple so it can continue in more fitting service to God. The fig tree is not pruned so it can bear fruit; it dies. Similarly, the act in the temple is to be understood, Mark makes clear, as the announcement of its end as well."[87] The other "sandwiched" stories also need to be interpreted in the light of their counterpart.

Chiasm

Chiasm, too, can cover lengthy literary units as well as smaller units. We have already seen the proposals that the entire Gospels of Mark, Matthew, and John are each constructed according to a chiastic pattern. Regardless of our view of an overall chiastic pattern, it is beyond doubt that all Gospel writers make considerable use of chiasm within their Gospels.[88] Just a few samples will make this point clear. The first example is Mark 3:20-35, another passage in which Mark has "sandwiched" one story within another: in this case the story of the scribes' accusation that Jesus is possessed by Beelzebul is set within a story of the concern of Jesus' family and friends. Not only is the first story encircled by the second, but together they make an impressive chiasm:

A. The friends (family) of Jesus seek him	3:20-21
B. Accusation: he is possessed by Beelzebul	3:22a
C. Accusation: by the prince of demons	3:22b
D. Logion on Satan	3:23-26
C'. Response to the second accusation	3:27
B'. Response to the first accusation	3:28-29
A'. The true relatives of Jesus	3:31-35[89]

John 13:36–14:31 provides us with a clear example of chiasm from the Gospel of John.

A Peter claims that he can follow Jesus now (13:36-38)
  B Let not your hearts be troubled (14:1-7)
    C Philip asks a question. Jesus' answer: My words are the Father's (14:8-14)
      D If you love me, keep my commandments (14:15-21)
    C' Judas asks a question. Jesus' answer: My word is the Father's (14:22-27)
  B' Let not your hearts be troubled (14:27-30)
A' Jesus follows the Father's commandment and goes forth (14:31)

---

87. Achtemeier, *Mark*, 33. On "intercalations or analeptic narrative constructions" in Mark, see also Kermode, *Genesis of Secrecy*, 127-37.

88. See already in 1931, Lund, "The Influence of Chiasmus upon the Structure of the Gospels," *ATR* 13 (1931) 27-48.

89. See W. Harrington, *Mark* (Wilmington: Michael Glazier, 1979), 43.

A final example of chiasm is taken from Luke 15:11-32 in order to show that Jesus' parables, too, are often structured chiastically.

A   One son takes his inheritance; conversation between Father and son (vv. 11-12)
   B   One son goes out; his conduct (vv. 13-16)
      C   The well-being of the Father's servants recalled; "I perish" *(apolly-mai)* (v. 17)
         D   I will say "I have sinned" (vv. 18-19)
            E   At the point of *crisis*, the Father runs to meet his son and is compassionate (v. 20)
         D' The son says "I have sinned" (v. 21)
      C' The Father instructs the servants to make well; the lost *(apololos)* is found (vv. 22-24)
   B' One son refuses to go in: his conduct (vv. 25-30)
A' One son promised his inheritance: conversation between Father and son (vv. 31-32)

The function of chiasm is not only to mark the limits of the unit, as inclusion does, but especially to *focus* the unit so that its message cannot be mistaken. The chiasm of "the parable of the prodigal son," as it is popularly known, shows clearly that the parable is not about one son but about two sons as well as a father. The chiastic structure reveals further that the focal point of the parable is the father's compassion.[90]

Other Literary Devices

FOR purposes of Gospel interpretation and preaching, it is important to be acquainted with a few more literary devices used by the Gospel writers.

Parallelism

In Chapter 10 we considered poetry and its utilization of various forms of parallelism. The hermeneutical significance of detecting parallelism is that the parallel lines explain each other. In the Gospels parallelism is found primarily in John in the discourses, and in the Synoptics in the words of Jesus and the songs.[91] For example, *synonymous* parallelism is found in the Song of Mary (Luke 1:46-47):

> My soul magnifies the Lord,
> and my spirit rejoices in God my Savior.

90. Welch, "Chiasmus in the NT," 241 and 239. See pp. 233-49 for many other examples from the Gospels. For chiasms in John, see Ellis, *Genius of John*; and Edwin C. Webster, "Pattern in the Fourth Gospel," 230-57.
91. Brown, *Gospel According to John*, I, cxxxii.

In John we find it, for example, in Jesus' words in 6:35:

> He who comes to me shall not hunger,
> and he who believes in me shall never thirst.

Antithetic parallelism is found, for example, in the familiar words of John 3:18:

> He who believes in him is not condemned;
> he who does not believe is condemned already.

Synthetic parallelism, which advances the thought in the second half line, comes to expression in John 8:44:

> You are of your father the devil,
> and your will is to do your father's desires.

Double Meaning

Double meaning is a feature to watch for particularly in the Gospel of John. Smalley explains that "since the Word has become flesh, material facts of created existence can convey spiritual reality."[92] Thus "born again" ("from above") has a double meaning (John 3:3-8), as does "living water" (4:10), "bread" (6:32-60), "blind" (9:39-41), and being "lifted up" (3:14; 8:28; 12:32-34). Double meaning is also found in Matthew, for example, where the "mountain" (5:1; 17:1; 28:16) denotes not only a geographical location but also "the place of revelation."[93] Naturally, one must be careful not to read double meanings where none is intended or one will be caught up in spiritualizing and allegorizing.

Irony

John's ambivalence often leads to irony in dialogue, for Jesus speaks at one level while his opposite, say, the Samaritan woman, responds at another level. Irony also occurs in other ways. Raymond Brown notes that "the opponents of Jesus are given to making statements about him that are derogatory, sarcastic, incredulous, or, at least, inadequate in the sense they intend. However, by way of irony these statements are often true or more meaningful in a sense they do not realize. The evangelist simply presents such statements and leaves them unanswered . . . , for he is certain that his believing readers will see the deeper truth." For example,

---

92. Smalley, *John*, 87. See also p. 192: "John's thought always operates on two levels at once. Indeed, such is John's deliberate ambivalence that we are never quite sure at any one moment on which level he is to be understood—the earthly or the heavenly, in time or in eternity." Cf. Smith, *John*, 102-4; Ellis, *Genius of John*, 7-8.

93. Bruce, *Message*, 67. On "settings," see Kingsbury, *Matthew as Story*, 27-29; and Rhoads, *JAAR* 50/3 (1982) 419.

John 8:22 reports: "Then said the Jews, 'Will he kill himself, since he says, "Where I am going, you cannot come?"'"[94]

Irony is also found in the Synoptics. Tannehill brings out the irony in Mark's passion story. For example, in the mocking of the soldiers, "the irony . . . actually has two levels. The soldiers act and speak ironically; outwardly they proclaim Jesus King of the Jews but actually they are rejecting his kingship. However, the reader is meant to take the soldiers' irony ironically, i.e., as pointing to hidden truth. This reading is supported by the repeated references to Jesus as Christ and king in the passion story."[95]

The "Divine Passive"

A final literary feature of some weight for interpreting and preaching the Gospels is known as the "divine passive," that is, the use of the passive voice of the verb "to denote the hidden action of God as the agent responsible for the activity."[96] Martin explains that this usage of the passive began "as a reverential way of avoiding the use of the sacred name of God," was next picked up in apocalyptic literature, and then became customary so that we find Jesus using it over 100 times. Just as we can substitute "kingdom of *God*" for Matthew's "kingdom of heaven," therefore, we ought mentally to add the name of God whenever we hear a "divine passive": "Blessed are those who mourn, for they shall be comforted [by God]" (Matt 5:4); "Why, even the hairs of your head are all numbered [by God]" (Luke 12:7). Although these examples are obvious, the addition clarifies the theocentric focus of these sayings. Moreover, sometimes these additions will clarify the author's intentions. For example, we find the passive in Mark 1:14: "Now after John was arrested [literally, "handed over," by God], Jesus came." Martin observes that "Mark's intention is to suggest a deliberate parallel between John's fate and the destiny of the Son of man who will at last be delivered by God into the hands of sinners (Mk. 9:31, 14:41)."[97]

GUIDELINES FOR PREACHING THE GOSPELS

THE Gospels are inherently suited for preaching because their origin lies in the preaching of Jesus and of the early church and the goal of their

---

94. Brown, *Gospel According to John*, I, cxxxvi. Other examples given are John 4:12; 7:35, 42; and 11:50.

95. Tannehill, *Semeia* 16 (1979) 79. For irony in Luke-Acts, see idem, *Narrative Unity*, I, 194, 282-84.

96. Martin, "Approaches to NT Exegesis," 237.

97. Ibid.

composition is preaching, kerygma.[98] In this section on guidelines for preaching the Gospels, we shall follow the steps of sermon preparation as discussed more generally in Chapters 3–8 above.

Text Selection

As with the preaching of other genres of literature, so in preaching the Gospels, the preaching-text must be a unit. In the Gospels the basic units are called "pericopes" (paragraphs). In the light of the discoveries of form criticism, one might tentatively formulate the general rule that for preaching the Gospels the preaching-text ought to be a pericope. At times, however, key verses may serve as a suitable preaching-text, though these verses must, naturally, be interpreted in the context of their pericope. Moreover, especially with scenic narrative, it may be advisable to preach on a number of consecutive pericopes. One cannot advocate, therefore, that every preaching-text from the Gospels be a pericope, but one can advise that every preaching-text, whether large or small, be a unit. Frequently, rhetorical structures such as repetition, inclusion, and chiasm are pointers to ideal preaching units.

Since these textual units today are constitutive parts of the written Gospels, they must be interpreted in the light of their Gospel context. This rule implies that it is inadvisable to create one's own preaching-text by combining pericopes or verses from different Gospels, for this procedure mixes decidedly different literary and historical contexts and intentions. For example, combining verses from Mark, Luke, and John in order to preach a Good Friday sermon on "The Seven Words from the Cross" fails to do justice to the Gospel context of each of these words.

The Gospels are ideally suited for series of sermons. One may prepare series of sermons not only on scenic narratives but also on discourses. The composite discourses of Matt 5–7, 10, 13, 18, and 24–25 lend themselves especially well to series of sermons. William Hull suggests, for example, a series of eight sermons on the Sermon on the Mount:

1. The Keys of the Kingdom (5:3-6)
2. The Creativity of Conflict (5:7-10)
3. Great Expectations (5:13-16)
4. The New Morality (5:17-48)
5. The Secret of True Religion (6:1-18)
6. The Priority of the Spiritual (6:19-34)
7. The Journey Inward (7:1-12)
8. The Great Divide (7:13-29)

---

98. Cf. Smith, *Interpreting the Gospels,* 20: "When the pericopes of the Gospels are taken as texts for preaching, one is in close touch with their original intent and purpose."

The other four composite discourses on various aspects of the kingdom of God lend themselves equally well to series of sermons.[99]

Once the preaching text has been selected, it must be interpreted holistically, that is, justice must be done to all of its dimensions. Since this holistic interpretation needs to cover more dimensions than were treated by the traditional grammatico-historical method, we shall approach it from three angles: the literary, historical, and theological.

Literary Interpretation

IN literary interpretation one seeks to ascertain the meaning of a passage by focusing on the words. Questions here concern grammar, syntax, figures of speech, double meaning, divine passive, repetition, parallelism, inclusion, chiasm—whatever will help to uncover the author's intended meaning. With narratives, one must also consider questions concerning plot, scenes, characters and their words and actions, the narrator and his point of view, and narrative techniques.

Literary Contexts

Literary interpretation also reminds the preacher of the need for understanding the preaching-text in its literary context. The immediate context may make one aware of a theme of which the preaching-text is a part, or a narrative or saying which contrasts with or parallels the text. The literary context of the whole Gospel provides opportunity to discover how the text functions meaningfully as a part of the whole; how it, in its own way, conveys the author's meaning and fulfills his purpose. All these procedures are similar to those in literary interpretation of other genres.

Comparing Parallel Passages

More than with any other genre, literary interpretation of the Gospels affords an opportunity to compare parallel accounts, for all four Gospels relate basically the same events and teachings, albeit in different ways. The object of comparing parallel accounts is not to try to discover what happened precisely or to harmonize the Gospels,[100] but to discover the specific message of the chosen text in its own particular Gospel. Comparing parallel pericopes offers at least two benefits: "First, the parallels will often give us an appreciation for the distinctives of any one of the Gospels. After all, it is precisely their distinctives that are the reason for having four gospels in the first place. Second, the parallels will help us to be aware of the different kinds of contexts in which the same or similar

99. Hull, "Preaching on the Synoptic Gospels," 177-78; see pp. 178-80 for further suggestions.

100. For a critique of harmonizing the Gospels, see my *Sola Scriptura*, 205-7.

materials lived in the ongoing church."[101] Thus the differences among the Gospels are not a drawback for preachers but an aid that can be utilized for discerning the specific point of the text.

Preachers will most frequently compare parallel pericopes in the Synoptic Gospels, though the Gospel of John, too, can sometimes be fruitfully compared with the Synoptics (e.g., its placement of the cleansing of the temple).[102] As far as the Synoptics are concerned, scholarly opinion generally holds that Mark wrote first and that Matthew and Luke used Mark (and other sources) so that any differences among parallel passages indicate that Matthew or Luke purposefully omitted the pericope, rearranged it, or modified it. Thus any differences would reflect the purposes of Matthew or Luke.

The origin of the Gospels is more complex, however, than Matthew and Luke simply writing their Gospels with Mark's Gospel open before them. Morna Hooker raises some pertinent questions: "Is it the text of Mark as we know it . . . that was used by the later evangelists? Where they diverge from Mark, is it because their theological motives compel them to make changes? Are the alterations due to other reasons—perhaps stylistic or accidental? Most important of all, are such divergences perhaps not primarily alterations of Mark, but due to the fact that an evangelist has chosen to follow a tradition other than Mark's, even where the two Gospels are to some extent parallel?"[103] With these questions unresolved, it is more prudent to follow Grant Osborne in focusing on the "differences between the gospels rather than depending on a too-rigid theory regarding the direction of the influence."[104]

The question remains how one goes about analyzing the differences among the Gospels. In explaining the use of Aland's *Synopsis Quattuor Evangeliorum*, Gordon Fee suggests that one "should be looking for four things: (1) rearrangements of material . . . , (2) additions or omissions of material, (3) stylistic changes, (4) actual differences in wording. A combination of these items will usually lead you to a fairly accurate appraisal of the author's interests."[105] Consequently, the following questions are appropriate for a Gospel text: Is this pericope (the preaching-text) found in other Gospels? If not, does its inclusion in this Gospel (like the parables of the Rich Fool and the Rich Man and Lazarus in the Gospel of Luke) point to the author's interests and purposes? If it is found in another Gospel but in a different context, does the different arrangement of the preaching text shed light on the purpose of its author? Has the author "added or omitted

---

101. Fee and Stuart, *How to Read the Bible*, 110.
102. See Fee, *NT Exegesis*, 112-13.
103. Hooker, "In His Own Image?" 32.
104. Osborne, *JETS* 28/4 (1985) 405.
105. Fee, *NT Exegesis*, 113. For practical hints on using a synopsis, see pp. 103-16.

anything? What verbal changes has he made? Are they merely stylistic? Are they more substantive? Do the changes reveal the author's interests? his unique emphases? Does the adaptation of . . . [the] pericope align with a series of such changes, either in the larger context of . . . [the] pericope itself or in the whole Gospel?"[106] These questions probe for the specific point of the text. For it is that unique message that must be proclaimed, not, as Bastiaan Van Elderen puts it, "a forced and watered-down harmonization. In some cases where an event is recorded in the triple tradition, three distinct, although related, interpretations are possible. The homilete must choose that interpretation which meets the needs of his audience, just as the Gospel writer interpreted the event to meet the needs of his readers."[107]

The fact that one compares Gospels in one's exegesis does not mean, however, that the sermon will necessarily highlight such differences. Much exegetical work never reaches the pulpit but remains in the study. Walter Liefeld advises pointedly that "differences that are inconsequential to the purposes of the sermon and that are unlikely to be a problem . . . in the minds of the congregation, should not intrude into the sermon."[108] Nevertheless, when the contrast with another Gospel clarifies the point of the preaching-text, it may be beneficial to share this insight with the hearers so that they, too, can see the reasons for the particular focus of the message and may learn, moreover, to appreciate the fact that the Lord gave us four Gospels instead of only one.

Historical Interpretation

HISTORICAL interpretation directs our attention specifically to the author, his audience, the historical-cultural background, and the occasion and purpose for writing. All four Gospels, it is clear, have different authors, different audiences, and were written against varied historical-cultural backgrounds and for different occasions and purposes. In the light of these differences, the wonder is not that the Gospels are so different but that they are so similar!

Historical interpretation seeks to understand the text as it was understood by its original audience. Narrative criticism tends to bracket out the historical dimension and concentrate on the self-contained story-world. But, as explained in Chapter 4 above, historical interpretation is the only objective point of control against subjective and arbitrary interpretations. Moreover, historical interpretation leads to better understanding of a text because it looks for the historical question (the question or perceived need of the original audience) to which the text is the answer.

---

106. Ibid., 39-40.
107. Van Elderen, "Teaching of Jesus and the Gospel Records," 115.
108. Liefeld, NT Exposition, 152.

Two Horizons

A complication in historical interpretation of the Gospels is that the preacher is confronted by two historical horizons (in addition to his own), the life-setting of the historical Jesus and that of the Gospel writers. Actually, redaction critics speak of three life-settings: that of the historical Jesus, that of the primitive church which transmitted the tradition, and that of the Gospel writers. Homiletically, however, the significant life-settings are those of Jesus and of the Gospel writers. With these two settings, preachers face the question of which horizon to use in their exposition. Many preachers almost automatically opt for the life-setting of Jesus. For example, the missionary discourse of Matt 9:35–10:42 receives an explication regarding Jesus instructing his disciples and an application for the church today. In other words, the sermon has two historical foci: in the past, Jesus instructing his disciples, and in the present, the contemporary church. Such sermons, however, neglect the significance of the life-setting of the Gospel writer addressing the early church. Kingsbury argues that "the missionary discourse of Jesus, like all of his great discourses, is meant to communicate at two levels: At the level of the story Matthew tells, it is the earthly Jesus in each speech who is addressing himself to the disciples or to the Jewish crowds; but at the level of Matthew's own historical situation, it is the resurrected Jesus in each speech who is addressing himself to the Christians of his church."[109] Hence the question facing the preacher is, Which historical level do I use in sermonic exposition?

Some homileticians allow for sermons to be based on either level. For example, Leander Keck writes, "In principle, where the same material is found in all three Synoptists, four sermons are possible: one from each of the Evangelist's treatment and one that focuses on Jesus in his situation."[110] But can one focus on Jesus' situation without acknowledging the viewpoint of the Gospel writer? Can the present text be used simply as a window offering a neutral view of the words and deeds of the historical Jesus? Fee and Stuart remind us that *"the Gospels in their present form are the Word of God to us; our own reconstructions of Jesus' life are not."* Should one, then, ignore the level of the historical Jesus and opt solely for the canonical level? Fee and Stuart suggest that "good interpretation may require appreciating a given saying first in its original historical context as a proper prelude to understanding that same word in its present canonical context."[111]

---

109. Kingsbury, *Int* 33 (1979) 369.
110. Keck, *Bible in the Pulpit*, 110.
111. Fee and Stuart, *How to Read the Bible*, 113 and 114. More emphatically, Ridderbos posits that "it is necessary first of all to ask what the original sense of the passage was, and the later ecclesiastical interpretation must not obscure or obliterate the historical meaning, but as much as possible take its starting point in that historical mean-

In seeking to come to terms with the two horizons, preachers ought to place themselves in the sandals of the Gospel writer and from that position survey the scene. They will observe, on the one hand, that the Gospel writer addresses his Gospel to a specific community and shapes it to meet that community's circumstances and needs. They will observe, on the other hand, that the Gospel writer accomplishes his purposes by turning to the immediate past and relating what Jesus said and did. Thus the Gospels indeed present two horizons, neither of which can be understood without the other. For purposes of interpretation, however, the life-setting of the Gospel writer is primary. As Van Elderen puts it, "The *Sitz im Leben* in the Gospels is that of the Evangelist, and it is in that perspective that the Gospels should be interpreted. The *Sitz im Leben Jesu* [life-setting of Jesus] can elucidate details, but the interpreter must always realize that he is seeing the event or saying through the eyes of the Evangelist—in the *Sitz im Leben des Verfassers* [life-setting of the writer]."[112]

In approaching the text, then, the life-setting of the Gospel writer is primary, but it, in turn, leads the preacher to the life-setting of Jesus. Consequently, in preaching one need not choose one life-setting over another but must do justice to both as they come to expression in a particular Gospel. This procedure will frequently be quite natural since the purpose of the Gospel writer is usually an extension of the purpose of Jesus. Dwight Moody Smith strikingly expresses this view by calling Jesus the "redactor" of Mark, that is, "Mark expresses Jesus' intention over against his original disciples. . . . Jesus warns his disciples that the gospel is centered in suffering and death, not in miracles. . . . Mark has composed his work exactly as intended, so that the purpose of Jesus might shine through.[113]

---

ing" (*Studies*, 45). Cf. p. 55: "This picture is not in the first place the result of reflection and interpretation only in behalf of the cares and problems of a specific local or regional church, but, on the contrary, an attempt to bring these specific and different aspects of the church's *Sitz im Leben* into the wide horizon of the redemptive history of Jesus' life, death, and resurrection, as these have been the very core and heart of the existing tradition."

112. Van Elderen, "Teaching of Jesus," 115. Cf. idem, *CTJ* 1/2 (1966) 174-75: "Greater stress should be laid on the *Sitz im Leben des Verfassers*, and since we have only the documents as they arose in the *Sitz im Leben des Verfassers*, this should be our point of departure in interpreting a passage. This will deliver us from artificial harmonizations and unnecessary attempts to remove so-called discrepancies in the Gospel accounts." James Dunn acknowledges that a word of the historical Jesus "may well speak to present day hearing of faith with greater force than Matthew's version, but inevitably the control against the danger of an imaginative reconstruction of the level of the historical Jesus (as in the 19th century Lives of Jesus) must be the canonical form of the Gospels themselves" (*HorBT* 4/1 [1982] 45).

113. Smith, *Interpreting the Gospels*, 40-41; cf. pp. 50-51. Concerning Matthew, Ridderbos writes similarly, "Matthew's intention above anything else is to give a cross-section of the miracles of Jesus in which his omnipotence is revealed with great

How, then, does one do justice to both life-settings? Suppose that the preaching text is the missionary discourse of Matt 10. It would be quite natural for the preacher to begin the sermon at level 1 with Jesus' instructions to his disciples, to continue to the expansion of level 2 with the risen Lord's instructions to the early church, and from there to move to the Lord's instructions for his church today. In other words, moving in the sermon from level 1 (the disciples) to level 2 (the early church) naturally forms a bridge to reaching level 3 (the church today). This example does not mean to imply, however, that the two horizons in the text can always be easily distinguished, for frequently the horizon of the Gospel writer is not apparent but gives way to the horizon of Jesus—Jesus and his disciples, Jesus and the Pharisees, Jesus and the Samaritan woman, etc. If one were to formulate a general rule it would be that one must indeed preach Jesus' deeds and teachings, but always from the viewpoint of the particular Gospel writer and as the text functions in his Gospel and not from a self-made historical reconstruction.

The Purpose of the Author

Historical interpretation also raises the question of the author's purpose. This purpose may be discerned most easily when the life-setting of the author and his audience is known, for the author seeks to proclaim Jesus and his words and deeds as a focused response to the questions and issues faced by the community he addresses. Unfortunately, little is known about the recipients of the Gospels except for what can be discovered from the Gospels themselves. Nevertheless, careful research in and comparison of the Gospels will reveal something about the community addressed and the purposes of the author.[114] For example, Mark likely wrote from Rome to some Gentile constituency.[115] One of the major purposes of Mark is to show that "Jesus, the Messiah, had chosen to suffer."[116] This purpose is clearly enunciated by the structure of Mark: "The first eight chapters are dominated by the Messianic secret (e.g., Mark 1:34, 44;

---

diversity, including his dominion over the powers of nature. This is the primary and dominant viewpoint. That this is used by the later church in its own situation to instil faith and give consolation does not conflict with that point of view and we should do justice to that viewpoint in our own preaching about this passage" (*Studies*, 46-47).

114. Fuller, *NT in Current Study*, 86, suggests that "we must pay very close attention to their editorial redactions—the connecting links they forge between the pericopes, their arrangement of the pericopes, the alterations they make to their sources where we have them. . . . Also their selection and omission of material is significant." See also Chapter 3 above on redaction criticism.

115. See Martin, *NT Foundations*, I, 214-16. For the pros and cons of Rome, see also Achtemeier, *Mark*, 128-31.

116. Davies, *Invitation*, 206.

3:12; 5:43; 7:36). But at the watershed in Mark 8:27–9:1, the secret is out, namely, that Jesus as the Son of Man will suffer and die. Therefore, the last eight chapters are dominated by the Messianic suffering (e.g., Mark 8:31; 9:31; 10:32-34; 14:22-25). In that sense, Mark is a martyrology which defines faith in terms of a cross, i.e., as the willingness to save one's life by losing it (Mark 8:35)."[117] Other themes in Mark are illuminated by that overall purpose, themes such as the messianic secret, the cost of discipleship, the passion, and the parousia.

Matthew addressed a Jewish Christian community for the purpose of giving assurance that Jesus of Nazareth was indeed the promised Messiah, the long-awaited King of Israel. This purpose elucidates underlying themes such as fulfillment of prophecy, the authority of Jesus, God with us, the kingdom of heaven, references and allusions to Moses, the mountain, the law, the missionary mandates (chaps. 10 and 28), and Jesus' promise to remain with his church.

Luke addressed the Greek Theophilus and probably other Greeks. He states his purpose in so many words (1:4): "that you may know the truth concerning the things of which you have been informed." Thus the purpose of Luke is to present Jesus as the Savior of Gentiles as well as Jews, particularly those of "low estate" (1:48). Consequently, Luke places his Gospel in the context of world history (Luke 2:1; 3:1, 38) and records Jesus' concern for the sick, the poor, women, Samaritans, tax collectors and sinners,[118] as well as Jesus' mandate for the church to bring the good news "to the end of the earth" (Acts 1:8).

John probably addressed a mixed audience which included "Jews of the Dispersion."[119] Like Luke, he also states his purpose in so many words (20:31): "These [signs] are written that you may believe that Jesus is the Christ, the Son of God, and that believing you may have life in his name." The purpose of calling his hearers to faith in Jesus the Christ elucidates subsidiary themes such as his anti-docetic emphasis on the incarnation (1:14 and 6:51-56) and his emphasis on faith as communicated in series of stories about belief and unbelief, sight and blindness. John's purpose of showing the way to eternal life ties in with the purpose of Jesus' own coming, "I came that they may have life, and have it abundantly" (10:10), his being "the way" (John 14:6), and with the theme of experiencing eternal life here and now.

117. Hull, "Preaching on the Synoptic Gospels," 180. See pp. 182-83 for the *inclusio* of five controversy stories in the beginning of Jesus' ministry (2:1–3:6) and five near the end (11:27–12:37), thus underscoring that Mark is "an apologia for the message of the cross."

118. See O'Toole, *Unity of Luke's Theology*, 109-48.

119. Harrison, *Introduction*, 226. Cf. Ladd, *NT and Criticism*, 161-62.

Universal Kingdom History

Historical interpretation should also remind preachers of the relation of the passage to the universal scope of kingdom history. Although this connection is frequently overlooked, it is homiletically significant because kingdom history links the historical horizons of the text with the horizon of the contemporary church, thus bringing into view the text's relevance for today. In contemporary biblical studies, this kingdom history is sometimes referred to as "story time": "Mark's narrative (narrative time) is part of a much larger story (story time), and its purpose is to show the meaning of that larger story by taking a small part of it and showing how that small part reveals the meaning of the whole."[120] That larger "story," actually history from creation (Mark 10:6) to parousia (13:24-27), includes the church today and thus forms a direct link between the message for the church then and the church today. For example, Kingsbury points out that Mark sees "salvation history" as two epochs: the time of Old Testament prophecy and "the time of the gospel (1:1, 14-15; 13:10). The time of the gospel extends to the end of time. . . . In Mark's perspective it is Jesus himself who is pivotal to the whole of the history of salvation. . . . The claim that Mark advances by means of his scheme of the history of salvation is that the cross of Jesus is pivotal to the entire history of God's dealings with humankind."[121] With this vision of kingdom history, preachers need not search far and wide for the relevance of the cross of Jesus, for the church they are addressing is historically related directly to that cross.

Luke is better known for his view of "redemptive history." He divides world history into three epochs, "first the era of the Law and the prophets, lasting until the appearance of John the Baptist. From then to the Resurrection and Ascension is the era of the Gospel, the 'middle of time' (16:16). This links on to the era of the church, in which Luke is writing and which will last until the parousia, the second coming of Christ."[122] Whether the Gospel writers divide world history into two epochs or three, however, several important similarities should be noted: first, the Gospel writers do not merely tell a closed, self-sufficient story as frequently assumed by narrative criticism but relate their "story" to world history; second, they teach that Jesus' history on earth is central in and pivotal for world history; and third, they show that the (historical) church is a direct result of the Christ event. Thus the Gospel narratives are inher-

120. Achtemeier, *Mark*, 45.

121. Kingsbury, *Int* 33 (1979) 364-65. Cf. p. 368: "But whereas Mark construes the time of fulfillment as the time of the gospel, Matthew construes it simply as the time of Jesus (earthly—exalted). This time of Jesus extends from his birth (1:23) to his parousia (25:31; 28:20)."

122. Koch, *Book of Books*, 127.

ently relevant for the church of all ages, for they tell the story of the church's Founder and Lord.

Theological Interpretation

THEOLOGICAL interpretation reminds preachers not to lose sight of the essence of the Gospels: the Gospels are the good news *of* God *about* God. In the Gospels, of course, that good news about God is the good news that God has come to us in Jesus Christ.

Christocentric Interpretation

In the Gospels Jesus is presented as "God with us" (Matt 1:23). "All things have been delivered to me by my Father," he says, "and no one knows the Son except the Father, and no one knows the Father except the Son and any one to whom the Son chooses to reveal him" (Matt 11:27). "He who has seen me has seen the Father," he says (John 14:9). Jesus is the Son of God, one with the Father and the Holy Spirit. Although the Gospels also make a clear distinction between Jesus and God the Father, their identity shows that Christocentric interpretation is ultimately theocentric.

In our description of the Gospels, we have already noted the centrality of Jesus Christ. Jesus has been called "the protagonist," "the central figure," "the subject around which every narrative turns."[123] The objective of all four Gospels is to relate what "Jesus began to do and to teach" (Acts 1:1). The turning point in all four Gospels is a confession of Jesus as the Christ.[124] Most importantly, the climax of all four Gospels is the resurrection of Jesus. Moreover, the centrality of Jesus in the Gospels can also be inferred from the fact that Jesus' resurrection accounts for the very existence of the Gospels.

With so many indications that the Gospels are centered on Jesus Christ, it is strange that many sermons on the Gospels center on Mary, Anna, Peter, or Judas and thus turn out to be anthropocentric rather than Christocentric. The usual reasons for concentrating on these "minor characters" are variety, interest, and relevance: "These people of many kinds and varied backgrounds constitute a rich source of material for the development of sermons which speak to life as it is actually lived. Since most people identify more readily with other people than with principles and abstractions, sermons based upon the figures in the story will appeal strongly to many."[125] However noble the purpose may be, when bio-

---

123. Achtemeier, *Mark*, 53.

124. See Frye, "Jesus of the Gospels," 78 (cited in n. 60 above). Note that Christocentricity does not detract from an underlying theocentricity. On the theocentricity of Luke-Acts, see Craddock, *Gospels*, 97.

125. Edwards, *SWJT* 21/1 (1978) 64-65.

graphic or character preaching lifts these characters out of their place in the Gospels and makes them the focal point of the sermon, it is no longer true to the nature and purpose of the Gospels because it detracts from the centrality of Christ. This is not to say, of course, that these characters have no place in the sermon, but that their place can never be center stage. For the Gospel writers never present these minor characters for their own sake or for their value as moral examples but for the sake of showing who Jesus is: his love, compassion, power, sonship, teaching, and mission. The arguments of Chapters 5 and 9 above against anthropocentric preaching need not be repeated here;[126] suffice it to say that Christocentric interpretation and preaching demands that the focus of the sermon be ultimately on Jesus Christ.

The Context of the Canon

Theological interpretation also is a reminder to view the message of the text in its broadest possible literary context, that of the canon. As Matthew makes abundantly clear with his theme of fulfillment, his Gospel is intended to be understood against the background of the Old Testament. And not only Matthew, but the other Gospels as well need to be interpreted in the context of the Old Testament. This procedure is required not only because all the Gospels proclaim Jesus as the fulfillment of God's Old Testament promises (e.g., John 19:24, 36-37 speak of fulfillment just as Matthew does) but also because all the Gospels are filled with references and allusions to the Old Testament. Missing these references and allusions may well mean missing the point of the text. We can understand the Gospels correctly only "via the detour of the Old Testament."[127]

The message of the Gospel text must also be compared with the New Testament writings. We have already seen how comparing parallel pericopes can sharpen the point of the message. Subsequently comparing that message with other New Testament writings is not intended to tone down the specific point of the preaching-text but to corroborate and strengthen that point with the witness of the entire canon.

Theme Formulation

WHEN the text has been investigated from all angles, one is ready for the definitive formulation of its theme. Formulating the theme of a Gospel text is no different from formulating the theme of Hebrew narrative: it must be an assertion (subject and predicate) that articulates the unifying idea of the text as intended by its author (from the viewpoint of the nar-

---

126. From another angle, see Buttrick's arguments against the "I Nicodemus" type of sermon, the dramatic monologue (*Homiletic*, 333-35).

127. Frederikse, "De Verhalende Prediking," 113-14.

rator). For example, the theme of Matt 2:1-12 might be formulated as "Gentiles Worship the King of the Jews"; 7:13-14 as "Enter by the Narrow Gate"; 9:35-38 as "Pray for More Harvesters"; 11:1-6 as "Jesus' Deeds Reveal that He Is the Promised Messiah"; 28:5-7 as "Jesus Has Risen: Come, See; Go, Tell."

Once the theme of the text has been established, one needs to determine whether it can serve as the theme of the sermon or requires some adjustment because of possible further development in the canon. Sometimes the historical-cultural setting of the present congregation may also necessitate revision of the theme in order truly to communicate for this day and age the original message according to its canonical intent (see Chapter 6 above). In contrast to the theme of an Old Testament text, however, the theme of a New Testament text seldom requires major revision precisely because the text comes from the *New* Testament.

Once carefully formulated, the sermon theme can function as a guide for outlining and forming the sermon. As Fred Craddock puts it, "That one central idea provides a natural control over which materials are admissible into the sermon and which are not, the theme serving as a magnet to attract only the appropriate."[128]

The Form of the Sermon

THE sermon's form should enhance its message. Guidelines for selecting the form of a sermon on New Testament narratives are the same as those for Old Testament narratives (see Chapter 9 above). The most appropriate form is a narrative which follows the development (story line) of the text. Following the sequencing of the narrative avoids casting the text into a foreign mold which might distort its message. Moreover, it enables the preacher to highlight the major components of the narrative and signal the climax as these occur in the narrative. For example, "in the familiar story of Jesus sleeping in the boat during a storm, the climax is not, as so often preached, in the calming of the wind and waves. It is rather the disciples' question at the end of the story: 'Who is this? He commands even the winds and the water, and they obey him' (Luke 8:25)."[129] Thus the conclusion of this sermon can hardly be the assurance, true as this may be, that Jesus calms the storms in our lives, but the question (if not the answer to): "Who is this?"

In preaching the Gospel discourses, too, it is advantageous to follow the textual sequence. Sometimes rhetorical structures such as repetition and chiasm reveal natural breaks; more often, however, the contents itself

128. Craddock, *Preaching*, 156.
129. Liefeld, *NT Exposition*, 64.

will reveal where shifts take place. In any event, since many discourses are of a composite nature, there appears to be little merit in changing the original order of the composition for contemporary preaching purposes. On the contrary, by closely following the development of the text, one not only honors the original composition but also derives the fringe benefit that the hearers are better able to follow the exposition in their Bibles.

The main guideline for creating a form for the sermon is to use a form that simultaneously shows respect for the ancient text and is effective in communicating its message for today's hearers. In thinking of the contemporary audience, as we have seen in Chapter 7, one should select a form that creates interest, shows movement, and involves the listeners from beginning to end.

The Relevance of the Sermon

THE relevance of a sermon on the Gospels is given already in the fact, observed above, that the Gospels relate the story of the Founder and Lord of the church. That relevance is enhanced by the fact that the Gospels as a whole as well as in their parts are open-ended and include Christians today. According to Amos Wilder, "These stories, long or short, in one way or another carry over into the future. The rounding off is usually in some sense still to come. The hearer or reader finds himself in the middle of the action. We are in the middle of the play. . . . God's last word is still to be spoken. . . . The Gospels end with attention eagerly directed to the future."[130]

When one sees the real relevance of the Gospels, one will no longer need to establish it by questionable means such as enjoining the listeners to imitate or shun the behavior of the minor characters, or by moralizing, psychologizing, or spiritualizing (see Chapter 8 above). The relevance of the Gospels is given in the revelation of Jesus Christ, our Savior and Lord.

That basic relevance of the Gospels can be made more concrete, however. One way to do this is to discover the original relevance of a passage and make use of the parallels between the early church to whom the passage was originally addressed and the church today. Consequently, one should ask, How was this passage relevant for the church the Gospel writer addressed? If this relevance is not immediately evident, it can usually be discovered by viewing the passage in the light of the context and purpose of the whole Gospel. For in its context, every passage has a purpose since every passage seeks a response from the audience—a response of faith, trust, repentance, obedience, thanksgiving, praise. . . . The re-

---

130. Wilder, *Early Christian Rhetoric*, 59-60. Cf. O'Day, *JBL* 105/4 (1986) 668, concerning the Gospel of John: "The reader does not observe the narrative but moves with it."

sponse sought indicates past relevance. Once a passage's relevance for the early church has been established, that relevance can be transferred to the contemporary church via the analogies that exist between the church then and the church today.

Another way to concretize the Gospel's relevance is to utilize the principle of hearer identification with a certain character in the narrative. As we observed in Chapter 8, however, this way is strewn with pitfalls. In order to avoid arbitrary and subjective identifications, one needs to defer to the intention of the author (narrator) in seeking to establish with whom the hearer should identify. Even so, difficulties remain. For example, Tannehill claims that "the implied author of Mark shapes a story which encourages the reader to associate himself with the disciples."[131] Paul Achtemeier disagrees, however, and argues that, "attractive as such an understanding is, . . . it is flawed at several critical points."[132] Kingsbury takes a more circumspect approach with the Gospel of Matthew: "Because the disciples possess conflicting traits, the reader is invited, depending on the attitude Matthew as narrator or Jesus takes toward them on any given occasion, to identify with them or to distance himself or herself from them."[133] Clearly, the question of identification with certain characters is not easy to resolve and can easily lead to arbitrary decisions. The only control we have is to inquire after the author's intention. With every narrative one ought, therefore, to raise the question: With which character, if any, did the author intend his audience to identify? With which character did the first recipients identify? Thus historical interpretation (again) functions as an indispensable control of subjective and arbitrary identifications. Whenever such historical interpretation validates identification with a certain character, one can seek to narrate the story in such a way that the present-day audience also identifies with this character and thus becomes involved in the story.

The difficulties of substantiating proper listener identification should not detract, however, from the most significant form of identification for relevant communication—the continuity between the contemporary church and the early church addressed by the Gospel writers. Smith summarizes this point well: "Today's preacher and congregation have an invitation and a right to stand where Mark and his congregation or readers stood. So, as Mark addressed his church, preachers may also address their congregations. The preacher stands where Mark stands, who stands where Jesus stood. The responsibility is awesome! . . . We preachers do

131. Tannehill, *JR* 57 (1977) 394. Cf. idem, *Semeia* 16 (1979) 82: "Christian readers must struggle with the fact that their heroes and representatives, those who share with them the call to follow Jesus, have failed the test."
132. See Achtemeier, *Mark*, 47-49.
133. Kingsbury, *Matthew*, 13.

not, of course, assume the prerogatives of Jesus, or even of the evangelist. We simply convey their word. So for the preacher to enter into this relationship is not presumptuous. Indeed, the presumption is to presume to preach without standing in this relationship to the text, to its author, and to Jesus."[134]

134. Smith, *Interpreting the Gospels*, 54.

CHAPTER 12

Preaching Epistles

THE genre of epistle covers 21 of the 27 New Testament books. Like the other genres discussed, epistle, too, contains other genres of literature. For example, we find the narrative genre in Gal 1:13–2:21; apocalyptic in 1 Thess 4:13–5:11; a hymn in Phil 2:6-11; and wisdom in Gal 5:9; 6:7; 1 Cor 15:33; and 2 Cor 9:6.[1]

The impression is sometimes given that it is more difficult to preach the Epistles than other biblical genres: "These letters are often closely argued documents. They are full of detailed truth and careful shades of meaning. In them every single word is full of significance. Expounding them therefore calls for hard work by the preacher before he can even begin to put a message together."[2]

In another sense, however, preaching the Epistles is less complicated than preaching, say, the Gospels, for the Epistles generally have only one historical horizon—that of the author addressing the early church. Even though the authors of the Epistles, too, make use of earlier material,[3] in practically every case that material is used not to focus on the past but to make a point for the present. For example, whatever function the hymn of Phil 2:6-11 may have had in the horizon of the liturgy of the early church, in his letter Paul focuses that hymn entirely on the horizon of the Philippians and turns it into an exhortation for their situation: "Have this mind among yourselves, which you have in Christ Jesus." In 1 Cor 11:23-34

---

1. The wisdom passages are suggested by Roetzel, *Letters of Paul*, 48. See p. 44 for traces of hymnody in Col 1:15-20; 1 Tim 3:16; and Eph 5:14. Goulder argues that Phil 2:6-11 is not a pre-Pauline hymn but Paul's own writing, the noble theme leading him "to lapse into the poetic cadences of Hebrew parallelism" ("Pauline Epistles," 501).

2. Lane, *Preach the Word*, 47.

3. See Guthrie, *NT Introduction*, 658-61; and Keck, *Paul*, 27-29.

Paul even uses such a foundational tradition as Jesus' institution of the Lord's Supper not so much to report on this past event as to warn the Corinthians: "Whoever, therefore, eats the bread or drinks the cup of the Lord in an unworthy manner will be guilty of profaning the body and blood of the Lord." Hence, while interpretation of the Epistles may be somewhat more difficult because of their closely argued, condensed nature, the fact that one usually deals with only one textual horizon simplifies interpretation considerably. Our discussion in this chapter reflects this simplification in that we need to examine only the genre of epistle and its literary characteristics before moving on to the guidelines for preaching epistles.

THE GENRE OF EPISTLE

THE genre of epistle was well-known in the Greek world. Paul was the first to adapt this genre for communicating with Christian churches. Some consider Paul's modifications so innovative that they speak of the apostolic letter "as a literary genre created by Paul" on a par with Mark's creation of the gospel genre.[4] We shall see, however, that Paul's contribution consisted of modification of an existing genre rather than creation of a new one. Moreover, it is important to remain aware of the old form of epistles, for a comparison between the old form and that of the New Testament Epistles discloses changes which may be significant for understanding the latter's purpose and meaning.

A fruitful entrance into the debate about the essence of this genre is Deissmann's question whether the biblical Epistles are epistles or letters.

Epistles or Letters

AT the turn of the century, Adolf Deissmann proposed a technical distinction between "epistle" and "letter." An "epistle" was a document written "for publication or for artistic effect." By contrast, a "letter" was a private document and written "purely for the momentary needs of situations." This distinction having been made, Deissmann concluded that Paul's letters "should be read as informal private notes, 'the outcome of a definite situation, which could not be repeated, and [which referred] only to this particular situation.'"[5]

From the New Testament Epistles themselves it is clear, however, that they cannot be categorized simply as occasional, private letters. Even Paul's most private letter, that to Philemon, is addressed also to "the

4. Raymond Collins, *Introduction to the NT*, 218.
5. Doty, *Letters in Primitive Christianity*, 24-25, quoting Deissmann's *Paul: A Study in Social and Religious History*, trans. W. E. Wilson, 2nd ed. (repr. New York: Harper & Brothers, 1957), 12.

church in your house." Moreover, Paul commands that his letter to the Thessalonians "be read to all the brethren" (1 Thess 5:27; cf. 2 Thess 3:14). And he instructs the Colossians: "When this letter has been read among you, have it read also in the church of the Laodiceans; and see that you read also the letter from Laodicea" (Col 4:16). Furthermore, as Ralph Martin points out, "Apostolic authority runs through the major epistles of Paul showing that he was conscious of his teaching office as 'apostle to the Gentiles'"[6] (cf. 2 Cor 1:1). Evidently, these letters were hardly intended as personal, private notes but as documents that were to be read in the church addressed and even to be shared with other churches. Thus, as far as the writer was concerned, the letters certainly transcended the "particular situation" which occasioned them. Nevertheless, we should not overlook the valid insight that the New Testament Epistles were in the first instance "*occasional* documents," that is, letters written for specific occasions, to respond to particular concerns.[7]

Treatises or Sermons

ANOTHER way to discern the essence of the New Testament Epistles is to raise the question whether they are treatises or sermons. Sometimes letters such as Romans are read as theological treatises, but Fee and Stuart rightly contend that "the occasional nature of the Epistles also means that they are *not* first of all theological treatises; they are not compendia of Paul's or Peter's theology. . . . It is always theology at the service of a particular need."[8] In that sense, the "theology" in the Epistles is always limited by the purpose of the Epistle, restricted by its focus. Moreover, a treatise calls to mind a systematic exposition, a methodical discussion. William Barclay judges that "Paul's letters are sermons far more than they are theological treatises. It is with immediate situations that they deal. They are sermons even in the sense that they were spoken rather than written. . . . They were poured out by someone striding up and down a room as he dictated, seeing all the time in his mind's eye the people to whom they were to be sent."[9]

Although this picture of prompt dictation to meet the immediate situation does not hold true for every letter of Paul, the suggestion that one view the letters as sermons is helpful. Aside from the observations that

6. Martin, "Approaches to NT Exegesis," 232. Cf. Harrison, *Introduction,* 257. See also the critique of Deissmann's distinction by Aune, *NT in Its Literary Environment,* 160.

7. See Fee and Stuart, *How to Read the Bible,* 45.

8. Ibid., 46.

9. Barclay, "A Comparison of Paul's Missionary Preaching and Preaching to the Church," 170. Cf. Aune, *NT in Its Literary Environment,* 197: "In the ancient world written letters and oral discourse . . . were closely related."

most letters were spoken before they were written and that they were aimed at a specific audience, further comparisons can be made between a letter and a sermon. In the Greek tradition, a letter was a stand-in for its author. Since Paul was removed some distance from a particular church and could not be present in person, his letters would function as "a direct substitute, and were to be accorded weight equal to Paul's physical presence."[10] Listening to the letter, then, was like listening to Paul. Hence one can characterize the New Testament Epistles as long-distance sermons.

The letters are like sermons also because several of them contain a summary of apostolic preaching. Richard Longenecker suggests that the body of Romans (1:18–15:13) can be viewed "as something of a précis of Paul's preaching in Jewish synagogues of the Diaspora and at Jewish-Gentile gatherings, . . . which, when directed to Rome, was supplemented with an epistolary introduction (1:1-17) and the personal elements of chapters 15 and 16." Ephesians was likely "originally meant to be a précis of Paul's teaching on redemption in Christ and the nature of the church." James, likewise, was probably "first a sermon representative of James's teaching—perhaps extracts drawn from a number of his sermons—and only later given a salutation." Similarly, 1 Peter "seems to be a compendium of Petrine sermonic and catechetical materials," as 1 John is of John's preaching.[11]

Pastoral and Tractate Letters

BECAUSE of the variety of New Testament Epistles, it is difficult to capture their essence under one head. All are occasional but some (e.g., Philemon) are more occasional than others (e.g., Romans). All are more like sermons than like theological treatises, but some (e.g., Romans) show more characteristics of a systematic treatise than do others.

To do some justice to the range of New Testament Epistles, Longenecker makes a distinction between pastoral letters and tractate letters. He identifies as pastoral letters 1 and 2 Corinthians, Galatians, Philippians, Colossians, Philemon, 1 and 2 Thessalonians, 1 and 2 Timothy, Titus, 2 Peter, 2 and 3 John, and Jude. The distinguishing mark of these pastoral letters is that their message is "more circumstantially than systematically delivered" since they arise "from a particular situation and speak . . . to that situation."

By contrast, the tractate letters "were originally intended to be more than strictly pastoral responses to specific sets of issues arising in particular places." These letters are more systematic in their presentation and probably contain primarily the typical preaching of the apostle concerned.

10. Doty, *Letters*, 36.
11. Longenecker, "On the Form, Function, and Authority of NT Letters," 104-5.

The tractate-type letters are Romans, Ephesians, Hebrews, James, 1 Peter, and 1 John.[12]

Whatever distinction we make among the Epistles, it is clear that all are in some sense occasional and that all therefore require historical interpretation as a prerequisite for valid interpretation. It is also clear that all Epistles are very closely related to apostolic preaching and hence are ideal sources for preaching today.

LITERARY CHARACTERISTICS OF THE EPISTLES

THE occasional character of the Epistles no doubt influenced their literary characteristics. One would hardly expect to find elaborate literary structures in letters drafted for a specific occasion and possibly in haste. Moreover, as customary in those days, the letters were frequently dictatèd to secretaries ("amanuenses"; see Rom 16:22; 1 Cor 16:21; Gal 6:11; Col 4:18; 2 Thess 3:17). In spite of these factors, many of the New Testament Epistles evidence careful crafting and contain intricate literary structures. Of course, these literary structures may have been in the sources used for the letters—sources such as hymns and summaries of preaching.

The most obvious literary characteristic of Epistles is their overall form. This form shows up, to a greater or lesser extent, in every Epistle. We shall first examine this overall form of the Epistles and next the rhetorical structures and other literary devices.

The Form of Epistles

The Standard Greek Form
Just as we today follow a basic form in writing our letters, so the ancient Greeks followed a standard form. The standard form of "nonliterary 'true letters' in the Greco-Roman period" consisted of three parts:

1. An introduction, prescript, or salutation, which included the name of the sender, the name of the addressee, greetings, and often a wish for good health.

2. The body or text of the letter, introduced by characteristic formulae.

3. A conclusion, which included greetings to persons other than the addressee, a final greeting or prayer sentence, and sometimes a date.[13]

The Standard Biblical Form
Paul modified this basic form by adding two new parts. After the introduction he would generally add a section of thanksgiving,[14] and after the

---

12. Ibid., 104-6.
13. Ibid., 103. Cf. Aune, *NT in Its Literary Environment*, 162-64, 183.
14. Some parallels have been found in Hellenistic-Jewish letters and first-century

body of the letter he would add a section of exhortations (parenesis). Thus the basic form of the New Testament Epistles consists of a five-part structure:

1. Opening
2. Thanksgiving
3. Body
4. Exhortations
5. Closing

It may be helpful to demonstrate the existence of this structure in actual letters. The following chart lists the major parts in three letters of Paul, two pastoral and one tractate:[15]

FORMAL PARTS OF NEW TESTAMENT LETTERS

	1 Corinthians	Galatians	Romans
1. OPENING			
a. Sender	1:1	1:1-2a	1:1-6
b. Addressee	1:2	1:2b	1:7a
c. Greeting	1:3	1:3-5	1:7b
2. THANKSGIVING	1:4-9	——	1:8-17
3. BODY	1:10–4:21	1:6–4:31	1:18–11:36
4. EXHORTATIONS	5:1–16:12	5:1–6:10	12:1–15:13
	16:13-18	6:11-15	15:14-32
	(closing	(personal	(travel plans
	parenesis)	summary)	and parenesis)
5. CLOSING			
a. Peace Wish	——	6:16	15:33
b. Greetings	16:19-21	——	16:3-16, 23
c. Warning	16:22	6:17	16:17-20a
d. Benediction	16:23-34	6:18	16:20b

The Value of Discerning the Form

Although there is little scholarly consensus on the details, the value of recognizing the standard form of New Testament letters is evident. First, the form of the letter discloses the basic outline of the letter. This outline enables the interpreter to see each part of the letter in the context of the whole. Second, the standard form of the letter makes one aware of any omissions. For example, the omission of the thanksgiving part in the let-

---

Greek papyri. See Aune, *NT in Its Literary Environment*, 177, 186. Cf. Goulder, "Pauline Epistles," 479.

15. The chart is adapted from Roetzel, *Letters of Paul*, 40, and Doty, *Letters*, 43. Note that their charts are quite different in detail, partly because of lack of consensus about the demarcation line between formal parts and partly because Roetzel has a broader view of parenesis than does Doty.

ter to the Galatians is highly significant. Third, knowing the standard form of the letter enables the interpreter to discern the writer's deliberate alterations. These alterations, in turn, provide clues to the author's intention and meaning. As Calvin Roetzel puts it, "We now know that the use of the letter-writing conventions of his time was just as natural . . . for Paul as for us. But his use of those conventions was hardly mechanical, for Paul, just as writers do today, altered the traditional epistolary forms to suit his own purposes. And it is the alterations he made that tell us most about Paul's self-understanding, his intentions, and his theology."[16] We shall look more closely at some of these alterations in the various parts of the letters.

Opening

The opening lends itself to a variety of significant alterations. In several letters Paul changes his opening line (that of the Sender) in anticipation of the main burden of his letter. For example, writing to the Romans, a church which he had never visited, Paul identifies himself as "Paul, a servant of Jesus Christ, called to be an apostle, set apart for the gospel of God," and continues for another five verses with a summary of this gospel. But writing to the Galatians, who had begun to question his apostleship, he identifies himself as "Paul an apostle—not from men nor through man, but through Jesus Christ and God the Father." In his letter to Philemon regarding the slave Onesimus, Paul introduces himself as "Paul, a prisoner for Christ Jesus."

Similar clues to the point of the letter may be found in variations in naming the addressee. For example, in his first letter to the church in the wicked city of Corinth, Paul addresses his letter, "To the church of God which is at Corinth, to those sanctified in Christ Jesus, called to be saints." Paul also changes the opening greeting from the standard Greek *chairein* (greeting) to *charis* (grace) and adds the word "peace" (probably in imitation of the *shalom* of Jewish letters). Thus the neutral Greek "Greeting!" becomes the profound "Grace to you and peace."

Thanksgiving

If the opening may contain clues to the intent of the letter, such clues may be anticipated even more in the thanksgiving section. It is generally acknowledged that "the thanksgiving period introduces 'the vital theme of the letter' or 'the epistolary situation.'"[17] For example, in 1 Cor 1:7 Paul mentions the spiritual gifts which play such a large role in this letter, and in v. 8 he touches on the subsequent theme of conduct by speaking of

16. Roetzel, *Letters of Paul*, 29.

17. Martin, "Approaches to NT Exegesis," 233, quoting P. Schubert's *Form and Function of the Pauline Thanksgiving* (Berlin: Töpelmann, 1939).

being "guiltless in the day of our Lord Jesus Christ." By contrast, the thanksgiving in Rom 1:16-17 speaks of the power of the gospel and the righteousness of God, thus highlighting the theme of Romans.

Body

The body of the letter meets the various concerns head on. Although its contents are frequently diverse and difficult to outline, the different letters generally do reveal a similar pattern. Roetzel observes that "a request or disclosure formula ('I beseech you . . . ,' or 'I would not have you ignorant . . .') serves as the threshold of the body, while the end is marked by an announcement of Paul's travel plans." Further, Paul usually relates something about himself near the beginning of the body. "In each case this autobiographical note is fully integrated into his theological argument. The report on his situation is made to impinge directly on the situation of his readers. By reciting the demands made on him as an apostle of Christ, Paul is apprising his hearers that like demands may be made of them."[18]

Exhortations

There is some disagreement as to what constitutes a section of parenesis (exhortation). Roetzel suggests that Paul's letters reveal three types of ethical instruction: "First there is the cluster of unrelated moral maxims, strung together like beads on a string." Second, "lists of virtues and vices." Third, "a prolonged exhortation or homily on a particular topic." According to Roetzel it is the parenetic section that "knits together the body of the letter and stretches to the conclusion (Gal., Rom., 1 Thess., and possibly 1 Cor. and Phil.). Although some of this instruction or exhortation has little specific relevance for any particular church, Paul often tailors general ethical traditions to fit particular needs."[19]

Closing

Finally we note how the closing, too, can be changed to fit the theme or situation. The peace wish in Rom 15:33 is extended to all: "The God of peace be with you all." By comparison, the peace wish in Gal 6:16 is decidedly restricted: "Peace and mercy be upon all who walk by this rule, upon the Israel of God." Moreover, it is followed in v. 17 by the pointed warning, "Henceforth let no man trouble me; for I bear on my body the marks of Jesus." The peace wish in 1 Thess 5:23-24 has a different tone again, alluding to the concern of the Thessalonians about members dying before the Lord's return: "May your spirit and soul and body be kept

---

18. Roetzel, *Letters*, 34 and 35.
19. Ibid., 35-36. Cf. Aune, *NT in Its Literary Environment*, 194-97.

sound and blameless at the coming of our Lord Jesus Christ. He who calls
you is faithful, and he will do it."

Rhetorical Structures

ALTHOUGH one might expect few rhetorical structures in occasional letters dictated to a secretary, one must also remember that these letters included traditional materials such as hymns, creeds, and doxologies—
forms which frequently were highly structured. Another consideration is
that the letters were intended to be forms of aural communication. "Because letters were read in the assemblies and therefore prepared for the
ear rather than the eye, they employ literary forms designed to aid the
listener's understanding and memory. Paul, for example, makes frequent
use of the inclusion . . . , the chiasm . . . , tables of household duties, antitheses, and other noticeable literary patterns."[20] We shall observe, in
turn, repetition, inclusion, chiasm, climax, and dialogue.

Repetition
Repetition occurs at many different levels in the Epistles. It can consist
simply of the repetition of a word in order to emphasize a point. For example, the sevenfold repetition of the word *one* in Eph 4:4-6 is used to underscore the fundamental unity of the church: "There is one body and one
Spirit. . . ."
Repetition also occurs in structural patterns. For example, the argument in Rom 6–7 is held together by a series of questions. Although the
questions are not identical, the simple repetition of questions carries the
argument forward: "What shall we say then? Are we to continue in sin
that grace may abound?" (6:1); "What then? Are we to sin because we are
not under law but under grace?" (6:15); "What then shall we say? That the
law is sin?" (7:7); "Did that which is good, then, bring death to me?"
(7:13).
Another level where repetition takes place is the level of thought or
ideas. In Gal 5:1, for example, Paul speaks of Christian freedom: "For freedom Christ has set us free." The same thought is reiterated in v. 13, "For
you were called to freedom." This repetition not only emphasizes the
theme of Christian freedom but also provides Paul opportunity for
further elaboration.
Walter Liefeld suggests that whether the repetitions be thought patterns or structural patterns or verbal patterns, "such patterns running
through a passage . . . give a sense of direction like tire tracks across wet
cement. Following the imprint provides continuity."[21] Moreover, repeti-

---

20. Craddock, *Preaching*, 171.
21. Liefeld, *NT Exposition*, 32.

tion frequently highlights what the author wishes to emphasize. It also forms the basis of other structural patterns such as inclusion and chiasm.

Inclusion

Many New Testament Epistles are encircled by an inclusion. Paul opens his letters with "Grace to you and peace" and closes with the peace wish followed by "The grace of our Lord Jesus Christ be with you." Many letters therefore show the following inclusion: "(opening) grace and peace; (closing) peace and grace."[22] An example of inclusion within a letter would be the (external) inclusion setting off 1 Cor 13. Paul concludes his discussion on spiritual gifts with the statement "Earnestly desire the higher gifts" (1 Cor 12:31). After the chapter on love, 1 Cor 14:1 resumes the earlier discussion with similar words, "Earnestly desire the spiritual gifts." One could probably argue for the existence of an internal inclusion encircling chap. 13 in the opening words, "I will show you a still more excellent way" (12:31b) and the concluding words, "But the greatest of these is love" (13:13).

Chiasm

1 Corinthians 12–14 also provides an example of a simple ABA' chiasm. This structure shows that chap. 13 is the focal point in this discussion on spiritual gifts.

A. Spiritual gifts (12:1-31a)
   B. Love, the greatest gift (12:31b–13:13)
A'. Spiritual gifts: prophecy and tongues (14:1-40)

Galatians 4:1-7 provides a good example of a chiastic structure in a single paragraph:

(a) The *heir* remains a *child* and *servant* (4:1)
   (b) Until the time appointed of the *father* (4:2)
      (c) When that time came, *God* sent forth his *Son* (4:4)
         (d) Made under the *law* (4:4)
         (d')To redeem those under the *law* (4:5)
      (c') Because ye are sons, *God* sent forth the Spirit of his *Son* (4:6)
   (b') That ye cry Abba, *Father* (4:6)
(a') That ye are no more a *servant* but a *son* and *heir* (4:7)[23]

---

22. Roetzel, *Letters of Paul*, 37.
23. Welch, "Chiasmus in the NT," 214. See pp. 211-33 and Ellis, *Seven Pauline Letters*, for more examples, many of them attempts to view whole Epistles as chiastic structures. While the value of discovering chiastic structures is self-evident, the attempt to structure whole Epistles as chiasm easily leads to forcing a structure on the text and ignoring its primary structure, the form of the letter.

For a chiastic structure within a paragraph, 1 John 1:6-7 provides a good example:

A: If we say we *have fellowship with* him
  B: and [yet] *walk in the darkness,*
    C: we lie and do not do the truth
  B': If we *walk in the light* as he is in the light,
A': *we have fellowship with* one another.[24]

Climax

Repetition sometimes shows step-by-step progression and frequently culminates in a climax. We see repetition reaching a climax, for example, in Eph 4:4-6, where the seventh recurrence of the word *one* reaches a culmination and then blossoms into a threefold repetition: "one God and Father of us all, who is above all and through all and in all." 1 Cor 13, which itself is already the focal point of the chaps. 12–14, builds through a series of triads to the climax, "but the greatest of these is love." Just like chiasm, therefore, climax can reveal the focus of the author's thought.

Dialogue

In the Epistles, dialogue takes the form of a debate with opponents: "But some one will ask, 'How are the dead raised? With what kind of body do they come?' You foolish man! What you sow does not come to life unless it dies" (1 Cor 15:35-36). This form of dialogue has been called "the device of *diatribe* by which a speaker or writer enters into imaginary debate with an interlocutor, raising points which he would make and objections he would voice, which are then answered and refuted."[25] Rom 3:27-31 provides a compact example of this Hellenistic debating style: "Then what becomes of our boasting? It is excluded. On what principle? On the principle of works? No, but on the principle of faith. . . . Do we then overthrow the law by this faith? By no means! On the contrary, we uphold the law" (cf. Rom 2–3, 1 Cor 9, Jas 2).

Other Literary Devices

Parallelism

One should also be aware of various forms of parallelism in the Epistles. Parallel structures are not always the work of the writer but may be constituent parts of a hymn or creed which the writer quotes. For example, 1 Tim 3:16 probably contains an early Christian hymn:

24. Breck, *BTB* 17 (1987) 72. See there also for chiastic structures of Phil 2:5-11 centered on "unto death, death on a cross," and of Rom 8:9-11.
25. Martin, "Approaches to NT Exegesis," 247. Cf. Aune, *NT in Its Literary Environment,* 200-202.

He was manifested in the flesh,
    vindicated in the Spirit,
seen by angels,
    preached among the nations,
believed on in the world,
    taken up in glory.

1 Corinthians 15:55 is a good example of synonymous parallelism:

O death, where is thy victory?
    O death, where is thy sting?

1 Pet 2:22 shows inverted parallelism:

He committed no sin;
    no guile was found on his lips.

Rom 4:25 is a good example of antithetic parallelism:

Who was put to death for our trespasses
    and raised for our justification.[26]

Although parallelism is not a major feature in the Epistles, the examples above show that it may be more prevalent than generally expected.

Antithesis

A major literary feature of the Epistles is antithesis or contrast. We find contrasts between Adam and Christ (Rom 5:12-21), between being in Adam and being in Christ (1 Cor 15:20-50), between flesh and Spirit (Rom 8:2-11; 2 Cor 5:16-17; Gal 5:19-23), between present suffering and future glory (Rom 8:18-39), between physical body and spiritual body (1 Cor 15:42-54), between light and darkness (Eph 5:8-14), etc. The prevalence of antithesis in the Epistles is probably best demonstrated by 2 Cor 4:16-18, which in only three verses sets forth three different contrasts:

Though our outer nature is wasting away,
    our inner nature is being renewed every day.
For this slight momentary affliction is preparing for
us an eternal weight of glory beyond all comparison,
because we look not to the things that are seen
    but to the things that are unseen;
for the things that are seen are transient,
    but the things that are unseen are eternal.

Metaphor

The Epistles are replete with powerful metaphors. Readers are encouraged to run the race to obtain the prize (1 Cor 9:24), to lay aside what

---

26. Cf. 1 Cor 13:6: "It [love] does not rejoice at wrong, but rejoices in the right."

would hinder and "run with perseverance" (Heb 12:1). They are told to put on "the whole armor of God," including breastplate, helmet, shield, and sword (Eph 6:11-17). James exposes the destructive power of words with the unforgettable metaphor, "the tongue is a fire" (3:6).

W. D. Davies requires an entire chapter to explain "the great Pauline metaphors." He categorizes Paul's metaphors into four groups according to the realm from which they are derived: (1) the Exodus, (2) the Creation, (3) the Sacrificial System, and (4) the Law. This analysis shows that the Epistles contain many more metaphors than one generally perceives—metaphors such as redemption, adoption, liberty, the new creation, peace, expiation, and justification.[27] How often do we not read over these words, and others like them, without realizing that they are metaphors? Yet being aware that a word is a metaphor enriches one's understanding. Moreover, metaphors readily lend themselves to elucidation in the sermon so that, like illustrations, they begin to function as windows to the truth.

Although more literary features could be mentioned,[28] the above will suffice to set the stage for guidelines for preaching Epistles.

GUIDELINES FOR PREACHING THE EPISTLES

IN this section we shall discuss the conclusions of Chapters 1–8 above as these apply specifically to preaching Epistles. We shall once again follow the order of sermon preparation: text selection, interpretation, theme formulation, form selection, and relevant preaching.

Text Selection

A Literary Unit
In selecting a text from the Epistles, the importance of selecting a unit cannot be overestimated. Especially for those inclined toward preaching doctrine, the temptation is great to select only part of a unit. In preaching on Phil 2, for example, it may seem attractive to select as a text the hymn and to preach on Christ's states of humiliation and exaltation. But in Paul's letter, the hymn functions in the context of v. 5, "Have this mind among yourselves, which you have in Christ Jesus." And this verse, again, is part

---

27. Davies, *Invitation to the NT,* 310-26. Cf. Tilley, *Story Theology,* 3: "The key concepts of Christian faith—creation, fall, incarnation, atonement, church, eternal life, trinity—are all metaphors at rest, metaphors which have become Christian doctrines." See also Goulder, "Pauline Epistles," 485-87, 496.

28. See, e.g., John Paul Pritchard, *A Literary Approach to the New Testament* (Norman: University of Oklahoma, 1972). See Aune, *NT in Its Literary Environment,* 206-7, for the "antithetical style": "a technique that amplifies thought by contrasting ideas using negation, antonyms, and other devices."

of a unit that begins at v. 1, "So if there is any encouragement in Christ, any incentive of love." The textual unit, therefore, is Phil 2:1-11.[29]

To take another example, one may be inclined to select as a preaching-text Eph 1:4a, "even as he chose us in him before the foundation of the world," and preach a sermon on predestination. The text continues in v. 4b, however, "that we should be holy and blameless before him." This verse, in turn, is part of vv. 3-14—a section which is not only a unit but in Greek a single sentence. This passage demonstrates the complexity of selecting a preaching-text from a densely written thanksgiving section. One might well select vv. 3-14 as a text and focus in turn on the work of the Father, the Son, and the Holy Spirit. In any event, one cannot simply select v. 4a to preach a sermon on predestination.

The Focal Point

Both examples above show that the proper or improper selection of a preaching-text will have repercussions down the line, all the way to the relevance of the sermon. A sermon on the states of Christ may be interesting, but how is it to be applied to the congregation? A sermon on predestination may be thought-provoking, but what is the point for the congregation? Both passages, however, include that focal point: Paul encourages the Philippians to have the mind of Christ and the Ephesians to be holy and blameless before God. Although that focal point may not always be so obvious, when it is present in a passage it ought to be included in the preaching-text, for it will subsequently guide not only the interpretation of the text but also the formulation of the sermon theme, possibly the form of the sermon, and certainly the articulation of the relevance of the sermon.

Substantiation

Whenever feasible the preaching-text should also include the textual substantiation of a particular claim or demand. Suppose one considers selecting as a preaching-text Rom 8:28, "We know that in everything God works for good with those who love him, who are called according to his purpose." Although this is a comforting text, in isolation it will raise more questions for suffering parishioners than it answers. Paul, however, goes on to substantiate his claim that God works for good: "For those whom

---

29. Note that Craddock, *Preaching*, 119, leaves it up to the preacher to decide at which level to preach the text, "to preach Christology or preach Christian attitude and conduct based upon that Christology." A case similar to Phil 2:1-11 is found in 1 Pet 2, where Peter introduces a poetic unit on the vicarious death of Christ (vv. 22-24) with v. 21: "For to this you have been called, because Christ also suffered for you, leaving you an example, that you should follow in his steps." See Ericson, "Interpreting Petrine Literature," 251.

he foreknew he also predestined to be conformed to the image of his Son [suffering?]. . . . And those whom he predestined he also called; and those whom he called he also justified; and those whom he justified he also glorified" (8:29-30). These verses not only substantiate the claim that God works for good in everything, they also put this claim in a different light than when seen in isolation.[30]

Literary Interpretation

The Literary Context

In literary interpretation, one seeks to determine the meaning of the words in their literary context. Here one pays attention not only to the details of grammar, syntax, figures of speech, etc., but also to the overall view of the letter. Letters are intended to be read through in one sitting, and biblical letters are generally no different. While this complete reading may not be feasible in the pulpit, certainly in one's study one ought to read through the entire letter in order to get the flavor of the whole. After reading through the letter, it is well to skim it once more in order to locate the various formal parts and note any alterations. The changes in the sub-sections of Sender and Addressee may hint at issues to be covered in the letter. The thanksgiving section frequently brings out the purpose for writing; even its omission in Paul's letter to the "foolish Galatians" speaks volumes, for their perversion of the gospel of grace leaves Paul little room for thanksgiving.

The Point of the Text

After gaining an overall view of the letter and its parts, one must determine how the chosen preaching-text fits in and functions in the context of the whole. A natural question here is whether the text is part of the opening, the thanksgiving, the body, the exhortations, or the closing, and what difference that makes in its interpretation. For example, if the text belongs to the more formal parts, the question should be raised, "How much has the form itself determined the content?"[31] This is also the time for detailed exegesis and for determining the point of the text in relation to its immediate context. Once the particular message has been determined, one should check if this issue is raised or worked out elsewhere in the letter, for Epistles tend to come back to the same issue, and every part, of course, should be understood in the context of the whole.

Exhortations

A problem area for understanding in context is a text chosen from the ex-

---

30. For more examples of substantiation, see Liefeld, NT Exposition, 70-71.
31. Fee, NT Exegesis, 33.

hortations.[32] As we saw earlier, some of these exhortations have been described as consisting of either "a cluster of unrelated moral maxims, strung together like beads on a string" (e.g., Rom 12:9-13), or a list of virtues and vices which "have only the most casual relationship to each other" (e.g., Gal 5:19-23).[33] If these exhortations do indeed exist in virtual isolation, the question must be raised whether one may select such an exhortation and interpret and preach it without any concern for its literary context. In other words, may one preach Rom 12:13, "Contribute to the needs of the saints," as a timeless truth that need not be related to its specific context?

This question is related to the broader question whether one may preach the imperative of exhortations without the indicative of what God in Christ has done for us. The danger of such preaching, clearly, is that it would lead to legalism. Moreover, it is striking that in the Epistles the imperatives never function without the indicative. In fact, the indicative constantly precedes the imperative. This order is evident not only in the form of the Epistles, where the thanksgiving and body precede the section of exhortations, but also in the details. After a detailed study, Herman Ridderbos concludes that "the imperative is grounded on the reality that has been given with the indicative, appeals to it, and is intended to bring it to full development."[34] Thus there is an intimate connection between the imperative and the preceding indicative. Note, however, that this connection is more than the one flowing from the other. Allen Verhey articulates the intricate interrelationship as follows: "The indicative mood has an important priority and finality in the proclamation of the gospel, but the imperative is by no means merely an addendum to the indicative or even exactly an inference drawn from the indicative. Participation in Christ's cross and resurrection (the important priority of the indicative) and anticipation of the new age of God's unchallenged sovereignty (the important finality of the indicative) are *constituted* here and now by obedience to God's will (the imperative)."[35]

When one's text is an exhortation, therefore, one cannot proclaim this imperative in isolation from the indicative. Hence in literary interpretation, too, one is driven back to the context to search for the connection between the exhortation and the indicative that is expressed in the letter. Recent research is uncovering some connections between supposedly iso-

32. See DeJong, *Pro Rege*, 10/4 (1982) 26-34.

33. Roetzel, *Letters of Paul*, 35-36.

34. Ridderbos, *Paul*, 254-55; cf. pp. 253-58, e.g., 254-55: "In each case the imperative follows the indicative by way of conclusion (with 'thus,' 'therefore'; Rom. 6:12ff.; 12:1; Col. 3:5, *et al.*). In each case following the calling of the new life is set forth as the object of the positive redemptive pronouncements ('so that,' 'in order to,' etc.; cf. Rom. 7:4; 2 Cor. 5:15, *et al.*)." See Longenecker, *Paul*, 174-75.

35. Verhey, *Great Reversal*, 104-5.

lated exhortations and specific situations. For example, "the vice list . . . in 2 Corinthians 12:20-21 deals with divisive behavior (bickering, pettiness, arrogance, etc.), antisocial acts (anger, selfishness, slander, gossip, etc.), and sexual immorality—all of which characterize Corinthian behavior mentioned elsewhere."[36] Thus the connection between a seemingly isolated exhortation and the literary context can frequently be established, even if it is via the historical context.

Historical Interpretation

As the last example shows, historical and literary interpretation cannot be separated from each other but go hand in hand. Historical interpretation seeks to understand each letter in its own historical-cultural context. Important questions here concern the occasion for writing, the purpose of the author, and historical-cultural conditioning.

The Occasion

Listening to a letter without being aware of its historical situation has been likened to hearing only one side of a telephone conversation:[37] one hears the answers but does not know the specific questions. Yet for a comprehensive understanding, one must know the questions to which the letter responds. William Doty remarks: "Often it is almost impossible to interpret Paul correctly until we have gained some sense of the background of the community to which he is writing."[38]

Fortunately, the letters themselves frequently provide sufficient information for gaining a general idea of the historical situation. In 1 Corinthians Paul even provides conspicuous indicators regarding some of the questions being raised: "Now concerning the matters about which you wrote" (7:1); "Now concerning food offered to idols" (8:1); "Now concerning spiritual gifts" (12:1). But usually the historical picture must be put together from bits and pieces and various sources. Norman Ericson makes the interesting observation, "What was most familiar to the original recipients is not specified in the letters, and thus the modern reader is not informed of these matters"—matters such as politics, society, economics, church life, difficulties. Yet "finding out this kind of information will clarify nuances, qualify statements, and provide the reader with a feeling

36. Roetzel, *Letters of Paul*, 47. Cf. pp. 47-48 on the parenesis of 1 Thess 5:16-18.
37. For example, Keck, *Paul*, vii.
38. Doty, *Letters*, 37. Cf. Roetzel, *Letters of Paul*, 50: "Once we realize how the ferment in the churches prescribed the scope if not the content of Paul's writings, then it is obvious why in considering Paul we must treat not simply his thought, but also the situation in the churches." Stendahl adds, "It is as letters to specific churches, . . . written in answer to specific situations that these writings form part of the Bible" ("Preaching from the Pauline Epistles," 306).

for the original context in which the authors delivered their instruction or exhortation. With this information the interpreter will be able to give proper stress to the elements which were stressed by the author."[39]

It is important, therefore, to have some understanding of the situation of the church being addressed. The letters were frequently written to counter a specific problem or threat: in Thessalonica, a high-strung expectation of Jesus' immediate return; in Galatia, inroads made by Judaizers; in Corinth, factionalism and libertinism; in Colosse, the threat of an early form of Gnosticism; and so on. To gain a better understanding of the recipients and their situation, one should seek to answer the following questions: "What is said explicitly? What is implied? Are they involved in behavior that needs correcting? Is the problem one of theological misunderstanding? or lack of understanding? Are they in need of comfort? exhortation? correction?"[40] Discovering the question behind the letter is like discovering the entrance into the letter.

The Purpose of the Author

The occasion for writing and the author's purpose are related as question and answer: the one informs the other. The goal of the interpreter is to use the historical situation to gain a clearer understanding of the author's purpose as this comes to expression in the letter. For example, Ericson suggests that "I Peter is written to encourage believers who are facing intense persecution. II Peter is a denunciation of false teachers who have surreptitiously entered the churches. . . . Jude can best be understood as a polemic tractate."[41] Such comments are helpful in delineating the main purpose of the author: to encourage, to denounce, to contend for the faith, or whatever.

Within the overall purpose, however, there may be any number of subsidiary purposes. For example, although the main purpose of 1 Thessalonians is to address the issue of the second coming of Christ (parousia), Paul makes use of the occasion to defend his conduct, to encourage his readers in their trials, to instruct new converts in godly living, to admonish his readers to continue working, and to assure them concerning believers who died before the Lord's return.[42] Several of these purposes are related to the issue of the parousia, but others have little or nothing to do with it. Thus our concern to preach a text in the light of the writer's purpose must be sufficiently flexible to recognize more than one purpose in a letter and not to force the text into a single-purpose mold.

39. Ericson, "Interpreting Petrine Literature," 249.
40. Fee, NT Exegesis, 33.
41. Ericson, "Interpreting Petrine Literature," 244-45.
42. See Harrison, Introduction to the NT, 262.

Since Hebrews and 1 John are anonymous and the identity of the authors of some other Epistles is disputed, the question may be raised if any uncertainty regarding the author's identity interferes with establishing his purpose. On the one hand, it must be admitted that knowledge of the author offers some aid in determining his purpose in a particular letter.[43] On the other hand, the author's purpose is to be gleaned from the letter and not from the person and his reputation. Hence the identification of the author is not absolutely necessary for establishing his purpose. For example, the generally accepted fact that Hebrews was not, as previously thought, written by Paul should make little difference in understanding and preaching Hebrews since the author's purpose must be determined from the letter under consideration and not from his other writings.

Cultural Conditioning

Historical interpretation also brings out the culturally conditioned character of the Epistles. To say that the Epistles are culturally conditioned is not the same as saying that they are culturally *bound*. A document that is culturally bound does not transcend its own historical horizon and hence has no message beyond its own time. By contrast, the Epistles transcend their own historical-cultural horizon and thus continue to speak to the church today. But they are culturally *conditioned*, that is, they are shaped and molded by the culture(s) of their author and original recipients. In fact, without cultural conditioning, these letters could hardly have been relevant for their original recipients.

The New Testament Epistles show their culturally conditioned character straight away in their use of the Greek language and all that it entails. They also show this character when they command certain behavior patterns which are foreign to our culture. A few examples from 1 Corinthians will demonstrate this point: "If any one sees you, a man of knowledge, at table in an idol's temple, might he not be encouraged . . . to eat food offered to idols?" (8:10); "Therefore, my beloved, shun the worship of idols" (10:14); "Any woman who prays or prophesies with her head unveiled dishonors her head. . . . Does not nature itself teach you that for a man to wear long hair is degrading to him, but if a woman has long hair, it is her pride?" (11:5, 14-15); "Greet one another with a holy kiss" (16:20). In preaching these passages, contemporary preachers come

---

43. Cf. Longenecker, "Form, Function, and Authority," 112: "Anonymity may be a frustrating phenomenon for us today as we seek to reconstruct situations and purposes." Regarding the so-called pseudepigrapha, Longenecker (p. 111) contends that a good case can be made "for the internally claimed and traditionally accepted authorship" by "taking into consideration the difference of topic in these letters, the altered situation presupposed by them for the apostle at the time of writing, and the probable use of an amanuensis."

face to face with the famous historical-cultural gap. Yet it must not be overlooked that these very features made these passages relevant in their own time and place.

Günther Bornkamm puts the issue in terms of contemporaneity: "The letters are truly contemporary in character. The experiences and problems, the language, opinions, and modes of thought, both of the author and of his recipients, belong to the world in which they lived and are no longer exactly the same as our own." He also cautions, however, against any hasty attempts to bridge the historical distance, for in that very attempt one is "actually preventing the early writers from saying what they have to say."[44] The preacher's first responsibility is not to look for applications to the present audience but to hear the author as he spoke in that foreign culture and at that particular time. "Temptations are considerable to grab hold of so-called Pauline themes and get ever more general in our repeating the obvious," says Krister Stendahl, but "the power of biblical preaching grows out of a grasp of the specifics of the text."[45]

Universal Kingdom History

Historical interpretation discloses not only historical *dis*continuity but also the continuity required for relevant application today. That continuity comes to expression in the apostolic teaching of kingdom history, which began with Adam, centers in Jesus Christ, and will come to completion at Jesus' parousia. Paul writes: "For as in Adam all die, so also in Christ shall all be made alive. But each in his own order: Christ the first fruits, then at his coming those who belong to Christ. Then comes the end, when he delivers the kingdom to God the Father" (1 Cor 15:22-24). The continuity between past and present is clear: past and present are parts of the history of God's coming kingdom. All the messages of Paul are given—and hence must be read—against the background of this all-encompassing history.

In Colossians Paul shows how this kingdom history is centered in Christ, more specifically in the cross of Christ: "In him all things were created, . . . all things were created through him and for him. . . . For in him all the fulness of God was pleased to dwell, and through him to reconcile to himself all things, whether on earth or in heaven, making peace by the blood of his cross" (Col 1:16, 19-20; cf. Eph 1:9-10). In addition, Paul emphasizes throughout his letters that this universal history will come to completion at the second coming of Christ, for in all his letters the "subsections tend to build toward an eschatological note."[46]

---

44. Bornkamm, *The NT*, 74-75.
45. Stendahl, "Preaching from the Pauline Epistles," 306.
46. Keck, *Paul*, 19.

Moreover, this redemptive history encompasses the whole world, the physical as well as the spiritual. Paul writes in Rom 8:11, "If the Spirit of him who raised Jesus from the dead dwells in you, he who raised Christ Jesus from the dead will give life to your mortal bodies also through his Spirit which dwells in you." Redemption for human beings, then, is not a redemption *from* the body but a redemption *of* the body (Rom 8:23; cf. Phil 3:21). Not even the world we live in is excluded, for "the creation itself will be set free from its bondage to decay and obtain the glorious liberty of the children of God" (Rom 8:21; cf. Rev 21:1-4). Hence the history of God's coming kingdom includes not only the spiritual but also the physical, and not only the past but also the present. Since both the church addressed in the past and the contemporary church are caught up in the same kingdom history, this universal history provides the fundamental continuity for relevant proclamation of historically conditioned letters.

Theological Interpretation

THE Epistles, too, can be characterized as messages *of* God and messages *about* God—God's kingdom, his redemption, his covenant, his will, his presence, etc. Theological interpretation is a reminder not to get so caught up in the local situation and the human characters that one neglects the theocentric focus of the Epistles.

Although the apostles were witnesses of Jesus Christ, it is striking that neither Paul nor any other author of a New Testament Epistle details the history of Jesus as do the Gospels. Roetzel points out, however, that "though Paul expresses little interest in Jesus' ministry or the content of his preaching, he does lay heavy stress on three historical facts: the cross, resurrection, and Jesus' imminent return."[47] In fact, Paul characterizes his own preaching as "Jesus Christ and him crucified" (1 Cor 2:2).

Christocentric Interpretation

What does Paul mean when he writes, "I decided to know nothing among you except Jesus Christ and him crucified" (1 Cor 2:2)? Does he mean that he spoke about nothing else but Jesus' crucifixion? G. C. Berkouwer comments, "As is clear from all his preaching (e.g., I Tim. 1:15; II Tim. 2:8), Paul does not have in mind a quantitative reduction of the gospel according to his own yardstick, a reduction of many truths to the one 'truth,' leaving other truths in the wings; yet in striking manner we find here expressed a decisive centralization, a concentration (Rom. 15:18)."[48] Moreover, Leander Keck points out that in 1 Thess 1:10 and Rom 10:9

---

47. Roetzel, *Letters of Paul*, 45.
48. Berkouwer, *Holy Scripture*, 179.

Paul mentions only Jesus' resurrection but that this "does not mean that Paul shifted content; rather, because cross and resurrection constituted a single meaning-complex, he could mention one and imply the other, depending on which aspect was most germane to the point being made at the moment."[49]

The meaning of "I decided to know nothing among you except Jesus Christ and him crucified" is elucidated by Col 1, where, as we saw, Paul proclaims that kingdom history is centered in the cross of Christ. "Jesus Christ and him crucified" refers literally to the crux, the heart and center, of this kingdom history which encompasses all things. Whatever point Paul raises, therefore, or whatever advice he gives, is related to the death and resurrection of Jesus Christ. As Paul sees it, everything in the world has to do with Jesus Christ—especially everything in the church, for the church is the body of Christ through which his life continues on earth.

All of Paul's statements, therefore, must be interpreted in the light of his Christocentric viewpoint. Even the exhortations which seem rather isolated from their context have to do with Christ: a list of virtues is "infinitely more than a list of 'do's' as opposed to a list of don't's. They describe the embodiment of the gospel in God's people. As paraenetic commands they call forth the presence of the Lord in his church. They provide a vivid description of what it means to live in Christ and to have Christ living in us."[50]

The Context of the Canon

Theological interpretation is also a reminder to move beyond mere literary and historical interpretation and consider the passage in the light of God's ultimate purpose as this comes to expression in the whole canon. Epistles, too, need to be interpreted in the context of the canon of which they now form a part. In comparing Scripture with Scripture, one can compare, for example, parallel passages between Ephesians and Colossians, or 1 Peter and James, and thus sharpen the focus of a particular message. Further, whenever Paul or James quotes or alludes to a word of the Lord, one can make comparisons with similar sayings in the Gospels (e.g., Rom 12:1–15:7 with Matt 5–7; 1 Cor 7:10-11 with Mark 10:11-12; James with Matt 5–7).[51]

Comparing Scripture with Scripture will also provide the necessary

---

49. Keck, *Paul*, 34.

50. DeJong, *Pro Rege* 10/4 (1982) 33. Cf. Ridderbos, *Paul*, 258-265, on "The Theocentric Point of View": "The theocentric point of view—so we may conclude—constitutes the great point of departure of the Pauline paraenesis" (260).

51. On Paul, see Roetzel, *Letters of Paul*, 45-46; on James, see Kistemaker, *JETS* 29/1 (1986) 55-56.

balance for the sermon even as it provides canonical depth and support. Although preachers should not tone down the point of their passage, they are responsible for evaluating each particular message in the context of the canon. For example, Paul's message in Rom 13:1-7, "Let every person be subject to the governing authorities," must not only be interpreted historically as requiring subjection to the Roman government as "God's servant" but must also be compared with passages such as Rev 13:1-10, which shows the government to be demonic, and Acts 5:29, where the apostles declare, "We must obey God rather than men." The point is that one cannot simply proclaim as gospel truth whatever is found in only one passage.[52] Although preachers should not blunt the point of their preaching-text by squaring it with every possible alternative, for responsible preaching they have no choice but to compare Scripture with Scripture and to check for progression of revelation.[53] Thus the point of the text needs to be determined in the context of the entire canon.

Theme Formulation

THE necessity of checking the message of the preaching-text in the context of the entire canon implies the necessity of distinguishing between the theme of the text and the theme of the sermon.

The Theme of the Text

The text's theme consists of a summary statement of the main thought of the text in its epistolary and historical contexts. It stands to reason that this theme can be formulated in its final version only after adequate literary, historical, and theological interpretation. Yet the formulation of this theme is not so much sudden insight at the end of holistic interpretation as it is a gradual process of clarifying the point of the text while going back and forth between the whole and its parts. In order to avoid misinterpretation, Denis Lane suggests that one should have the main thrust of a passage clearly in mind before interpreting the details: "A grasp of the main argument and an understanding of the problem with which the apostle was dealing will keep you from unbalanced presentation. Attention to the main verbs will help you . . . here, for they hold the whole passage together."[54]

---

52. Cf. L. Berkhof, *Principles of Biblical Interpretation*, 165, to the effect that one must take into account "the number of passages that contain the same doctrine," "the unanimity or correspondence of the different passages," "the clearness of the passage," and "the distribution of the passages."

53. See, e.g., Longenecker, "On the Concept of Development in Pauline Thought," 195-207.

54. Lane, *Preach the Word*, 48.

The Theme of the Sermon

Although the theme of a preaching-text from the Epistles can usually function as the sermon's theme, the example from Rom 13:1-7 (above) shows that the text's theme may require some adjustments or qualifications in view of other passages in the canon. Such alignments are also required when the culturally conditioned character of the text is reflected in its theme, as, for example, in 1 Cor 8:1-13: "Christians Are Free to Eat Food Offered to Idols."

The theme of the sermon should be an assertion, such as "The Gospel Is the Power of God for Salvation" (Rom 1:16-17), "God Gives Victory over Death" (1 Cor 15:50-58), "Live the Resurrection Life!" (Col 3:1-4), "Do More and More What You Are Doing!" (1 Thess 4:1-12). In distinction from a subject or from a catchy title for the church bulletin, the sermon theme should assert in summary form the text's message for the church today. This assertion is the single point the sermon needs to get across to its hearers. Hence the theme functions as a guide in outlining and writing the sermon.

Since passages from the Epistles are frequently crammed with details, it is easy for preachers to go off on a tangent. In view of this possibility, it may be worthwhile to go over the sermon after it is finished and to use the theme as a knife to cut out all ideas, illustrations, and images that do not support the theme. It undoubtedly takes courage to eliminate good ideas, but in the end it is better to communicate one theme well than to clutter up the sermon with many different ideas that obscure its very point.

The Form of the Sermon

THE sermon's form needs to enhance the text's message. Since texts in the Epistles vary from thanksgiving to polemics and from doctrine to ethics, one cannot prescribe any one particular form. We shall look at a few possibilities.

The Didactic Form

When a passage combats certain erroneous views or sets forth a particular point of doctrine, the didactic form is valuable in teaching the congregation the point at issue in a logical, systematic way. The sermon should still have only one point and the subpoints should be taken from the text and not from other passages or systematic theology. The development of the point and subpoints can be deductive, inductive, or a combination of both (see Chapter 7 above). With deductive development, one may state the theme at the beginning, but one should normally avoid announcing all the subpoints at this time, since this enumeration interferes with the flow of the sermon. Whenever suitable, one can state each subpoint at the appropriate place in the sermon and possibly mention all of them together in the conclusion. Care must be taken that the sermon does not lose the forward momentum of the text and that it does not turn into a lecture but remains a relevant expository sermon.

The Narrative Form

The didactic form is not the only form for a doctrinal passage; sometimes the narrative form is more appropriate for driving home its point. James Cox observes that "a vibrant story lies just beneath the surface of many an epistle text." As an example he mentions Eph 2:8-10, "For by grace you have been saved through faith; and this is not your own doing, it is the gift of God."

Think of the drama in Ephesians 2:8-10:

I. We try to get on good terms with God by our good works. (The situation.)
II. But works "don't work." (The complication.)
III. God saves us in spite of our weakness, failure, and sin, saves us by his grace through our faith in Jesus Christ, which produces good works. (The resolution.)

This is a story of the Apostle Paul. It is our story, too, and the story of many of our hearers. Those who hear such a sermon can identify with at least its first movement. . . . Then some of these hearers could identify with the second movement. . . . The last movement could well be precisely the word of salvation for such hearers, the light at the end of a long, dark tunnel.[55]

Sometimes even a sermon on an exhortation can be shaped in a narrative form. Ronald Allen suggests that "one can preach from a Pauline ethical exhortation in the story genre just as one can preach from the story of blind Bartimaeus. Ethics, after all, is part of the human story."[56]

One can also try to combine the didactic and narrative forms, using the didactic form to exposit the passage and the narrative form to drive it home. But however preachers seek to utilize the narrative form, they must be especially careful that the sermon does justice to the passage and that it clearly brings across the point of the passage.

Textual Forms

Instead of the didactic or narrative form, one should usually give priority to the textual form since it not only conforms with the text but also best enables the hearers to follow the exposition in their Bibles. "The golden

55. Cox, *Preaching,* 155.
56. Ronald Allen, unpublished paper, as quoted by Rice, *The Drew Gateway* 46/1-3 (1975-76) 24.

rule for sermon outlines is that each text must be allowed to supply its own structure. The skilful expositor opens up his text, or rather permits it to open itself before our eyes."[57] This rule requires the preacher to search the text itself for a structure that can form the main components of the sermon outline. In this endeavor literary interpretation lends its aid, for it frequently reveals the text's structure in the repetition of words, phrases, or questions, in chiastic structures, dialogue, parallelism, or antitheses.

If none of these rhetorical structures is in evidence, one can usually discover the structure of the text by a close reading of the passage, paying attention to its main and subordinate clauses, its major affirmations, and its sequence of ideas.[58] To that end Walter Liefeld makes a helpful distinction between exegesis and exposition: "In exegesis, one studies each part of the Greek sentence, doing careful analysis with a view to understanding each truth presented accurately. In large measure this is done line by line. In exposition, on the other hand, the passage is studied as a whole, and with attention to the flow of thought or sequence of events."[59] In searching for the text's structure, one studies the passage as a whole, "with attention to the flow of thought."

Whatever form is chosen for the sermon, one must keep in mind that the preaching text is part of an Epistle, and that this Epistle is more than likely a *pastoral* letter which responds pastorally to specific issues. This pastoral tone should also color our sermons on these texts.[60] In some passages Paul may express anger or frustration or concern, but all these expressions are within the context of a pastoral letter that begins with "Grace to you and peace" and ends with the wish of peace and the benediction of grace.

The Relevance of the Sermon

ALTHOUGH we discussed the question of relevance extensively in Chapter 8, it may be well in this final chapter to reiterate and augment a few points. On the one hand, we have seen that historical interpretation makes us aware of the culturally conditioned character of the Epistles and the discontinuity between then and now. On the other hand, historical, as well as theological, interpretation also makes us aware of the continuity

---

57. Stott, *Between Two Worlds*, 229.
58. See Liefeld, *NT Exposition*, 46-54.
59. Ibid., 20. Cf. Buttrick, *Homiletic*, 369: "With Paul . . . we must begin by discerning the structure of the passage; first, major shifts in thought and, then, subordinate shifts."
60. Cf. Carl, "Shaping Sermons by Structure," 129: "Paul's entire message is pretty strong, but given with a pastoral understanding. That tone must be retained in the sermon itself. Rather than chiding or whining, this is a fervent appeal from one who believes that with Christ's help and in Christ the community will come together."

between then and now—a continuity which assures the continued relevance of the Epistles today.

Continuity

The continuity between past and present is guaranteed by a faithful covenant God and realized by one covenant people in the context of the one history of God's coming kingdom. This continuity is borne out by the fact that many preaching-texts from the Epistles have such immediate relevance for the church today that we are hardly aware of their age. This sense of immediacy is conveyed particularly by passages in the more general Epistles such as Ephesians, Hebrews, and 1 Peter. The reason for this direct relevance lies in the purpose of these Epistles. "To be useful to a circuit of churches, the admonitions based on the apostolic gospel should be very general in nature. Thus the admonitions of I Peter are not detailed, do not address either specific persons or specific situations, but declare the perspectives and criteria by which Christians in any situation can determine what behavior is honorable before God."[61] In other Epistles, too, the more general admonitions transfer readily to the church today.

The Purpose of the Passage

This sense of immediacy is not always present, however, for one will run head-on into discontinuity in passages such as 1 Cor 8:1-13, "Now concerning food offered to idols . . . ," or Eph 6:5-9, "Slaves, be obedient to those who are your earthly masters. . . ." When preachers select such passages they face the question of how to cross the historical-cultural gap. Instead of the common tendency to generalize the specifics so as to obtain a message for today, one should concentrate first on the specifics, especially the purpose of the passage.

All passages, even the so-called doctrinal passages, are focused responses to specific historical needs. John Bettler remarks pointedly that "Scripture grew out of real life situations."[62] For example, Paul uses "eschatology" in 1 and 2 Thessalonians to comfort bereaved Christians and to admonish those who quit their jobs to await the return of Christ. He formulates "Christology" in Col 1 to combat heresy and uses "Christology" in Phil 2 to encourage humility. In Galatians he articulates the doctrine of justification by faith to correct those who seek salvation partially by works, while in Rom 8 he uses the doctrine of providence to encourage suffering Christians.

The contemporary relevance of these doctrinal passages may become clear when we concentrate on their original relevance. Instead of experi-

---

61. Ericson, "Interpreting Petrine Literature," 246.
62. Bettler, "Application," 335.

encing the culturally conditioned character of the Epistles as a negative factor, therefore, we should see it as a positive indication that the Epistles indeed spoke relevantly in their own time.[63] Since the discovery of a text's past relevance can be a pointer to discovering its present relevance, one should inquire after its original purpose. Bettler calls this search for the text's purpose "the most critical point of applicatory preaching. The application must be that of the text. It must be aimed at the change the Holy Spirit intended. If I do not know the purposes of a text, I cannot apply it."[64] Discovering the historical purpose of a text is only a first step, however. The next question is, How does one transfer a past purpose to a contemporary congregation?

Analogies between Then and Now

In attempting to apply a past purpose to a contemporary congregation, one may well run into the historical-cultural gap. Paul's purpose to regulate master-slave relations or the issue of eating food offered to idols cannot be transferred directly to today. The question is bound to come up, What is the purpose of these culturally conditioned passages for the present? How can we transfer them responsibly across the historical-cultural gap?

The only way to cope with the historical-cultural gap is to see the text's *dis*continuity in the context of the all-encompassing continuity of one faithful covenant God, one covenant people, and one kingdom history. This all-embracing continuity provides the bridge across the historical-cultural gap. We can make use of that bridge by spotting analogies between the church addressed then and the church today.[65]

When we do not share any obvious comparable particulars, we must seek to discover such analogies. Here the emphasis of historical interpretation on the *occasion* for writing pays dividends. Keck remarks that "the interpreter needs to penetrate not only Paul's 'answer' but also the 'question' until what becomes apparent is the extent to which today's readers share the same problem as the original ones. . . . In the long run it is precisely the particularity of the occasions that makes Paul's letters perennially significant."[66]

---

63. Cf. Bornkamm, *The NT*, 75: "The time-conditioned character of the letters does not justify us in dismissing them as no longer relevant. Rather, it points up their relevance, showing that the letters do not deal with the Christian message in a timeless vacuum."

64. Bettler, "Application," 339.

65. As we saw in Chapter 8, "Whenever we share comparable particulars (i.e., similar specific life situations) with the first-century setting, God's Word to us is the same as His Word to them" (Fee and Stuart, *How to Read the Bible*, 60).

66. Keck, *Paul*, 16-17.

Principle and Practice

Whenever the passage is so culturally specific that it yields no analogies with the contemporary situation, one can seek to redefine the specific issue (see Chapter 8 above) or try to discover the principle entailed in the recommended practice. Once one has discovered this principle, one can apply it to the present historical-cultural setting in an analogous way. For example, concerning food offered to idols (1 Cor 8:1-13), George Ladd admits frankly that "this particular historical problem does not have application to the modern Western world (it is still a problem in parts of Asia), but the principles involved have a permanent validity." These principles are those of Christian freedom and of loving consideration of one's neighbor. "In various cultural situations, certain practices are considered quite innocent by devout believers but are offensive to others. In such matters, the two biblical principles of freedom and loving consideration ought to prevail. The essential principles embodied in the ancient historical situation have permanent validity, even though the particular historical problem has passed away with the ancient world."[67] Naturally, applying these principles in our contemporary setting with any degree of specificity is a delicate and complex issue. In connection with 1 Cor 8, for example, the question is bound to come up, "What is the difference . . . between simply 'annoying' one's neighbor and 'destroying' that neighbor? . . . The interpreter is forced to make some judgment about biblical principles, modern society, and contemporary behavior."[68]

Addressing the Whole Person

Relevance is further enhanced by realizing that the Epistles address the whole person. Ridderbos speaks of "the totalitarian character of the new obedience" demanded by Paul's parenesis. "As sin is a totalitarian regime that claims the whole man for itself (Rom. 6:12, 13; 7:14), so the new man must place his body (himself) and all his members (all his actions and potentialities) at the disposal of God."[69] As Paul addressed the whole person, so preachers today ought to address the whole person. They must do so not by addressing separately the intellect, the will, and the emotions, but, holistically, the entire person at once. As Ian Pitt-Watson puts it, "In our preaching as in our living, we have got to get together the truth that we think, the truth that we feel, and the truth that we do."[70]

Addressing the whole person implies that the audience will hear the word as it applies to every area of their lives and thus perceive its perva-

67. Ladd, *NT and Criticism*, 173.
68. Efird, *How to Interpret*, 125.
69. Ridderbos, *Paul*, 265.
70. Pitt-Watson, *Primer*, 101.

sive relevance. For the gospel speaks not only to the spiritual area of life but to every area. "Although Scripture is not as a whole a political tract, an economic treatise or a moral homily, it does fundamentally speak to our political, economic, and moral life out of and in terms of the ultimate horizon of faith."[71] Preachers need not spell out the precise political and economic implications of a particular passage, but they should provide the groundwork for the hearers to work out these implications for their occupations and areas of expertise.

Being Concrete

Relevance has to do not only with breadth of coverage but especially with being concrete. Concreteness requires that the sermon not stay with generalities but become as specific as feasible. This specificity will be enhanced when the preaching-text includes the focal point (the purpose) and the substantiation (see Text Selection above).

Further, being concrete means that one should avoid abstract theoretical language as much as possible and instead use concrete language which stimulates the imagination of the hearers. A metaphor in the text can frequently serve as a vehicle to make the whole sermon concrete. "Metaphors are locomotives of meaning," says Terrence Tilley. "They bear the freight of insight from place to place. . . . The arrival of a powerful metaphor alters the geography of our thoughts and forces us to redraw our conceptual maps."[72] Thomas Troeger suggests,

> Next time you prepare a sermon, go through the notes with your nose. Do you smell anything?
> Go through the notes with your body. Do you feel anything?
> Go through the notes with your eyes. Do you see anything?
> Go through the notes with your mouth. Do you taste anything?
> Go through the notes with your ears. Do you hear anything?[73]

Using Illustrations

One will need to use illustrations especially with nonnarrative sermon forms. Like narrative, illustrations can make the sermon come alive for the audience. Illustrations may be derived from any number of sources. "Karl Barth liked illustrations from the daily newspaper, James Stewart from literary classics, autobiography, and hymns, Eduard Schweizer from homely incidents in everyday life."[74] Others prefer personal illustrations.[75] Whatever the source, one ought to select illustrations not simply

---

71. Olthuis, *Hermeneutics*, 25.
72. Tilley, *Story Theology*, 1.
73. Troeger, *Creating Fresh Images*, 65-66.
74. Cox, "Seven Questions," 237.
75. Bettler, "Application," 348-49. On illustrations, see Buttrick, *Homiletic*, 127-51.

to create interest but to elucidate the truth or to concretize the application of a particular passage.

James Cox provides a good summary for the issue of relevance: "If the sermon is not interesting, preachers need to go back and see if they have been talking about the real needs of the people, if they have used supportive material (illustrations and examples) with which the people can identify, if they have laid out their ideas in a logical way that makes good sense, and if they have couched their thoughts in words and sentences that people can understand. You should have sound exegesis; your theology should be sound. No doubt about that! But how shall they hear except they be interested."[76]

How shall they hear? The preacher stands at the intersection of the ancient Scriptures and the contemporary congregation and has a responsibility to both. We began this book with Paul's charge to Timothy, "Preach the word, be urgent in season and out of season, convince, rebuke, and exhort, be unfailing in patience and in teaching" (2 Tim 4:2). The word which needs to be preached is the word of God. In the final analysis, this word is Jesus Christ, the Word made flesh. To preach this Word is the ultimate responsibility of Christian preachers. As Paul puts it in 2 Cor 4:5, "What we preach is not ourselves, but Jesus Christ as Lord." The implications of such preaching are staggering—for the church as well as for the world.

76. Cox, "Seven Questions," 238.

SELECT BIBLIOGRAPHY

Abraham, William J. *Divine Revelation and the Limits of Historical Criticism.* Oxford: Oxford University, 1982.

Achtemeier, Elizabeth. "The Relevance of the Old Testament for Christian Preaching." In *A Light unto My Path: Old Testament Studies in Honor of Jacob M. Myers.* Ed. Howard H. Bream, R. D. Heim, and C. A. Moore. Philadelphia: Temple University, 1974. Pp. 3-24.

_____. *Creative Preaching: Finding the Words.* Nashville: Abingdon, 1980.

_____. "Preaching from Isaiah, Jeremiah, and Ezekiel." In *Biblical Preaching: An Expositor's Treasury.* Ed. James W. Cox. Philadelphia: Westminster, 1983. Pp. 119-32.

Achtemeier, Elizabeth, and Paul Achtemeier. *The Old Testament and the Proclamation of the Gospel.* Philadelphia: Westminster, 1973.

Achtemeier, Paul J. *Mark.* 2nd ed. Philadelphia: Fortress, 1986.

Adams, Jay E. *Preaching with Purpose.* Grand Rapids: Baker, 1982.

Albrektson, Bertil. *History and the Gods.* Coniectanea Biblica 1. Lund: Gleerup, 1967.

Alexander, T. Desmond. "Jonah and Genre." *TynBul* 36 (1985) 35-59.

Allen, Ronald J. "Shaping Sermons by the Language of the Text." In *Preaching Biblically: Creating Sermons in the Shape of Scripture.* Ed. Don M. Wardlaw. Philadelphia: Westminster, 1983. Pp. 29-59.

Allen, Ronald J., and Thomas J. Herin. "Moving from the Story to Our Story." In *Preaching the Story.* Ed. Edmund A. Steimle, Morris J. Niedenthal, and Charles L. Rice. Philadelphia: Fortress, 1980. Pp. 151-61.

Allmen, Jean-Jacques von. *Preaching and the Congregation.* Trans. B. L. Nicholas. Richmond: John Knox, 1962.

Alter, Robert. *The Art of Biblical Narrative.* New York: Basic Books, 1981.

_____. *The Art of Biblical Poetry.* New York: Basic Books, 1985.

_____. "The Characteristics of Ancient Hebrew Poetry." In *The Literary Guide to the Bible*. Ed. Robert Alter and Frank Kermode. Cambridge: Harvard University, 1987. Pp. 611-24.

Anderson, Bernhard W. "The New Frontier of Rhetorical Criticism." In *Rhetorical Criticism: Essays in Honor of James Muilenburg*. Ed. J. J. Jackson and M. Kessler. Pittsburgh: Pickwick, 1974. Pp. ix-xviii.

_____. *Understanding the Old Testament*. 3rd ed. Englewood Cliffs: Prentice-Hall, 1975.

_____. *The Eighth Century Prophets: Amos, Hosea, Isaiah, Micah*. Philadelphia: Fortress, 1978.

Armerding, Carl E. "Prophecy in the Old Testament." In *Dreams, Visions and Oracles: The Layman's Guide to Biblical Prophecy*. Ed. Carl E. Armerding and W. Ward Gasque. Grand Rapids: Baker, 1977. Pp. 61-73.

_____. *The Old Testament and Criticism*. Grand Rapids: Eerdmans, 1983.

Aune, D. E. "The Problem of the Genre of the Gospel." In *Gospel Perspectives: Studies of History and Tradition in the Four Gospels*. Vol. 2. Ed. R. T. France and David Wenham. Sheffield: JSOT, 1981. Pp. 9-60.

_____. *The New Testament in Its Literary Environment*. Philadelphia: Westminster, 1987.

Baird, J. Arthur. "Genre Analysis as a Method of Historical Criticism." *SBL Proceedings*, 1972. Vol. 2, 385-411.

Barclay, William. "A Comparison of Paul's Missionary Preaching and Preaching to the Church." In *Apostolic History and the Gospels: Biblical and Historical Essays Presented to F. F. Bruce*. Ed. W. Ward Gasque and Ralph P. Martin. Grand Rapids: Eerdmans, 1970. Pp. 165-75.

Bar-Efrat, Shimon. "Literary Modes and Methods in the Biblical Narrative in View of 2 Samuel 10–20 and 1 Kings 1–2." *Immanuel* 8 (1978) 19-31.

_____. "Some Observations on the Analysis of Structure in Biblical Narrative." *VT* 30 (1980) 154-73.

Barr, James. *The Bible in the Modern World*. New York: Harper & Row, 1973.

_____. "Story and History in Biblical Theology." *JR* 56 (1976) 1-17.

Barth, Karl. *The Word of God and the Word of Man*. Trans. Douglas Horton. New York: Harper & Row, 1957.

_____. *The Preaching of the Gospel*. Trans. B. E. Hooke. Philadelphia: Westminster, 1963.

Barton, John. *Reading the Old Testament: Method in Biblical Study*. Philadelphia: Westminster, 1984.

_____. "Classifying Biblical Criticism." *JSOT* 29 (1984) 19-35.

Bass, George M. *The Song and the Story*. Lima, Ohio: C.S.S., 1984.

Beardslee, William. *Literary Criticism of the New Testament*. Philadelphia: Fortress, 1970.

Berkhof, Hendrikus. *Christian Faith: An Introduction to the Study of Faith*. Trans. Sierd Woudstra. Grand Rapids: Eerdmans, 1979.

Berkhof, Louis. *Principles of Biblical Interpretation*. Grand Rapids: Baker, 1950.

Berkouwer, G. C. *Holy Scripture*. Trans. and ed. Jack B. Rogers. Grand Rapids: Eerdmans, 1975.

Berlin, Adele. *Poetics and Interpretation of Biblical Narrative*. Sheffield: Almond, 1983.

_____. *The Dynamics of Biblical Parallelism*. Bloomington: Indiana University, 1985.

Best, Ernest. *From Text to Sermon: Responsible Use of the New Testament in Preaching*. Atlanta: John Knox, 1978.

_____. *Mark: The Gospel as Story*. Edinburgh: T. & T. Clark, 1983.

Bettler, John F. "Application." In *The Preacher and Preaching*. Ed. Samuel T. Logan. Phillipsburg, NJ: Presbyterian and Reformed, 1986. Pp. 331-49.

Blackwood, Andrew W. *Preaching from the Bible*. New York: Abingdon, 1941.

_____. *The Preparation of Sermons*. London: Church Book Room, 1948.

_____. *Preaching from Prophetic Books*. New York: Abingdon-Cokesbury, 1951.

Bloede, Louis W. "Preaching and Story." *Iliff Review* 37 (Fall 1980) 53-61.

Boersma, T. *Is the Bible a Jigsaw Puzzle . . .: An Evaluation of Hal Lindsey's Writings*. St. Catherines, Ont.: Paideia, 1978.

Bornkamm, Günther. *The New Testament: A Guide to Its Writings*. Trans. R. H. Fuller and I. Fuller. Philadelphia: Fortress, 1973.

Braaten, Carl E. *History and Hermeneutics*. Vol. 2 of "New Directions in Theology Today." London: Lutterworth, 1968.

Breck, John. "Biblical Chiasmus: Exploring Structure for Meaning." *BTB* 17/2 (1987) 70-74.

Bright, John. *The Kingdom of God: The Biblical Concept and Its Meaning for the Church*. Nashville: Abingdon, 1953.

_____. *Early Israel in Recent History Writing*. SBT 1/19. London: SCM, 1956.

_____. *The Authority of the Old Testament*. Nashville: Abingdon, 1967.

_____. *Covenant and Promise: The Prophetic Understanding of the Future in Pre-Exilic Israel*. Philadelphia: Westminster, 1976.

Brooks, R. T. *Communicating Conviction*. London: Epworth, 1983.

Brown, Raymond E. "The History and Development of the Theory of a Sensus Plenior." *CBQ* 15/1 (1953) 141-62.

_____. "The 'Sensus Plenior' of Sacred Scripture." S.T.D. Dissertation, St. Mary's, Baltimore, 1955.

_____. "The *Sensus Plenior* in the Last Ten Years." *CBQ* 25 (1963) 262-85.

_____. *The Gospel According to John (I–XII)*. AB. Garden City, NY: Doubleday, 1966.

Bruce, F. F. *The New Testament Documents: Are They Reliable?* 5th ed. Grand Rapids: Eerdmans, 1960.

_____. *The Message of the New Testament*. Grand Rapids: Eerdmans, 1973.

Bullock, C. Hassell. *An Introduction to the Old Testament Prophetic Books*. Chicago: Moody, 1986.

Bultmann, Rudolf. "Is Exegesis without Presuppositions Possible?" In *Existence and Faith: Shorter Writings of Rudolf Bultmann*. Trans. Ogden Schubert. New York: Meridian, 1960. Pp. 289-96.

Buss, Martin J. "The Meaning of History." In *Theology as History*. Ed. J. M. Robinson and J. B. Cobb. New York: Harper, 1967. Pp. 135-54.

_____. "Understanding Communication." In *Encounter with the Text: Form and History in the Hebrew Bible*. Ed. Martin J. Buss. Philadelphia: Fortress, 1979. Pp. 3-44.

Buttrick, David G. "Interpretation and Preaching." *Int* 35/1 (1981) 46-58.

_____. *Homiletic: Moves and Structures*. Philadelphia: Fortress, 1987.

Caird, G. B. "Redaction Criticism." *ExpTim* 87 (1976) 168-72.

Campbell, Doris B. J. *The Synoptic Gospels: A Commentary for Teachers and Students*. London: Murray, 1966.

Carl, William J. "Shaping Sermons by the Structure of the Text." In *Preaching Biblically: Creating Sermons in the Shape of Scripture*. Ed. Don M. Wardlaw. Philadelphia: Westminster, 1983. Pp. 121-36.

Carson, D. A. "Redaction Criticism: On the Legitimacy and Illegitimacy of a Literary Tool." In *Scripture and Truth*. Ed. D. A. Carson and J. D. Woodbridge. Grand Rapids: Zondervan, 1983. Pp. 119-42.

Casserley, J. V. Langmead. *Toward a Theology of History*. London: Mowbray, 1965.

Childs, Brevard S. *Biblical Theology in Crisis*. Philadelphia: Westminster, 1970.

_____. "The Old Testament as Scripture of the Church." *CTM* 43 (1972) 709-22.

_____. *The Book of Exodus*. OTL. Philadelphia: Westminster, 1974.

_____. "The Canonical Shape of the Prophetic Literature." *Int* 32 (1978) 46-55. Repr. in James Luther Mays and Paul J. Achtemeier, eds. *Interpreting the Prophets*. Philadelphia: Fortress, 1987. Pp. 41-49.

_____. *Introduction to the Old Testament as Scripture*. Philadelphia: Fortress, 1979.

_____. "Response to Reviewers of *Introduction to the Old Testament as Scripture*." *JSOT* 16 (1980) 52-60.

_____. "Some Reflections on the Search for a Biblical Theology." *HorBT* 4/1 (1982) 1-12.

_____. *The New Testament as Canon: An Introduction*. Philadelphia: Fortress, 1984.

_____. *Old Testament Theology in a Canonical Context*. Philadelphia: Fortress, 1986.

Christensen, Duane L. "Andrzej Panufnik and the Structure of the Book of Jonah: Icons, Music and Literary Art." *JETS* 28/2 (1985) 133-40.

_____. "The Song of Jonah: A Metrical Analysis." *JBL* 104/2 (1985) 217-31.

Clark, D. J., and J. de Waard. "Discourse Structure in Matthew's Gospel." *Scriptura* Special 1 (1982) 1-97.

Clements, Ronald E. "History and Theology in Biblical Narrative." *HorBT* 4-5 (1982-83) 45-60.

Clines, David J. A. *I, He, We, and They: A Literary Approach to Isaiah 53*. Sheffield: JSOT, 1976.

_____. *The Theme of the Pentateuch*. Sheffield: JSOT, 1978.

_____. "Story and Poem: The Old Testament as Literature and as Scripture." *Int* 34/2 (1980) 115-27.

_____. "Methods of Old Testament Study." In *Beginning Old Testament Study*. Ed. John Rogerson. London: SPCK, 1983. Pp. 26-43.

Clowney, Edmund P. *Preaching and Biblical Theology*. Grand Rapids: Eerdmans, 1961.

_____. "Preaching Christ From All the Scriptures." In *The Preacher and Preaching*. Ed. Samuel T. Logan. Phillipsburg, NJ: Presbyterian and Reformed, 1986. Pp. 163-91.

Coats, George W. *Genesis: With an Introduction to Narrative*. FOTL I. Grand Rapids: Eerdmans, 1983.

_____. "Theology of the Hebrew Bible." In *The Hebrew Bible and Its Modern Interpreters*. Ed. Douglas A. Knight and Gene Tucker. Philadelphia: Fortress, 1985. Pp. 239-62.

Collins, John J. "Introduction: Towards the Morphology of a Genre." *Semeia* 14 (1979) 1-20.

Collins, Raymond F. *Introduction to the New Testament*. Garden City, NY: Doubleday, 1983.

Combrink, H. J. Bernard. "The Structure of the Gospel of Matthew as Narrative." *TynBul* 34 (1983) 61-90.

Conroy, Charles. *Absalom Absalom! Narrative and Language in 2 Samuel 13–20*. Rome: Pontifical Biblical Institute, 1978.

Cox, James W. *A Guide to Biblical Preaching*. Nashville: Abingdon, 1976.

_____. *Preaching*. San Francisco: Harper & Row, 1985.

_____. "Seven Questions About Sermon Structure and Content." In *Heralds to a New Age*. Ed. Don M. Aycock. Elgin, IL: Brethren, 1985. Pp. 233-38.

Craddock, Fred B. *Overhearing the Gospel*. Nashville: Abingdon, 1978.

_____. *As One Without Authority*. Nashville: Abingdon, 1981.

_____. *The Gospels*. Nashville: Abingdon, 1981.

_____. "Occasion—Text—Sermon." *Int* 35/1 (1981) 59-71.

_____. *Preaching*. Nashville: Abingdon, 1985.

Cullmann, Oscar. *Christ and Time: The Primitive Christian Conception of Time and History*. Rev. ed. Trans. Floyd V. Filson. Philadelphia: Westminster, 1962.

Culpepper, R. A. "Story and History in the Gospels." *RevExp* 81/3 (1984) 467-78.

Daane, James. *Preaching with Confidence: A Theological Essay on the Power of the Pulpit*. Grand Rapids: Eerdmans, 1980.

Danielou, Jean. *The Lord of History: Reflections on the Inner Meaning of History*. Trans. N. Abercrombie. London: Longmans, 1958.

Davies, W. D. *Invitation to the New Testament: A Guide to Its Main Witnesses*. Garden City, NY: Doubleday, 1969.

Davis, Henry Grady. *Design for Preaching*. Philadelphia: Fortress, 1958.

DeJong, James A. "Principled Paraenesis: Reading and Preaching the Ethical Material of New Testament Letters." *Pro Rege* 10/4 (1982) 26-34.

Diemer, Johann H. *Nature and Miracle*. Trans. Wilma Bouma. Toronto: Wedge, 1977.

Dijk, K. *De Dienst der Prediking*. Kampen: Kok, 1955.

Dillard, Raymond B. "The Literary Structure of the Chronicle's Solomon Narrative." *JSOT* 30 (1984) 85-93.

Dodd, C. H. *The Apostolic Preaching and Its Development*. New York: Harper, 1964.

Dooyeweerd, Herman. *A New Critique of Theoretical Thought*. 4 vols. Ed. David H. Freeman and William S. Young. Philadelphia: Presbyterian and Reformed, 1953-1958.

Doty, William G. *Contemporary New Testament Interpretation*. Englewood Cliffs, NJ: Prentice-Hall, 1972.

_____. *Letters in Primitive Christianity*. Philadelphia: Fortress, 1973.

Dunn, James D. G. "Levels of Canonical Authority." *HorBT* 4/1 (1982) 13-60.

Edwards, Glen. "Preaching From Mark's Gospel." *SWJT* 21/1 (1978) 55-69.

Efird, James M. *How to Interpret the Bible*. Atlanta: John Knox, 1984.

Eichrodt, Walther. *Theology of the Old Testament*. Vol. 1. Trans. J. A. Baker. OTL. Philadelphia: Westminster, 1961.

Ellis, Peter F. *The Yahwist: The Bible's First Theologian*. Notre Dame: Fides, 1968.

_____. *Matthew: His Mind and His Message*. Collegeville: Liturgical, 1974.

_____. *Seven Pauline Epistles*. Collegeville: Liturgical, 1982.

_____. *The Genius of John: A Composition-Critical Commentary on the Fourth Gospel.* Collegeville: Liturgical, 1984.

Ericson, Norman R. "Interpreting Petrine Literature." In *The Literature and Meaning of Scripture.* Ed. Morris A. Inch and C. Hassell Bullock. Grand Rapids: Baker, 1981. Pp. 243-66.

Eybers, I. H. "Some Remarks Concerning the Composition of the Historical Books of the Old Testament." In *De Fructu Oris Sui: Essays in Honour of Adrianus Van Selms.* Ed. I. H. Eybers, et al. Leiden: Brill, 1971. Pp. 26-45.

Fackre, Gabriel. "Narrative Theology: An Overview." *Int* 37/4 (1983) 340-52.

Fee, Gordon D. *New Testament Exegesis: A Handbook for Students and Pastors.* Philadelphia: Westminster, 1983.

Fee, Gordon D., and Douglas Stuart. *How to Read the Bible for All Its Worth: A Guide to Understanding the Bible.* Grand Rapids: Zondervan, 1982.

Ferguson, Duncan S. *Biblical Hermeneutics: An Introduction.* Atlanta: John Knox, 1986.

Fohrer, G. *Introduction to the Old Testament.* Trans. David E. Green. New York: Abingdon, 1968.

Fokkelman, J. P. *Narrative Art in Genesis: Specimens of Stylistic and Structural Analysis.* Amsterdam: Van Gorcum, 1975.

_____. "Genesis." In *The Literary Guide to the Bible.* Ed. Robert Alter and Frank Kermode. Cambridge: Harvard University, 1987. Pp. 36-55.

Fowler, Robert M. "Using Literary Criticism on the Gospels." *The Christian Century* 99 (26 May 1982) 626-29.

France, R. T. "Scripture, Tradition and History in the Infancy Narratives of Matthew." *The Scottish Evangelical Theological Society Bulletin* 1 (1980) 2-20. Repr. in *Gospel Perspectives: Studies of History and Tradition in the Four Gospels.* Vol. 2. Ed. R. T. France and David Wenham. Sheffield: JSOT, 1981. Pp. 239-66.

Frederikse, Th. C. "De Verhalende Prediking." In *Wegen der Prediking.* Ed. C. W. Mönnich and F. J. Pop. Amsterdam: Holland, 1959. Pp. 57-126.

Freeman, Harold. "Making the Sermon Matter: The Use of Application in the Sermon." *SWJT* 27/2 (1985) 32-37.

Frei, Hans W. *The Eclipse of Biblical Narrative.* New Haven: Yale University, 1974.

Friedrich, Gerhard. *"kēryx, kēryssō, kērygma, prokēryssō."* In *TDNT.* Vol. III. Ed. G. Kittel. Trans. Geoffrey W. Bromiley. Grand Rapids: Eerdmans, 1965. Pp. 683-718.

Froehlich, Karlfried. "Biblical Hermeneutics on the Move." *Word and World* 1/2 (1981) 140-52. Repr. in Donald A. McKim, ed. *A Guide to Contemporary Hermeneutics.* Grand Rapids: Eerdmans, 1986. Pp. 175-91.

Frör, Kurt. *Biblische Hermeneutik.* München: Kaiser, 1964.

Frye, Roland M. "A Literary Perspective for the Criticism of the Gospels." In *Jesus and Man's Hope*. Vol. 2. Ed. Donald G. Miller and Dikran Y. Hadidan. Pittsburgh: Pittsburgh Theological Seminary, 1971. Pp. 193-221.

_____. "The Jesus of the Gospels: Approaches through Narrative Structure." In *From Faith to Faith: Essays in Honor of Donald G. Miller*. Ed. Dikran Y. Hadidan. Pittsburgh: Pickwick, 1979. Pp. 75-89.

Fuller, Reginald H. *The New Testament in Current Study*. New York: Scribners, 1966.

_____. *Interpreting the Miracles*. London: SCM, 1972.

Furnish, Victor Paul. "Prophets, Apostles, and Preachers: A Study of the Biblical Concept of Preaching." *Int* 17/1 (1963) 48-60.

Gadamer, Hans-Georg. *Truth and Method*. New York: Crossroad, 1975.

Gamble, Connolly. "The Nature of Biblical Theology: A Bibliographical Survey." *Int* 5/4 (1951) 462-67.

_____. "The Literature of Biblical Theology: A Bibliographical Study." *Int* 7/4 (1953) 466-80.

_____. "The Method of Biblical Theology." *Int* 9/1 (1955) 91-99.

Garrett, Duane A. "The Structure of Amos as a Testimony to Its Integrity." *JETS* 27/3 (1984) 275-76.

_____. "The Structure of Joel." *JETS* 28/3 (1985) 289-97.

Goetz, Stewart C., and Craig L. Blomberg. "The Burden of Proof." *JSNT* 11 (1981) 39-63.

Goldingay, John. "That You May Know that Yahweh Is God: A Study of the Relationship between Theology and Historical Truth in the Old Testament." *TynBul* 23 (1972) 58-93.

_____. *Approaches to Old Testament Interpretation*. Downers Grove, IL: IVP, 1981.

_____. "Interpreting Scripture." *Anvil* 1/2-3 (1984) 153-62, 261-81.

Gottwald, Norman. "Poetry, Hebrew" In *IDB*. Vol. III. Ed. George Arthur Buttrick. Nashville: Abingdon, 1962. Pp. 829-38.

Goulder, Michael. "The Pauline Epistles." In *The Literary Guide to the Bible*. Ed. Robert Alter and Frank Kermode. Cambridge: Harvard University, 1987. Pp. 479-502.

Gowan, Donald E. *Reclaiming the Old Testament for the Christian Pulpit*. Atlanta: John Knox, 1980.

Greenstein, Edward L. "Biblical Narratology." *Prooftexts* 1 (1981) 201-8.

Greenwood, David. "Rhetorical Criticism and Formgeschichte: Some Methodological Considerations." *JBL* 89/4 (1970) 418-26.

Greidanus, Sidney. *Sola Scriptura: Problems and Principles in Preaching Historical Texts*. Toronto: Wedge, 1970.

_____. "Human Rights in Biblical Perspective." *CTJ* 19/1 (1984) 5-31.

_____. "On Criticizing Sermons." *The Banner* 119 (13 August 1984) 8-9.

_____. "The Universal Dimension of Law in the Hebrew Scriptures." *SR* 14/1 (1985) 39-51.

Gundry, Robert. *Matthew: A Commentary on His Literary and Theological Art.* Grand Rapids: Eerdmans, 1982.

Gunn, David M. *The Story of King David: Genre and Interpretation.* Sheffield: JSOT, 1978.

_____. *The Fate of King Saul: An Interpretation of a Biblical Story.* Sheffield: University of Sheffield, 1980.

Guthrie, Donald. *New Testament Introduction.* 3rd ed. Downers Grove, IL: IVP, 1970.

Hagner, D. A. "Biblical Theology and Preaching." *ExpTim* 96 (1985) 137-41.

Hall, Thor. *The Future Shape of Preaching.* Philadelphia: Fortress, 1971.

Hanson, Anthony. "The Quandary of Historical Scepticism." In *Vindications.* Ed. Anthony Hanson. London: SCM, 1966. Pp. 74-102.

Harris, Murray J. *Easter in Durham: Bishop Jenkins and the Resurrection of Jesus.* Exeter: Paternoster, 1985.

Harrison, Everett F. *Introduction to the New Testament.* Grand Rapids: Eerdmans, 1964.

Harrison, R. K. *Biblical Criticism: Historical, Literary and Textual.* Grand Rapids: Zondervan, 1978.

Hasel, Gerhard F. "Biblical Theology: Then, Now, and Tomorrow." *HorBT* 4/1 (1982) 61-93.

_____. *Old Testament Theology.* 3rd ed. Grand Rapids: Eerdmans, 1982.

_____. "Major Recent Issues in Old Testament Theology 1978-1983." *JSOT* 31 (1985) 31-53.

Herion, G. A. "The Role of Historical Narrative in Biblical Thought: The Tendencies Underlying Old Testament Historiography." *JSOT* 21 (1981) 25-57.

Heschel, Abraham. *The Prophets.* 2 vols. New York: Harper & Row, 1969 and 1975.

Hicks, R. Lansing. "Form and Content: A Hermeneutical Application." In *Translating and Understanding the Old Testament: Essays in Honor of Herbert Gordon May.* Ed. Harry Thomas Frank and William L. Reed. Nashville: Abingdon, 1970. Pp. 304-24.

Hirsch, E. D. *Validity in Interpretation.* New Haven: Yale University, 1967.

Hoekstra, H. *Gereformeerde Homiletiek.* Wageningen: Zomer & Keuning, 1926.

Holwerda, B. "*. . . Begonnen Hebbende van Mozes. . . .*" Terneuzen: Littooij, 1953.

Hooker, Morna D. "Christology and Methodology." *NTS* 17 (1970-71) 480-87.

_____. "On Using the Wrong Tool." *Theology* 75 (1972): 570-81.

_____. "In His Own Image?" In *What about the New Testament?* Ed. Morna D. Hooker and Colin Hickling. London: SCM, 1975. Pp. 28-44.

_____. "What Do We Preach about Jesus Christ?" *Epworth Review* 3/1 (1976) 49-56.

Hull, William E. "A Teaching Outline of the Gospel of Matthew." *RevExp* 59/4 (1962) 433-44.

_____. "Preaching on the Synoptic Gospels." In *Biblical Preaching: An Expositor's Treasury.* Ed. James W. Cox. Philadelphia: Westminster, 1983. Pp. 169-94.

Hultgren, A. J. "Interpreting Scriptures in a Theological Context." *Dialog* 21/2 (1982) 87-94.

Jennings, James E. "Interpreting the Historical Books." In *The Literature and Meaning of Scripture.* Ed. Morris A. Inch and C. Hassell Bullock. Grand Rapids: Baker, 1981. Pp. 39-55.

Jensen, Richard A. *Telling the Story: Variety and Imagination in Preaching.* Minneapolis: Augsburg, 1980.

Jepsen, Alfred. "The Scientific Study of the Old Testament." Trans. John Bright. In *Essays on Old Testament Hermeneutics.* Ed. Claus Westermann. Richmond: John Knox, 1963. Pp. 246-84.

Johnson, C. E. *Verbum Vocale: Biblical Preaching Today.* Ann Arbor, MI: University Microfilms, 1965.

Kahmann, J. *The Bible on the Preaching of the Word.* Trans. T. J. Holmes. DePere, WI: St. Norbert Abbey, 1965.

Kaiser, Walter C. *The Old Testament in Contemporary Preaching.* Grand Rapids: Baker, 1973.

_____. *Toward an Exegetical Theology: Biblical Exegesis for Preaching and Teaching.* Grand Rapids: Baker, 1981.

Kantzer, Kenneth S. "Redaction Criticism: Is It Worth the Risk?" *Christianity Today* 29/15 (18 October 1985) 55-66.

Keck, Leander E. *The Bible in the Pulpit: The Renewal of Biblical Preaching.* Nashville: Abingdon, 1978.

_____. *Paul and His Letters.* Philadelphia: Fortress, 1979.

Keifert, Patrick R. "Mind Reader and Maestro. . . ." *Word and World* 1/2 (1981) 153-68. Repr. in Donald K. McKim, ed. *A Guide to Contemporary Hermeneutics.* Grand Rapids: Eerdmans, 1986. Pp. 220-35.

Kermode, Frank. *The Genesis of Secrecy: On the Interpretation of Narrative.* Cambridge: Harvard University, 1979.

Kessler, Martin. "A Methodological Setting for Rhetorical Criticism." *Sem* 4 (1974) 22-36.

_____. "Inclusio in the Hebrew Bible." *Sem* 6 (1978) 44-49.

Kikawada, Isaac M. "Some Proposals for the Definition of Rhetorical Criticism." *Sem* 5 (1977) 67-91.

Kingsbury, Jack Dean. "The Gospel in Four Editions." *Int* 33 (1979) 363-75.

_____. *Matthew as Story.* Philadelphia: Fortress, 1986.

Kirkland, Bryant M. "Expository Preaching Revitalized." *Pulpit Digest* 45 (1965) 9-14.

Kistemaker, Simon J. "The Theological Message of James." *JETS* 29/1 (1986) 55-61.

Kitchen, K. A. *Ancient Orient and Old Testament.* Chicago: IVP, 1966.

_____. "Historical Method and Early Hebrew Tradition." *TynBul* 17 (1966) 63-97.

_____. *The Bible in Its World: The Bible and Archaeology Today.* Downers Grove, IL: IVP, 1977.

Kline, Meredith. *The Treaty of the Great King.* Grand Rapids: Eerdmans, 1963.

Klooster, Fred H. "Historical Method and the Resurrection in Pannenberg's Theology." *CTJ* 11/1 (1976) 5-33.

Knierim, Rolf. "Criticism of Literary Features, Form, Tradition and Redaction." In *The Hebrew Bible and Its Modern Interpreters.* Ed. Douglas A. Knight and Gene Tucker. Philadelphia: Fortress, 1985. Pp. 123-65.

Koch, Klaus. *The Book of Books: The Growth of the Bible.* Trans. Margaret Kohl. Philadelphia: Westminster, 1968.

Krentz, Edgar. *The Historical-Critical Method.* Philadelphia: Fortress, 1975.

Kromminga, Carl G. "Remember Lot's Wife: Preaching Old Testament Narrative Texts." *CTJ* 18/1 (1983) 32-46.

Kugel, James. *The Idea of Biblical Poetry: Parallelism and Its History.* New Haven: Yale University, 1981.

_____. "On the Bible and Literary Criticism." *Prooftexts* 1/3 (1981) 217-36.

Ladd, George Eldon. *The New Testament and Criticism.* Grand Rapids: Eerdmans, 1966.

_____. "The Search for Perspective." *Int* 25 (1971) 41-62.

_____. *I Believe in the Resurrection of Jesus.* Grand Rapids: Eerdmans, 1975.

Lane, Denis J. V. *Preach the Word.* Manila: Overseas Missionary Fellowship, 1976.

Lane, William L. "Redaktionsgeschichte and the De-historicizing of the New Testament Gospel." *BETS* 11 (1968) 27-33.

LaSor, William S. "Prophecy, Inspiration and Sensus Plenior." *TynBul* 29 (1978) 49-60.

_____. "The Sensus Plenior in Biblical Interpretation." In *Scripture, Tradition, and Interpretation: Essays Presented to Everett F. Harrison.* Ed. W. Ward Gasque and William S. LaSor. Grand Rapids: Eerdmans, 1978. Pp. 260-77. Repr. in Donald K. McKim, ed. *A Guide to Contemporary Hermeneutics.* Grand Rapids: Eerdmans, 1986. Pp. 47-64.

LaSor, William S.; David A. Hubbard; and Frederic Wm. Bush. *Old Testament Survey: The Message, Form, and Background of the Old Testament.* Grand Rapids: Eerdmans, 1982.

Latourelle, René. *Finding Jesus through the Gospels.* New York: Alba House, 1979.

Lawson, LeRoy. *Matthew.* Cincinnati: Standard, 1986.

Leaney, A. R. C. "Historicity in the Gospels." In *Vindications.* Ed. Anthony Hanson. London: SCM, 1966. Pp. 103-34.

Lemke, Werner E. "Revelation Through History in Recent Biblical Theology." *Int* 36/1 (1982) 34-46.

Licht, Jacob. *Storytelling in the Bible.* Jerusalem: Magnes, 1978.

Liefeld, Walter L. *New Testament Exposition: From Text to Sermon.* Grand Rapids: Zondervan, 1984.

Limburg, James. *Old Stories for a New Time.* Atlanta: John Knox, 1983.

Lischer, Richard. "The Limits of Story." *Int* 38/1 (1984) 26-38.

Lloyd-Jones, D. Martyn. *Preaching and Preachers.* Grand Rapids: Zondervan, 1971.

Lohfink, Gerhard. *The Bible: Now I Get It!* Trans. Daniel Coogan. Garden City, NY: Doubleday, 1979.

Lonergan, Bernard. *Method in Theology.* New York: Seabury, 1971.

Long, Burke O. *I Kings: With an Introduction to Historical Literature.* FOTL IX. Grand Rapids: Eerdmans, 1984.

Longenecker, Richard N. *Paul, Apostle of Liberty.* New York: Harper & Row, 1964.

_____. "On the Concept of Development in Pauline Thought." In *Perspectives on Evangelical Theology.* Ed. Kenneth S. Kantzer and S. N. Gundry. Grand Rapids: Baker, 1979. Pp. 195-207.

_____. "On the Form, Function, and Authority of New Testament Letters." In *Scripture and Truth.* Ed. D. A. Carson and J. D. Woodbridge. Grand Rapids: Zondervan, 1983. Pp. 101-14.

Longman III, Tremper. "The Literary Approach to the Study of the Old Testament: Promise and Pitfalls." *JETS* 28/4 (1985) 385-98.

_____. *Literary Approaches to Biblical Interpretation.* Grand Rapids: Zondervan, 1987.

Lorenzen, Thorwald. "Responsible Preaching." *SJT* 33/5 (1980) 453-69.

Lowry, Eugene L. *The Homiletical Plot: The Sermon as Narrative Art Form*. Atlanta: John Knox, 1980.

Lund, N. W. "The Influence of Chiasmus upon the Structure of the Gospels." *ATR* 13 (1931) 27-48.

Lundbom, Jack. *Jeremiah: A Study in Ancient Hebrew Rhetoric*. Society for Biblical Literature Dissertation Series. Missoula: Scholars, 1975.

Lyon, Robert W. "Evangelicals and Critical Historical Method." In *Interpreting God's Word for Today*. Ed. W. McCown and J. E. Massey. Anderson, IN: Warner, 1982. Pp. 135-64.

Macky, Peter W. "The Coming Revolution: The New Literary Approach to New Testament Interpretation." *The Theological Educator* 9 (Spring 1979) 32-46. Repr. in *A Guide to Contemporary Hermeneutics*. Ed. Donald K. McKim. Grand Rapids: Eerdmans, 1986. Pp. 263-79.

Man, Ronald E. "The Value of Chiasm for New Testament Interpretation." *BSac* 141 (1984) 146-57.

Marcel, Pierre. *The Relevance of Preaching*. Trans. Rob Roy McGregor. Grand Rapids: Baker, 1963.

Marshall, I. Howard. *Luke: Historian and Theologian*. Grand Rapids: Zondervan, 1970.

_____. "Historical Criticism." In *New Testament Interpretation: Essays on Principles and Methods*. Ed. I. Howard Marshall. Grand Rapids: Eerdmans, 1977. Pp. 126-38.

_____. *I Believe in the Historical Jesus*. Grand Rapids: Eerdmans, 1977.

Martin, Ralph P. *Mark: Evangelist and Theologian*. Grand Rapids: Zondervan, 1972.

_____. *New Testament Foundations: A Guide for Christian Students*. Vol. 1. Grand Rapids: Eerdmans, 1975.

_____. "Approaches to New Testament Exegesis." In *New Testament Interpretation: Essays on Principles and Methods*. Ed. I. Howard Marshall. Grand Rapids: Eerdmans, 1977. Pp. 220-51.

Marxsen, Willi. *Mark the Evangelist: Studies on the Redaction History of the Gospels*. Trans. James Boyce. Nashville: Abingdon, 1969.

Matera, Frank J. "The Plot of Matthew's Gospel." *CBQ* 49 (1987) 233-53.

Merkley, Paul. "The Gospels as Historical Testimony." *EvQ* 58/4 (1986) 319-36.

Merrill, Eugene H. "Ebla and Biblical Historical Inerrancy." *BSac* 140 (1983) 302-21.

_____. "Literary Genres in Isaiah 40–55." *BSac* 144 (1987) 144-56.

Mickelsen, A. Berkeley. *Interpreting the Bible*. Grand Rapids: Eerdmans, 1963.

Milgrom, Jacob. "'You Shall Not Boil a Kid in Its Mother's Milk.'" *Bible Review* 1/3 (1985) 48-55.

Miller, Donald G. *Fire in Thy Mouth*. Nashville: Abingdon, 1954.

_____. *The Way to Biblical Preaching*. Nashville: Abingdon, 1957.

Miller, J. Maxwell. *The Old Testament and the Historian*. Philadelphia: Fortress, 1976.

Miller, Marlo B. "Restoring the Story." *Word and World* 3/3 (1983) 284-93.

Miscall, Peter D. *The Workings of Old Testament Narrative*. Philadelphia: Fortress, 1983.

Mitchell, Henry H. "Preaching on the Patriarchs." In *Biblical Preaching: An Expositor's Treasury*. Ed. James W. Cox. Philadelphia: Westminster, 1983. Pp. 36-52.

Moessner, David P. "'The Christ Must Suffer': New Light on the Jesus—Peter, Stephen, Paul Parallels in Luke-Acts." *NovT* 28/3 (1986) 220-56.

Morris, Leon. *I Believe in Revelation*. Grand Rapids: Eerdmans, 1976.

Mosley, A. W. "Historical Reporting in the Ancient World." *NTS* 12 (1965) 10-26.

Muilenburg, James. "A Study in Hebrew Rhetoric: Repetition and Style." *VTSup* 1 (1953) 97-111.

_____. "Form Criticism and Beyond." *JBL* 88/1 (1969) 1-18. Repr. in Vincent L. Tollers and John R. Maier, eds. *The Bible in Its Literary Milieu: Contemporary Essays*. Grand Rapids: Eerdmans, 1979. Pp. 362-79.

Müller, Jac. J. "Exegesis and Kerygma." In *Biblical Essays*. Ed. A. H. Van Zyl. Potchefstroom: 1966. Pp. 230-38.

Nations, Archie L. "Historical Criticism and the Current Methodological Crisis." *SJT* 36/1 (1983) 59-72.

Newing, Edward George. "A Rhetorical and Theological Analysis of the Hexateuch." *SEAJT* 22/2 (1981) 1-15.

Newsom, Carol A. "A Maker of Metaphors: Ezekiel's Oracles against Tyre." *Int* 38/2 (1984) 151-64. Repr. in *Interpreting the Prophets*. Ed. James Luther Mays and Paul J. Achtemeier. Philadelphia: Fortress, 1987. Pp. 188-99.

Nichols, J. Randall. *The Restoring Word: Preaching as Pastoral Communication*. San Francisco: Harper & Row, 1987.

Noth, Martin. "The 'Re-presentation' of the Old Testament in Proclamation." Trans. James Luther Mays. In *Essays on Old Testament Hermeneutics*. Ed. Claus Westermann. Richmond: John Knox, 1962. Pp. 76-88.

O'Day, Gail R. "Narrative Mode and Theological Claim: A Study in the Fourth Gospel." *JBL* 105/4 (1986) 657-68.

Olthuis, James. *A Hermeneutics of Ultimacy: Peril or Promise?* Lanham, MD: University Press of America, 1987.

Osborne, Grant R. "The Evangelical and Traditionsgeschichte." *JETS* 21/2 (1978) 117-30.

_____. "The Evangelical and Redaction Criticism: Critique and Methodology." *JETS* 22/4 (1979) 305-22.

_____. "Genre Criticism—Sensus Literalis." *Trinity Journal* 4/2 (1983) 1-27.

_____. "Preaching the Gospels: Methodology and Contextualization." *JETS* 27/1 (1984) 27-42.

_____. "Round Four: The Redaction Debate Continues." *JETS* 28/4 (1985) 399-410.

O'Toole, Robert F. *The Unity of Luke's Theology: An Analysis of Luke-Acts.* Wilmington, DE: Michael Glazier, 1984.

Padilla, C. René. "The Interpreted Word: Reflections on Contextual Hermeneutics." *Themelios* 7/1 (September 1981) 18-23. Repr. in *A Guide to Contemporary Hermeneutics.* Ed. Donald K. McKim. Grand Rapids: Eerdmans, 1986. Pp. 297-308.

Palmer, Richard E. *Hermeneutics.* Evanston, IL: Northwestern University, 1969.

Pannenberg, Wolfhart. "The Revelation of God in Jesus of Nazareth." Trans. Kenneth Grobel. In *Theology as History.* Ed. J. M. Robinson and J. B. Cobb. New York: Harper, 1967. Pp. 101-33.

_____. "Response to the Discussion." Trans. William A. Beardslee, et al. In *Theology as History.* Ed. J. M. Robinson and J. B. Cobb. New York: Harper, 1967. Pp. 221-76.

_____. *Jesus—God and Man.* 2nd ed. Trans. Lewis L. Wilkins and Duane A. Priebe. Philadelphia: Westminster, 1968.

_____. *Basic Questions in Theology.* Vol. 1. Trans. George H. Kehm. Philadelphia: Fortress, 1970.

Parunak, H. Van Dyke. "Oral Typesetting: Some Uses of Biblical Structure." *Bib* 62/2 (1981) 153-68.

_____. "Some Axioms for Literary Architecture." *Sem* 8 (1982) 1-16.

Patrick, Dale. "Political Exegesis." In *Encounter with the Text: Form and History in the Hebrew Bible.* Ed. Martin J. Buss. Philadelphia: Fortress, 1979. Pp. 139-52.

Payne, J. Barton. *Encyclopedia of Biblical Prophecy: The Complete Guide to Scriptural Predictions and Their Fulfillment.* New York: Harper & Row, 1973.

Payne, Philip B. "The Fallacy of Equating Meaning with the Human Author's Intention." *JETS* 20/3 (1977) 243-52.

_____. "Midrash and History in the Gospels with Special Reference to R. H. Gundry's *Matthew*." In *Gospel Perspectives: Studies in Midrash and Historiography.* Vol. 3. Ed. R. T. France and David Wenham. Sheffield: JSOT, 1983. Pp. 177-215.

Pennington, Chester A. "Response to 'Preaching and Story.'" *Iliff Review* 37 (1980) 63-64.

Perrin, Norman. *Rediscovering the Teaching of Jesus*. New York: Harper & Row, 1967.

_____. *What Is Redaction Criticism?* Philadelphia: Fortress, 1969.

_____. *The New Testament: An Introduction*. New York: Harcourt Brace Jovanovich, 1974.

_____. *The Resurrection According to Matthew, Mark, and Luke*. Philadelphia: Fortress, 1977.

Perry, Lloyd M. *A Manual for Biblical Preaching*. Grand Rapids: Baker, 1965.

Pitt-Watson, Ian. *Preaching: A Kind of Folly*. Edinburgh: St. Andrews, 1976.

_____. *A Primer for Preachers*. Grand Rapids: Baker, 1986.

Polzin, Robert. *Moses and the Deuteronomist: A Literary Study of the Deuteronomic History*. New York: Seabury, 1980.

_____. "Literary and Historical Criticism in the Bible: A Crisis in Scholarship." In *Orientation by Disorientation: Studies in Literary Criticism and Biblical Literary Criticism Presented in Honor of William A. Beardslee*. Ed. Richard A. Spencer. Pittsburgh: Pickwick, 1980. Pp. 99-114.

Poythress, Vern S. "Philosophical Roots of Phenomenological and Structuralist Literary Criticism." *WTJ* 41/1 (1978) 165-71.

_____. "Structuralism and Biblical Studies." *JETS* 21/3 (1978) 221-37.

_____. "Analyzing a Biblical Text: Some Important Linguistic Distinctions." *SJT* 32/2 (1979) 113-37.

Rad, Gerhard von. *Old Testament Theology*. 2 vols. Trans. D. M. G. Stalker. New York: Harper & Row, 1962, 1965.

_____. "The Beginnings of Historical Writing in Ancient Israel." In *The Problem of the Hexateuch and Other Essays*. Trans. E. W. Trueman Dicken. Edinburgh: Oliver & Boyd, 1966. Pp. 166-204.

_____. *Biblical Interpretations in Preaching*. Trans. John E. Steely. Nashville: Abingdon, 1977.

_____. *God at Work in Israel*. Trans. John H. Marks. Nashville: Abingdon, 1980.

Radday, Yehuda T. "Chiasmus in Hebrew Biblical Narrative." In *Chiasmus in Antiquity*. Ed. John W. Welch. Hildesheim: Gerstenberg, 1981. Pp. 50-117.

Ramm, Bernard. *Protestant Biblical Interpretation: A Textbook of Hermeneutics*. 3rd ed. Grand Rapids: Baker, 1970.

Ramsey, George W. *The Quest for the Historical Israel: Reconstructing Israel's Early History*. Atlanta: John Knox, 1981.

Rendtorff, Rolf. *The Old Testament: An Introduction*. Trans. John Bowden. Philadelphia: Fortress, 1985.

Rhoads, David. "Narrative Criticism and the Gospel of Mark." *JAAR* 50 (1982) 411-34.

Rhodes, Arnold B. *The Mighty Acts of God.* Atlanta: John Knox, 1964.

Rice, Charles. "Preaching as Storytelling." *The Drew Gateway* 46 (1975-76) 11-28.

Richard, Ramesh P. "Levels of Biblical Meaning." *BSac* 143 (1986) 123-33.

Richardson, A. *History Sacred and Profane.* London: SCM, 1964.

Ridderbos, Herman. "Tradition and Editorship in the Synoptic Gospels." In *Jerusalem and Athens: Critical Discussions on the Theology and Apologetics of Cornelius Van Til.* Ed. E. R. Geehan. Philadelphia: Presbyterian and Reformed, 1971. Pp. 244-59.

_____. *Paul: An Outline of His Theology.* Trans. John Richard De Witt. Grand Rapids: Eerdmans, 1975.

_____. *Studies in Scripture and Its Authority.* Grand Rapids: Eerdmans, 1978.

Riegert, Eduard Richard. "Preaching: Where We're Going." *Consensus* 8/2 (1982) 11-18.

Robbins, Vernon K. "Summons and Outline in Mark: The Three-Step Progression." *NovT* 23/2 (1981) 97-114.

Robertson, David. "The Bible as Literature." In *IDBSup.* Ed. Keith Crim. Nashville: Abingdon, 1976. Pp. 547-51.

Robinson, Haddon W. "What Is Expository Preaching?" *BSac* 131 (1974) 55-60.

_____. *Biblical Preaching: The Development and Delivery of Expository Messages.* Grand Rapids: Baker, 1980.

Robinson, James M. "Revelation as Word and as History." In *Theology as History.* Ed. J. M. Robinson and J. B. Cobb. New York: Harper, 1967. Pp. 1-100.

_____. "On the *Gattung* of Mark and John." In *Jesus and Man's Hope.* Vol. 1. Ed. David G. Buttrick. Pittsburgh: Pittsburgh Theological Seminary, 1970. Pp. 99-130.

Roetzel, Calvin J. *The Letters of Paul: Conversations in Context.* Atlanta: John Knox, 1975.

Rogerson, John. *Old Testament Criticism in the Nineteenth Century: England and Germany.* Philadelphia: Fortress, 1984.

Rosenberg, Joel. "Jeremiah and Ezekiel." In *The Literary Guide to the Bible.* Ed. Robert Alter and Frank Kermode. Cambridge: Harvard University, 1987. Pp. 184-206.

Roth, Robert. *Story and Reality: An Essay of Truth.* Grand Rapids: Eerdmans, 1973.

Rowley, H. H. *The Re-Discovery of the Old Testament.* London: James Clarke, 1945.

Runia, Klaas. "What Is Preaching According to the New Testament?" *TynBul* 29 (1978) 3-48.

_____. "The Hermeneutics of the Reformers." *CTJ* 19/2 (1984) 121-52.

Ryken, Leland. *The Literature of the Bible*. Grand Rapids: Zondervan, 1974.

_____. "The Bible as Literature." In *The Christian Imagination: Essays on Literature and the Arts*. Ed. Leland Ryken. Grand Rapids: Baker, 1981. Pp. 173-85.

_____. *How to Read the Bible as Literature*. Grand Rapids: Zondervan, 1984.

Sanders, James. *God Has a Story Too*. Philadelphia: Fortress, 1979.

Sandmel, Samuel. *The Enjoyment of Scripture: The Law, the Prophets, and the Writings*. New York: Oxford University, 1972.

Savran, George. "1 and 2 Kings." In *The Literary Guide to the Bible*. Ed. Robert Alter and Frank Kermode. Cambridge: Harvard University, 1987. Pp. 146-64.

Schmidt, W. H. "dābhar." In *TDOT*. Vol. III. Ed. G. J. Botterweck and H. Ringgren. Trans. John T. Willis and Geoffrey W. Bromiley. Grand Rapids: Eerdmans, 1978. Pp. 94-125.

Scotland, Nigel. *Can We Trust the Gospels?* Exeter: Paternoster, 1979.

Scott, M. Philip. "Chiastic Structure: A Key to the Interpretation of Mark's Gospel." *BTB* 15/1 (1985) 17-26.

Scroggs, Donald H. *The Value of the Historical-Critical Method upon Preaching the Old Testament*. Dallas: Perkins School of Theology, 1984.

Shuler, Philip L. *A Genre for the Gospels: The Biographical Character of Matthew*. Philadelphia: Fortress, 1982.

Smalley, Stephen S. "Redaction Criticism." In *New Testament Interpretation: Essays on Principles and Methods*. Ed. I. Howard Marshall. Grand Rapids: Eerdmans, 1977. Pp. 181-95.

_____. *John: Evangelist and Interpreter*. Exeter: Paternoster, 1978.

Smart, James D. *The Strange Silence of the Bible in the Church: A Study in Hermeneutics*. Philadelphia: Westminster, 1972.

Smend, Rudolf. "Questions about the Importance of the Canon in Old Testament Introduction." *JSOT* 16 (1980) 45-51.

Smith, Dwight Moody. *Interpreting the Gospels for Preaching*. Philadelphia: Fortress, 1979.

_____. *John*. 2nd ed. Philadelphia: Fortress, 1986.

Spina, Frank W. "Canonical Criticism: Childs versus Sanders." In *Interpreting God's Word for Today: An Inquiry into Hermeneutics from a Biblical Theological Perspective*. Ed. W. McCown and J. E. Massey. Anderson, IN: Warner, 1982. Pp. 165-94.

Stanton, Graham H. *Jesus of Nazareth in New Testament Preaching*. London: Cambridge University, 1974.

_____. "Presuppositions in New Testament Criticism." In *New Testament Interpretation: Essays on Principles and Methods*, Ed. I. Howard Marshall. Grand Rapids: Eerdmans, 1977. Pp. 60-71.

_____. "Interpreting the New Testament Today." *Ex Auditu* 1 (1985) 63-73.

Steimle, Edmund A. "The Fabric of the Sermon." In *Preaching the Story*. Ed. Edmund A. Steimle, Morris J. Niedenthal, and Charles L. Rice. Philadelphia: Fortress, 1980. Pp. 163-75.

Stein, Robert H. "What Is Redactionsgeschichte?" *JBL* 88/1 (1969) 45-56.

_____. "The Proper Methodology for Ascertaining a Markan Redaction History." *NovT* 13/3 (1971) 181-98.

_____. "The 'Criteria' for Authenticity." In *Gospel Perspectives: Studies of History and Tradition in the Four Gospels*. Vol. 1. Ed. R. T. France and David Wenham. Sheffield: JSOT, 1980. Pp. 225-53.

Stek, John H. "The Message of the Book of Jonah." *CTJ* 4/1 (1969) 23-50.

_____. *The Former Prophets: A Syllabus*. Grand Rapids: Calvin Theological Seminary, 1985.

_____. "The Bee and the Mountain Goat." In *A Tribute to Gleason Archer: Essays on the Old Testament*. Ed. Walter C. Kaiser and Donald F. Youngblood. Chicago: Moody, 1986. Pp. 53-86.

_____. "When the Spirit Was Poetic." In *The NIV: The Making of a Contemporary Translation*. Ed. Kenneth L. Barker. Grand Rapids: Zondervan, 1986. Pp. 72-87.

Stendahl, Krister. "Preaching from the Pauline Epistles." In *Biblical Preaching: An Expositor's Treasury*. Ed. James W. Cox. Philadelphia: Westminster, 1983. Pp. 306-26.

_____. *Meanings: The Bible as Document and as Guide*. Philadelphia: Fortress, 1984.

_____. "The Bible as a Classic and the Bible as Holy Scripture." *JBL* 103/1 (1984) 3-10.

Sternberg, Meir. *The Poetics of Biblical Narrative*. Bloomington: Indiana University, 1985.

Stevenson, Dwight E. *Preaching on the Books of the Old Testament*. New York: Harper, 1961.

_____. *In the Biblical Preacher's Workshop*. Nashville: Abingdon, 1967.

Stock, Augustine. "Chiastic Awareness and Education in Antiquity." *BTB* 14/1 (1984) 23-27.

Stott, John R. W. *Between Two Worlds: The Art of Preaching in the Twentieth Century*. Grand Rapids: Eerdmans, 1982.

Stroup, G. W. *The Promise of Narrative Theology: Recovering the Gospel in the Church*. Atlanta: John Knox, 1981.

Stuart, Douglas. *Old Testament Exegesis*. Philadelphia: Westminster, 1980.

Stuhlmacher, Peter. *Historical Criticism and Theological Interpretation of Scripture:*

Towards a Hermeneutic of Consent. Trans. Roy A. Harrisville. Philadelphia: Fortress, 1977.

Talbert, Charles H. *What Is a Gospel? The Genre of the Canonical Gospels.* Philadelphia: Fortress, 1977.

Talmon, Shemaryahu. "Ezra and Nehemiah." In *The Literary Guide to the Bible.* Ed. Robert Alter and Frank Kermode. Cambridge: Harvard University, 1987. Pp. 357-64.

Tannehill, Robert C. *The Sword of His Mouth.* Philadelphia: Fortress, 1975.

_____. "The Disciples in Mark: The Function of a Narrative Role." *JR* 57 (1977) 386-405.

_____. "The Gospel of Mark as Narrative Christology." *Semeia* 16 (1979) 57-95.

_____. *The Narrative Unity of Luke-Acts: A Literary Interpretation.* Vol. 1. Philadelphia: Fortress, 1986.

Taylor, Gardner. "Shaping Sermons by the Shape of Text and Preacher." In *Preaching Biblically: Creating Sermons in the Shape of Scripture.* Ed. Don M. Wardlaw. Philadelphia: Westminster, 1983. Pp. 137-52.

Thiselton, Anthony C. "Structuralism and Biblical Studies: Method or Ideology?" *ExpTim* 89 (1978) 329-35.

_____. *The Two Horizons: New Testament Hermeneutics and Philosophical Description.* Grand Rapids: Eerdmans, 1980.

_____. "Reader-Response Hermeneutics, Action Models, and the Parables of Jesus." In *The Responsibility of Hermeneutics.* Ed. Roger Lundin, Anthony C. Thiselton, and Clarence Walhout. Grand Rapids: Eerdmans, 1985. Pp. 79-113.

Thompson, William D. *Preaching Biblically: Exegesis and Interpretation.* Nashville: Abingdon, 1981.

Tilley, Terrence W. *Story Theology.* Wilmington, DE: Michael Glazier, 1985.

Toombs, Lawrence E. "The Problematic of Preaching from the Old Testament." *Int* 23 (1969) 302-14.

Travis, Stephen H. "Form Criticism." In *New Testament Interpretation: Essays on Principles and Methods.* Ed. I. Howard Marshall. Grand Rapids: Eerdmans, 1977. Pp. 153-64.

Trimp, C. "The Relevance of Preaching (in the Light of the Reformation's 'Sola Scriptura' Principle)." *WTJ* 36 (1973) 1-30.

Troeger, Thomas H. *Creating Fresh Images for Preaching: New Rungs for Jacob's Ladder.* Valley Forge, PA: Judson, 1982.

Troeltsch, Ernst. "Geschichte und Metaphysik." *ZTK* 8 (1898) 1-69.

_____. "Über historische und dogmatische Methode in der Theologie." In *Zur religiösen Lage, Religionsphilosophie und Ethik: Gesammelte Schriften.* Vol. 2. Tübingen: Mohr, 1913. Pp. 729-53.

Trompf, G. W. "Notions of Historical Recurrence in Classical Hebrew Historiography." *VTSup* 30 (1979) 213-29.

Tucker, Gene M. *Form Criticism of the Old Testament*. Philadelphia: Fortress, 1971.

Turner, David L. "Evangelicals, Redaction Criticism, and Inerrancy Crisis." *GTJ* 4 (1983) 263-88.

Turner, H. E. W. *Historicity and the Gospels*. London: A. R. Mowbray, 1963.

Unger, Merrill F. *Principles of Expository Preaching*. Grand Rapids: Zondervan, 1955.

VanderGoot, Henry. *Interpreting the Bible in Theology and the Church*. Toronto: Edwin Miller, 1984.

Van Elderen, Bastiaan. "New Perspectives in Biblical Research." *CTJ* 1/2 (1966) 165-81.

_____. "The Teaching of Jesus and the Gospel Records." In *Jesus of Nazareth: Saviour and Lord*. Ed. C. F. H. Henry. Grand Rapids: Eerdmans, 1966. Pp. 109-19.

Van Seters, John. *In Search of History: Historiography in the Ancient World and the Origins of Biblical History*. New Haven: Yale University, 1983.

Vaux, Roland de. *The Bible and the Ancient Near East*. Trans. Damian McHugh. New York: Doubleday, 1972.

Verhey, Allen. *The Great Reversal: Ethics and the New Testament*. Grand Rapids: Eerdmans, 1984.

Volbeda, Samuel. *The Pastoral Genius of Preaching*. Compiled and edited by R. Evenhuis. Grand Rapids: Zondervan, 1960.

Vorster, W. S. "Kerygma/History and the Gospel Genre." *NTS* 29 (1983) 87-95.

Vos, Geerhardus. *Biblical Theology: Old and New Testaments*. Grand Rapids: Eerdmans, 1948.

Voskuil, Louis J. "History: Sound and Fury Signifying Nothing?" *Pro Rege* 16/3 (1988) 2-12.

Vriezen, Th. C. *An Outline of Old Testament Theology*. Trans. S. Neuijen. Oxford: Blackwell, 1962.

Walhout, Clarence. "Texts and Actions." In *The Responsibility of Hermeneutics*. Ed. Roger Lundin, Anthony C. Thiselton, and Clarence Walhout. Grand Rapids: Eerdmans, 1985. Pp. 31-77.

Wardlaw, Don M. "Eventful Sermon Shapes." In *Preaching and Story*. Compiled for the 1979 Meeting of the Academy of Homiletics. Des Plaines, IL: Academy of Homiletics, 1979. Pp. 40-47.

_____. "The Need for New Shapes." In *Preaching Biblically: Creating Sermons in the Shape of Scripture*. Ed. Don M. Wardlaw. Philadelphia: Westminster, 1983. Pp. 11-25.

_____. "Shaping Sermons by the Context of the Text." In *Preaching Biblically: Creating Sermons in the Shape of Scripture.* Ed. Don M. Wardlaw. Philadelphia: Westminster, 1983. Pp. 60-83.

Watts, John D. W. "Preaching on the Narratives of the Monarchy." In *Biblical Preaching: An Expositor's Treasury.* Ed. James W. Cox. Philadelphia: Westminster, 1983. Pp. 72-83.

Webb, Barry G. *The Book of the Judges: An Integrated Reading.* Sheffield: JSOT, 1986.

Webster, Edwin C. "Pattern in the Fourth Gospel." In *Art and Meaning: Rhetoric in Biblical Literature.* Ed. D. J. A. Clines, et al. Sheffield: JSOT, 1982. Pp. 230-57.

Weinfeld, M. "Berîth." In *TDOT.* Vol. II. Ed. G. J. Botterweck and H. Ringgren. Trans. John T. Willis. Grand Rapids: Eerdmans, 1975. Pp. 253-79.

Welch, John W. "Chiasmus in the New Testament." In *Chiasmus in Antiquity.* Ed. John W. Welch. Hildesheim: Gerstenberg, 1981. Pp. 211-49.

_____. "Introduction." In *Chiasmus in Antiquity.* Ed. John W. Welch. Hildesheim: Gerstenberg, 1981. Pp. 9-16.

Wenham, Gordon. "History and the Old Testament." In *History, Criticism and Faith: Four Exploratory Essays.* Ed. Colin Brown. Downers Grove, IL: IVP, 1976. Pp. 13-75.

West, James K., and Donald J. Selby. *Introduction to the Bible.* New York: Macmillan, 1971.

Westermann, Claus. "The Interpretation of the Old Testament." Trans. Dietrich Ritschl. In *Essays on Old Testament Hermeneutics.* Ed. Claus Westermann. Richmond: John Knox, 1963. Pp. 40-49.

_____. *Basic Forms of Prophetic Speech.* Trans. Hugh C. White. Philadelphia: Westminster, 1967.

_____. *What Does the Old Testament Say about God?* Atlanta: John Knox, 1979.

_____. *Elements of Old Testament Theology.* Trans. Douglas W. Stott. Atlanta: John Knox, 1982.

Whitesell, Faris D. *Preaching on Bible Characters.* Grand Rapids: Baker, 1955.

Whybray, R. N. "On Robert Alter's *The Art of Biblical Narrative.*" *JSOT* 27 (1983) 75-117.

Wilcoxen, Jay A. "Narrative." In *Old Testament Form Criticism.* Ed. J. H. Hayes. San Antonio: Trinity University, 1974. Pp. 57-98.

Wilder, Amos. *Early Christian Rhetoric: The Language of the Gospel.* Cambridge: Harvard University, 1971.

_____. "Story and Story-World." *Int* 37 (1983) 353-64.

Willimon, William H. *Preaching and Leading Worship.* Philadelphia: Westminster, 1984.

Willis, John T. "Dialogue between Prophet and Audience as a Rhetorical Device in the Book of Jeremiah." *JSOT* 33 (1985) 63-82.

Wingren, Gustaf. *The Living Word: A Theological Study of Preaching and the Church.* Trans. V. C. Pogue. London: SCM, 1960.

Wink, Walter. *The Bible in Human Transformation: Toward a New Paradigm for Biblical Study.* Philadelphia: Fortress, 1973.

Winward, Stephen F. *A Guide to the Prophets.* Atlanta: John Knox, 1976.

Wolff, Hans Walter. *The Old Testament: A Guide to Its Writings.* Trans. Keith Crim. Philadelphia: Fortress, 1973.

_____. "Prophecy from the Eighth through the Fifth Century." Trans. W. S. Towner with Joy E. Heebink. *Int* 32/1 (1978) 17-30. Repr. in *Interpreting the Prophets.* Ed. James Luther Mays and Paul J. Achtemeier. Philadelphia: Fortress, 1987. Pp. 14-26.

_____. *Confrontations with Prophets.* Philadelphia: Fortress, 1983.

Woudstra, Marten H. "Event and Interpretation in the Old Testament." In *Interpreting God's Word Today.* Ed. Simon Kistemaker. Grand Rapids: Baker, 1970. Pp. 51-72.

_____. *The Book of Joshua.* NICOT. Grand Rapids: Eerdmans, 1981.

Yoder, Perry. *From Word to Life: A Guide to the Art of Bible Study.* Scottdale, PA: Herald, 1982.

Young, Edward J. *An Introduction to the Old Testament.* Grand Rapids: Eerdmans, 1960.

Zimmerli, Walther. *The Law and the Prophets: A Study of the Meaning of the Old Testament.* Trans. R. E. Clements. New York: Harper & Row, 1967.

Zylstra, Carl Eugene. "God-Centered Preaching in a Human-Centered Age: The Developing Crisis Confronting a Conservative Calvinist Reformed Church, 1935-1975." Ph.D. diss., Princeton University, 1983.

SUBJECT INDEX

Acts of God. *See* God acting in history
Aesthetic interpretation. *See* Interpretation: aesthetic and literary
Ahistorical tendencies, 35, 56, 79, 192-93, 264, 268-70, 273-74
Allegorizing, 35, 111-12, 118, 159-60
Ambassador, 4, 8, 12
Analogies between past and present, 172-75, 179-81, 261-62, 309, 338
Analogy, principle of, 26, 30-32, 37, 41-42
Ancient standards of history writing, 88-92, 191, 272-73
Anthropocentric interpretation. *See* Interpretation: anthropocentric
Anthropocentric preaching. *See* Preaching types: anthropocentric
Antithesis (contrast), 322
Apocalyptic literature. *See* Genre: apocalypse
Apostle, 3-7, 313, 317
Application, 72, 100-101, 107, 117, 120-21, 125, 140, 144, 150, 160, 166-67, 169-70, 173, 182-84, 196-97, 221, 224, 330, 338-41
Art forms. *See* Literary art, ancient
Atomism, 48-49, 54, 56, 67, 79, 100, 136, 153, 213, 221, 250 (*see also* Reductionism)
Audience. *See* Church; Original hearers
Aural literature, 60, 197-98, 203, 209, 251, 319
Author, 55-56, 58, 78-79, 329 (*see also* Narrator)
    divine and human, 71, 104, 106
    purpose of. *See* Purpose of the author
Authority of preaching, 2, 9, 12, 77, 123-24, 161, 166

Bible, 26, 29, 43 (*see also* Canon)
    as criterion of preaching, 9, 14-15
    as proclamation (kerygma), 13, 14, 20, 57, 76-77, 87, 90-94, 102-3, 158, 182, 222-23, 228, 266-67, 272, 295, 313-15
    as source for preaching, 5, 8, 12-14, 315 (*see also* Preaching types: expository)
Bible characters. *See also* Characters; Preaching types: biographical
    as examples, 117-18, 161-63, 216-18, 290
    identifying with, 175-81, 309
Biblical forms. *See* Forms, biblical; Genre; Sermon forms
Biblical preaching. *See* Preaching types: biblical
Biblical theology, 67-74
    and preaching, 72
Biographical preaching. *See* Preaching types: biographical
Broken structures, 65, 203, 208-9
Burden of proof, 30, 45-46, 191-92, 277

Canon, 13-14, 74-76, 105
Canonical approach, 49, 73-79, 254
    and preaching, 76-77
Canonical context. *See* Context: canonical
Canonical criticism, 73, 78
Character sermons. *See* Preaching types: biographical
Characters. *See also* Bible characters
    character description, 161, 200, 286
    contrasted characters, 200, 286
    number of characters, 177, 199, 212
    parallel characters, 200-201, 286-87

SCRIPTURE INDEX